M000223803

*The Lost Tradition of Economic Equality
in America, 1600–1870*

The Lost Tradition
of Economic Equality in
America, 1600–1870

DANIEL R. MANDELL

LIBRARY OF
CONGRESS
SURPLUS
DUPLICATE

Johns Hopkins University Press

Baltimore

© 2020 Daniel R. Mandell

All rights reserved. Published 2020

Printed in the United States of America on acid-free paper

2 4 6 8 9 7 5 3 1

Johns Hopkins University Press

2715 North Charles Street

Baltimore, Maryland 21218-4363

www.press.jhu.edu

Library of Congress Cataloging-in-Publication Data

Names: Mandell, Daniel R., 1956– author.
Title: The lost tradition of economic equality in America, 1600–1870 /
Daniel R. Mandell.
Description: Baltimore : Johns Hopkins University Press, 2020. |
Includes bibliographical references and index.
Identifiers: LCCN 2019022472 | ISBN 9781421437118 (hardcover : alk. paper) |
ISBN 9781421437125 (electronic) | ISBN 1421437112 (hardcover : alk. paper) |
ISBN 1421437120 (electronic)
Subjects: LCSH: Equality—United States—History. | Social classes—United
States—History. | Income distribution—United States—History. |
United States—Economic conditions—To 1865.
Classification: LCC HN90.S6 M326 2020 | DDC 305.50973—dc23
LC record available at https://lccn.loc.gov/2019022472

A catalog record for this book is available from the British Library.

*Special discounts are available for bulk purchases of this book. For more information, please
contact Special Sales at specialsales@press.jhu.edu.*

Johns Hopkins University Press uses environmentally friendly book materials,
including recycled text paper that is composed of at least 30 percent post-consumer
waste, whenever possible.

For all my ancestors and teachers, my sons and students
M'dor l'dor

CONTENTS

Because this book covers a wide swath of time and topics and took many years to research and write, many groups and individuals have provided critical assistance. In particular, I received two sabbaticals from Truman State University: the first in 2007–8 at the beginning of this project, when I was considering the broader question of the idea of equality in American history; and the second in 2015–16 toward its conclusion, during which I finished about half of the chapters and sketched out the remainder. During that first sabbatical I also received an Andrew Mellon Foundation Research Fellowship from the Library Company of Philadelphia and the Historical Society of Pennsylvania, which allowed me to spend a wonderful January working at those two fine institutions, gain guidance from the Library Company's James Green, and live at the Company's lovely Cassatt House. I have also been fortunate to work with the supportive and skilled library staff at Truman, particularly with Lori Allen in Interlibrary Loan, who labored to track down and borrow rare works from distant libraries and archives. I am particularly grateful to my history department colleagues for supporting me in many ways throughout this project, including leaves of absence in 2012–13 and 2018–19.

That first leave allowed me to accept a critical long-term research fellowship funded by the American Antiquarian Society (AAS) and the National Endowment for Humanities (NEH). Ten months at the AAS in Worcester, Massachusetts, allowed me to accomplish much of the research for this project and to draft the first three chapters. In addition to daily access to the society's incomparably vast holdings of printed materials, I benefited from the expert support and guidance of its staff, including Paul Erickson, Ashley Cataldo, Vincent Golden, Lauren Hewes, Marie Lamoureaux, Denis Laurie, Elizabeth Pope, Laura Wasowicz, and S. J. Wolfe. (My apologies to those I've neglected here.) Also, living next door at the Fellow's Residence provided a unique, wonderful, and fruitful opportunity to meet, learn from, and dine with wonderful scholars at various stages of their careers, including David Anthony, John Demos, Neil Kamil, Jessica Linker, Jen Manion, Scott McLaren, Dawn Peterson, Christina Snyder, and Gloria Whiting. As the long-term resident that year, I also enjoyed serving as maître d'hôtel and experiencing special events such as the twenty-four inches of snow delivered by winter storm Nemo. The fellowship also allowed me to participate during that year in seminars at the Massachusetts Historical Society and Princeton Institute for Advanced Study and to give a lecture from chapter 3 at Western Connecticut State University.

While I started studying the idea of American equality during my first sabbatical, I began to narrow my focus while participating in a summer 2011 NEH research seminar in Philadelphia, "The Problem of Governance in the Early American Republic," which was the last seminar of many organized and run by John Larson and Michael Morrison (ה"ע). In addition to attending daily meetings at the Library Company to read and dissect the best published scholarship in the field and taking tours of the city's historic sites and pubs, seminar members worked on and shared our individual projects. At this critical juncture, after a couple of years during which my work on the general idea of equality had stalled, the advice and support of my seminar colleagues—Patrick Bottiger, Melissa Bullard, Christopher Childers, Thomas Cox, Andrew Fagal, Gregory King-Owen, Helen Knowles, Albert Koschnik, Gabriel Loiacono, Patrick Peel, Andrew Schocket, Nora Pat Small, Sarah Swedberg, and John Van Atta—encouraged me to renew the project and focus on the issue of *economic* equality. I owe a particular debt to Gabe for suggesting the title.

Later, the overall project and early versions of two chapters benefited from seminars organized and led by Danielle Allen at the Princeton Institute for Advanced Study (IAS): my project overview and chapter 3 in January 2013 (with special thanks to Patchen Markell, who told me about Eric Nelson's *Hebrew Republic*, particularly important for chapter 1) and chapter 4 in April 2015 as part of participating "virtually" in the IAS Social Science 2014–15 seminar, "Egalitarianisms." Both seminars involved outstanding scholars from a range of disciplines. I also benefited from conversations about my work with Jonathan Israel and Michael Walzer, faculty at the IAS. My occasional visits to the IAS were wonderful in so many ways, including the amazing luncheon seminars, famous afternoon teas with scrumptious cookies, the pilgrimage to the library where Einstein had worked, and even my attempts during the frigid winter to solve the malfunctioning "smart energy" functions of the newly constructed visitors' apartment.

I have also been fortunate to participate in many other seminars in which participants read early drafts and prepared comments that helped me develop and sharpen this project. The Early American Seminar Series hosted by the Massachusetts Historical Society read chapter 3 in February 2013; the comments offered by participants helped immensely, particularly those offered by official commenter Brendan McConville, and I appreciate everyone waiting as I made the dash in a fast taxi from Logan after snow delayed my flight. Participants in a similar workshop closer to home, the Missouri Regional Seminar in Early American History, provided a very helpful discussion of chapter 4 in February 2015. The great FREAC folks (Front Range Early American Consortium) read the first draft of chapter 5 in October 2015 and gave me extremely useful suggestions for improvements. Finally, the Grim Group, an informal faculty reading circle at Truman, read and gave me comments on an early version of chapter 1 in January 2013 and a draft of a conference paper on the Jubilee (Sabbath gadol) that connected segments of chapters 1, 3, 4, and 9. Marc Becker, Anton Daughters, and Jason McDonald were there for both; William Ashcraft, Margaret Edwards, and Caleb Owen made it for one.

Some chapters also benefited substantially from close readings by individual colleagues. Michael Winship of the University of Georgia helped sharpen chapter 1 and pointed me toward recent scholarship on seventeenth-century England. Richard Brown took time out from his project on equal rights, *Self-Evident Truths*, to give a close and fruitful reading to chapter 3, and he provided additional suggestions at various points along the way. Laura Wasowicz, curator of Children's Literature at the AAS, opened my eyes years ago to the potential of children's literature in historical research and helped with chapter 5. Doug Egerton at Le Moyne College, who had recently written *The Wars of Reconstruction*, was kind enough to read and provide useful comments on a draft of chapter 9. Because I wanted the book to appeal to a broad readership, I also asked interested and willing cousins to read and comment on chapters; Craig Mautner, an independent software engineer, tackled chapter 2, and Gail Mautner, a lawyer with Lane Powell in Seattle, helped with chapter 7. Of course, I am responsible for all interpretations, omissions, and errors.

This work is much stronger because I was able to present pieces at conferences where colleagues offered much-appreciated comments and support. I presented pieces of what became chapter 3 at the meeting of the Society for Historians of the Early Republic (SHEAR) in July 2009, at the meeting of the Omohundro Institute for Early American History and Culture in June 2012, and at Western Connecticut State University in the fall of 2012. I presented an overview of chapter 6 at the second conference on the Histories of Capitalism in America, at Cornell University in September 2016; sections of chapter 5 at the SHEAR meeting in July 2017; and the paper on "The American Great Jubilee" at the Religion and Politics in Early America Conference at St. Louis in March 2018. I also benefited from twice describing the entire project to audiences that included a range of academics: first to the Truman Faculty Seminar in spring 2017 and then in the keynote lecture for the Kinder Institute on Constitutional Democracy Summer Seminar, University of Missouri, August 2018.

I was fortunate to spend 2018–19 as Distinguished Research Fellow at the Kinder Institute. While my focus that year was starting a new research project and participating in the cornucopia of Kinder seminars and lectures, I was also able to revise the book manuscript far more quickly than would have been possible with the usual teaching and administrative responsibilities. This fellowship and the others I received during the past decade were only possible because of colleagues who regularly wrote recommendations—in particular, Danielle Allen, John Brooke, Richard Brown, and Christopher Clark—for those and many others for which I applied but did not receive. Thank you!

Like other scholars, I wove this book around my family; they have my gratitude for their support and my apologies for absences and absence-mindedness. When I started the project, David and Joshua were in middle school, and Barbara was senior editor for Truman State University Press. As it developed, David's senior year in high school fell during my AAS-NEH fellowship in Worcester, and I became quite familiar with Cape Air's eight-passenger Cessna from STL to IRK, Kirksville's airport. Joshua's senior year, on the other hand, came during the last sabbatical, which I spent at home writing, and I was therefore able (and happy) to take him on college campus visits. As I finished the manuscript, David had finished his zoology B.S. and became involved in a series of internships, Joshua was heading toward finishing his history B.A. at Brandeis, and Barbara (now director) was in the process of shutting down the press due to Missouri's cuts in financial support for public higher education. Such cuts are, of course, one of the elements in this country's problem with the growing gap between the wealthy and everyone else.

The Lost Tradition of Economic Equality
in America, 1600–1870

Introduction

By the early twenty-first century, the United States of America reached some of the highest levels of wealth and income inequality in the world. Recent judicial decisions give the spending of money to influence elections the same protection as speech and seem to grant corporations more power than that held by individual citizens. Although Americans cherish political and social equality, at least rhetorically, a large percentage opposes measures that would limit corporate power and wealth and is hostile to progressive taxes that would redistribute wealth downward. Most more generally view the individual accumulation of great wealth as evidence of talent and hard work and one of the cherished freedoms guaranteed by the Founding Fathers. In fact, as this book shows, the United States was shaped in part by the radical tradition of economic equality and the notion that the health and stability of a republican commonwealth required avoiding extremes of great wealth or terrible poverty.

I began this study while finishing an earlier book on Native Americans in southern New England from the Revolution through Reconstruction in which (among other things) I delved deeply into economic concerns. The widening gulf between rich and poor in the United States was becoming a major public concern, decried in a growing number of policy studies and articles in national publications. Few considered the history of the issue, and those that did, at best, went back to the Gilded Age for what the writers assumed was the origin of concerns over economic inequality. Such ignorance was unfortunate, as I knew from past research that during the Revolution and for decades afterward Americans believed that widespread property ownership was essential to republican government and worried about the corrupting influence of concentrated wealth. Yet I also knew that Congress during Reconstruction had rejected egalitarian land reforms while extending the vote to freedmen, which seemed to mark a substantive ideological shift. My research into how and why that shift occurred led to this book.

The ideas and passions that shaped the tradition of economic equality in America began in early modern England. In the 1400s, the feudal paradigm of a "godly hierarchy" that should forever monopolize wealth as well as power was fatally undermined by the Renaissance, with its expansion of trade, growth of cities, invasion of the Americas, and the rediscovery of Roman accounts of efforts to end corrupting power by limiting wealth. A century later, that weakened edifice was doomed by the Protestant revolt against Catholic hierarchy, with the rapid spread of subversive literature printed in everyday language. Perhaps most noteworthy for our story, new translations of Jewish texts featured discussions of the Jubilee (Great Sabbath) held every half-century, during which all debts were forgiven, all slaves freed, and all land returned to its original owners. These secular and sacred notions of equality, economic as well as social and political, exploded into prominence during England's civil war in the late 1640s, when the Diggers established a commune near London and denounced private landholding as the Original Sin. Although the Diggers were soon squashed, the radical notion of economic equality approached reality in the American colonies, particularly in New England, thanks largely to the weak colonial hierarchy and the abundant land "provided" (unwillingly) by indigenous peoples. Natives also helped shape ideas of equality at the turn of the century: Enlightenment writers depicted Indians as "noble savages" representing the virtues of Eden, and some Indians visitors to England were quoted criticizing the vast gap between rich and poor.

These notions of economic equality gained strength with the outbreak of the American Revolution and continued to swell afterward, possibly cresting in the 1790s, even as the opposing liberal defense of individual property rights emerged and gained prominence. When the War for Independence erupted, price regulation efforts reflected traditional concepts of the "just price" and more radical egalitarian republican ideals. Americans generally embraced equality instead of regarding it as dreaded anarchy and saw their new country as the most egalitarian nation on earth. But at the same time, they began to view capital as a source of corrupting affluence, vehemently opposed the creation of corporations as a source of privileged power, were increasingly concerned that an aristocracy of wealth could endanger the republic, and called for measures to ensure a future of independent households and widespread property ownership, most commonly by ending primogeniture. These values formed the tradition of American economic equality. Some Americans even advocated legal limits on individual property. In the 1790s, anxieties about inequality intensified with the new national institutions, the increasing wealth and influence of a relatively few men, passions over the French Revolution, and the emergence of warring political parties. Some became convinced that the nation needed a stabilizing hierarchy. Instead, in 1800 a "passion for equality" swept Thomas Jefferson into the presidency.

But the tradition of economic equality was increasingly challenged by new developments in the country's culture and economy. Americans saw education as a critical route to socioeconomic equality, with widespread literacy necessary to maintain virtue and republican government. To fulfill that demand, printers produced not only newspapers, political literature, and sermons but also books for children. Long-standing habits and no copyright laws meant that, until the 1830s, these works originated mostly in England, written by gentry to instruct laboring children that inequalities in wealth and power were "natural" and should be embraced. The American conservatives who advocated formal schooling for children appreciated that such literature taught self-discipline and social duty as well as skills and, when they began to write schoolbooks, generally echoed the prescription to work hard and accept the authority of wealthy men. The adult literature dealing with similar concerns, on the other hand, generated much more debate with a wide range of prescriptions. On one side, a growing body of American writers, particularly ministers and merchants, rejected older ideas of republican virtue and pushed Adam Smith's ideas to new extremes, stating with scientific certainty that individual greed and wealth were good, and poverty the result of natural inequalities. On the other side, the shocking and impoverishing rise of unstable unskilled wage labor caused many to urge either minimum wages and other measures to support laboring men, in order to preserve republican patriarchal household independence, or a radical vision of collective enterprise and democratic socialism as the only way to achieve economic equality.

As Americans argued over the best course for the nation's economy, the political system that would enact such policies was changing dramatically. Between 1800 and 1830, states eliminated from their constitutions property requirements to vote and hold office. Today we celebrate this democratic shift despite the racial strictures adopted at the same time. But there was another dark side to the change, discussed at the time but unnoticed since: it severed the traditional links between political and economic power. By the time Andrew Jackson with Martin Van Buren forged his Democratic Party, American wage-workers without property could vote (unlike their English counterparts), allowing them to participate seemingly as equals in electoral politics and join with the wealthy and middle class in party solidarity, weakening labor organizing and making the ballot box "the coffin to class consciousness." Thus, even as Jackson celebrated the simultaneous victory of his candidacy and the democracy, Americans increasingly assumed that inherited power and lifelong wage labor were normal and unalterable aspects of their republic.[1]

At the same time, the country's increasingly concentrated wealth and terrible poverty generated a new surge of efforts to revive and recharge the American tradition of economic equality. One new current in the surge was the sudden flourishing of a communitarian movement, in which many Americans embraced communal property and labor in an effort to transcend the polity's limits on managing the problems of the early industrial market economy. That effort began with a few devout religious groups like the Shakers and mushroomed in the 1820s and 1830s with secular quasi-socialist settlements organized on Owenite or Fourierist principles. A different reaction was to call for fundamental reforms in the way the nation managed its vast western territories. In 1844 that call became a movement with the formation of the National Reform Association (NRA) by labor organizers with the aim of abolishing the current "Land Monopoly," opening free homesteads to settlers with limits on size (160-acres) and inheritances, and imposing a ten-hour workday for laborers. While the NRA's vision reached back to the Diggers, with an end to absolute landownership, its policies sought to solve urban labor poverty by reviving the American tradition of economic equality through egalitarian farming households. The organization grew rapidly by forging connections with labor groups and communes, and its leaders would help form the Free Soil Party and spawn the 1862 Homestead Act.

Unfortunately, the marginalization of that American tradition became clear with Congress's unwillingness to confiscate and redistribute plantation land to freedmen during Reconstruction. During the Civil War, Republicans considered measures to free human and landed property from Confederate leaders. In 1865, in the wake of the Thirteenth Amendment ending slavery, they gave the new Freedmen's Bureau the duty to rent up to forty acres to freedmen at very low rates, and in the occupied southeast coast General Sherman provided black families with forty-acre allotments from lands "abandoned" by Confederate owners. But after Lincoln's assassination, President Andrew Johnson ordered the return of land to the former rebels, and Congress, despite urgent proposals, rejected confiscation and redistribution, trusting in wage labor and the free market, and choosing to extend only civil rights and the vote to freedmen. While clearly racism was a factor, their decision also highlighted the new paradigm that political power and economic power were distinct and showed that the American tradition of economic equality had been supplanted by an ideology of sacred private property and virtuous wage labor. Until the 1800s, Americans assumed that a citizen needed economic independence in order to exercise his proper political role in a virtuous republic, but by the end of the Civil War they overwhelmingly believed that citizens needed only the vote.

The tradition of economic equality developed between 1600 and 1880 not as a straight path with a coherent ideology but as a wandering stream of related ideas. That course is hardly surprising, given the dramatic changes in the United States with national independence and new governments; the country's dramatic expansion and growing power; international revolutions in politics, technology, and finance; the rise of mass production, cities, and wage labor; and the growing authority of democratic political and social ideals. The stream ranged between two very different shores—on one side, the belief that all property should be held in common, and on the other, the assumption every household should have enough property to avoid dependence and that government should prevent extremes of terrible poverty or excessive wealth. There were also many different intellectual sources for that stream: theology was certainly significant, most notably radical Protestant egalitarianism and idealized Jewish traditions, although more noticeable were the secular sources, particularly classical republican ideals and the Enlightenment's labor theory of value.

Yet there were also persistent currents in this stream. The most constant was the notion that a virtuous republic requires widespread ownership of property, along with avoiding extreme wealth or poverty and corrupting connections between wealth and power (i.e., corporations). That ideal was extremely powerful during the Revolution and early Republic but faced a fundamental challenge with the rise of mass production and wage labor. Concerned Americans tried to answer that challenge with various forms of communitarianism—labor associations, calls for limits on inheritance, Fourierism, the international socialist movement—and by the NRA's calls to use western federal lands for family homesteads and to bar speculation. Biblically based calls for economic equality were significant primarily at the beginning of this story, with the Diggers who saw landownership as the Original Sin and New England puritans who barred individual greed, although the Jewish concept of a Great Jubilee continued to serve as a touchstone for ultimate economic justice and, for African Americans, included the end of slavery. The one "native" egalitarian vision, the Edenic Indian, celebrated by many European intellectuals during the Enlightenment, was universally rejected by Americans during this period, although (as noted in the epilogue) it would emerge as a noticeable trope in the mid-twentieth century. In light of the continued American concern about rising inequality, frequent worshipful references to Founding Fathers, and recent discussion of reparations for African Americans, this history needs to become more familiar.

CHAPTER ONE

English Origins

The American tradition of economic equality began in mid-seventeenth-century England with the idea that that every man had the right to land as well as the right to participate in politics. This egalitarian ideology had its roots, ironically, in the ancient assumption that all forms of power were connected, even though that paradigm for centuries had been used to justify autocratic authority, whether feudalism or absolute monarchy. But when the English Civil War exploded in the 1640s, driven by antimonarchical anger and Protestant desires for religious reform, that old assumption spawned the radical notion that Englishmen should have economic as well as political equality. The concept was first broadcast by a group of London-based "middling" men who became known as the Levellers and, soon after, in a more refined and radical form by the Diggers, or, as they called themselves, "true Levellers." James Harrington put those ideas at the core of his novel *The Commonwealth of Oceana*, published in 1656, and they can be glimpsed in England's American colonies, particularly (and ironically) in New England, and in the Glorious Revolution of 1688. That connection between economic and political equality became so deeply embedded in Anglo-American thought and culture that it became an ideological tradition.

At the start of the seventeenth century, most Europeans still believed in the necessity of a rigid social hierarchy where a comparatively few "well bred" men dominated the reins of government and the engines of wealth. The intertwined nature of power in this pyramid-shaped hierarchy was often depicted as a Great Chain of Being that began with God and stretched downward through monarchs to aristocrats, yeomen, and servants to insects and rocks. Men inherited the authority that God had granted Adam—namely, to rule over those below them in that Chain; even the lowliest peasant exerted power over his wife and children. That assumption accompanied those who went to America. In April 1630, as John Winthrop sailed aboard the *Arbella* toward New England, he penned in his diary a sermon describing the goals for the Massachusetts Bay Colony that he would govern. "GOD ALMIGHTY in His most holy and wise providence," he began, "hath so disposed of the condition of mankind, as in all times some must be rich, some poor, some high and eminent in power and dignity; others mean and in submission."[1]

Winthrop like most Englishmen assumed that his country's prosperity depended on the stability of this hierarchy, and those with power and property enforced that presumption. At the top was the king, who in theory was the owner of the entire domain and its source of law—and was therefore exempt from those laws. This ideology gained strength after 1527 when Henry VIII pulled the kingdom out of the Catholic orbit, placed himself at the head of the Church of England, and seized lands held by Catholic monasteries and officials. The Church of England's first *Book of Common Prayer* (1549) emphasized that God required obedience to superiors and particularly to the king. A later version of its catechism pledged, "To love, honour, and succor my father and mother. To honour and obey the kyng and his ministers. To submitte my selfe to all my governours, teachers, spiritual pastours and maisters. To ordre my selfe lowly and reverentelye to all my betters." Henry's daughter Elizabeth I ruled from 1558 until her death in 1603; she named as successor her nephew James, already Scotland's king. Both Elizabeth and James maneuvered to increase the Crown's power by rewarding supporters with titles of nobility and punishing opponents with poverty or prison.[2]

The wealthiest men other than the monarch wielded the power of service in Parliament. Titled nobility automatically served in the House of Lords. As a result, noblemen controlled the wealth and power from the huge country estates and city homes that came with their titles; in addition, they also "owned" manor courts; maintained and controlled large households of relatives, domestics, and laborers; and held the power to appoint clergy for the parishes on their estates. Knights and other titled gentry held less land and power and did not sit in the House of Lords, but they were still considered gentlemen and prime candidates for Parliament's elected branch, the House of Commons. Those who served in either house knew they were subservient to the monarch: while officially they had the sole power to propose new laws and approve new taxes, the monarch could independently issue rules and, at will, dismiss and recall Parliament. Wealth and its power were limited by primogeniture: the eldest son inherited the whole of the father's title, estates, and power, whereas younger sons entered the military or the church. Even the minor power to vote was limited by property, as only about 25 to 30 percent of adult men had the requisite 40-shillings worth of land or other income.[3]

During the 1500s, England's hierarchical system had developed social and economic tensions. The king and Parliament largely ignored the growing cities, the high migration rate within the country, and the increasingly powerful role of merchants, artisans, and others who did not fit the old political structure. Outside the kingdom, Spain's "discovery" of the Americas meant that England shifted from the edge of the Mediterranean-focused world of trade to the center of the increasingly lucrative transatlantic world of conquest and commerce. Inside the kingdom, the rising population, now bouncing back from the ravages of the Black Death, met the declining harvests due to the Little Ice Age, resulting in frequent famines and shorter lifespans. Landowners began implementing improvements that reduced the commons, most notably consolidating and hedging pastures, which allowed more intensive agriculture, raising sheep for the wool trade, and exerting more control over pastoral and sylvan regions.[4]

England's economy did improve somewhat toward the end of the century. Despite the drag of corruption along with resistance from those more concerned with local conditions, the country's expansion of domestic and international trade gradually integrated its markets, which helped manage crop shortfalls even as harvests improved. Unlike the rest of Europe, in England the nobility as well as the gentry was deeply involved in these developments, and the king remained central to the economy because he held the power to grant corporate charters and licenses to trade and produce. Those included a growing roster of monopolies—over glass, coal, iron, brushes, combs, pins, and many other consumer goods—that pushed up prices and benefited mostly men who already had power and wealth through their connections to the Court. But those at the top of the hierarchy feared more threatening changes, and Henry and Elizabeth with Parliament's blessing issued laws to stabilize prices, wages, and labor itself. "Vagrants" and "masterless men" were threatened with whippings, branding, mutilation, hanging, slavery, and transportation to the colonies in servitude. "Liberties" remained privileges granted by superiors to particular groups, not inherent rights held by all citizens in the country.[5]

Decades later, in 1688, the first attempt to survey the population and income in England and Wales depicted a stark pyramid of wealth and power. At the top, the "temporal lords," 160 households with 6,400 members, had annual incomes averaging £3,200; below them were the 520 "spiritual lords" (Church of England bishops) with annual incomes averaging £1,300. Then barons (£800 per year), knights (£650), justices of the peace (£450), "gentle-men" (£280), "persons in greater offices and places" (£240), and those in "lesser offices" (£120). The next rank, "eminent merchants and traders by sea," had the relatively high annual income of £400; "lesser merchants" earned £198; and lawyers obtained £154. The remaining fifteen ranks—two levels of cler-gymen, two types of freeholders, tenant farmers, scholars, shopkeepers, arti-sans, naval and army officers, seamen, laborers, paupers, soldiers, and vagrants—included more than half of the country's population and obtained less than £75 per year—slightly over 2 percent of the income at the top, and 26 percent of a gentleman's income. Although the details were almost certainly different than they would have been earlier, there is no doubt that the larger, most meaningful pattern would be the same: social and political ranks were closely correlated to wealth.[6]

Beneath the authoritarian English hierarchy lay a subversive ideological un-dercurrent that would blossom into broad demands for human equality, in-cluding wealth. Some scholars argue that the concept of human rights did not develop until the second half of the eighteenth century, with the emergence of empathy along with sharpened notions of autonomy and privacy in West-ern culture, and therefore challenges to hierarchical power awaited the devel-opment of broad self-conscious political theories. But there were clear prede-cessors. In fifteenth-century Europe generally, the Renaissance undermined old assumptions about a sacred hierarchy in various ways, including the spread (through the new printing press) of Roman historians who praised the virtue of republican government. In England, this classical republican ideal became part of the simmering conflict between renters, gentry, and aristocrats: an ex-panding field of civil rights derived from the Magna Carta; communitarian traditions of land use rights; and an increasingly powerful commonwealth ethos that the state should serve the common good. Yet none of these elements challenged England's socioeconomic hierarchy until political conflicts linked with radical Protestant ideas intensified in the second quarter of the seven-teenth century.[7]

During Elizabeth's reign (1558–1603) and the early decades of Stuart rule, tenants and villagers faced swelling rents and new restrictions on the commons as aristocrats and gentry enclosed pastures and drained fens. A noticeable number resisted, often with traditional tactics of poaching or targeted violence against property, sometimes encouraged or directed by gentry allies with their own agendas. This violence seemed to crest in mid-1607, when thousands of protesters in the Midlands calling themselves "Diggers" rioted against the widespread enclosures in two counties by a particularly unpopular family; local militia refused to oppose the actions, and the residents of Leicester threatened to join until the landowners used their employees to squash the uprising. For the next two years, sympathetic anti-enclosure actions shook the kingdom. Similarly, protests in the rapidly growing city of London increased and shifted from local concerns (such as the supply and price of grain) to issues of national significance, often venting hostility to a royal official or tax. Many lords, gentry, and tenants saw the country's order and stability under siege; the cottagers and laborers put on trial for rioting against enclosures were accused of being "levelers" of the kingdom's social structure as well as its hedges and fences.[8]

Although the fears of disorder are understandable, and some of these protests may have been directed at England's hierarchy, the protesters' more obvious goal to preserve the common good fit fundamentally conservative commonwealth ideals. The continued power of the commonwealth is highlighted in the way that traditional land-use rights were occasionally successfully defended in court, particularly when backed by a sympathetic patron, until Parliament passed laws in the 1600s giving landowners new powers to raise rents and enclose lands. Some aristocrat intellectuals boasted that English yeomen and gentry had far more economic and social mobility than their peers in France or elsewhere in Europe. Although the upper levels of the country's hierarchy controlled the legal system, Englishmen regardless of class were able to claim some civil rights from the Magna Carta and other sources, including trials by peers in which the jury often had the power to decide law as well as fact. In addition, during this period the myth emerged that, before the Norman invasion, Anglo-Saxons boasted democracy and broad landholding and that those ancient ways remained deeply rooted in England. This story made its first appearance in Edward Coke's *Institutes of the Lawes of England* (1628), would later appear in many important Anglo-American publications, and offered a potential cultural support for broader economic and political rights.[9]

But the most important challenges were driven by the Reformation's rejection of Catholic hierarchy and power. Growing numbers of intellectuals, gentry, and merchants called for the Bible to be translated in the vernacular so that all could read and understand God's Word; at the same time, the increasing availability and declining cost of printing encouraged literacy and facilitated the rapid mass publication of writings. This revolution was not limited to spiritual concerns. As perhaps best highlighted by the creation of the Church of England, lawmakers and lawbreakers alike saw no distinction between church and state or ecclesiastical and constitutional concerns; this included economic matters such as landholding, labor, and moral behavior in the market. The growing "priesthood of believers" eagerly read and argued over an expanding corpus that examined theology, church government, and human relations; thus, *religion* contained the ideological and social meanings that a century later became imbedded in *politics*.

In 1607, when the Scottish King James ascended to the English throne, he initially seemed open to those who sought deeper institutional, ritual, and theological reforms in the Church of England; however, he quickly made it clear that he regarded those puritans as an illegitimate challenge to his authority. The reformers were also divided among themselves: many sought only to eliminate the formal rituals and trappings continued by the Church; "Independents" insisted that each parish should have the power to govern itself, including the right to choose its minister and discipline members; and Presbyterians wanted a national ecclesiastical structure without autocratic bishops, as in Scotland. Both James and the Presbyterians feared that the Independents gave too much power to ordinary people. Independents would later be targeted by Charles and his archbishop William Laud, and many would flee to Massachusetts where they established their desired congregational church structure.[10]

Even the Independents feared and opposed the radical reformers who envisioned full human equality. One of the most infamous such groups was the Familists, the Family of Love, which had emerged during the previous century from the anticlerical Lollard movement in northern Europe. Its founder Hendrick Niclaes preached the mystical message that members should follow all aspects of Christ, including an escape from earthly sin to perfection. Familists came from a wide range of classes and occupations and, while remaining in the Church of England, formed secret groups to read Scriptures and to restore in their lives the innocence of the Garden of Eden. Many authorities considered the Familists heretical and suspected that they rejected "proper" arrangements of wealth and power and held all goods in common. One of Niclaes's best-known works, *Terra Pacis* (1572), encouraged such suspicions: it described a pilgrim's progress to the land of peace without a rigid hierarchy and where "no man that claims anything to be his own, as to possess the same to his own private use . . . but all whatsoever is free."[11]

Broader discontent began to swell in the 1620s, as first James and then Charles (after becoming king in 1625) increasingly insisted on control of foreign policy and domestic spending and tried to impose new taxes, fees, and customs duties. James was used to the more accommodating Scottish Parliament, wished like the absolutist Catholic monarchs of Spain and France to rule without elected assemblies, and disliked the disruptive threat seemingly posed by puritans; Charles *believed* that God had given him unconditional authority and that he need answer to no man. The House of Commons, on the other hand, maneuvered to increase its power and influence through the impeachment of prominent courtiers and pressed Charles to accept the Petition of Right forbidding the king from imposing taxes or martial law without its approval, in exchange for funds to pay past war debts. This political conflict had a strong religious component. Charles edged toward toleration of Catholics—his wife was French Catholic—and wished to increase the Church of England's power to control parishes and enforce doctrines and rituals. The Commons was dominated by puritans who feared a Catholic conspiracy, detested the extravagance of the king's courtiers, and aimed to reduce the Church's administration (and expenses) and reform its rituals.[12]

Cornered, in 1628 Charles accepted the Petition of Right but then acted in ways that intensified conflict. He dismissed Parliament and sought to rule without it, raised money in various ways including selling new contracts to drain the Fens (destroying resources needed by thousands of cottagers), and expanded efforts to punish religious dissidents. Frustrated lawyers, merchants, and gentry supported the increasingly radical calls by puritan preachers and writers to reduce the power of the monarch and Church. In 1637 Charles sought to incorporate the Church of Scotland, but the Scots resisted and by 1640 defeated the king's forces, captured Newcastle, and forced Charles to pay their war debts along with a daily "fee" not to push further south. The king still hoped to suppress the Scottish rebellion and called another Parliament in order to obtain more money. Parliament took the opportunity to force reforms that severely reduced the king's power, including an end to his right to dissolve Parliament or to levy duties or fees without its permission. But the House of Commons also faced problems, particularly a widening gap between "conservatives" and "radicals," with tradition and fear of popular political passions favoring the former. In November 1641 the king's ambivalent response to the Irish Revolt generated bitter debates in the House before a bare majority passed the Grand Remonstrance denouncing Charles's policies and demanding parliamentary approval of his ministers. Bolstered by the apparently strong support of a large "moderate" royalist faction in Parliament, in early January Charles took four hundred soldiers into Parliament to arrest John Pym, the leader of the radicals, and four other prominent opponents for treason; when that effort failed, Charles fled London, fearing the hostile city populace. Negotiations between the king and Parliament became increasingly acrimonious and in August exploded into civil war.[13]

The war let loose and intensified festering grievances about injustice and oppression, which began to transform religious platitudes about human equality into social and political ideologies. Initially the conflict was limited: most Englishmen were neutral, and Parliament's conservative alliance of gentry, lawyers, and merchants wanted a restricted constitutional monarchy, not a revolution that could endanger its power. But as the war spread and intensified, more egalitarian ideas gained strength, often expressed in religious, even apocalyptic terms. The press became an important part of the movement, as the conflict destroyed the mechanisms of censorship, and printers became able, willing, and even eager to produce a much wider range of political and religious publications. Some of the most prominent radical writers were Levellers, a loosely knit group based primarily in London that had coalesced in the 1640s and agitated for popular sovereignty, egalitarian natural rights, and deep reforms in the common law in order to eliminate tyrannical flaws that they thought had been imposed by the Normans in 1066. The most prominent Levellers, like John Lilburne, were well educated and came from "middling" families in the City. Now middle-aged, they had been deeply involved in dissenting congregations before the war and anti-Presbyterian activities during the conflict, and from the opening salvo they challenged England's constitution and social hierarchy. In 1646, at the height of the war, Lilburne affirmed: "All and every particular and individual man and woman, that ever breathed in the world, are by nature all equal and alike in their power, dignity, authority and majesty, none of them having (by nature) any authority, dominion or magisterial power one over or above another."[14]

Perhaps the most significant element in England's political hothouse was the New Model Army, established by Parliament in 1645 to be a full-time professional national force, with rank and honors determined by proficiency rather than status or wealth. Many joined for ideological reasons, including experienced soldiers who were strongly puritan, Independent ministers, and apprentices and artisans from London with more drastic ideas. It was more a remodeling of the old than a completely new entity, and much of its organization and officers remained the same, but the New Army's political purpose made it very different from previous forces. Overall the New Army fought to separate the king from his imagined evil advisers and to compel religious reforms; either meant reducing the king's power, so not surprisingly the Army became a nursery for more radical political, social, and economic ideas, as many chaplains and some in the ranks preached sermons that the ordinary soldiers would help establish God's kingdom and equal justice for all.[15]

The passions and burdens of civil war soon moved these soldiers to insist on popular sovereignty and broader civil liberties. By March 1647, under the leadership of Sir Thomas Fairfax and Oliver Cromwell, the Army had destroyed most of the royal forces. In May, Charles sought refuge with the Scottish forces in England, hoping to create an alliance against Parliament, but instead the Scots turned the king over to Parliament, which imprisoned him. Army rank and file became increasingly worried that Presbyterian conservatives in the legislature were negotiating a peace with Charles that would preserve Presbyterian privileges and an established church. The tension worsened in the spring of 1647 as Parliament moved to disband much of the Army and send the rest to campaign in Ireland without paying months of back wages. In response, troops called for a new constitution with broad political participation. Each regiment elected two Agitators and demanded that Fairfax gather all of them at a rendezvous outside London. These Agitators developed close relations with Lilburne and other Levellers who viewed the Army as the only legitimate authority in the land until they could deliver that power to the people. On June 3, one day before the rendezvous, Cornet Joyce Jr. led a company of mounted troopers to seize the king from Parliament's supervision. One day later, all agreed to create a council that included officers and Agitators; on June 5 they issued *A Solemne Engagement of the Army*, read to the Army and directed at Parliament, agreeing not to disband until their grievances were met.[16]

During the summer, it became clear that Parliament, along with Cromwell and his son-in-law, General Henry Ireton, preferred to reach a very different, more "moderate" agreement with the king. Outraged, five cavalry regiments elected new Agitators to push for stronger measures: they wrote a manifesto, *The Case of the Armie Truly Stated*, calling for no king or House of Lords; a Parliament subordinate to the people elected every two years with representation determined by population; and complete freedom of religion and no special privileges in the law. In order to maintain the unity of the Army, the council agreed to a debate on the proposals, to be held at the end of October in Putney, then six miles from London and now in its southwest sector. By that time, *The Case* had been taken up by a larger gathering of Agitators, now joined by the Levellers, and reissued as *The Agreement of the People*, which became the focus of the Putney Debates. At the end of October, the *Agreement* was presented to the council, which agreed to hold the debate.[17]

When the debates began on October 28, it quickly became clear that economic issues had become a major concern. Edward Sexby, one of the Levellers who had helped capture the king, insisted that "the poor and meaner" soldiers had the right to vote because they had saved the nation, and Colonel Thomas Rainsborough similarly argued that all men in the realm should be allowed to vote because they were equally affected by the laws enacted by government. On the other side, Henry Ireton and Cromwell (who led a politically power-ful group of officers known as the Grandees) urged a plan that met many of the Army's concerns while limiting political power to those "possessed of the permanent interest in the land" to make sure voters could not "destroy property" by passing laws making "an equality of goods and estate." That position not only followed prewar paradigms but may have also reflected their alarm that earlier in the month some soldiers were calling for the income of any remaining lords to be limited to £2,000 per year, with that of other classes to be comparably limited. Thus, whereas the Levellers focused far more on polity than property, gentry officers embraced the traditional view that those elements were closely linked. The debates ended abruptly on Novem-ber 11 when word reached the camp that Charles had escaped, renewing the civil war; the Agitators agreed to consider a revision of *The Agreement*, but Fairfax and Cromwell maneuvered successfully to suppress the radicals by promising a few vague reforms and squashed an incipient spark of rebellion.[18]

By the end of the following year Parliament and the Grandees would also win the second civil war, and in January 1649 Charles I was executed for trea-son. But calls for broader and more radical reforms continued, economic as well as political, particularly as the chaos of the war was followed by a bad harvest, and Cromwell's forces crushed those who again called for back wages and fulfillment of *The Agreement*. In early December 1648 a group of radical Levellers in Buckinghamshire published *Light Shining in Buckinghamshire*, condemning enclosure and private property as original sin, and called for "Common Rights and Equity . . . A just portion for each man to live, that so none need to beg or steal for want, but everyone may live comfortably." The following March the group issued *More Light*, calling enclosure "the cause of all oppressions, whereby many thousands are deprived of their rights which God hath invested them withal, whereby they are forced to beg or steal for want." By then Gerrard Winstanley, a failed London cloth merchant who had been working for five years as a cow herder in Surrey, reached an epiphany that led the mystic to repudiate wage labor and embrace communism as the only way for mankind to gain freedom from Adam's Curse. He convinced other laborers and another former merchant, William Everard, to begin that process of liberation. On Sunday morning, April 1, just a few days after publication of *More Light*, they gathered at St. George's Hill, an area of wasteland between Cobham village and Surrey near south London, where enclosure had been particularly harmful. Here, once they set up homes and began digging and planting a commons, their numbers quickly swelled to around fifty. Although they called themselves True Levellers, they soon became known as the Diggers.[19]

On April 14, fifteen of the men published *The True Levellers Standard Advanced*, which began by declaring: "In the beginning of Time, the great Creator Reason, made the Earth to be a Common Treasury, to preserve Beasts, Birds, Fishes, and Man." Since Adam, they wrote, "the Earth hath been enclosed and given to the Elder brother Esau"—by tradition the rebellious son who sold his birthright for a pot of stew, and a clear reference to primogeniture. Through the generations, this mythical elder brother had "held the Earth in bondage" through the use of violence and "subtle selfish Counsels," resulting in the hierarchical arrangement of "Honor, Dominion and Riches . . . the curse the Creation groans under, waiting for deliverance." But they, as True Levellers, sought "by laboring the Earth in righteousness together . . . to lift up the Creation from that bondage." By their work and their words they hoped to "lay the Foundation of making the Earth a Common Treasury for all, both Rich and Poor, That every one that is born in the land, may be fed by the Earth his Mother that brought him forth according to the Reason that rules in the Creation. Not Inclosing any part into any particular land, but all as one man, working together . . . all looking upon each other, as equals in the Creation." They also highlighted the myth of an egalitarian Anglo-Saxon past and, while celebrating Parliament's overthrow of the corrupting monarchy, worried that the body had only "pretended to throw down that Norman yoke.[20]

The Diggers fulfilled the deepest fears of the Grandees by calling for an egalitarian nation of small villages holding all property in common, claiming to speak for laborers, servants, and paupers. Those gentry were not reassured when on April 19 Everard and Winstanley told Lord Fairfax and others in Whitehall that "their intent was to restore the Creation to its former Condition," especially when the delegation (apparently including a woman) failed to doff their hats and, when challenged, replied that Fairfax was "but their fellow Creature." One year later, Winstanley wrote more optimistically that Parliament's elimination of the monarchy and the House of Lords "takes away the Tirany of [Norman] conquests . . . and restores *England* to their Creation right," and he foresaw that "the Land of England shall be a common Treasury to all English men without respect of persons. . . . neither hedging in the elder, nor hedging out the younger brother." While the local landlord used gangs to beat the Diggers and the court to compel them to leave in August, they

The Declaration and Standard of the Levellers of England, 1649, titlepage. Courtesy of
The Bodleian Libraries, The University of Oxford, shelfmark G. Pamph 1371 (6).

simply moved a short distance away and created a settlement on land belonging to a more sympathetic gentleman—although he, too, turned and harassed
them until they left in April 1650. Other Digger settlements briefly appeared
in at least nine other counties, totaling several hundred inhabitants, uncoor-
dinated but inspired by common needs, common anger against "the great
Landlords . . . who are continually crucifying their poor Brethren by oppression, cheating, and robbery," and a common vision that with their help God
would bring back Edenic Creation so there would be no private estates or
poverty.[21]

The Digger movement quickly collapsed due to the violent opposition of
landlords, but the aspiration for economic equality even affected the original,
more moderate Levellers. For years John Lilburne had vigorously denied any
intention to level property, but in 1653, after reading Roman sources, Milton,
and Machiavelli, he published *The Upright Man's Vindication*, urging the right
of laborers to participate in politics and agrarian reforms that would redistribute land to soldiers and poor householders. Winstanley himself published
one more pamphlet, *The Law of Freedom in a Platform* (1652), in which he envisioned a democratic, patriarchal, communist society, with annual elections,

state-owned trading operations, no established church, and no private property or wages. After a long dedication to Cromwell, he began by insisting, "True commonwealth's freedom lies in the free enjoyment of the earth," and he connected the private ownership of land—and the creation of ministers and lawyers, as well as the evils of servitude and poverty—to William the Conqueror's victory over the English. Once the bondage of the people and the land was lifted, one of Parliament's main duties was to ensure that the land was not again "so entangled in bondage upon a new account."[22]

Winstanley's *Platform* supported another radical idea—that government had the right and even the duty to redistribute property, generally known as agrarian law, in order to create and maintain a moral commonwealth. Agrarian law had roots in two very different ancient Mediterranean traditions, Roman and Jewish. Renaissance philosophers and lawyers like Thomas More learned of the first tradition through the fifth-century chroniclers of Cicero, who condemned the Senate's application of agrarian law as subverting public order and helping to bring about the fall of the Republic. Not surprisingly, More and others wrote about land redistribution with horror. A century later, the Jewish version found its way into the various publications by Dutch Protestant intellectuals who had developed a strong interest in Hebrew and Jewish scholarship, most notably the Talmud and its most famous interpreter, Moses Maimonides (1135–1205). These writers became fascinated by ancient Jewish land laws described in the Torah and explicated by the Talmud, particularly the Sabbath Gadol, the Great Sabbath (also called the Great Jubilee), held every forty-nine years, when, with a shofar blast "proclaiming freedom throughout the land to all its inhabitants" (Lev. 25:10), all land was to be returned to its original owners (and slaves freed), which meant all land was essentially leased rather than sold. The most famous book on the topic, *De Republica Hebraeorum* (The Hebrew Republic), written by Peter van der Kun (pen name Petrus Cunaeus, 1586–1638), set out a schematic of the ancient Hebrew kingdom, described it as the best model for republican government, and highlighted the importance of the Sabbath Gadol; he rejected the older scholarship and instead argued that Rome's *lack* of regular agrarian laws had doomed its republic. *De Republica Hebraeorum* went through seven editions between 1617 and 1700 and was translated into French and English.[23]

Van der Kun's encouraging view of agrarian law along with the Roman tradition of republican equality entered the English political sphere through James Harrington's *Commonwealth of Oceana* (1656). In that novel, which quickly gained fame and would be frequently reprinted through the early nineteenth century, Harrington dared recommend an agrarian constitution that gave land to all and placed an explicit limit on income and wealth because "equality of estates causes equality of power," and "where there is inequality of Power, there can be no Commonwealth." *Oceana* depicted a society whose republican government (with a separate house to isolate the nobility) was grounded on a law that mandated partible (divided) inheritance and barred individuals from obtaining lands producing more than £2,000 per year (the precise amount some Army troopers advocated a decade earlier); anyone who somehow obtained enough land to gain a larger income was required to give the "overage" back to the state.[24]

Harrington is regarded as the originator of a strain of constitutional thought that shaped the Commonwealthmen, exemplified by the essays of John Trenchard and Thomas Gordon, written as articles in the 1720s and eventually collected and published under the title *Cato's Letters.* The essays are viewed as critical in shaping Anglo-American fears of political corruption and parliamentary tyranny leading to the American Revolution. Harrington's views on wealth and power also resonated with John Adams, one of the Revolution's leading legal minds, who told a friend in May 1776 that "Harrington has Shewn that Power always follows Property," which led him in turn to believe that "the Ballance of Power in a Society, accompanies the Ballance of Property in Land." Adams like Harrington saw land as the only source of wealth and power and therefore ignored the threat of excessive accumulation of capital. Of course, the potential for such a problem was far more apparent in the late eighteenth century than 120 years earlier. In the late 1650s, such radical ideas as well as calls for more moderate reforms were beaten down by a gentry increasingly alarmed about the country's stability and its own power. Yet at that very moment, aspects of the egalitarian vision shared by the Levellers and Harrington were developing in English colonies in North America.[25]

England's leaders first looked to the Americas toward the end of Elizabeth's reign as a means of increasing their international power and wealth, particularly in the deadly competition with Catholic Spain. The nation's establishment of overseas colonies would also relieve the dire threats to the nation's political, social, and economic order. Richard Hakluyt emphasized in *A Discourse Concerning Western Planting* (1584) that such "plantings" would provide "the manifold imployment of nombers of idle men" and keep good mariners from the poverty that forced them into piracy; this would rescue "many men of excellent wits and of divers singuler giftes" who "for trifles" such as the theft of bread might "be devoured by the gallowes." Perhaps most importantly, "the frye [children] of the wandringe beggars of England, that growe upp ydly

[idly], and hurtefull and burdenous to this Realme, may there be unladen [and] better bredd upp."[26] Anxious aristocrats and gentry saw America as the kingdom's safety valve, ensuring the kingdom's stability and their authority and wealth.

English organizers of colonization certainly intended to maintain strong hierarchies in what they perceived as the edge of the world. As glimpsed in the contemporary Familist movement, radical egalitarian ideas lay close to the surface, and the country's ruling elites were worried that those ideas would find fertile ground in the "wilderness" (actually a cornucopia of food and resources) because it lacked the institutions and people to enforce a "civilized" socioeconomic order. The potential appeared early, in the summer of 1609, when, after a massive storm, the flagship of a fleet sent to relieve Jamestown wrecked on Bermuda, an island in the Caribbean without any people. One of many survivors, Stephen Hopkins, used the Bible to persuasively argue that the colonists had returned to an Edenic state and could therefore ignore the governor and charter carried on the ship, ignore the demands by that governor and Virginia investors to build a ship to continue the trip, do only what was necessary to support their immediate families, and write a compact to govern themselves. Hopkins was arrested and the mutiny squashed, although eleven years later he returned to America on board the *Mayflower* and was among the signers of the Plymouth compact. The Bermuda episode became the source for *The Tempest* (1611), in which Shakespeare described the survivors' return to a state of nature (as John Locke would call it eight decades later), envisioned as a completely egalitarian society in which the nobility had to labor alongside the lowest.[27]

Despite this potential, the first long-term North American English settlement, Jamestown, established in 1607 by the Virginia Company, initially presented a simple struggle to survive. The company was financed by noblemen, merchants, and gentry to create an outpost where settlers might find and process precious metals; it could also be used to raid Spanish shipping to the south and develop trade with the Natives. Jamestown barely got through its first few years, for various reasons: its poor water quality (where salt and fresh water mixed), the poor judgment and unfounded expectations of its organizers, quarreling leadership, and its apprehensive and sometimes hostile relations with Natives. Disease and starvation decimated the English, especially in the winter of 1609 after food supplies shrank and Natives besieged the fort; in June 1610, the survivors abandoned the fort and headed toward the sea, but there they met with a fleet bringing four hundred men and supplies for a year, which rescued the colony. A year later, Sir Thomas Gates and Sir Thomas Dale arrived and imposed martial law; in response, "dyvers" settlers "did runne away unto the Indians," despite fears of a nasty death at the hands of the Powhatans. Those recaptured were executed in nasty ways.[28]

The colony's socioeconomic condition and its promise suddenly changed after John Rolfe introduced the lucrative crop of tobacco in 1612, and the Virginia Company decided to offer land to all colonists in 1619. Landownership in the English system carried social and political privileges as well as economic benefits, and in Virginia the political benefits were immediate because the company also authorized those now landowning colonists to elect an assembly, the House of Burgesses, that would decide issues of local concern. Settlers who had lived in the colony for at least three years were granted a hundred acres each; future settlers who stayed for at least three years would be granted "headrights": fifty acres for every person for whose passage they paid. Initially, indentured servants were promised fifty acres after they gained their freedom. In England, landownership was impossible for the poor, the middling, and even (because of primogeniture) the younger sons of nobility and gentry. Not surprisingly, young Englishmen rushed to Virginia, despite continued high mortality rates, especially after the Powhatans nearly destroyed the colony in 1622. In response, the settlers then decimated the Indians and limited the survivors to small reservations. Thus, land taken from Natives not only led to plantations scattered along the rivers and no additional towns in the colony but fueled a social, economic, and political structure more egalitarian (for white men) than in England.[29]

While the Crown took over the colony in the wake of the first Powhatan War, free land and lucrative tobacco continued to fuel the growth of Virginia and, beginning in 1634, neighboring Maryland. One study shows that 16,000 to 20,000 people entered Virginia every decade between 1650 and 1680, the equivalent of the population of Bristol, England's second largest city. But the mortality rate remained high: although 120,000 settlers went to the Chesapeake during the century, only about 70,000 whites lived there in 1700. A very high proportion (perhaps 80 percent) of the English that came to the Chesapeake region came as indentured servants, facing seven years of harsh forced labor with only some support from English law and social networks but also (at least until the 1660s) the likelihood of owning land at the end. About half of the indentured came from the lower ranks of English society; the rest were the young with nothing to lose. Of course, those positioned to make the most of the colonies' opportunities were free and fairly well-off. Few already powerful men survived more than a couple years, which meant that the gentry and merchants who did well became not only wealthy but powerful: they became justices of the peace, around whom neighborhood networks formed, and advisers to the royal governor—and therefore were able to claim more land and more power.[30]

By the 1660s a relatively stable hierarchy developed in the two Chesapeake colonies that, in a simplified and irregular fashion, echoed the order back in England. Although an unusually high percentage of the settlers continued to die quite young, the colony's demographics, sociopolitical leadership, and landownership stabilized as death rates began to fall and birth rates rose. The gentry in Virginia and Maryland increasingly regarded itself as an elite class deserving political, social, and economic power, including control of provincial offices and large swaths of the best land along the broad navigable rivers from the Potomac to the James. On the other notch of this socioeconomic order, indentured servants gaining their freedom found declining opportunities for economic and social mobility; most would end up as tenants or laborers. Evidence from defamation lawsuits filed in Virginia county courts shows an increasingly powerful, confident, and instrumentalist gentry class as generations of colonists became more deeply imbedded in social and economic networks headed by the wealthier "better sort."[31]

At the same time, landownership remained far more widespread in the Chesapeake area than back in England. For example, in Maryland's Charles County, in 1660 about 80 percent of white men owned land, and although that percentage did decline, in 1690 landownership in the county still stood at 60 percent of white men. Similarly, about 65 percent of the heads of households in Surrey County, Virginia, and 75 percent of those in Talbot County, Maryland, owned farms, and those percentages remained basically unchanged in 1704. As important was the *amount* of land owned, since a successful tobacco plantation required at least 100 acres, and all but a few Chesapeake farmers owned more. In 1705, when the land boom ended in eastern Virginia—and the importation of slaves from Africa skyrocketed—the average planter in the colony owned a farm of 225 acres, and just 10 percent of landowners held less than the requisite 100 acres.[32]

Because property ownership was joined to political participation, voting became far more extensive in the Chesapeake than in England, and after Bacon's Rebellion in 1675 the House of Burgesses even lowered the bar of property ownership. Governors dispatched from London to manage the colonies were horrified at this republican tendency. In 1712 Virginia governor Alexander Spotswood complained that because (supposedly) one had to own but half an acre in the colony to vote, "the Mob of this Country" in the last election had "generally chosen representatives of their own Class" who refused to raise taxes despite his urgent request. Three years later, he bemoaned that the half-acre standard meant that "the meaner sort of People will ever carry ye Elections," since "ye Vulgar People" inevitably chose those "such men as are their most familiar Companions," who "dare in Assembly do nothing that may be disrelished out of the House by ye Common People." More-distanced historians see Chesapeake gentry as wielding effective socioeconomic authority (as well as support and favors) through their overseas connections and positions as justices, militia officers, and vestrymen. In addition, voting was quite public, so those with relatively little land tended in the occasional elections to (literally) stand by the gentleman to whom they owed social obligations. As a result, contrary to Spotswood's grumblings, Virginia operated not as a democracy open to all but as a republic, in which elections tended to confirm the authority of the wealthy who had proved their worthiness to lead the community.[33]

Governor Winthrop's Massachusetts and the other New England colonies developed quite differently. As Winthrop warned settlers, theirs was a religious errand to this "good land," to create a godly community as an example for all Christendom "as a citie upon a hill." Instead of scattering along rivers as in Virginia, people were expected to live "under a due form of government both civil and ecclesiastical." The General Court that governed the colony insisted that people settle in chartered towns, where they could keep a loving watch on each other to ensure that sin did not take root and risk God's wrath on the community. Winthrop also emphasized that they should not expect to get rich in Massachusetts, for although God had established mankind's hierarchical condition, His will was that the wicked should be restrained so "the rich and mighty should not eat up the poor, nor the poor and despised rise up against and shake off their yoke."[34]

In keeping with this mission, Massachusetts, like Plymouth and later Connecticut and New Haven, insisted on having a congregational (independent) church established at the center of every town; usually the meetinghouse was the first building constructed and was used for all community gatherings, including church services and town meetings. The *Massachusetts Laws and Liberties*, in 1641 the first codified body of criminal law in an English colony, referenced the biblical sources that made crimes from adultery to witchcraft to bestiality punishable by death, although that ultimate penalty was rarely imposed. The puritan colonies were not precisely theocracies, because ministers were barred from holding office in order to focus on ecclesiastical duties, but (with the notable exception of Rhode Island) there were close links between church and state, including regular fast and feast days and requirements that everyone attend church. By 1658 it was recommended (Plymouth) or mandated (Massachusetts, Connecticut, and New Haven) that every town establish a school so that boys *and girls* (and, later, slaves) would learn to read the Bible. Most strikingly, only in Rhode Island was it necessary to own property to vote; voting in Massachusetts was restricted to full church members; in Plymouth, to any man designed as "a freeman" by the assembly; and in Connecticut, to all free men.[35]

New England's demographics and environment were also very different from the Chesapeake's. Between 1620 and 1640, about 13,700 colonists crossed the Atlantic to New England, and then suddenly the stream ended as the English Civil War began. Most arrived in cohesive households, and in some cases entire village groups migrated together, resulting in balanced sex ratios and stable families and communities. Their success rested on the terrible decimation of the Native population by European epidemics and wars, and the Native lands and resources that the colonists resettled, bought, stole, and reshaped. After an initial "starving period," the English raised good crops and abundant cattle in a relatively disease-free environment unlike the warm Chesapeake's, which produced dysentery as well as tobacco. The result was astonishingly long lives and large families. For example, Judith Coffin died in Newbury, Massachusetts, in 1705 at the age of *eighty*, after bearing at least 10 children who lived past infancy. She had her last child in 1669, at the age of forty-four, and lived to see 177 of her progeny. With many like Judith Coffin, by the 1670s the English population in New England rose to more than 60,000, greatly outnumbering the Natives who remained after the devastating King Philip's War.[36]

New England puritan sermons and policies emphasized that a stable socioeconomic hierarchy was necessary to fulfill God's ordinances. Various public privileges reinforced the standing and authority of elites who were expected to shepherd and improve the community. When towns divided land, larger holdings were given to the minister, church elders, merchants, judges, and those financing the settlement. Meetinghouse seats were assigned according to social rank within the community, usually reflecting wealth and prestige, and those with the best seats were expected to provide more support for the minister as well as other communal needs. Until the mid-eighteenth century, Harvard College and later Yale assigned each incoming student a rank based not on academic achievement but on his family's social standing, although one could be downgraded by particularly egregious behavior. The *Massachusetts Laws and Liberties* was surprisingly even-handed, yet even it gave the "better sort" one particular privilege: whereas no man could be whipped more than forty stripes, neither a "true gentleman, nor any man equal to a gentleman," could be whipped at all "unless his crime be very shameful, and his course of life vicious and profligate."[37]

Adherence to traditional commonwealth tenets was viewed as similarly necessary for "ordered liberty," and town officials were charged with monitoring individual and household behavior. But sexual transgression was not their only concern; as important was regulating commerce and household management. Winthrop in his 1630 sermon emphasized that "the care of the public must over sway all private respects. . . . For it is a true rule that particular estates cannot subsist in the ruin of the public." At the start of settlement, the Massachusetts General Court issued various economic regulations, such as forbidding merchants from selling imported commodities at more than 33 percent of the market price in England, fixing the price of corn in the winter of 1633–34, and frequently using public monies for a granary whose contents could be sold during shortages at reduced prices. In 1637 Robert Keayne, one of the wealthiest and most prominent Bostonians, was fined £200 for overcharging. A decade later, the colony authorized town meetings "to set the prices and rates of all workmen's labors and servants' wages" and to prosecute violators. Towns throughout the region set weights and prices for bread, places and times for markets, and hours and prices for taverns and ferries. In this spirit, the "warning out" of poor strangers was as much about regulating residents who might hire or host outsiders as providing notice under the law that the town had no obligation to provide support.[38]

This commonwealth ethos was the major factor shaping widespread landholding in southern New England, with a smaller gap between the rich and poor than in any other part of British North America. When the General Court chartered a town, the initial proprietors (including the investors and most adult male settlers) met and allotted enough of the area so that every head of household had a house lot and shares in meadow and uplands. In 1635 Concord became the first inland Massachusetts settlement and an excellent example of this process. The rich land and fishing resources within the six-mile-square township had supported a sizable Native population (perhaps five hundred) until European epidemics in 1613 and 1633 left a small group of survivors who apparently made formal sale of the territory in August 1637 and later moved to nearby Nashoba. The English settlers moved into the abandoned area and took up clustered house lots that averaged six acres and meadow and upland sections that averaged less than a hundred acres scattered in large unfenced commons. In 1653 the householders decided to allot most of the land within the initial town boundaries, giving the men three acres for every one already owned. Yet even after this second division, the gap in cumulative landholdings between community elites and the "average" (yeoman) farmer remained small. One of the town's gentry, Humphrey Barrett, had a very large 12-acre house lot and a total of 316 acres, whereas two yeomen, William Hartwell and Luke Potter, had house lots of 9 and 6 acres respectively, and total holdings of 285 and 253 acres. The handful of wealthy men who had paid for surveying, building the meetinghouse, hiring the minister, and other initial needs received much larger, consolidated holdings; for example, merchant Thomas Flint and the Reverend Peter Bulkley were each given 750-acre farms.[39]

Similarly, when Andover was settled in the early 1640s, each of eighteen heads of households received house lots of 4 to 20 acres, clustered around the center where the meetinghouse was built. By 1662, after four more land divisions, the town had forty-two heads of households who owned between 100 and 600 acres including meadow and swampland. The coastal towns more involved in fishing and shipbuilding made much smaller allotments: in Essex County, Rowley proprietors each took on average less than 20 acres; in Salem, 20 acres; and in Newbury, 33 acres. One exception to the general rule of widespread landownership was Springfield, Massachusetts, established and dominated by the Pynchon family, with perhaps half of the town's men either tenants of or laborers for the Pynchons. But that was indeed an exception. Most New England men owned farms; in fact, a problem that quickly emerged was a shortage of laborers in the region, which meant that farmers had to depend on their sons. One effect was that fathers tended to delay giving land to their sons for years after they married, so that landownership and status became particularly skewed by age. For example, in those three Essex County towns, only half of the men owned land by age thirty, but nearly all (95 percent) did by age thirty-six.[40]

New England puritan leaders saw no conflict between this widespread landownership and their belief in hierarchical social relations; after all, ministers and other elites were given more land and in other ways given recognition as the "better sort." But the potential dissonance could be glimpsed soon after initial settlement in Massachusetts. On December 11, 1634, Boston's freemen met to choose seven men to allot the town's land. That election was highly unusual and controversial: not only did the electors insist on secret ballots, but they spurned the leaders of the colony and instead elected a deacon and (according to Governor John Winthrop) "the rest infearior sortes." Some of the men explained that they voted in that way because they feared "that the richer men would give the poorer sort no great proportion of land." After discussing the matter, with the magistrates exerting not-so-subtle pressure, the meeting agreed to a new election on another day, at which time they followed the proper order and elected Winthrop and other elites.[41]

Puritan anxieties about radicalism resulted in the expulsion of Anne Hutchinson and her allies in 1637 and, less famously but just as controversial at the time, stronger hostility against Samuel Gorton in the 1640s. Gorton arrived in Plymouth in 1637, but his strong, unorthodox, and loudly expressed opinions got him expelled from that colony and then from two different settlements in Rhode Island (Roger Williams thought him a Familist). Finally, after seemingly safe on land he purchased in 1643 from two Native sachems, he was arrested, tried, and banished by Massachusetts authorities. Back in England, in 1646 he published an assault on the Bay Colony, *Simplicity's Defence Against Seven Headed Policy*, that reflected the egalitarian ideas espoused by English Familists and Anabaptists. Edward Winslow, in London to defend the colonies, immediately published a slashing reply, initially titled *Hypocrisie Unmasked*, but three years later—after the crushing of the Army radicals—it was republished as *The Danger of Tolerating Levellers in a Civil State*.[42]

Massachusetts ministers and magistrates tended to condemn dissidents as dangerous radicals at least in part to reassure themselves as well as their supposed audience in England about their orthodoxy. In 1647 Nathaniel Ward complained in *The Simple Cobler of Aggawam* that they were considered a rabble "of wild Opinionists, swarmed into a remote wilderness to find elbowroom for our Fanatical Doctrines and Practices," but wished to "proclaim to the World" that "Familists, Antinomians, Anabaptists, and other Enthusiasts" should stay away. In the late 1650s, Quakers, whose insistent egalitarian preaching reflected Familist roots, targeted Massachusetts and refused to stay out even after four were hung in Boston. At the height of this controversy, the foremost Boston minister John Norton published a pamphlet warning of "the irregenerate & hungry multitude . . . changing places with their Superiours, and possessing themselves with their power, honour & estates"; connecting the Quakers to radicals like Thomas Muntzer, who in the 1520s became leader of a chaotic German peasant revolt with the message of "parity amongst men, rejection of Dignities, [and] Community of goods"; and implying that God might allow similar horrors in New England if they forgot "that Originally they are a Plantation Religious, not a plantation of Trade." The same alarm would be sounded in the jeremiads that New England ministers often preached in the last quarter of the century. In 1673, for example, Urian Oakes in *New-England Pleaded With* warned his congregation that the monster of absolute equality was appearing their midst, born of excessive love of profits and unchained social climbing, exhibited in part by the way that many "average" people were wearing expensive clothing despite long-standing sumptuary laws.[43]

England's experiment in republicanism lasted only about a decade. In 1660, following Cromwell's death and then two years of intrigue, including the reappearance of Agitators in the Army, an alarmed Parliament restocked with royalists invited Charles, son of the "martyred" king, back from France to restore the Crown. During that decade, Parliament sought to return to the "ancient constitution" before the Civil War, while King Charles II tried to increase his prerogatives and to expand the English empire by establishing feudal-style proprietary colonies in North America. In 1664 a fleet was sent to take New Netherlands, which was renamed New York and assigned a royal governor without an assembly; that governor made huge grants of land and manorial powers to favored political allies. Five years later, John Locke and the Earl of Shaftesbury wrote the *Fundamental Constitutions of Carolina* for a new colony established by colonists from Barbados, which envisioned a government "made most agreeable to the Monarchy" in order to "avoid erecting a numerous Democracy." Although its vision of a three-tiered nobility and manorial system never took root, its plan for religious toleration, racial slavery, and an elite that dominated wealth and power found a home in Carolina and other southern Anglo-American colonies.[44]

The older colonies also became, eagerly or reluctantly, part of this new British empire. In Virginia, Sir William Berkeley, adviser to the first Charles I, who had appointed him governor in 1641, sought after the Restoration to create a neofeudal regime by recruiting the younger sons of English noble families who used the headright system and political influence to gather most of the good tobacco lands along with many servants and slaves. When the situation exploded in 1675, in what became known as Bacon's Rebellion, Charles II took the opportunity to exercise tighter controls over the colony, and its gentry turned increasingly from plantation laborers to slaves brought by the Royal African Company. Massachusetts initially managed to resist the Crown's effort to bring it to heel, but in 1676 the existential threat of a broad Native uprising (King Philip's War) forced the colony's leadership to ask England for help and provided an opening for Charles II. In 1682 the Crown formally challenged the Massachusetts charter in *quo warranto* proceedings, which encouraged dissidents in and outside the colony. Four years later, Charles II put all the New England colonies along with New York under the absolute authority of Sir Edmund Andros, who then challenged the town charters, in turn endangering all of the allotments made by those towns.[45]

Back in England, tensions developed in the 1670s between Charles and Parliament. The conflict was primarily driven by distrust of the king's foreign policies and fear that his younger brother James, strongly suspected of being Catholic, would become his successor. The split opened a space for Whig writers, including Shaftesbury and Locke, who felt forced by the threat to argue for English republicanism, based in part on Leveller ideas, and, as the exclusion crisis intensified, to encourage if not organize public rallies calling for limitations on the king's power and keeping James from the throne. Royalists argued that such challenges to authority threatened to undermine the English constitution and let loose anarchy. One writer noted that if republican arguments were taken seriously, "the very rabble" would become "magistrates and legislatures," which would put Levellers in power and "encourage every poor man to 'plunder his wealthy neighbor.'"[46]

After James ascended to the throne in 1685, the crisis reached a boiling point in mid-1688 when a boy was born to the king. A group of noblemen asked William, the Dutch Protestant leader married to James's daughter Mary, to intervene. William was already planning to invade, and his landing with a huge navy and army triggered waves of anti-Stuart rioting throughout England. James decided to flee for France, and Parliament "persuaded" William to accept the Bill of Rights, which recognized the assembly as a coequal part of the government, marking what became known as the Glorious Revolution. Uprisings erupted in Maryland, New York City, and Boston; in the latter, local leaders with popular acclaim placed Governor Andros under arrest and shipped him back to England, and New Englanders resumed their (somewhat more tentative) control of colonies and towns.[47]

In December 1689 John Locke anonymously published *Two Treatises of Government*, which in the mid-eighteenth century would become a significant source for American political thought and resistance to imperial measures. Locke claimed that he wrote to justify the Glorious Revolution, although there is evidence that it was written six to ten years before. The first *Treatise* is a thorough refutation of the absolutist argument in Sir Robert Filmer's *Patriarcha* that the king's authority was granted by God. The second *Treatise* argued that "all Men by Nature are equal" and that government rested on a voluntary contract made by men to protect their "natural rights" to "life, liberty, or estate [property]." The Levellers had similarly argued that all men had inherent political rights, and the Diggers pushed that to include the right to land; their opponents, such as Ireton and Crowell at Putney, condemned both ideas as threatening what they saw as necessary social, political, and economic distinctions. Locke also echoed the myth, embraced by Levellers and Diggers, that the Normans had imposed feudalism on an egalitarian Anglo-Saxon culture, and added the argument that such imposition had no validity past the first generation.[48]

Locke's contract theory of government rested on the necessity for consent, which was derived in part from Protestant ideas of grace, and emphasized *understanding* instead of *property*. Thus, all men should have access to power and opportunity instead of just those with sizable amounts of property, which seemed in concord with Leveller ideas about widening the franchise and ensuring equal rights under the law. But although Stuart persecution may have pushed Locke (and his patron Shaftesbury) away from the feudal slave system envisioned in the *Fundamental Orders of Carolina* and toward more liberal ideas, he continued to believe in socioeconomic hierarchy. After discussing natural equality, Locke noted that "Age or Virtue may give Men a just Precedency," and "Excellency of Parts and Merit may place others above the Common Level: Birth may subject some, and Alliance or Benefits others."[49]

At various points the English lawyer and political philosopher celebrated the individual's inalienable right to property. In chapter 5, "Of Property," he held that an individual's inalienable right to property was derived from the labor put into it and that land held in common was far less productive than that held privately. A few chapters later, in discussing the development of human society, he concluded that men had given up their state of nature, which by implication included equality, in order to ensure the protection of their property. Thus, although *Two Treatises* reflected some radical ideas from the Civil War period, Locke rejected those espoused by Winstanley and other "True Levellers." Yet at the same time, like the Diggers, he believed that wasteland regardless of title could be claimed by the landless, who would farm it. In mid-1698 Locke on behalf of the Board of Trade recommended sweeping reforms in Virginia, including confiscating the huge uncultivated estates held by the colony's elite and redistributing the land in fifty-acre parcels to new landless immigrants. This echoed his broader point in *Two Treatises* that there was one place with huge open spaces where Englishmen could go and create property for themselves. That place was America, including New England's biblical republic with widespread landownership and little poverty, coming close to Winstanley's vision of a "true commonwealth," and Virginia's rough-and-tumble opportunities for free landless men. In addition, as Locke and many other Englishmen believed, America was also the Edenic place where Natives lived in the proverbial state of nature.[50]

CHAPTER TWO

Indians and Anglo-American Egalitarianism

In 1708 Thomas Nairne, Scottish trader and Indian agent for the new colony of South Carolina, trekked from Charlestown to the Mississippi River, meeting and developing connections with Muskogee (Creek) and Chickasaw communities. A letter that he wrote in mid-April from a Chickasaw village described the tribe's matrilineal social system, which traced ancestry and authority through women rather than men, and then remarked that neither Plato nor any other republican theorist could imagine "a Government where the equality of mankind is more Justly observed than here among the savages." Nairne joked that John Lilburne, the infamous Leveller leader during the English Civil War of the 1640s, must have "been in America, or if not, might thence have been furnished with excellent presidents [precedents]. He would have seen a prince, nobility, and the Mobb all at work or play together, and so equally dressed that an able Arithmetician could scarce have told whose Cloths was of the most value, and the same in their diet house and furniture. If this be not Compleat leveling, at least in fact, I don't know what it is." The Chickasaws, according to Nairne, were relatively equal in all ways—political, economic, social—creating a unified system of power that seemed to serve as a mirror image (for better or for worse) to the one in Europe.[1]

This perceived nature of the indigenous people of North America meant that descriptions of those like the Chickasaws played significant roles in the evolution of Anglo-America ideas of economic equality. Writers on both sides of the Atlantic increasingly depicted Indians not as wild men with few redeeming qualities but as noble savages whose innocence denoted the virtues of Eden. Such an image became a common trope among Enlightenment political philosophers. In addition, Indians visiting England were widely quoted criticizing the vast gap that they saw between rich and poor and the way that the wealthy and powerful abused or ignored the poor. Indigenous people also "provided" (to be precise, had taken from them) the resources—land, water, wood, food, minerals—that created the potential for socioeconomic equality in North America. In England, land had long served as the primary determinant of wealth and power, and American equality would be grounded on widespread landownership. As the French-soldier-turned-New York-farmer J. Hector St. John de Crevecoeur enthused, "What should we American farmers be without the distinct possession of that soil?" The "true and the only philosophy of an American farmer," he imagined, was that "this formerly rude soil has been converted by my father into a pleasant farm, and in return, it has established all our rights; on it is founded our rank, our freedom, our power as citizens."[2] In fact, through the end of the nineteenth century, free or inexpensive land taken from Native Americans would in large part serve as a substitute for economic reforms when class conflicts and other social tensions developed.

In some ways this reflects one of the most famous interpretations of American history, Frederick Jackson Turner's 1893 "The Significance of the Frontier in American History." Turner rejected the dominant "germ theory" of American politics—that the country's democratic culture had its roots in the Germanic tribes of northern Europe—and instead argued that America's unique culture was shaped by "the existence of an area of free land" that served as "a gate of escape from the bondage of the past" and fostered an egalitarian democratic culture as the country pushed to the Pacific. Turner turned the decades-old dream of the West as an escape valve, and the Jacksonian mythology of its (white) settlers as rugged independent frontiersmen, into the explanation for the entire course of American history. He depicted America as an Edenic wilderness to be reshaped and Indians as obstacles to overcome. Of course, in reality most of the suitable "wilderness" was already utilized by Native peoples; as a result, America's relations with indigenous peoples reflected a fundamental tension between the ideal of economic equality and the reality of expropriation and violence.[3]

As Europeans explored and exploited the Americas, they sought to make sense of the people living there. For these devout Christians, one of the most important initial questions was how Native Americans fit into Genesis, particularly coming on the heels of the "discovery" and development of trade with Sub-Saharan Africa. Had God perhaps conducted two or more creations? Perhaps human appearance changed after the Tower of Babel, if one assumes, of course, that Europeans represented the initial and therefore "purest" human genotype. But once past that essentialist question, Europeans focused on making sense of indigenous societies and cultures, including their distinctive notions of status, power, and property.

European perceptions of Indians had their roots in the notion of the savage man, solitary and uncivilized in the wilderness, which probably developed alongside the society and culture of the city. The earliest known example is Enkidu, Gilgamesh's antithesis and friend. Enkidu was raised by animals in natural innocence, wandering and hunting with them, but he was rejected after his seduction by a prostitute, became a shepherd, and then went to the city to meet and wrestle with its king Gilgamesh—after which the two became friends (and perhaps lovers) until Enkidu was killed by the gods. Greek and Roman writers described anthropoid apes that were black and hairy like bears, part of the wild areas where they lived, driven by carnal desires without limits, hunting and gathering, wielding stone tools, unforgiving of injury or insult. Wild men were often part of European medieval pageantry, and during the Renaissance the ancient accounts from Pliny and others were resurrected and given wide currency. During the sixteenth century, the many published stories and reports from various parts of England and Europe indicate that the wild man was believed to live in the dangerous "wastelands" between villages and cities. Not surprisingly, European explorers and traders found in the wild man useful imagery for describing Native Americans to their countrymen. By the end of the century, the imagery of the wild man was almost completely replaced by images of the American savage.[4]

Savagery meant that Europeans defined Native Americans largely by what they seemed to lack: writings, aristocracy, possessions, sophisticated technology, theology, a social hierarchy, and clear gender roles. That was particularly important because Europe and England had, during the Renaissance, embraced material refinement as the touchstone of civilized culture and the primary indicator of where one stood in the social, economic, and political hierarchy. In the sixteenth century, books of costume began to be published that differentiated dress from different occupations, classes, and nationalities. Color, cut, material, and ornamentation became symbols for rank and authority, and the widest difference appeared between the silk-ennobled European aristocrat and the naked Native American. In that hierarchy, nakedness meant bestiality and disorder. But Europe also had the tradition of nakedness as the mark of innocence in the Garden of Eden, and the nude figure had long been used to denote the virtuous rejection of corrupting wealth and power.[5]

In fact, the turmoil of the Renaissance and Reformation, with societies and cultures torn by ceaseless wars and religious conflict, and long-distance trade and the developing money economy, drove a deep longing for a lost Golden Age. Even as many Europeans enjoyed the higher standard of living facilitated by long-distance trade and technological developments like movable type, they yearned for a lost precapitalist innocence and found it in the American noble savage. That trope, like that of the wild man, had its roots at least partly in classical writings, some of which described the predecessors of modern European countries. For example, Justin noted that the Scythians, in southern Russian, "desire nothing they do not possess," and if others did the same, "there would not have been waged so many wars throughout the ages in all lands." Julius Caesar praised the Germans in his *Chronicles of the Gallic Wars* because "no one possesses any definite amount of land, nor has any private property. . . . They are not, therefore, anxious to acquire large estates, nor are they strongly tempted to dispossess the weak." These historical concepts in the early seventeenth century became part of the mythology of England's Saxon inheritance. But they became even more important elements in many descriptions of Indians.[6]

Descriptions of Edenic sharing in the New World began at the beginning, in Columbus's initial reports. The admiral noted the "guileless" and "generous" character of the people he called Indians and praised how "they refuse nothing that they possess" but instead "invite any one to share it." He was not even sure if they had any sense of private property. Such tropes became widespread in the sixteenth century. Peter Martyr, the Italian-born Spanish historian, in *Decades of the Newe Worlde* (1511–30), one of the first books on America printed in English (in 1555), also praised their communitarian virtues. "'Mine' and 'Thine' (the seeds of all mischief) have no place with them. They are content with so little that, in a so large a country, they have rather superfluity than scarceness. So that (as we have said before) they seem to live in a Golden World, without toil, living in open gardens, not entrenched with dikes, divided with hedges, nor defended with walls." Similarly, the Dominican friar Bartolome de Las Casas described the indigenous Americans as "virtuous," lacking the desire "to possess worldly wealth." French philosopher and statesman Michel de Montaigne waxed enthusiastically after hosting one of the Brazilians visiting Rouen; he decided that these Americans were blessed to have neither riches nor poverty and had never heard of "lying, treachery, dissimulation, avarice, envy." In 1584 Arthur Barlowe, exploring the coast of what later became North Carolina, similarly described Algonquins in the area as "gentle, loving, and faithful," living "after the manner of the Golden Age . . . without toil or labor." These chroniclers were primarily concerned about the nature of the Natives and the "new" land because they were interested in commerce, colonization, and conversion. At the same time their descriptions pointed to egalitarian and communitarian economies as important elements of Native virtues. All these ideas became part of the concept of the noble savage.[7]

On the other hand, like the story of the wild man, the American savage archetype had its dark side. Columbus found the Caribs, who were "very fierce and who eat human flesh," rampaging through the Indies to "pillage and take whatever they can." De Montaigne included his visitor's account of "continual" brutal warfare along with ritual cannibalism, although he ended that passage by emphasizing the far more barbaric Portuguese method of executing prisoners. Among the English, this archetype came in part from the long effort to conquer Ireland, with Elizabethan commentators justifying their army's vicious tactics by depicting the Irish as living "like beastes, voide of law and all good order." Not surprisingly, some of the devout fearful New England puritans took the savage stereotype to its extreme, viewing the Indians around them as part of the cosmic battle between God and the Devil; the Natives lay deep in Satan's embrace, evinced not only by their fierce opposition to God's people but also by their seeming rejection of property and civilized hierarchy.[8]

Some of the earliest English descriptions of indigenous American societies emphasized strong hierarchies and wealthy rulers, apparently to prove the sophisticated and orderly nature of indigenous people. John Smith praised the Indians of Tidewater Virginia for the power that their "Magistrates" wielded and, with admiration, noted Powhatan's overflowing treasury of "skinnes, copper, pearle, and beades," stored for the ruler's elaborate burial. His people, Smith thought, believed the Native ruler to be "not only as a king but as halfe a God," and even "his inferior kings" had the "power of life and death." Smith's account would not have been encouraging to those who yearned for an Edenic New World, though it was probably more so for Smith's patron King James I, who would have been attracted to the potential wealth. Whereas Pocahontas was treated as royalty during her visit to England in 1616, indigenous Americans were generally regarded as savages, either innocent or beastly.[9]

These perceptions of Native Americans were reshaped during the Enlightenment, the intellectual movement that emerged in the early seventeenth century and continued through the 1780s. Enlightenment writers disagreed about much, but they all embraced empiricism, critical thinking, and notions of individual rights; in turn they questioned many social assumptions and religious orthodoxy. Enlightenment political philosophers were particularly interested in how and why human institutions took their present form and questioned the relevance (if not the veracity) of biblical depictions of the development of societies, polities, and laws. One of their most common methods was to begin with the assumption that at some point in the distant past humans lived in a "state of nature," in which there were few people, no government, no clear laws, and little social control. These writers would often point to American Indians (or at least popular concepts about Natives) as one of the few examples of contemporary human existence that resembled that condition.

The trope began with English philosopher and scientist Thomas Hobbes, who wrote the groundbreaking *Leviathan* during the English Civil War, when men fought over the structure, authority, and power of the state. Not surprisingly, he concluded that fear of violent death and the desire to protect property led men to create the authoritarian government necessary to wield effective power, and he pointed to "the savage people in many places of *America*" as examples of how, before this social contract was forged, "the life of man [was], solitary, poor, nasty, brutish, and short." Several decades later, John Locke in *Two Treatises of Government* tackled many of the same issues but (as noted previously) depicted government as an alterable contract and man's labor as necessary to give land value—and therefore worthy of legal and political protection. Like Hobbes, Locke pointed to Indians as examples of the state of nature, noting they "are rich in land, and poor in all the comforts of life . . . for want of improving it by labour," so that "a king of a large and fruitful territory" in America eats and lives "worse than a day-labourer in England." For Locke, this emphasized the important role of commerce in encouraging labor and cultivation, for Native Americans lacked such motivation. "Thus in the beginning all the world was America," he concluded, "for no such thing as money was any where known."[10]

Locke was quite knowledgeable for an Englishman of the time about the indigenous peoples of America. He was heavily involved in his country's American efforts, read reports of voyages and invested in those efforts, and during the late 1660s served as secretary of the Board of Trade and Plantations as well as secretary to the Lords Proprietor of Carolina—and helped draft a new charter for that colony in 1669. His *Second Treatise* reflected widespread assumptions about the vast "empty" land in North America, and his theory of labor value along with his perceptions of indigenous polities and economies supported the colonialist theory of *vacuum domicilium*—that Native

Americans were wandering hunters without a legal right to much of the land. At the same time, Locke's depictions of men in the state of nature, and by extension Native Americans, were more Edenic than "brutish" and "savage." His writings therefore provided a far more promising and inviting view of America to prospective emigrants and investors than Hobbes had done in *Leviathan.*[11]

During the eighteenth century, as Europeans began to feel more at home in eastern North America, the Indian as noble savage became *the* symbol for human equality: social, political, and (especially) economic. That paradigm was an extension of earlier depictions of America as a Garden of Eden, and indigenous Americans as free of the corrupting desire for wealth and power. Increasingly, writers who wished to critique their country's inequalities and decadence found actual Indian communities and cultures to be useful models. Some Native people, whether at home or visiting London, used these ambivalent notions as a means to critique the Euro-American obsession with individual wealth and to highlight the superiority of their society and culture.

The trope of the Native critic first appeared in English translations of French works. De Montaigne's account of the visit of Brazilian Indians to Rouen noted how, after their tour of the city, they told their hosts that they were amazed at how so many people, "half-starved with hunger and poverty," were willing to "suffer so great an inequality and injustice" without striking back against the few extremely wealthy. De Montaigne's *Essays* were published in London in 1603, and one century later similar sentiments appeared in the Baron Lahonton's *New Voyages to North-America.* The baron, Louis Armand de Lom d'Arce, an officer in the French military in America in the 1690s, noted that the "the *Savages* are utter Strangers to distinctions of property," and they thought it bizarre and immoral that one man should own more than another, that the rich should be given more authority than the poor. Those who had visited France "are continually teazing us with the Faults and Disorders they observ'd in our Towns, as being occasion'd by Money." As with subsequent critiques, these views attributed to Indians may have been shaped by the writer's concerns about European corruption.[12]

Other than Pocahontas and her entourage, few Indians visited England before Lahonton's work was published there in 1703. But during the eighteenth century, as England sought to cement and extend its empire in North America, a steady if small stream of Native delegations traveled to London. Those Indian leaders believed that meeting the king and his advisers personally, instead of representatives in America, would better secure their trade and military connections with England. No doubt some also thought this would bypass the more mercurial, greedy, and often hapless provincial leaders, who seemed more interested in grabbing their land than controlling colonial trespassers. The king's advisers saw these visits as an excellent means to impress the Indians with England's large populace, growing power, and swelling opulence. That populace was clearly impressed by the visitors: crowds surrounded them in public places, the "better sort" clamored for private meetings, and London's newspapers and periodicals were filled with news and gossip about Indian dress, itineraries, speeches, and manners. But it is difficult to determine whether the English saw the Natives as more than (very) exotic diplomats and sources of entertainment and knowledge. Were the visitors an attractive model for egalitarianism where the legal, economic, and social gap between the many poor and the powerful few was so immense?[13]

One of the first and most famous Native delegations was the four "Kings of Canada"—three Mohawks and one Mahican—who traveled from Iroquoia (New York) in April 1710. For five weeks the English newspapers and periodicals were filled with news of their appearance and movements, including an audience with Queen Anne on April 19, attendance of theatrical performances, and meetings with the Board of Trade. Although only their formal address to the queen was recorded, in the wake of their trip accounts by English commenters were published in various forms. The most meaningful was probably a series published by the *Spectator* a year later, written by one of the famous magazine's founders, Joseph Addison. Addison pretended to have found a bundle of papers left behind by one of the Indians that, once translated, lampooned England's church as dull, its politics as barbarous (with the two main factions Whigs and Tories depicted as savage animals), and its men as exceedingly lazy because they were carried around in sedan chairs. Soon a group of rakes in London adopted the label "Mohowks" and misbehaved in ways that spawned stories of gleeful mayhem and violence; at the same time, writers began to refer to some seemingly disruptive political elements as Mohawks.[14]

In mid-1730 seven Cherokees spent about three months in England on a diplomatic tour organized and led by the slightly mad nobleman Sir Alexander Cuming. Their doings filled the country's newspapers: they started in Windsor, where they met four times with King George II, then went to London at the king's expense, where (according to the *Daily Journal*) they sought "to see all the Curiosities here." That meant the Tower, fairs at Tottenham Court, the baths at Richmond Wells, and various theaters. They became a huge attraction in the capital: at least one theater featured them on the day's billings, and the *Daily Courant* on August 7 reported that their stroll in St. James's Park drew "a numerous Crowd of Spectators." It took another month for the actual business, a formal treaty between the Cherokee and England, to be consummated. As in the visit of the four Kings of Canada, the Cherokees left few comments about London or its social and cultural conditions, although four decades later trader and historian James Adair would note that members of the tribe considered the English "covetous" because they did not give the poor "such a share . . . as would keep them from want."[15]

The Cherokee visit impressed General James Oglethorpe, member of Parliament. Three years later, when Oglethorpe led the first shipload of colonists to Georgia, England's last colonial effort along the Atlantic coast, he sought to forge good relations with the Yamacraws living nearby. During the negotiations he proposed that the tribe's leader (Tomochichi) form a delegation to visit London. The large group landed in England in mid-June 1734 and in London became celebrities. Its members met many times with the men behind the Georgia colony, hammering out the details of trade and political relationships and gathering for a group portrait; and in August they had a formal audience with the king and his family. Like the Cherokees, the Yamacraws became both tourists and attractions, visiting all the famous places and attending a series of plays, including some advertised "For the Entertainment of Tomo Chachi." They attracted crowds of the curious and were the subject of frequent articles in London's newspapers and periodicals. The Yamacraws also traveled to Oglethorpe's estate outside the capital, where "a great number of Country People" gathered to glimpse the exotic Americans. After being taken through the palace, Tomochichi supposedly commented that the English "knew many things his Country men did not, but doubted if [the English] were happier. Since [they] live worse than [we], and [we] more innocently."[16]

Some historians have cited these comments as evidence that, while Natives were impressed by the large population, soaring churches, huge buildings, powerful military, and sophisticated culture of Georgian England, they were also critical of the immense and immoral gap that existed between the many poor and the few wealthy and powerful. This view raises the intriguing possibility that the Indian delegations, brought to London as a means of building up the empire, were somewhat subversive of its fundamental hierarchy. But Native criticisms of the glaring gap between massive poverty and opulent wealth were not explicit and were rarely published at the time. This was even true of the most straightforward example of an Indian visitor disparaging England's inequality: Samson Occum's comment during his 1766 tour that "the Sight of the Nobility put me in mind of Dives and the Rich Glutton. . . . What great Difference there is Between the Rich and the Poor—and What Difference there is and will be, Between God's poor and the Devil's Rich." His

Audience Given by the Trustees of Georgia to a Delegation of Creek Indians (detail), by William Verelst, 1734–35, London, England. Oil paint on canvas. Courtesy, Winterthur Museum, Gift of Henry Francis du Pont, 1956.567.

disgust was clearly shaped by deep evangelical Christian beliefs, colored by generations of Mohegan efforts to survive Anglo-American domination; but it existed only in his journal and was not published during his lifetime. It is possible, since "folk" nonliterate culture remained a significant (perhaps dominant) force in England, that stories about the feathered visitors whose communities shared everything circulated in parts of the country and inspired some with a vison of alternative possibilities. Unfortunately, there is no evidence for such stories, and Anglo-Americans generally continued to demonstrate scorn for indigenous Americans. On the other hand, during the eighteenth century the idea of the Indian was clearly influential in shaping how some English and European elites conceived of economic equality, putting America and its indigenous peoples at the center of the concept.[17]

By the mid-eighteenth century, Enlightenment political philosophers agreed that human societies evolved through four essential stages, each shaped by the primary means of subsistence. Humans began as primitive hunter-gatherers with no need or knowledge of property; became tribes of nomadic herdsmen or shepherds who owned only their herds; became in turn settled farmers who owned or leased their land; and finally embraced commerce and manufacturing, with long-distance trade, extensive division of labor, large-scale manufacturing, and great luxury. In this schematic, subservience and corruption were in large part an unavoidable outgrowth of human progress and the growth of the arts. Such analysis lent itself to social criticism, and some writers highlighted how Europe's "advanced" civilization had inherent problems. In 1754, for example, Jean-Jacques Rousseau wrote in *Discourse on the Origin and Foundations of Inequality among Men* that "the savages of America" lived in a state of equality without the knowledge of property-in-land that (like the fruit of knowledge in Eden) resulted in slavery, misery, violence, "the breakdown of equality" with "the usurpations of the rich, [and] the banditry of the poor." Some Scottish Enlightenment writers like David Hume defended the "civilizing" effects of commerce, holding that the dangers were outweighed by the benefits of a constructive society built on the pursuit of luxuries. But most, including Adam Smith, feared that a society built on commerce would be fundamentally corrupt and destructive of human relationships.[18]

Across the Atlantic Ocean in eastern North America, England's colonists, joined by an increasingly diverse crowd of enslaved Africans, Huguenots, Scots-Irish, Germans, and others, were noticeably hostile to notions of the noble savage. While that concept would in the long run shape American ideas of equality, until the early nineteenth century the Indian generally represented a devilish threat. Yet Native peoples did contribute (reluctantly if not forcibly) a foundational element to the American tradition of economic equality: the land and its resources. Land had long served as the primary determinant of power and authority in England and Europe, and the Anglo-American passion for social equality and a decent living has its roots in widespread land-ownership. During the colonial period, the lands taken from Indians, worked by indentured servants, African slaves, or family members, allowed Euro-American households to expect if not experience a level of economic and social equality impossible elsewhere. In the eighteenth century, lands along the Appalachians and in the Ohio Valley proved subversive to the efforts of elites to maintain a more stable and hierarchical society. When class conflicts did develop, the possibility of acquiring free or inexpensive land served as a substitute for more systemic reforms.

When the English began to establish permanent colonies in eastern North America, they did consider whether they had the moral and legal right to land. One of the more explicit reflections came from John Winthrop in 1629, a year before he led his puritan flock to New England: "We have noe warrant to enter uppon that land wch hath been soe long possessed by others." His answer to this objection was the Roman concept of *vacuum domicilum*: "That wch lies common & hath never been replenished or subdued is free to any that will possess and improve it," and since New England's Natives "inclose noe land neither have any settled habitation nor any tame cattle," if we leave them enough land to use then "wee may lawfully take the rest." For Winthrop and many others, the ancient concept seemed quite applicable to the Indians; after all, didn't early explorers depict them as living in Edenic abundance without private landholding? But not all English agreed: in 1609 a minister in Virginia preached that his people did not have right to take land from Indians, and more famously in 1635 Roger Williams was expelled from Massachusetts in part for attacking as sinful the Bay Colony's claims. By the end of the century colonial leaders mostly accepted the reality that Native communities possessed delineated territory that they used for crops, game, and other needs. That acceptance arose at least in part from the competition between European powers and among the proprietors of different English colonies, so that a written deed from an Indian leader became the best card to play.[19]

Regardless of the legalities, English colonists tended to locate settlements on the sites of recently abandoned Native villages. Such sites provided open house lots, relatively cleared fields, and ready access to streams for transportation as well as fish and waterfowl. Native villages, and the English communities that replaced or succeeded them, were also often located along regional pathways, although rivers and estuaries were for all peoples more significant for travel and moving goods. Edward Winslow noted in 1621 that his infant Plymouth colony had found "very good" land, "being for the most part cleared" by the Indians who had "died in a great plague not long since." When the puritans began to establish settlements away from the coast, they continued to obtain and use sites already shaped by Natives for homes and crops, as with Concord in 1635 and Deerfield in 1665. Virginia colonists sought similar sites: for example, in the mid-seventeenth century, a group bought land from Chicaocans and set its plantations on the fields already cleared by Indians.[20]

While the colonists sought land shaped by Native villages, their distinctive economy and agriculture quickly changed that land. The colonists felled forests at a much higher rate than did the Natives, allowing them to build larger homes, home fires, and ships and to export large amounts as timber or potash; they also cut in order to simply clear more land for farming and pasture. As a result, watersheds were altered such that large areas were dried out or became flooded. Plants and animals brought by the settlers pushed out native flora and fauna. The greatest change came with English cattle and pigs, for Natives had domesticated only the dog. Cattle required much more land for pasture than was needed for food crops, multiplying the colonists' seemingly constant demand for more territory. The English enclosed their crops rather than their pastures, allowing wandering cattle to find food and water more easily and breed faster. They insisted that the Indians do the same, but the Indians had never constructed fences and thought that the English should instead erect barriers around their animals. Colonists refused, resulting in wandering cattle that ate Indian corn and consumed wild food needed by the deer hunted by Natives.[21]

These changes happened very rapidly. In mid-1642 Miantonomo, sachem of the Narragansetts, perhaps the most powerful tribe in southern New England, went with his counselors to the Montauks on eastern Long Island to forge an alliance against the increasingly numerous and powerful English. In one of the most famous Native speeches from this period, he told the Montauks that "we [must] be one as they are, otherwise we shall be gone shortly, for you know our fathers had plenty of deer and skins, our plains were full of deer, as also our woods, and of turkies, and our coves full of fish and fowl. But these English having gotten our land, they with scythes cut down the grass, and with axes fell the trees; their cows and horses eat the grass, and their hogs spoil our clam banks, and we shall all be starved."[22] Native peoples tried to adapt in various ways, taking on English housing as local materials became scarcer, complaining to justices of the peace about English violations, or hunting or laboring for the colonists. Some took on animal husbandry, which in European culture served as the ultimate symbol of civilized landholding, particularly favoring pigs that needed little care and, when allowed to go feral, would be hunted by men, thereby fitting traditional indigenous gender roles.[23]

Such efforts were largely for naught, as the English insisted on expanding their control as well as their land, and a series of wars erupted. In Virginia in 1622 the Powhatans tried getting rid of the colonists and in 1644 hit them again with less success, and in 1676 Doegs, Susquehannas, and other back-country Indians became targets in an effort by Nathaniel Bacon and western colonists to get more land. In New England in 1636 the colonists forged an alliance with the Narragansetts, Wampanoags, and Mohegans and nearly wiped out the Pequots, and in 1675–76 engaged in all-out war with Wampanoags (led by "King Philip"), Nipmucs, Pocumtucks, and Wabanakis. The English managed to win all of these wars, often inflicting huge losses on their enemies; the surviving Natives headed for the borderlands, where Indian groups continued to dominate, or sought ways to maintain communities on pieces of their home territories, including lands protected by provincial laws in an effort to keep order and prevent new conflicts. Those who remained maintained many aspects of their traditional economies, including communitarian landholding, subsistence farming, and hunting. A growing number became part of the Anglo-American economy by working as laborers, mariners, or craftsmen.[24]

The colonists gained much from the indigenous peoples of eastern North America. While gold or silver was nowhere to be found, the lush furs from beavers and other small mammals were so valuable that the French poured considerable resources into its outposts in Canada; the Dutch similarly worked hard to maintain trading posts in New Netherlands, and the English in various northern colonies fought to tap into the trade. Those furs came almost entirely through Native peoples: men trapped the animals, women processed the skins, and then men traded the furs for European goods, including (disastrously) rum and brandy. The European desire for pelts and Native desire for guns and other manufactured goods nearly drove the beaver to extinction, fundamentally transformed indigenous cultures, and spawned horrific wars and terrible violence within communities. During the eighteenth century, the same thing happened with the deerskin trade in the Southeast.[25]

Timber was also a valuable export commodity: wood was sent to England, southern Europe, and especially to the West Indies where, since few trees remained, planters focused on sugar. The Royal Navy prized and protected the tall straight pines in northern New England as well as the tough live oaks along the southeast coast, and it was a heavy user of the pitch and turpentine from North Carolina. By the end of the seventeenth century, large amounts of timber were feeding the growing shipbuilding industry in Boston and Salem. Those ships were essential for New England's shipping and fishing industries, both of which continued to play major roles in that region's economy through the late nineteenth century. Of course, the most important resource by far was the huge abundance of land, some of it already cleared, that would fuel the astonishingly rapid expansion of the Euroamerican population and produce massive amounts of tobacco, wheat, beef, cotton, and other riches.[26]

Although the export of fur and timber was dominated by a relatively few prominent merchants, many colonists at all socioeconomic levels were involved. Even before European colonization began, fisherman drying their catch along the shore traded for pelts that they brought home and sold. During the seventeenth century, many small-scale farmers in Virginia, southern New England, and New Netherlands occasionally traded their produce for pelts. The Dutch West Indies Company tried to eliminate such free agents but with little success; further east, the Pynchon family similarly held a legal monopoly on the trade along the Connecticut River and employed farmers, who also carried on a little trade for themselves, to serve as its agents. This pattern would repeat in the eighteenth century as colonists moved into the borderlands, as far west as the Ohio Valley and the Great Lakes.[27]

More significant in its egalitarian (and ecological) effect was the timber trade. The colonists cut trees to prepare and enlarge fields and, particularly during slack seasons, turned those trees into essential goods that could be sold locally or carried to regional markets to be exchanged for imported or manufactured goods. Colonial fireplaces were huge and required lots of wood, and scattered records show that it was common for farmers to cut cordwood for others within their villages and increasingly for the growing port towns that had exhausted local supplies. Some took the extra step of producing coal or potash. Farmers could earn even more by cutting shingles and barrel staves for use in the mushrooming settlements as well as for export overseas. Some found they could make a living by cutting timber, usually along the borderlands of settled areas, either for sale to local shipyards (particularly in New England, which at the turn of the century produced large vessels for the local carrying trade to the West Indies), and, increasingly, for export by turning the extractive enterprise into manufacturing and transportation industries that provided opportunities as well as employment for men from various backgrounds.[28]

But not surprisingly it was farmland taken from Native Americans that became the most significant source of American equality, both as a reality and as an ideal. The promoters of the colonies had to recruit adult male settlers in order to realize their dreams of wealth, power, or a godly commonwealth, and that meant promising those recruits the opportunity to gain the land and a "competency" impossible in England. The abundance of land, relatively small numbers of colonists, and the need to encourage emigration also meant that few wage laborers would be available, limiting the size of farms. In the Chesapeake the use of indentured labor—and, by the 1660s, African slavery—in growing the staple crop of tobacco allowed that hurdle to be overcome, but the ideal remained firmly established that the American colonies offered unique opportunities for free white men to own their own land, thereby gaining household independence and a political voice.

That assumption remained strong throughout the eighteenth century. As David Ramsey wrote in 1789, "In consequence of the vast extent of vacant land, every colonist was, or easily might be, a freeholder. Settled on lands of his own, he was both farmer and landlord—producing all the necessaries of life from his own grounds, he felt himself both free and independent. Each individual might hunt, fish, or fowl, without injury to his neighbors. These immunities which, in old countries, are guarded by the action of penal laws, and monopolized by a few, are the common privileges of all, in America." Through the end of the nineteenth century, the promise of abundant land and resources to the west—if you could take it from the Indians—remained a major factor in the expansion of the United States.[29]

While widespread landownership remained a powerful aspect of every British American province in the eighteenth century, a more "mature" class structure developed in the coastal areas as a result of increasing population, development of a creole elite with access to political and legal power, and increasing trade and cultural connections with England. Each colony went through three similar stages of development. At the start of English settlement, small populations, subsistence living, and weak political and legal institutions resulted in *social simplification*, marked by the lack of stable class structure and an open economy. As the colonial population became denser and the children of settlers raised their own families, the result was *social elaboration*, with the development of institutions and values that outwardly resembled those in England but were functionally distinct so local populations could manage without difficulty. Then, as the population density increased and the economy became more mature, the growing wealth and social complexity resulted in *social replication*, as the gentry and elite sought to replicate British society, culture, and politics.[30]

Indeed, in every mainland British colony a creole elite emerged in the early eighteenth century. At the local and provincial levels, the gentry combined social, economic, and political power. Militia rank corresponded with local and county offices, and titles of esquire, gentleman, master, and yeomen were reserved for particular social and economic ranks and carefully protected in court documents and lawsuits. Wealth, status, and offices were increasingly passed on to sons, reducing the chances for others to enter those ranks, amplifying the effects of reduced open agricultural land along the coast. Many wealthy elites were able to send their sons to London to gain sophistication and create closer connections with the center of power in the burgeoning empire. More consumer goods of all kinds entered the colonies, causing prices to plunge so more people at every level could afford ceramics and forks. Elites then distinguished themselves by buying silver, clocks, and even carriages and socializing at luxurious coffeehouses. Courts implemented more complex common-law rules of procedure and increasingly focused on providing a forum to adjudicate commerce. The growing port towns of Boston, New York,

Philadelphia, and Charleston became more like English cities, with a widening gap between very wealthy families and a permanently poor and mobile class of maritime laborers.[31]

Members of the southern gentry were at the forefront of the increasing tendency of the colonies to reproduce British society and culture. As they increasingly dominated the best land and locations along navigable rivers, they also became the intermediaries between poorer planters and overseas merchants, marketing their crops and serving as merchants for imported manufactured goods needed by planters—a role that increased their social, political, and economic clout. Their growing hunger for African slaves after 1680 was particularly significant for two reasons: the establishment and enforcement of racial slavery legitimated abusive power, and those who possessed the property and connections to buy African laborers were able to raise more tobacco and thereby obtain more wealth and authority.[32]

Members of the gentry put their brick multistoried great houses on hilltops to show their wealth and authority and located county courthouses, Anglican churches, and taverns nearby where networks of roads met. Church of England services were highly ritualized, with their format and liturgy reinforcing the authority of the men at the top of the hierarchical community. When a gentleman "stood" for election, finished leading militia drills, or won a horse race, he treated the middling and poor planters to ale and beef; this was not a bribe but the obligation of generosity and power. Perhaps most strikingly, the elaborate code of manners memorized by the gentry's adolescents, including a sixteen-year-old George Washington, emphasized the importance of noticing and acknowledging social rank in various ways.[33]

Although north of Virginia the gap between the rich and poor was much narrower and the middling class much larger, in those colonies the elites also generally strengthened their social, political, and economic power. Elected officials acted as community "fathers" as well as agents for the town in county business and the provincial assembly, and their political authority was closely connected to their social, economic, and moral authority. When one retired or died, a son was often elected in the father's place. Appointed offices— justices, judges, and governor's council—went to men with higher social standing, extraordinary wealth, and more education. Merchants involved in overseas trade were able to build substantial brick houses and fill them with luxuries. Such development was particularly prominent in Philadelphia, where wealthy Quaker traders dominated the city's booming economy and, while continuing to dress "plainly," managed to marginalize the movement's radical egalitarian elements. Church seating was by social rank within the community and, as already noted, students at Harvard and Yale were ranked by the status of their families.[34]

The assumption was, as Boston merchant John Saffin noted in 1700, that God "hath ordained different degrees and orders of men, some to be high and honourable, some to be low and despicable, some to be monarchs, kings, princes, and governors, masters and commanders, others to be subjects and to be commanded." Later, Jonathan Edwards wrote, "There is a beauty of order in society, as when the different members . . . have all their appointed offices, places, and station." In 1765 Cadwallader Colden, New York merchant and lieutenant governor, described his province as "distinguished into different ranks," with the manor lords at the top, "Gentlemen of the Law" second, merchants third, and farmers and craftsmen at the bottom—with slaves barely worth mentioning. One's station or order in the community was determined by the linked factors of wealth and "breeding" (social status).[35]

But even as urbanization, poverty, inequality, and racial slavery increased, British America continued to be distinguished by its extraordinary large number of households that owned enough productive land to achieve independent middling status, proportionally more than any other contemporary Western society. For most colonists, little changed in the daily and yearly rhythms of their lives between the end of the seventeenth and the mid-eighteenth century. About 75 to 85 percent were farmers who raised much of their own food along with some surplus for market. With very little currency or specie, informal neighborly networks and "book debt" anchored the local and regional economies, and without a banking system, personal honor and extended kinship networks remained critical for long-distance trade. On the other hand, households and communities became more deeply enmeshed in regional and international trade networks, benefiting from imported goods but also subject to the fluctuations of the increasingly global economy.[36]

Other significant social and economic changes emerged toward midcentury in the coastal areas first settled by the English. Particularly in southern New England, generations of large families and partible (divided) inheritances shrank farm sizes to the minimum, forcing more specialization in agriculture and causing sons to either wait for land, move to the frontier, or pursue a crafts trade in the nearest town. While the childbirth rates in those areas declined somewhat, they continued to be part of the dramatic demographic growth that marked the English colonies, attributed by observers to abundant food and other conditions facilitated by the relatively easy availability of land taken from the Indians. In 1751 Benjamin Franklin told imperial officials that because the Indians "were easily prevail'd upon to part with Portions of

Territory," land in America was so cheap that "a laboring Man . . . can in a short Time save Money enough to purchase a Piece of new Land sufficient for a Plantation" and thereby marry earlier than in Europe, with the result that "our People must at least be doubled every 20 Years." But North America was "so vast," he noted, "that it will require many Ages to settle in fully," and in the meantime every man would obtain a farm rather than labor for others. The continually expanding population and economy drove a steady growth in the gross annual product such that, by midcentury, it increased by 3.2 percent, twice the rate of England.[37]

British officials were increasingly concerned, in fact, that these conditions in the colonies could draw more Englishmen to America. In the 1580s that was celebrated as a means to relieve the pressures of overpopulation, but by the mid-eighteenth century the concern developed that America might gain at England's expense. America also represented a broader, egalitarian threat to England's socioeconomic hierarchy. Such anxiety was reflected in the report on conditions in the colonies written in 1760 by Boston customs officer Nathaniel Ware for the head of the Board of Trade. Ware warned that, should "the most useful and industrious amongst the lower orders" learn that the continent's climate was "temperate and healthy" and the soil productive of "great perfection and abundance" with only "very moderate labour," and that in the colonies "all mortifying distinctions of rank are lost in common equality," nothing would restrain them "from abandoning a necessitous and servile condition *here*, for property and independency *there*." In fact, by 1773 Parliament had received so many similar reports that it considered banning all emigration to its colonies in North America, although at the time it decided (as legislative bodies often do) to study the situation further.[38]

The widespread "property and independency" in the American colonies meant that in every province a much larger percentage of white adult men could vote than in England. In the "mother country" perhaps 20 percent of all adult men held enough property to vote (sufficient land or another source generating 40 shillings a year or more), although the percentage probably increased somewhat in the late sixteenth and early seventeenth centuries due to inflation. In America the percentages varied noticeably: 80 to 90 percent in newly settled areas; about 70 percent in long-settled farming towns like Concord, Massachusetts; and 40 to 50 percent in older coastal towns like Ipswich in Massachusetts, cities like Philadelphia and Boston, and some frontier settlements where many men lacked the money to buy land, as in Kent, Connecticut. Also, in many colonies different levels of property ownership were required to vote for either provincial or town offices, and in some cases local officials chose to let men participate and vote who did not qualify. But over-all, most British American men held enough property to vote, although that figure may have declined slightly after midcentury as coastal land rose in price and the economy in some areas fell into a depression.[39]

This Anglo-American tradition of widespread landholding and political participation was the primary reason that every province featured an elected assembly more inclusive and responsive to public opinion than any other gov-ernment in the known world. In addition, the colonies had no titled aristoc-racy with special privileges carved out in law, and its gentry class was gener-ally less wealthy and less powerful than its counterpart in England. New England was known for the modest homes and holdings of its rural "better sort" (although after 1700 they were likely to own a slave or two) and for its broad-based town meetings, held at least once a year, in which nearly all adult heads of households decided on taxes, spending, policy questions, and officers ranging from selectmen to fence viewers. Those offices did represent a socio-economic hierarchy: usually the selectmen, who met and made decisions for the town between meetings, held about twice as much land as "ordinary" farmers, whereas lower-level offices like fence viewers and hog reeves (moni-tors) went to poorer men, who were often relatively young since age was a ma-jor factor determining an individual's wealth. In New York, Pennsylvania, and New Jersey, great landowners and merchants had immense influence in provincial politics and officeholding, but because the governments in all three colonies had limited reach and were often paralyzed by intense factionalism, elected local officials and county commissioners made most of the important decisions. In the South, where elites flaunted their greater wealth to mark their authority, the gentry encouraged "middling" and poorer planters to partici-pate in elections and fostered a quasi-egalitarian ethos in some public settings (the tavern, racing, gambling) in exchange for social and political support— including support for African slavery.[40]

Not surprisingly, the British provinces in the eighteenth century seemed rife with tensions between their egalitarian and hierarchical tendencies. Some ac-counts, like Devereux Jarratt's recollections of his childhood in Virginia, stressed the deference that he and his neighbors gave to the wealthy planters, who, they thought, were "beings of a superior order." In 1730, Benjamin Col-man, one of the most prominent ministers in Boston, welcomed the new Mas-sachusetts royal governor Jonathan Belcher with a sermon that proclaimed, "The Great God has made the governments and rulers of the earth its pillars," and men should give "just deference one to another." Ten years later, Colman's associate William Cooper preached in his election sermon that "the Notion of Levelism has as little Foundation in Nature as in Scripture" and that, "in the political World, there are the Distinctions of Superiours and Inferiours, Rulers and Ruled." Other accounts, like the diary kept by William Byrd, the wealthiest and most powerful Virginian in the first half of the eighteenth century, highlighted the insults, contempt, and outright defiance of "ordinary" men and women. Such antagonism could be political as well as personal: in the 1720s, as George Keith sought the support of Philadelphia's craftsmen in his battle against the colony's proprietors, he published a pamphlet that included the warning to the city's wealthy merchants that they needed to again embrace Quaker moderation or risk having angered artisans force them to redistribute their wealth.[41]

The social and cultural tensions in British America became more apparent during the religious Awakenings that shook nearly every colony in the middle of the century. Revival rumblings became noticeable even before the famed George Whitefield made his way up the coast in 1739 and 1740. In New Jersey, a series of preachers including Presbyterians William Tennent and his son Gilbert began to connect the polyglot settlers—Dutch Reformed, New England puritans, Quakers, German pietists, and Scots-Irish Presbyterians—who increasingly resented efforts by the Church of England and Scottish proprietors to extend their influence. Some of their sermons were directly aimed at the wealthy gentry; Theodorus Frelinghuysen, for example, a pietistic Dutch Reform itinerant, thundered, "Go now, ye rich men, weep and howl, for your miseries will come upon you . . . Your gold and silver . . . Shall eat your flesh as if it were fire." Whitefield's sermons in northern Jersey united these dissenters and drew fire from Anglican gentry, which sought to use the pulpit and the law to squash the disorder. In response, local elites led their neighbors in a violent and successful resistance against the proprietors' efforts to enforce their authority and land claims. The clash reflected a developing trend in the colonies, in which beleaguered yeomen defended their right to land, drawing in part on religious egalitarianism and in part on Locke's theory that property rights were derived from one's labor (or the laborers one owned) against outside gentry that tried to impose a socioeconomic hierarchy based on grants from the Crown.[42]

The Awakening became disruptive in a different fashion in southern New England, as the ministers and political leaders who had initially welcomed Whitefield increasingly felt besieged by the exhorters and enthusiasts. Elites in the region were particularly troubled by the chord that the Awakening struck among the lower orders, including several communities of Indians that had previously spurned Christianity. At least one itinerant minister, James Davenport, who in March 1743 crossed Long Island Sound to preach in Connecticut, rallied his enthusiastic listeners to collect and burn expensive clothing and books written by more conservative ministers. Such explosive events were rare; more common were individual visions among ecstatic "New Lights" and the fracturing of churches between the New Light evangelicals who tended toward more antiauthoritarian attitudes and the more "conservative" members who preferred formal liturgy and sober sermons. The movement undermined the authority of ministers, judges, and merchants by insisting that the goal of salvation could not be gained by obeying the law or demonstrated by material success.[43]

The Awakening's egalitarian elements became particularly clear when Baptist preachers reached Virginia and North Carolina in the 1750s and 1760s. As noted previously, members of the southern gentry demonstrated their status through their formal manners, luxurious possessions, and easy ways with wealth; they cemented their authority in large part by providing liquor and entertainment (including horse races and card games) to poorer planters. Evangelical preachers and their followers became a subversive movement because they condemned gambling and drinking, sought to form a fellowship of equals in Christ, and demonstrated their faith through emotive conversion experiences with public confessions. Some congregations even accepted slaves and included poorer whites on disciplinary committees that might excommunicate a gentleman for sinful behavior. In backcountry North Carolina, where Euroamericans began settling in the 1740s, radical Protestantism became a wellspring of resistance to the legal, social, and economic order that local elites and absentee speculator landlords sought to impose on the backcountry. In the late 1760s, that resistance exploded in the Regulator movement. Its most famous member, Herman Husband, came from Maryland, was "awakened" by George Whitefield, became a Quaker, and wrote pamphlets insisting that true Christians were obligated to oppose tyranny. Elected to the provincial legislature in 1769, Husband pushed significant egalitarian measures, including requiring land speculators to pay every squatting farmer "the Value of his Labour, and Damages of moving to another Place."[44]

The Awakening emerged from a transatlantic "visionary culture" that began in Europe and made its way to America through the efforts of Englishmen like Whitefield and the large-scale immigration of pietistic German sects. The Moravians, probably the largest, became infamous for their liturgy that gave an equal role in the church to women, saw marital sex as a sacrament, and focused on Jesus' blood and wounds; they were also noted for their communal living and landholding. The first group came to the infant colony of Georgia in 1735, and many more immigrated in the 1740s and 1750s. Some moved to the North Carolina Piedmont (and became involved in the Regulator movement), but the movement focused most of its efforts in backcountry Pennsylvania and New York, establishing Bethlehem as their capital and building a series of missions near large Indian settlements. Moravians sought to treat the Indians as equals, to learn from them, and to find a middle ground that allowed converts to draw on existing social and cultural frameworks. Another radical German sect was the "New Baptists" or "Dunkers," some of whom created utopian communes like Ephrata in frontier Pennsylvania near Lancaster.[45]

But most German immigrants, as well as the Scots-Irish, who also flooded across the Atlantic in huge numbers, came to America in the second quarter of the century to escape poverty and war. Many of these newcomers entered through Philadelphia and, unable to obtain land in long-settled coastal areas, kept going to the eastern slopes of the Appalachians and then south as far as South Carolina; some pushed further west into the Ohio Valley. Some American-born sons who did not inherit land were similarly forced to seek land in the frontier or border areas further inland. These settlers spawned decades of bitter, savage warfare with Native Americans as they killed animals, cut timber, built cabins, and farmed in places used and claimed by Indians. That movement continued after the Revolutionary War. For example, in 1784 Benjamin Franklin urged (in an article published in France) "hearty young Labouring Men, who understand the Husbandry of Corn and Cattle" to come to America, because land was cheap with "the vast Forests still void of Inhabitants," and a farm of a hundred fertile acres "full of Wood" could be purchased "near the Frontiers" for only "eight to ten Guineas."[46]

Ironically, even as those moving to Appalachia and the Ohio Valley sought to wrest that land from the Indians who still lived on it, others found Indians useful allies or appropriate symbols to use against annoying landlords. The first situation was somewhat rare, but after midcentury New England farmers, who had settled on lands along the Hudson Valley, forged alliances with Mahicans and Wappingers that helped them resist, by law and by arms, efforts by New York manor lords to evict them or collect rents. The latter was more common, particularly after the Revolution. While Anglo-Americans generally scorned the idea as well as the reality of the noble savage, backcountry colonists embraced aspects of the Indian stereotype in order to anonymously resist absentee landlords attempting to challenge their land claims and impose "order" on their "lawless" society. These "white Indians" became particularly notorious after the Revolutionary War in Maine and the Wyoming Valley of Pennsylvania, and during the 1830s and 1840s along the upper Hudson River as farmers (many from western New England) continued to resist paying rent to New York landlords.[47]

After the Revolution, Native Americans would continue to serve as symbols of social and economic equality. During the war, British officer Jonathan Carver published an account of his *Travels* in America that emphasized how the Indians he met were "strangers to all distinction of property," thought it "irrational" that one man should be wealthier than another, and were particularly shocked at the idea that a person could be imprisoned for debt. In 1791 Delaware editor Robert Coram, in recommending measures to maintain economic and political equality in the United States, quoted extensively from Carver to emphasize how Indians saw unequal distribution of property as something that only European "savages" embraced. Six years later, Thomas Paine, in his notorious *Agrarian Justice*, pointed to Native Americans as superb examples of "the natural and primitive state of man" that has none of "those spectacles of human misery which property and want present to our eyes, in all the towns and streets of Europe. . . . The life of an Indian is a continual holiday, compared with the poor of Europe." But Carver was a foreigner, and Coram and Paine used the egalitarian image of the Indian solely to criticize what they saw as immoral European practices. Not until the early twentieth century would a noticeable movement emerge among Americans to improve their country's economy and society with Native American customs about equality.[48]

CHAPTER THREE

Revolutionary Ideologies and Regulations

On April 12, 1773, the town of New Haven, Connecticut, site of Yale College, gathered for the sermon that followed its annual elections. But this would not be the usual election sermon designed to instruct the new officials on their responsibilities and the people on their duty to obey. It had been, after all, five years after most New Englanders including the wealthiest had sworn to embrace a homespun brew and spurn English-taxed tea, and Boston radicals were pushing the common-law boundaries of governance. In the midst of this increasingly politicized climate, the Reverend Benjamin Trumbull addressed the town and its newly elected officers: "Every civil community" should "keep their rulers . . . intimately connected with them . . . to keep property as equally divided among the inhabitants as possible, and not to suffer a few persons to amass all the riches and wealth of a country." Should men "become possessors of the Wealth of a state," the minister warned, "it will be in their power to purchase, or by undue influence . . . thrust themselves into all places of honour and trust," enabling them "by fraud or force" to "oppress and tyrannize over their fellow-men." The best way to maintain free elections and the people's liberties, Trumbull emphasized, was to keep property "as equally divided as possible." In calling for a popular government with the power to redistribute property, the minister did more than reflect True Leveller ideas from the English Civil War and *Cato's Letters* from the 1720s: he highlighted an egalitarian commonwealth ideology that had become increasingly powerful in the colonies during the imperial crisis.[1]

After the War for Independence erupted, that egalitarian ideology became imbedded in the efforts by governments at the local, state, and national levels to manage the wartime economy, primarily through price and wage regulations. These regulations had practical purposes: to help soldiers to buy provisions and support families on their fixed salaries, prevent immoral behavior, ensure affordable supplies of "necessaries," and help stabilize the currency. But the connected ideologies became clear in the resulting battles over the rules. Supporters trumpeted not only old, cherished concepts of "just prices" and the commonwealth but also more radical egalitarian ideas, especially when the struggles intensified; in Philadelphia, some officials even insisted in proto-Marxian terms that laborers who helped build cargo ships had a right to the produce that those ships carried. Opponents initially emphasized the impracticality of regulations, but in May 1777 a piece in the *Connecticut Courant* argued that wage and price limits were "encroaching upon those natural and unalienable principles of liberty and property, which ought always to be sacred and inviolable in a free country." That view, which went beyond the liberal ideas in Adam Smith's recently published *Wealth of Nations*, was quickly embraced by many merchants. Their view seemed to triumph in state and national policies by the end of the war, although communitarian ideals remained influential on the local level and more broadly in American culture well into the nineteenth century. More importantly, equality became an ideal instead of dreaded anarchy or the Devil's work. At the same time, Americans continued to perceive power as an organic whole with interwoven economic, social, and political elements.[2]

For most British Americans, the daily and yearly rhythms of life in the mid-eighteenth century remained similar to what they had been a century before, although the provincial cultures and political systems had matured and become more like those in England, and the sudden uptick of immigration generated some disorienting changes, particularly in the middle colonies of Pennsylvania and New York and the western borderlands of the Carolinas and the Ohio Valley.[3] Anglo-Americans who wished to become effective legislators, lawyers, or judges studied moral philosophy, incorporating what today is distinguished as economics, sociology, or political science. Important sources included classical writers, particularly Cicero and Tacitus, who wrote about Rome's political troubles; James Harrington's *Oceana* and Algernon Sidney's praise of republics in *Discourses Concerning Government* (ca. 1680); Enlightenment political philosophers from Thomas Hobbes to David Hume; and the English radical Whigs who published a series of articles and books in the 1720s (most famously *Cato's Letters*) criticizing the corrupting ties between politics and wealth in the British Empire. The mythology that Anglo-Saxon egalitarianism remained deeply rooted in England became part of newer works such as Richard Bland's *Inquiry into the Rights of the British Colonies* (1766) and Obediah Hulme's *An Historical Essay on the English Constitution* (1771), reprinted in America and excerpted in newspapers. Many colonists embraced that mythology along with English radical Whig writings because both reflected an idealized conception of their present and past condition, as well as a warning that those virtues were endangered.[4]

Also important, and possibly more influential in the colonies, were the religious sources of republican ideas that had emerged out of the Reformation, from the small clique of Familists who pooled their resources to the more "mainstream" puritan reformers who sought to replace the vestiges of Catholic corruption with "Godly republicanism." New England election sermons not only trumpeted the need for hierarchy and deference, and a greater role for the "respectable" in government, but also celebrated the disinterested pursuit of the common good and condemned selfish pursuit of private ends. The Awakenings recharged these morals, particularly in the borderland conflicts between eastern elites and western settler communities that drew strong support from Scots-Irish Presbyterians, radical "Separate" Baptists, Moravians, and other dissenters.[5]

Anglo-Americans were particularly sensitive to the commonwealth ideal that ran through these secular and religious sources—that government, society, and every individual within a community existed to benefit all regardless of status—and after the midcentury they began to pay more attention to the egalitarian facets of that ideal. The radical current of economic equality in this republican stream appeared infrequently before the imperial crisis exploded, but it can be glimpsed in "The Love of One's Country," an excerpt from *Cato's Letters* (1721), published in the Boston *Independent Advertiser* in January 1748.

> As Liberty can never subsist without Equality, nor Equality be long preserved without an Agrarian Law, or something like it; so when Men's Riches are become immeasurably or surprising great, a People who regard their own Security, ought to make strict Enquiry, *how they came by them*, and oblige them to take down their own Size, for Fear of TERRIFYING THE COMMUNITY, OR MASTERING IT. In every Country, and under every Government, *particular Men may be too rich*. . . . But, will some say, is it a Crime to be rich? Yes, certainly. AT THE PUBLICK EXPENCE, or to the Danger of the Publick.[6]

These words could be considered the manifesto of the American tradition of economic equality. The *Advertiser* was published for two years, apparently at the behest of a small group of men, including Samuel Adams, explicitly for artisans and laborers concerned about the "rights and liberties of mankind" in the wake of the port town's successful resistance against impressment efforts by an English admiral and also worried by rising rates of poverty and unemployment. But these ideas were not unique to Boston; they found fertile ground in Anglo-American culture because property ownership and local political participation were quite widespread. Even as a gentry class developed, the colonies had no titled nobility, and the social and income gap between the wealthiest and poorest remained fairly narrow. That could be a source of political stability, as in New England, or instability, as in New Jersey or North Carolina.[7]

Although by midcentury poverty and socioeconomic inequality became more of a problem, most observers continued to insist that conditions in America were more equal than in England. James Otis's *The Rights of the British Colonies Asserted and Proved*, published in July 1764, while focusing on Enlightenment and English constitutional principles, proudly proclaimed that "Liberty and Property" were widely distributed in America. Later, as opposition to the Stamp Act flared, Joseph Warren of Boston told his friend Edmund Dana that the measure had "inflamed" America "to the highest degree" because, since "there is a more equal division of property" in America than in England, "influence and authority must be nearly equal, and every man will think himself deeply interested in the support of public liberty." To Anglo-Americans, the nemesis of "public liberty" was the corruption marked by intertwining of political and economic power, which became notorious in 1720 with the South Sea Bubble, and after 1760 growing numbers of colonists believed that their commonwealths were threatened by spreading corruption in the form of political control of property and wealth by conniving "courtiers."[8]

The fundamentally optimistic ideology of liberalism, which explored and celebrated the role of the individual in society, government, and the economy, emerged during the seventeenth century as England experienced years of good harvests, improved transportation networks, and increasingly inexpensive imports from America and Asia. Writers sketched an increasingly abstract model of the economy that emphasized patterns of exchange fixed in human nature, which governments could not control, even after Parliament following the Glorious Revolution implemented mercantilist policies that celebrated national interests. These liberal ideas were expanded by Enlightenment writers, beginning with John Locke's concept of government as a social covenant designed to protect life, liberty, and property, and blossoming after 1725 with the exploration by Scottish Enlightenment philosophers of the individual's moral and social sensibilities. While these intellectuals disagreed about many things, they generally saw human needs as the driving force for social evolution from hunting to pastoral, agricultural, and finally commercial activities; government had little positive influence on that process. Thus, David Hume praised Harrington's *Oceana* but dismissed the notion of an agrarian law because "men will soon learn the art . . . of concealing their possessions under other people's name." But they were not laissez-faire economists: from Francis Hutcheson to Adam Smith, they believed that selfishness was generally held in check by the individual's need for social bonds and approval.[9]

As the imperial crisis heated up, Anglo-Americans increasingly gave moral philosophy the attention once reserved for theology, and their words and actions reflected the communitarian ethos. With the Townshend duty boycotts in the late 1760s, following quickly on the Stamp Act crisis, artisans, laborers, shopkeepers, and women created associations at the neighborhood and county level to pressure reluctant individuals, often gentry or merchants, to demonstrate republican virtue and sociability. The "better sort" felt the need as never before to show support for the community not only by spurning the detested tea but also by wearing homespun and hiring local artisans to make products instead of buying more luxurious versions from England. In his 1768 almanac, the famed Boston publisher Nathaniel Ames began by offering his readers some useful advice: "How much more honor'd and esteemed by every true Patriot and Friend to his Country, is the Man, who, cloath'd in the Manufacture of his own House, comes to the City on his lofty Steed. . . . I say, how esteemed and much more useful to Society is such a one, than the empty idle Fop." At the end, facing the December calendar, he reprinted Boston's resolve calling for nonimportation. Loyalists faced increasing pressure from neighbors and associates to join the nonimportation and homespun movement. A few newspapers dared print letters mocking the effort as self-serving, but only the *Boston Chronicle* dared attack the "patriot' merchants (including John Hancock) by printing shipping manifests to show they were violating the agreement. The opponents and advocates of nonimportation apparently agreed on one thing: the virtue of the commonwealth.[10]

As tensions grew, a few radical republican voices spotlighted class conflict and condemned the connections between wealth and power. In 1767 a pamphleteer in New York City condemned the rich who had become powerful "by a pernicious trade at the expence and ruin" of the public. In April 1773 Benjamin Trumbull in his New Haven election sermon echoed the Diggers and *Cato's Letters* in calling for republican governments to have the power to redistribute property. One year later, on October 20, 1774, the First Continental Congress, meeting to coordinate opposition to the Coercive Acts, sought to organize market regulation in the boycott of British trade, asking that merchants and artisans maintain prices and a committee be chosen "in every county, city, and town" to enforce the measure. In Newburyport, Massachusetts, the committee of inspection and safety called on fellow merchants "to hold on their usual prices"; a few months later, Nathaniel Carter publicly apologized for raising prices on goods shipped to Boston. In New York City, a shaky coalition of artisans and merchants chose sixty men to inspect ships, seize those carrying forbidden cargo (at least twenty-one ships between November 1774 and February 1775), sell illicit goods at public auction, and take other substantive actions against violators. The Philadelphia committee set price limits for salt, tea, and other needs, but members were divided between objecting to those measures and urging strict and immediate enforcement, so they agreed to publicly shame violators.[11]

More radical republican and egalitarian currents reappeared as the colonies moved to open revolt. That was particularly apparent in Pennsylvania, where conservatives resisted independence until May, at which point revolutionary committees in Philadelphia took the reins (with Congress's blessing) and organized elections for a state constitutional convention. A committee of privates in the city's militia published a broadside urging voting for representatives who would maintain America's current "Happiness" of having "no Rank above that of Freemen." The country's "future Welfare and Tranquility" depended on preserving its supposedly classless society, they wrote; for "great and over-grown rich Men will be improper to be trusted, they will be too apt to be framing Distinctions in Society, because they will reap the Benefits of all such Distinctions." Unlike the Anglo-American mythology of an idyllic democratic Saxon past, this broadside presented a remarkable view of an egalitarian *present* and accessible (if threatened) future.[12]

The revolutionaries' campaign was successful: the men elected to the convention, which met upstairs from the Continental Congress, were mostly "middling" artisans and farmers, including the celebrated radicals Thomas Paine and Thomas Young. But it was the "moderate" Benjamin Franklin who apparently proposed the agrarian measure that would have given the legislature the power to take "excessive" property from individuals on the principle that concentrations of wealth were "a danger to the happiness of mankind." The proposal did not pass, but the final product was far more democratic than the constitutions written by other states. Among other elements, there were no property ownership requirements for either voters or legislators, just the mandate to pay "public taxes," usually the poll tax laid on every adult in the community. This measure, which went beyond the initial Leveller program during the English Civil War, was the first move to reject the traditional connection between political power and socioeconomic status since early puritan New England empowered all church members to vote.[13]

During the summer, after celebrating the Declaration of Independence, Americans waited for the next blow from the British Army and became increasingly concerned about the threat of Tories and economic malfeasance, including engrossing, forestalling, monopolizing, and price gouging. Farmers lost laborers to the military, mistrusted the currencies flooding the country, and faced increasingly uncertain markets; many would adapt as the war went on by turning to subsistence strategies, which reduced supplies to towns and the army. Local committees of safety not only demanded oaths of allegiance to the new state governments and nation but also sought to control the chaotic state of trade. The Pennsylvania constitutional convention authorized local committees of inspection to control prices, and when ninety Philadelphia merchants publicly scorned the measure, they were widely condemned. In late July and early August 1776, Philadelphia's committee seized green tea and salt being sold at inflated prices; in the latter case, it paid the merchants what it considered "just compensation." Elsewhere, violators of price regulations were fined, denounced as "enemies of the American cause," and their goods sometimes seized. In July 1776, men in Longmeadow, Massachusetts, blackened their faces and, led by the town's deacon, seized imported goods from Samuel Colton and had the town clerk sell the goods at a "just price." During this same critical period, crowds in several New York communities seized and distributed tea and in southern states took immediate action against merchants hoarding salt. More generally, Congress and the state legislatures issued currency and mandated that retailers accept the notes as specie.[14]

England and Europe generally had a long tradition of communities and guilds regulating wages, hours of work, prices, marketplaces, and the sizes, weights, or volume of necessities such as bread and ale. Tudor and Stuart legal codes barred forestalling (buying before the market was open to the public), regrating (buying for resale at the same or another market), and engrossing (buying a large amount of an article in an effort to obtain a monopoly), claiming as immoral such efforts to profit at the expense of the community. Regulation of the marketplace was viewed as a necessary part of police powers to ensure the public good; it was grounded in biblical commandments, feudal-era obligations, guild regulations, and other customs designed to manage necessaries, particularly during times of scarcity. English chroniclers describe crowds in markets insisting on paying the customary price for foodstuffs, which highlighted the sense that all members of a community were entitled to basic needs.[15]

Such regulation was more common and frequent in England than its colonies, but it was not unknown in America, particularly in port towns that became centers of commerce and population in the eighteenth century. Towns set prices and standards for necessities like bread and beer (known as assizes); mandated ferryman, lodging, and carting fees; appointed inspectors of products such as wood and leather; and set places, times, and standards of measurement for marketplaces. In 1684 New York City barred forestalling and engrossing; in 1741 the province barred the export of wheat to control prices because the poor were "distressed"; and in 1742 the city council renewed a broad set of market regulations. As a prominent group of men reminded the council in August 1763, "in all populous Cities the Regulation of the publick Markets respecting the Price of Provisions hath ever been esteemed a Matter of great Importance to the Inhabitants."[16]

The New England colonies had a particularly strong tradition of town governments enforcing regulations on prices, tavern rules, grain supply, and employment of outsiders, and such rules become more aggressive during the eighteenth century. For example, in 1709, and again in 1713, word circulated through Boston that merchant Andrew Belcher planned to make higher profit by selling his grain in the West Indies instead of in the town; both times, when the selectmen failed to dissuade him, angry crowds attacked his ships and emptied his warehouses. Colonies south of New York showed little interest in economic regulations, aside from brief efforts in the Chesapeake to control the production and quality of tobacco. But farmers in those regions at midcentury also demonstrated a strong desire for a more egalitarian society and economy, with the Baptist insurgence in Virginia and the antiproprietary struggles in New Jersey and the North Carolina Piedmont. Religious concerns shaped European economic regulations, and in Revolutionary America those practices fit squarely within the commonwealth paradigm that society and government had the right to set boundaries for individual initiative and action. The price and wage control measures also sought to meet the radical republican goal, last glimpsed during the English Civil War, to prevent any "great and over-grown rich Men."[17]

Not surprisingly, systematic regulatory efforts began in New England. In March 1776 thirteen towns in eastern Massachusetts asked the state assembly to deal with the "growing Evil" of "extravagant" prices "demanded" for "English Goods" and "sundry other Articles"; separately, a committee of representatives from eight towns in Essex County and four in southern New Hampshire asked the state for a quick "remedy" to the "evils" of "exorbitant prices" demanded by merchants and farmers. In Connecticut, that same month, a convention of committees of inspection in New London County acted on its own, drawing up its own list of price limitations to be enforced throughout the county. Apparently the northern committees became impatient with the slow pace of the state assembly, because in November they organized a series of meetings of "Committees and Agents" from twenty-seven towns and districts in northern Massachusetts and southern New Hampshire and, at the end of the month, sent petitions to both state legislatures asking for measures that would prevent price gouging. At that point, the Massachusetts legislature called for a convention of New England representatives to work out a regional approach to economic regulation and military preparation. Three days later, on November 19, the Connecticut legislature set statewide labor rates and prices for various commodities and agreed to send delegates to the regional meeting.[18]

At the meeting in Providence on December 25–31, the delegates approved a resolve that decried "the unbounded avarice of many persons" in raising prices and labor rates to "intolerably exorbitant" levels. Their greed could have "the most pernicious and fatal consequence" in discouraging the war effort and making it impossible for soldiers on fixed pay to support their families. The convention backed the resolve with broad wage and price guidelines and called for the states to set and enforce more detailed regulations. All four New England states quickly put these measures into force, and all but New Hampshire also embargoed the export of key commodities without a special permit. Such regulation fit quite well with New England's commonwealth tradition, and the avarice condemned by town committees and the legislatures was viewed as a broad moral failing. The Providence convention sent its resolves to Congress for its approval and recommendation to other states.[19]

The measure drew strong support in Philadelphia. The few congressmen who spoke against the regulation seem to have been those most directly connected to the Scottish Enlightenment with its liberal economic ideas. Benjamin Rush, who had studied at Edinburgh in the 1760s, cited (incorrectly) David Hume's description of English price regulations as "a monument of human folly"; John Wilson, who attended the University of St. Andrews before immigrating to Philadelphia in 1766, warned his colleagues that such regulations would "hang as a dead weight" on overseas trade; and College of New Jersey president John Witherspoon, also from Edinburgh University, proclaimed, "It is beyond the power of despotic princes to regulate the price of goods," noting that such regulations actually tended to create scarcities and therefore higher prices. Yet none of these men argued that such regulations violated an individual's natural rights, perhaps because they were concerned about pushing their opposition into unpopular territory. Most congressmen agreed with Richard Henry Lee and others who spoke in favor of the resolutions: the body voted to "recommend" that other states pass laws to limit "exorbitant prices" and called for two separate regional conventions of other states.[20]

Meanwhile, New Englanders, mostly through town committees, sometimes meeting in county conventions, were creating regulations that enforced and extended the state acts. The bustling shipbuilding commercial town of Newburyport, for example, "set and affixed" prices for a wide range of foodstuffs, textiles, lumber, shoes, and other goods; wages for maritime craftsmen, laborers, teamsters, and blacksmiths; charges at stables and taverns; and treatment of any items not listed to be in accordance with the "Usages and Customs which have heretofore been practiced in said Town."[21] The few records of the discussions on these measures highlight a strong belief in their political and moral necessity as well as their economic need. The Boston town meeting on February 6 called price limits "absolutely necessary for the effectual security of the essential Rights and Liberties of America," and two months later its officials mandated prices for many imported and domestic goods not enumerated in the state law, including fish, shoes, beaver hats, soap, loaf sugar, and hard cider. When Connecticut governor Joseph Trumbull heard that traders were avoiding the limits through "dissimulation & subterfuges," he called on all town officials to investigate every complaint "so that all such persons who prove themselves Enemies to their country, preferring their private gain to the Salvation of the States may meet with their just reward."[22]

At the same time, many disagreed on the value of price controls. The commercial farming community of Springfield in Massachusetts resolved that the primary reason for the rapid inflation was not price gouging but the huge amount of currency in circulation—which discouraged trade and industry, thus causing shortages and price increases. Nevertheless, the farmers agreed to carry out the state act. William Baylies of Dighton made the same point when he told Robert Treat Paine that the increase in prices was due to either scarcity or the recent flood of currency or both. The tension between those who focused on "avaricious" traders and those who viewed the economy in more mechanistic terms can be seen in the shifting proposals considered by

In Purſuance of an Act from the Great and General Court, of the State of Maſſachuſetts-Bay, entitled an " *Act to prevent Monopoly and Oppreſſion*," the Selectmen and Committee of the Town of NEWBURY-PORT, have ſet and affixed the following PRICES to the Articles herein after enumerated, which are to be taken and deemed to be the Prices of all ſuch Goods and Articles, in the ſaid Town of NEWBURY-PORT, and all other Articles not herein after particularly enumerated, to be in proportion thereunto, according to the Uſages and Cuſtoms which have heretofore been practiſed in ſaid Town.

GOOD merchantable WHEAT, at 7s. 6d. a buſhel. Good merchantable RYE, or RYE-MEAL, at 5s. a buſhel.

Good INDIAN-MEAL or CORN, at 4s. a buſhel.

Freſh PORK, weighing above ten ſcore, at 5d. a lb.

Ditto, under ten ſcore, 4d.

And, SALT PORK in the uſual proportion according to the price of Salt,

Good well fatted Graſs fed BEEF, at 3d. a lb. and Stall-fed Beef well fatted, at 4d. a lb. and Beef of an inferior quality in equal proportion.

MUTTON, LAMB, and VEAL, at 4d. a lb.

TURKEYS, Dunghill Fowls, and Ducks, to be ſold only by the pound, at 5d. a lb.

GEESE, at 4d. a lb. MILK, at 3d. a quart.

Freſh COD-FISH, at one penny a pound.

FLOUR imported from the Southern States, at 30s. a cwt.

FLOUR manufactured in this State, at 25s. a cwt.

PATATOES commonly called Spaniſh Patatoes of the beſt quality, at 1s. 2d. a buſhel in the Fall of the Year, and no more than 1s. 8d. a buſhel in any other ſeaſon, and other Patatoes in the uſual proportion.

PEAS, 8s. a buſhel. BEANS, 6s. a buſhel.

BUTTER, at 10d. a lb. by the ſingle pound, and 9d. by the Firkin. EGGS, 6d. a dozen.

Beſt CHEESE manufactured in America, 6d. a lb.

American manufactured CHOCOLATE, 1s. 8d. a lb.

Good merchantable imported SALT, at 10s. a buſhel. Salt manufactured from ſea-water in this State, at 12s. a buſhel.

Good merchantable Weſt-India RUM, at 6s. 8d. per gallon by the hogſhead, including the caſk, and 6s. 10d. by the barrel, excluſive of the barrel, and 7s. 8d. by the ſingle gallon, and 2s. by the quart, and ſo in proportion for a leſs quantity according to the former cuſtom and uſages for retailing ſmaller quantities.

New-England RUM, at 3s. 10d. a gallon by the hogſhead, or barrel, excluſive of 13s. 4d. for the hogſhead, or 4s. for the barrel, and 4s. 6d. by the ſingle gallon, if diſtilled in this Town, and ſo in like proportion for ſmaller quantities according to the old approved cuſtoms for retailing ſmaller quantities.

Beſt of Muſcovada SUGAR, at 54s. a cwt. by the hogſhead, and 3l. by the ſingle cwt. and 8d. a lb. by the ſingle pound.

Beſt COCOA, by 6l. 10s. a cwt.

COTTON, 3s. a lb. by the bag, and 3s. 8d. by the ſingle pound.

Good COFFEE, 2s. 4d. a lb. by the ſingle pound.

LIVER OYL by the barrel, 4s. a gallon.

BLUBBER Refined, 30s. a barrel.

Good merchantable White Pine BOARDS, not to exceed 45s. a thouſand,

Red Oak Hogſhead STAVES, 50s. a thouſand.

Good merchantable Shaken Hogſheads meaſuring 44 inches in length, at 4s. each, and others of different ſizes in proportion.

Good Shipping SHINGLE, at 11s. a thouſand, and all other kinds of Lumber in the ſame proportion.

BLOOMERY IRON, at 30s. a cwt. at the place of manufactory, and the ſame allowance to be made for tranſporting of Iron by land as is allowed for other articles.

Good Refined IRON, at 50s. a cwt.

Good merchantable SHEEPS WOOL, at 2s. a lb.

Good well dreſſed merchantable FLAX, 1s. a lb.

Good merchantable TOBACCO raiſed in this State, at 6d. a lb.

Meas beſt YARN STOCKINGS, at 6s. a pair, and in that proportion for an inferior quality.

Men's SHOES made of Neat's Leather, of the beſt common ſort, 8s. a pair, and for others the like price according to their fine and quality.

Good yard-wide TOW CLOTH, 2s. 3d. a yard, and other Tow Cloth in proportion according to its width and quality, and the price of coarſe Linens to be computed after the ſame rate.

Good yard-wide STRIPED FLANNEL, 3s. 6d. a yard, and other Flannels in proportion according to their widths and qualities, and other Woollen Cloth manufactured in America according to their widths and qualities.

PORK by the barrel, 220 wt. in a barrel, 4l. 12s.

BEEF by the barrel, 242 wt. in a barrel, 3l. 14s.

Good TRIED TALLOW, 7d. a lb. and Rough Tallow, at 5d. a lb.

RAW HIDES, at 3d. a lb.

RAW CALF SKINS, at 6d. a lb.

TANNED HIDES, at 11s. 4d. a lb.

CURRYING LEATHER, 5l. a Hide, Calves Skins, 1s. a piece, and other Leather in the ſame proportion.

CARPENTERS, at 5s. 4d. a day.

JOYNERS, at 4s. 8d. a day.

CAULKERS, at 6s. a day.

MASONS, at 6s. a day.

COOPERS finding and ſetting a hogſhead Hoop, 4d. finding and ſetting a barrel Hoop, 2d.½

BARBERS, ſhaving, 3d.

DAY LABOURERS finding themſelves, 4s. being found at 3s. a day, and all other tradeſmen's labour to be in the ſame proportion.

HORSE-KEEPING for a night, or twenty-four hours, with Engliſh hay, 2s. Keeping a yoke of Oxen, the ſame as a Horſe.

Engliſh HAY of the beſt quality not to exceed 4s. 6d. a cwt. and ſo in proportion for a meaner quality.

OATS, at 2s. a buſhel.

Haling a cord of Wood the diſtance of half a mile, or leſs, 1s. 9d.

Teamſter finding himſelf and Cattle, for one hand with Cart or Waggon, one yoke of Oxen and a good draught Horſe, or two yoke of Oxen, 12s. a day.

TRUCKAGE. Haling one hogſhead the diſtance of half a mile, or under, 1s. 4d. for a ſingle barrel, 6d.

HORSE-HIRE, 4d.½ a mile.

CHAISE-HIRE 3d.½ a mile.

SULKEY HIRE, 2d.½ a mile.

HORSE-SHOEING all round, with Steel Corks, 7s.

OX-SHOEING, in the ſame proportion.

Good CHARCOAL, 6d. a Buſhel.

DINNERS at Taverns for travellers, of boiled and roaſt Meat, with other articles equivalent, excluſive of Wine, 1s. 6d. Suppers and Breakfaſts 1s. each, Lodging 4d.

Good Eaſtern WOOD, landed on any Wharf in this Town, 21s. a Cord, including Wharfage and Cordage.

WHARFAGE of Wood, 5d. a cord.

Fulled Woolen cloth, of American Manufacture, common width, 9s. per yard.

Cotton and Linen yard wide, 3s. 6d. a yard.

Woolen Goods, coarſe Linens, Duck, Cordage, Ticklenburgs and Oznabrigs, ſhall not be ſold by wholeſale at a higher rate than in the proportion of £375 ſterling, for what uſually coſt £100 ſterling, in that part of Europe from whence they are imported ; and any other goods, wares or merchandize, excepting Hemp, waulke or military ſtores imported from thence or brought, or which ſhall be brought into any port in this State in any prize veſſel, ſhall not be ſold at a higher rate from the prime coſt as aforeſaid, than in the proportion of £450 ſterling, for what coſt £100 ſterling in Europe; and the ſeller by wholeſale, ſhall make out a bill of parcels at the ſterling coſt of the articles ſold, with his advance thereupon, and deliver the ſame to the bearer, under penalty of the ſum at which ſaid articles are ſo ſold by him; and the retailers of ſuch goods, wares and merchandize, ſhall not ſell them at a higher advance than 20 per cent upon the wholeſale price, and ſhall, if requeſted by the buyer, give a bill of parcels, with the ſterling coſt and advance.

NEWBURY-PORT: Printed by JOHN MYCALL, 1777.

GOOD merchantable WHEAT, at 7s. 6d. a buſhel. Good merchantable RYE, or RYE-MEAL, at 5s. a buſhel.

Good INDIAN-MEAL or CORN, at 4s. a buſhel.

Freſh PORK, weighing above ten ſcore, at 5d. a lb.

Ditto, under ten ſcore, 4d.

And, SALT PORK in the uſual proportion according to the price of Salt,

Good well fatted Graſs fed BEEF, at 3d. a lb. and Stall-fed Beef well fatted, at 4d. a lb. and Beef of an inferior quality in equal proportion.

MUTTON, LAMB, and VEAL, at 4d. a lb.

TURKEYS, Dunghill Fowls, and Ducks, to be ſold only by the pound, at 5d. a lb.

GEESE, at 4d. a lb. MILK, at 3d. a quart.

Freſh COD-FISH, at one penny a pound.

FLOUR imported from the Southern States, at 30s. a cwt.

FLOUR manufactured in this State, at 25s. a cwt.

PATATOES commonly called Spaniſh Patatoes of the

Good COFFEE, 2s. 4d. a lb. by the ſingle pound.

LIVER OYL by the barrel, 4s. a gallon.

BLUBBER Refined, 30s. a barrel.

Good merchantable White Pine BOARDS, not to exceed 45s. a thouſand,

Red Oak Hogſhead STAVES, 50s. a thouſand.

Good merchantable Shaken Hogſheads meaſuring 44 inches in length, at 4s. each, and others of different ſizes in proportion.

Good Shipping SHINGLE, at 11s. a thouſand, and all other kinds of Lumber in the ſame proportion.

BLOOMERY IRON, at 30s. a cwt. at the place of manufactory, and the ſame allowance to be made for tranſporting of Iron by land as is allowed for other articles.

Good Refined IRON, at 50s. a cwt.

Good merchantable SHEEPS WOOL, at 2s. a lb.

Good well dreſſed merchantable FLAX, 1s. a lb.

Good merchantable TOBACCO raiſed in this State, at 6d. a lb.

DAY LABOURERS finding themſelves, 4s. being found at 3s. a day, and all other tradeſmen's labour to be in the ſame proportion.

HORSE-KEEPING for a night, or twenty-four hours, with Engliſh hay, 2s. Keeping a yoke of Oxen, the ſame as a Horſe.

Engliſh HAY of the beſt quality not to exceed 4s. 6d. a cwt. and ſo in proportion for a meaner quality.

OATS, at 2s. a buſhel.

Haling a cord of Wood the diſtance of half a mile, or leſs, 1s. 9d.

Teamſter finding himſelf and Cattle, for one hand with Cart or Waggon, one yoke of Oxen and a good draught Horſe, or two yoke of Oxen, 12s. a day.

TRUCKAGE. Haling one hogſhead the diſtance of half a mile, or under, 1s. 4d. for a ſingle barrel, 6d.

HORSE-HIRE, 4d.½ a mile.

CHAISE-HIRE 3d.½ a mile.

SULKEY HIRE, 2d.½ a mile.

HORSE-SHOEING all round, with Steel Corks, 7s.

Price and wage regulations, Newburyport, 1777. Courtesy, American Antiquarian Society.

the other regional convention that met in late March 1777, with delegates from New York to Virginia. The first set of proposals it considered was couched in highly moralistic language and focused on price controls, whereas the second, a completely rewritten version, concentrated on reducing the currency in circulation and rejected price control measures. Gradually the perception grew that prices and currency were connected, so that in the fall a second wave of regulatory measures would seek to control both.[23]

One significant problem with the regulatory act quickly emerged, as long-standing tensions between port towns and surrounding farm villages flared, with city laborers and artisans suspecting farmers of taking their produce to other places where they could get higher prices, and farmers suspecting artisans of gouging on labor charges. In February 1777 Boston's committee of correspondence sent a circular to its rural counterparts to reassure them that goods in city markets would be priced according to the state law; city dwellers were worried that "false reports" had caused farmers "to withhold the usual and common supplies of Provisions." Similar problems were reported in Salem and Worcester. As winter ended, New Englanders increasingly complained about greedy merchants sending goods elsewhere and farmers refusing to bring produce to regulated markets. On April 21 Abigail Adams told her husband of the "general cry against the Merchants, against monopolizers &c. who tis said have created a partial Scarcity." The result, she told John, was that five hundred Bostonians "carted" six Salem merchants who had bid up prices and refused to take currency; the crowd had dumped the miscreants in Roxbury under threat of death if they returned. She noted that the disciplined crowd was led by the semi-mythical figure of Joyce, Junior, famous in puritan history for leading the capture of Charles I. This resurrection of a heroic figure from the English war against aristocracy points to potential tensions between those with more "conservative" notions of republican virtue and those who held more radical egalitarian goals. Regardless, prices continued to rise, and supplies continued to fall.[24]

New Englanders generally responded to the problem by allowing some adjustment for inflation while seeking stricter enforcement. For example, Massachusetts raised the price ceilings on some goods and services while authorizing town selectmen and committees of correspondence to fix wages and prices bimonthly and seize and sell goods in the market. On May 11 committees of safety from throughout Plymouth County gathered in Plympton to rally support for the new law. The convention mourned the decline of virtue and then passed a series of recommendations, beginning with a nod to the True Leveller principle that "an equitable exchange of the fruits of the earth . . .

in due proportion to that of another, is the basis on which the felicity, free-dom, and happiness of a community greatly depend." Of the eight measures the convention proposed, five urged severe enforcement of the act. Over the next six weeks, towns around the state tightened enforcement measures. As July drew to a close, Abigail Adams reported to John that "a new set of mo-bility" had taken the upper hand in Boston: crowds of women angered by high prices and scarce supplies broke into stores, took coffee and sugar to the mar-ket, sold it by the pound at a just price, and threatened any who tried to stop them. William Pynchon reported the same in Salem, and similar popular en-forcement occurred in other states.[25]

But perhaps more significant, though still very much a minority position, was the opposite response, as liberal opponents of economic regulation became increasingly emboldened to argue that men should not be told how to price or handle their property. On May 12 a writer in the *Connecticut Courant* ar-gued that regulating price with penal statutes was impossible "in a free coun-try" because men could not be limited "in the purchase or disposal of prop-erty," for to do so "must infringe those principles of liberty for which we are gloriously fighting." Subsidizing the families of soldiers directly would accom-plish the same purpose. This piece seems the first to make an explicit link between an individual's freedom in the marketplace and the Revolution's slo-gan of liberty. Two weeks later, a different writer condemned the regulating act as an imposition by farmers upon "labourers, mechanicks and traders." That same day, a Boston town meeting instructed state representatives to re-peal the regulatory act, partly for practical reasons but primarily from a strong liberal view of the economy. "For it has been a known & acknowledged Truth," the town emphasized, "that Trade must regulate itself; can never be clogged but to its ruin, & always flourishes when left alone." Not only did ef-forts to regulate trade result in "innumerable Evils," but they were also "di-rectly opposite to The Idea of Liberty." The largest city in the region, and the sparkplug of the American revolt against England, had for the first time con-nected economic freedom with the new country's struggle.[26]

This hyper-liberal notion of individual unrestricted liberty was potentially revolutionary. Enlightenment moral philosophers from Locke to Smith had viewed the heavy hand of aristocratic government as distorting the economy, inhibiting improvements, and (at least potentially) destructive of liberty. But at the same time, they viewed individuals as necessarily social creatures who not only needed the approval and company of other people but also felt sym-pathy for the needs of others and thus were compelled to act in altruistic ways. The writer of the first piece in the *Courant* derived his language from the collective demands of colonists against the measures imposed by Parliament, from the Sugar to the Tea Act, but extended the argument to individuals trading in local, state, and regional marketplaces. It would become a common perception remarkably quickly, probably in part because Americans had made the collective argument for more than a decade, and in part because many Americans were unhappy about the problems (especially the crowd "disorder") involved in the months of efforts to regulate price. Although certainly few Americans were philosophers, the Revolution was a particularly fertile period for new ways that all sorts of people used political language. For example, five months earlier, blacks in Boston had effectively wielded Enlightenment language of natural rights and references to the Declaration of Independence to argue that slavery should be abolished in Massachusetts.[27]

In the second half of 1777, the failure to stem inflation drove reconsiderations of economic laws and policies. Even as Massachusetts towns sought more strictly to enforce the act, the state assembly considered repealing it and finally decided to call for another regional convention; it met at the end of July, included commissioners from New York as well as the four New England states, and agreed to end the impractical wage and price controls and to limit inflation instead by calling in and "sinking" bills of credit. At the same time, strong public support for economic regulation remained: states continued to forbid engrossing goods and public auctions (which encouraged speculation in commodities), and city selectmen continued to regulate marketplaces. When Boston merchants refused to sell sugar at the prices offered by farmers bringing produce, a huge crowd forced them to sell it at a just price. A Providence town meeting in September, lamenting the "false Pretences of Scarcity," required anyone trading in the town to obtain a license and follow strict price limits; Connecticut enacted a similar measure in October.[28]

As prices and shortages continued to increase, writers argued that the problems were due to the "avaricious design" of their enemies or to excessive depreciated currency, or were just an inevitable result of the "natural right" of men "to value" property and sell or not as they pleased. Another retorted that, even if prices resulted from supply and demand, a magistrate could as readily "punish an extortioner or engrosser as to whip a thief or hang a murderer." The new state efforts to limit currency were also controversial: although such measures were generally supported by merchants and artisans in port towns, at least one inland town decried them for making trade much more difficult. A deeper fear came from the writer in the *Connecticut Courant* who charged that "fat and nasty" farmers and merchants were pressuring soldiers and their families to sell state and Continental bills of credit at huge discounts. He predicted that after the war those same "monopolists and engrossers" would force laws taxing the underpaid mechanics and laborers to repay those same notes, sparking an uprising that sounds remarkably similar to the one that actually did occur nine years later in western New England, known as Shays's Rebellion.[29]

For most of 1777, New England had been the focus for the expansive efforts to regulate wages and prices and the debates over the efficacy of such efforts. But on November 22, less than three months after those states repealed their regulations, as national inflation worsened even with the American victory at Saratoga and the possible salvation of a French alliance, Congress called for several regional conventions to enact price controls and new taxes for the war effort. In January 1778 the northern convention in New Haven, with delegates from New Jersey to New Hampshire, recommended taxes for currency reduction as the primary means to dampen inflation, but also urged price and wage controls and denounced the selfish motivations of those who would argue that such limits violated "principles of Trade & Liberty." But the convention also warned that regulations could be effective only if they were universally adopted. Connecticut did enact enabling legislation in mid-February, and New Jersey, New York, and Pennsylvania followed. However, Rhode Island, New Hampshire, and (perhaps most surprisingly) Massachusetts refused; in that last, a joint committee on April 27 reported that this "unhappy experiment" had convinced many that it was "impractical," and indeed the state would never again enact broad wage and price limits. Faced with this failure, in early May, a month after Congress called on other states to follow Connecticut's example, that state voted to repeal its act, and Pennsylvania followed three weeks later. Finally, on June 4 Congress not only acknowledged these failures but declared that price-control measures generally were "productive of very evil Consequences to the great Detriment of the public Service and grievous Oppression of Individuals." Dramatically reversing its previous positions, the national body embraced the hyper-liberal idea that market freedom was part of the Revolution's concept of liberty.[30]

But that was not the end of efforts to regulate prices. The American war effort gained morale and a critical ally with the arrival of French forces and European gold, and in mid-June 1778 the British decided to abandon Philadelphia, focus on a few other cities, and win the South. Unfortunately, the positive military developments also fueled a new wave of inflation that was particularly acute for foodstuffs, as the French navy and the Continental Army (now supplied with specie) offered ever higher prices for domestic crops. In early November, the congressional quartermaster committee suggested that legislatures should establish every month assizes of necessary commodities, and levy taxes on "engrossers" of 20 percent of their proceeds; no state responded, however, probably because of the experiences in 1777, and indeed the debates in Congress indicate that liberal economic paradigms had become even stronger among national and state legislators. The result was the resurgence in mid-1779 of *local* committees of correspondence and safety concerned with instituting wage and price controls for practical and egalitarian purposes.[31]

This new communitarian surge had its genesis in Philadelphia in 1776 when the convention on the Pennsylvania constitution had considered authorizing the legislature to confiscate excessive property from the very wealthy. As French troops and gold arrived in the city, prices on necessities rose rapidly, and class tensions became particularly intense, as some of the wealthiest merchants, including Robert Morris, organized a local caucus that sought to revise the state's constitution along less populist lines and demanded free-market liberties, and many in the city suspected the merchants of profiteering from political and military connections. On May 22 Quaker Elizabeth Drinker noted in her diary that her friends were "apprehensive of a mob rising" about prices; two days later a broadside warned: "You that have money, and you that have none, down with your prices, or down with yourselves. . . . We have turned out against the enemy and we will not be eaten up by monopolizers and forestallers." This signaled the reenergized committee movement, spearheaded by democratic political activists such as Timothy Matlock and David Rittenhouse and Philadelphia's radical militia.[32]

On May 25 a huge crowd gathered in the State House yard and elected as chair former congressman and militia officer Daniel Roberdeau, who then delivered a speech in which he condemned those who had become rich "sucking the blood of [their] country" and argued that, since merchants had banded together to raise prices, the city "had the "natural right to counteract such combinations" by imposing price controls. The gathering then discussed and passed two resolutions. The first declared the community's right to prevent suspected trade abuses by individuals and appointed a committee to ensure that Robert Morris in particular answered its questions. The second demanded that prices be returned to the levels they had been on May 1, with the goal of rolling prices back to levels at the start of the year, and appointed a committee to investigate and publish past prices and to receive complaints against merchants and the regulations. After the meeting, "thousands of common people" gathered along the Delaware River as a merchant, butcher, and "speculator" accused of raising prices were marched off to jail. On May 28 the committee published a schedule of prices for a range of goods, from coffee to whiskey to rice, and its chairman explained that, since the "evil" causes of the inflation were "too subtle" and "transitory" for legislation, solutions had to be imposed by local committees, and he urged the spread of similar efforts. One month later, the committee held a citywide meeting to announce fines for violations, permits to reexport goods worth more than £100, measures to halt forestalling, and distribution of food to the poor. They also encouraged other parts of the country to establish similar committees.[33]

This wave of democratic regulation did indeed quickly spread. On June 18 the town of York, a hundred miles west of Philadelphia, adopted the goal of rolling back prices to May levels, banned exports of necessaries, called for legislative controls on trade, and set up a monitoring and enforcement committee. New York communities up the Hudson River Valley also responded: Albany's committee of correspondence and safety met on June 20 for the first time in many months, and committees were also revived in various towns in Dutchess, Ulster, Tyron, and probably Orange counties, focusing on the same economic concerns as in 1777: forbidding distilling (to lower prices on grain for food), seeking out forestalling and hoarding, taking over police functions, and demanding statewide price controls. Their efforts crested with a state convention in Albany County in August that asked the legislature to impose heavier taxes (to soak up excess currency) and statewide price controls and to confiscate the property of traitors.[34]

Boston was also continuing to experience terrible shortages and prices, and not surprisingly it too embraced the populist movement. On June 16 residents awoke to find the broadside calling for a gathering at the Old South Meeting House the next morning to "Rouse and catch the Philadelphia spirit." The turnout was so huge that the meeting adjourned to Faneuil Hall, where a committee was dispatched to meet with the merchants, and a description of events in Philadelphia was read aloud as the crowd waited. The city's merchant elites were experienced enough to understand what the broadside portended, and the previous day had reached an agreement that they brought to the anxious meeting. Emphasizing their determination "to sacrifice . . . our private Interest to the public Good," it made seven promises, including not raising prices on current stock, taking only paper currency, and implementing the Philadelphia plan of rolling back prices *if* merchants in other port towns agreed to do the same.[35]

Boston's meeting embraced the merchant's "salutary plan," adopted a report that blamed the shortages and inflation on evil *"Hawkers & monopolizers"* masquerading as merchants, vowed to follow the Philadelphia example, and called for a statewide convention of town delegates at Concord on July 14 to agree on price and wage regulations. Neither the merchants nor anyone at the meeting dared mention the town's resolve, passed two years before, that efforts to govern trade were "opposite the Idea of Liberty." Boston's call created a new regulatory movement in New England that bypassed state governments. The Concord convention drew delegates from 151 towns, passed a set of wage and price limits, and urged towns to set other limits as necessary and "to keep a watchful Eye over *each other*" to prevent evasions and violations. At least seventy-five towns approved the resolves, set prices through local gatherings and county conventions, and created committees to enforce the rules. There was a similar statewide price-setting convention in Rhode Island on August 10, called by Providence; in New Hampshire on September 26; and in Connecticut on October 5, called by a Windham County convention that had met on September 6.[36]

The Philadelphia spirit even traveled south, to Williamsburg, Virginia, where residents awoke on July 15 to find broadsides calling for a meeting the next morning to discuss regulating prices and keeping regulated goods in town. That meeting chose a committee that drew up resolves celebrating the "virtue of the people at large [that] can easily redress what the laws cannot reach," and set prices for local produce and imported goods. Another meeting approved the resolves and appointed a committee to enforce the measures. This was the farthest south that the wage and price regulation movement traveled, probably because there were only a few southern towns with sizable populations and somewhat diversified economies.[37]

But as towns from New Hampshire to Virginia embraced the spirit of Philadelphia, tensions erupted within that city over its regulatory effort. Delaware Valley farmers and millers took their produce to other buyers, including the French and American armies. A noticeable opposition to the regime emerged in July, with a published protest by a large group of leatherworkers, strongly contested elections for various municipal offices, and publication of the hyper-liberal *Essay on Free Trade and Finance.* The anonymous author (later revealed as merchant Pelatiah Webster) began by declaring, "Freedom of trade, or unrestrained liberty of the subject to *hold* or *dispose* of his property as he pleases, is absolutely necessary to the prosperity of every community," and concluded by mourning that the price controls had created "greater restraints and abridgments of natural liberty" than the hated imperial measures that led to the Revolution. Many Philadelphia artisans and shopkeepers were having second thoughts about the regulations, and probably Webster's liberal arguments further weakened their support.[38]

One month later, eighty merchants including Robert Morris signed a long critique of the economic regulations, which they presented to the city's regulatory committee. Their petition challenged the morality as well as the practicality of regulating prices, argued that limits worsened shortages and thus increased prices, and even dared defend engrossing as benefiting the public because it caused the price of an item to rise through "artificial scarcity" and therefore prevented actual shortages. The merchants also criticized the bans on exports, which had become a common aspect of legislation in many northern states hoping to prevent scarcities, as endangering the union and more likely to produce shortages by discouraging commercial exchange. The merchants were particularly critical of limits on imported luxuries, providing a long account of the costs involved in the voyages; also, unlike their Boston counterparts, they refused to limit prices on current stocks, comparing such efforts to killing the goose that laid golden eggs.[39]

In September the city's price control committee published the merchants' letter with its reply. The committee's response began with the conservative, commonwealth justifications and noted that wage and price regulation had long been common on a wide range of commodities and services from tavern lodging to ferries, yet merchants had never before complained. The committee then directly challenged the memorandum's liberal paradigm by arguing that the rules of civil society require that "every right or power claimed or exercised by any man or set of men, should be in subordination to the common good." What the merchants really meant by their frequent references to free trade, committee members felt, was "freedom of extorting." Most intriguingly, the committee insisted that the laborers who had built ships for merchants retained "a right [to] the *service* of the vessel" (which therefore could be regulated) for they had done the work not just for wages but "the more beneficial purposes of supplying themselves and fellow citizens with foreign necessities." Their assertion could be seen as an expanded version of the contemporary labor theory of value, that is, that property rights originated in the act of individual labor, or as a proto-Marxist version of communitarianism.[40]

But this debate and the many frustrations of trying to control the economy apparently convinced the committee that the situation in Philadelphia was out of control. A week later it petitioned the state assembly to take charge, and when a bill was introduced in that body to ban the export of necessaries and prevent "foreclosing and engrossing," the committee voted to suspend its work; on September 28 the assembly enacted the measure. Six days later the tension in the city erupted in fatal gunfire. A company of militia, carrying out its long-standing pledge to uphold the committee's work, went to arrest various merchants who had not only opposed price controls but were suspected of having cooperated with the British during the occupation. Twenty to forty "gentlemen" outside City Tavern, some of whom were on the militia's list, saw the company headed in their direction and fled into the nearby home of James Wilson. As the militia passed Wilson's home, a shot was fired, and then those inside and outside began shooting. Ten minutes later the brief battle ended when some cavalry charged the militia, with one man killed inside and five to six militiamen dead.[41]

Meanwhile, tensions and suspicions between city consumers and country producers were hurting the regulatory effort in Massachusetts. On August 31 Bostonians who had attended the Concord convention wrote an open letter to their rural counterparts, mourning that farmers were spreading rumors that the city was withholding supplies and merchants were selling most of their goods in neighboring states, while the "general withdraw" of traders who normally supplied the Boston market made the city's inhabitants suspect the farmers were spurning the price controls and "would starve us into a breach to them." City and country towns looked to the state legislature to overcome these differences but soon called for another regional meeting. However, as the legislature considered an ancillary measure calling for free trade, members noticed an unusual number of oxen teams in Boston gathering to transport commodities from the city's market to other states, thought of how the price of cattle had recently suddenly doubled, and decided instead to add a long list of commodities to the existing export embargo.[42]

Commissioners from all four New England states and New York gathered at Hartford on October 20, 1779, and, after extended discussions, passed a resolution defending the necessity of price limits to control inflation and prevent "the engrosser, monopolizer, opulent farmer and trader" from raising prices faster than states could levy taxes. Without such regulation, the burden of the taxes that everyone agreed were necessary to support the currency would rest on "the poor and middling farmer." The commissioners also acknowledged that, in order to make such price limits "permanent and salutary," there needed to be an agreement among states at least as far south as Virginia, and they called for a national convention in Philadelphia in January 1780. But in the wake of the Hartford meeting, only Connecticut and New York adopted price limits, and both made them contingent on all five states doing the same. In the meantime, the New Jersey legislature had petitioned Congress for a national plan, and that body also received the Hartford resolutions. In mid-November, Congress passed a resolution decrying the "inequality and injustice" caused by economic instability and recommending a series of state economic reforms, including limits on commodities, farm produce, and labor.[43]

The national convention in Philadelphia began as scheduled on January 29, but despite the endorsement by Congress there were clear signals that nothing would result. Massachusetts instructed its delegates that they should remember how past limits had "discouraged Husbandry and Commerce and starved our Sea Ports" and generally created artificial scarcities and "a stagnation of Business." The convention barely met before it adjourned, never to meet again. On March 18 Congress devalued the Continental currency and authorized new bills redeemable in six years at 5 percent interest. This move did not end inflation, but it did signal a shift in economic plans and gave evidence that Robert Morris was becoming the director of financial policy in the country. Morris had been the target of Philadelphia's advocates of economic regulation, hated restrictions on commerce, and spoke for the business elites.[44]

Four years later, on August 30, 1784, the coda to the wartime economic regulatory efforts came with the Pennsylvania Council of Censors throwing out the state's anti-forestalling and price regulatory acts, arguing that the measures and other forms of price controls were "agrarian laws" that violated constitutionally guaranteed property rights. Of course, no state had actually seized and redistributed property, despite the calls early in the war for such measures and the occasional angry crowd actions in a few cities. But a growing number of Americans agreed that legislative measures to improve economic equality violated natural rights. A year and a half later, as the Pennsylvania Assembly debated whether to reauthorize the charter of the Bank of North America, Robert Morris challenged William Findley for supposedly arguing the "wicked" idea that agrarian laws could be legitimate in a democracy. An obviously uncomfortable, defensive Findley replied that he had said that "agrarian laws would be unjust in our present situation." Just a decade earlier, men like Findley along with Philadelphia artisans had come close to writing such a law into the state's constitution. In 1784 Findley was among the majority voting for the report that condemned the state's wartime wage and price regulation acts.[45]

The wartime experience of regulating wages and prices clearly fostered the liberal vision of individual economic freedom. This liberal ideology contained egalitarian elements, particularly an emphasis on equal opportunity. Findley rejected the Bank, for example, because the state charter gave wealth and power to a small group. Another liberal goal was widespread education, as Delaware newspaper editor Robert Coram acknowledged in his 1791 masterwork *Political Inquiries*. Although Coram clearly saw an egalitarian division of property as the ideal social condition and spent the first section detailing that vision, he concluded that he was "not quite so visionary" as to think Americans would seriously consider the idea. So, instead, he turned to the more "practicable" task of persuading his countrymen that living up to their ideal of equality required a publicly funded system of universal education.[46]

During the War for Independence, governments at the local, state, and national levels struggled to manage the wartime economy. The expansion of traditional price and wage limits was viewed as the best means to prevent greed, ensure affordable "necessaries," and help stabilize the currency. As with many other aspects of the Revolution, the struggles over those rules became a battleground for evolving political ideas. Supporters drew on old and cherished concepts of the egalitarian commonwealth, "just" prices, and republican virtues. Opponents emphasized newer ideals of liberal individualism and capitalism. These debates highlighted many important aspects of the new nation: tensions between city and country; the connections between local face-to-face networks and regional or international markets; the gap between northern and southern economies; and the concern among political leaders that economic regulation required dangerously popular enforcement. Efforts to finance the war drove a shift in the debates over the economy from a focus on prices to a broader concern about the relationship between prices and currency, to an emerging unease about the concentration of capital. Perhaps the most significant development was this fear that control of *capital* rather than control of *land* could become the greatest source of inequality and oppression. Feudalism had linked political power to land, and initially Americans feared manor lords rather than merchants. But concerns of class and alarm about the corrupting power of capital accumulation emerged by 1779. Recent work on American concerns about capital and class focuses on its origins in the postwar period, yet that clearly became an issue during the war, a decade earlier.[47]

In the state and national governments, liberal economic ideologies seemed to replace commonwealth or "just price" rhetoric by 1780. While this was clearly a result of the frustrating failures in trying to enforce price controls and the spread of liberal ideals, it was also more evidence of the postwar conservative social and political leanings among American intellectuals and elites that would result in the federal Constitution. Yet Americans continued to strongly believe in the need to maintain relative economic equality and guard against corrupting concentrations of wealth. Capital mobility and accumulation increasingly dominated the anxieties of people who felt victimized or endangered by economic and political power. In the countryside, these fears would be highlighted in the mid-1780s with Shays's Rebellion in western Massachusetts and again in the mid-1790s in the Whiskey Rebellion in the Ohio Valley. Town and city dwellers embraced the radical egalitarianism of the French Revolution, with new calls for property redistribution, and continued to insist on marketplace regulation and bread assizes into the mid-nineteenth century. While the vision of individual freedom in the marketplace blossomed during the Revolutionary War, its communitarian egalitarian counterpart did not disappear.[48]

CHAPTER FOUR

Wealth and Power in the Early Republic

When the War for American Independence officially ended in 1783, Johann Schoepf, chief surgeon of the Ansbach troops recruited by George III to fight the rebels, decided to explore the country and its people. For more than a year, the highly educated scientist trekked as far west as Pittsburgh and south to Florida, recording not only flora and fauna but the social habits, institutions, material cultures, and economies of the various areas where he traveled. At the beginning, visiting the national capital of Philadelphia, he was struck by the egalitarian attitudes of Americans. "People think, act, and speak here precisely as it prompts them; the poorest day-laborer on the bank of the Delaware holds it his right to advance his opinion, in religious as well as political matters, with as much freedom as the gentleman or the scholar." Degrees of wealth seemed to make no difference because "every man expects at one time or another to be on a footing with his rich neighbor." Toward the end of his journey, as he arrived in Charleston, South Carolina, he opined that generally "America knows no nobility, rather hates the thought of such a thing, and refuses any respect demanded by those whose only claim is that of descent and birth." But his travels had also made Schoepf more sensitive to the new nation's nuances: he added that there was "a class of citizens who by natural gifts, useful acquirements, or wealth" were clearly "superior to the rest," understood how to work the levers of power, and in many other ways "think and act precisely as do the nobility in other countries."[1]

As the United States achieved independence, Americans wrote and argued about the future of their new country. While those who were "white" generally believed that they lived in the most egalitarian conditions in the world, they were concerned about how wealth and power might reshape the infant republic. Most saw sufficient equality in the opportunities offered by the new country's rapidly changing economy, easily available land, and lack of titled nobility. Some elites feared that the Revolution had loosened dangerous "levelling" tendencies and sought to reestablish steadying influences, including a "natural aristocracy" based on talent rather than inheritance. But many at all levels began to fear the emergence of a new aristocracy of wealth and called for measures to ensure future or increased economic equality. Changing inheritance laws to end the British tradition of preserving large estates was particularly popular; every state with such laws abolished them by 1800. A strong consensus also urged universal education to allow any man access to opportunity and power, although states failed to impose the necessary taxes and structure to support such schools. Some called for limits on individual wealth, although all but a few avoided troubling specifics, probably due to the increasingly powerful belief that natural liberty included a man's right to control his property.

In the 1790s anxieties among white men about economic and social equality intensified with the establishment of new national institutions, the specter of public debt speculation, the increasing wealth and influence of a relative few, the popular passions over the French Revolution, and the emergence of warring political parties. As some elites sought state charters for banks, canals, roads, and manufacturing centers, many Americans protested that such privileges would enable a corrupt aristocracy of wealth. Men also called for more progressive tax laws, an end to property requirements for voting, and size limits on purchases from the public domain. The calls for limits on individual wealth were fewer and fainter than in the previous decade, for various reasons related to the shifting political and cultural milieu. But the broader political and ideological struggle convinced many involved in politics that the new nation needed to ensure socioeconomic as well as political stability; some suggested giving property a role in the government and forging a "natural aristocracy." By the end of the 1790s, this counterrevolution became so bitter that some openly scorned the very idea of equality. In part because of such overreach, the "passion for equality" swept Thomas Jefferson into the presidency and the Federalists from power.

After winning independence, Americans continued to embrace the "True Whig" paradigm that the widespread ownership of property facilitated the active and virtuous citizenry necessary for a just society and republican government. In 1780 Jacob Green, Presbyterian minister of Hanover, New Jersey, emphasized that "to maintain the freedom of elections, there should, as much as possible, be an equality among the people of the land"; ideally that meant "an equality of estate and property." Four years later and many miles to the west, Kentucky settlers petitioning Congress for statehood noted: "It is a well-known truth that the riches and strength of a free Country does not consist in Property being vested in a few Individuals, but the more general[ly] it is distributed, the more it promotes industry, population, and frugality, and even morality." Three years after that, Waterbury representative John Welton told his colleagues in the Connecticut assembly, during a debate over whether to make the state's currency legal tender, that natural law required a "popular government" to have "a good degree of equality among the people as to their property."[2]

During the imperial crisis that sparked the Revolution, many provincials perceived their "country" as nearly fulfilling that ideal, and this conceit remained important in the 1780s. "A True Patriot," writing in the *New Jersey Gazette* on April 25, 1781, addressed a wide range of state controversies, including class conflict, but assured his readers that "there is not under the whole canopy of heaven such another place as America, while free, for the encouragement of the poor, in their pursuits for obtaining comfortable livelihoods." In 1785 "Observator" in the *New Haven Gazette* noted that "the division of property is (perhaps) the most equal in this country, of any in the world." That same year, a writer in Boston's *Independent Chronicle* wrote a series of articles urging new taxes for rapid repayment of the country's debts and in one piece noted, "No people in the universe are so able to pay their taxes as the Americans, owing to their *equality of property*." In his 1787 Fourth of July oration in Boston, Thomas Dawes Jr. began by describing a European balloonist who had commented on the patterns of fields and suggested that, had such a daredevil soared over the fields of Massachusetts, he would have also enjoyed the "idea of *equality*." A South Carolina pamphleteer believed that "fortunate circumstances" had allowed America to stay close to the natural law that "an equality of property" was "just law" and "productive of happiness and safety." Recent scholarship confirms that this was indeed the experience of most white Americans during the period, particularly when they compared their lives to European counterparts.[3]

American writers generally connected the country's rough economic equality with its successful strike for independence and the republican nature of its governments. John Adams wrote many controversial things in his 1787 *Defence of the Constitutions of Government of the United States of America*, but uncontested was his point that the wide division of property "among the common people in every state" was the main reason for American victory. The future president estimated that "nineteen twentieths" of all property would long continue "in the hands of the commons" regardless of who held office. One of his frequently published critics, "A New Jersey Farmer," agreed, noting that "the landed property in the middle and northern states is nine-tenths in the hands of a yeomanry." Not surprisingly, the idea became part of the debate over the proposed federal constitution. When Noah Webster argued for ratification in his influential *An Examination into the Leading Principles of the Federal Constitution*, he emphasized that, because "*property* is the basis for *power*," America's "general and tolerably equal distribution of landed property" was "the whole basis" for the triumph of republicanism. A year later, Harrison Grey Otis concluded his July Fourth oration that mostly praised the proposed federal system by listing America's blessings including "equality of property."[4]

At the same time, this moralistic view easily generated fears about America's potential flaws and future dangers. Most scholars have focused on the discussion among the political elites about where the infant American republic belonged on the Scottish Enlightenment scale of social development ranging from hunter-gatherers to commerce. In the immediate aftermath of the war, as the British barred American produce from West Indian markets and the economy stalled, some began to detect troubling symptoms of corruption. In the long run, US leaders tended to either (like Thomas Jefferson) embrace agriculture as the source of American republican virtue or (like Alexander Hamilton) see commerce and manufacturing as the best future for the country.[5]

While such philosophical discussions were meaningful within an important circle of American elites, and in the 1790s would help shape the debates over the new nation's economic policies, in the 1780s most critics reflected Calvinist apprehensions of man's sinful nature. Such anxieties had driven the wartime price control efforts and remained strong: for example, in 1780 the Philadelphia Constitutional Society condemned the "vice, fraud, and extortion" committed by "forestallers and monopolizers." Some focused on traditional iniquities, such as sexual immorality. More commonly, ministers and orators tended to censure American fondness for tea and other imported "luxuries," often with misogynistic commentaries. Such secular jeremiads could be a source of satire, as when one Connecticut writer wrote that "the preservation of our liberties" depended on remaining in New England, where the "cold and uncomfortable region" ensured that "property, or rather poverty, will always be equally divided," and in the southern states where "sickly marshes and sandy plains" ensured that "no man, however, rich, can live long enough to form any ruinous design on the liberties of the people."[6]

Generally, observers saw more to praise than to censure. True Patriot admitted that there were class tensions in New Jersey but argued that there was no better place than America "for the encouragement of the poor, in their pursuits for obtaining comfortable livelihoods by industry and care." Two years later, an anonymous South Carolinian celebrated how, due to "fortunate circumstances . . . America has not yet departed far from the rule of right" and quoted *Cato's Letters* that "an equality of estate, will give an equality of power." David Daggett, in his 1787 July Fourth oration in New Haven, admitted deep flaws in America's past, particularly the "fraud and injustice" in "forcibly or fraudulently depriving the natives of their possessions," and mourned that the colonists' "simplicity of manners" had been lost to "luxury and its attending evils"—but concluded by celebrating "that equal distribution of property, and that general diffusion of knowledge which so effectually prevent oppression and slavery." Four years later, Robert Coram of Delaware idealized the egalitarian nature of Native American society, economy, and culture and complained about the influence of merchants in the United States, but still insisted that the country's inhabitants "are more upon an equality in stature, and powers of body and mind, than the subjects of any government in Europe," and that New Englanders in particular "enjoy the most perfect equality." Similarly, the earliest histories of the Revolutionary War emphasized the importance for America of a deep connection between widespread property ownership, republicanism, and liberty.[7]

Yet latent conflicts clearly nestled within this generally sunny consensus. Perhaps most significant was the tension between the two distinct socioeconomic paradigms that had emerged during the war and would for many decades shape US politics. One echoed the classical view that widespread property ownership ensured the public virtue necessary to elect a "natural aristocracy" that would properly wield social, economic, and political authority. For example, while Samuel Stillman in his May 1779 Massachusetts election sermon celebrated the present "happy era" when the "great principles of liberty" taught that a magistrate's authority was derived from the people, he urged people to choose "men of leisure and abilities"—which meant wealth and advanced education. In 1788, as the state ratification conventions gathered, a prominent Massachusetts political figure published a pamphlet in which he saw "a highly democratical government" rather than a propertied aristocracy as America's greatest threat and (like John Adams) hoped for means to empower a "natural aristocracy" made up of those "who by nature, education, and good dispositions, are qualified for government."[8]

Some pushed this further to endorse a strong socioeconomic hierarchy as necessary for a republic. In late August 1787, the Swedish Lutheran minister Nicholas Collin (under the name of the "Foreign Spectator") wrote a series in Philadelphia's *Independent Gazetteer* (reprinted in many northern newspapers) that emphasized the need to wean America from the "overdriven principle of equality" that had enabled a corrupting love of luxury, so that "the maid too often vies with her mistress, and a common laborer can with propriety dress like a governor." Although he "despise[d] aristocracies," Foreign Spectator told readers that "Almighty God has established an order in human affairs," reflected in differences in wealth that resulted from ability, industry, inheritance, and God's favor, and Americans needed to respect that arrangement in order to achieve "political happiness."[9]

The other paradigm presented a very different view of the wealthy and powerful and called for measures to break the traditional links between economic, social, and political authority. In 1782 Herman Husband, the Quaker farmer, preacher, politician, writer, and leader of the North Carolina Regulator movement before the Revolution, reemerged in western Pennsylvania with a set of radical *Proposals to amend and Perfect the Policy of the Government of the United States of America.* In past elections, Husband mourned, districts were so large that voters knew little about the candidates running for office and so were persuaded by "the Flattery of Men in Power and possessed of Wealth" that only the well-known, rich, and immoral tavern keepers, merchants, and lawyers could get elected. He urged instead more representatives in smaller districts and creating a system of luxury taxes in order to leave undisturbed "the laboring Part of Mankind, who waste nothing." In South Carolina in 1783, as the gentry struggled to reestablish a stable government, an anonymous writer condemned the assumption that "men who are indigent and low in circumstances" lacked sufficient independence to vote, for "none are more insatiable [greedy] than the rich," and a prominent judge, Aedanus Burke, condemned several anti-Loyalist measures as corrupt efforts by the wealthy to create a hereditary aristocracy.[10]

Concerns about class inequalities were also heard in New England. In early 1788 a writer in a Boston newspaper rejected the proposed federal constitution because only "the richest, most notable or most intriguing" could get elected, leaving unrepresented "that most numerous and most valuable part of the community, the commonality." He went on to opine that the rich felt "an involuntary bias towards those of their own rank," which made them "continually fearful of Agrarian laws, and the division of property," whereas "the poor have equal reason to dread the influence of the rich to produce monopolies."

In the fall of 1791 Connecticut shoemaker Walter Brewster explained the campaign to reform state tax policies as seeking to reverse the propensity of laws "to assist those who have property and power, against those who have none." These writers did not necessarily urge measures to ensure economic equality, but they clearly saw strong reasons to prevent the wealthy from dominating politics in the new republic.[11]

Calls to end slavery also developed during the early Republic in large part because of the Revolutionary rhetoric of liberty and equality. In 1777 Massachusetts towns rejected the proposed state constitution in part because it would have blessed slavery, although the institution was not proscribed until a pair of state court decisions in 1781 and 1783. Other northern states passed gradual emancipation laws in the late 1780s and 1790s, although even as late as the 1830s there were still some slaves in New York City. That agonizingly slow decline of slavery resulted from perhaps the most troubling irony of America's Revolutionary rhetoric: property was one of the "natural rights" embraced by Revolutionary leaders, and under existing law slaves were property.[12]

Americans also became increasingly sensitive that slavery marked a widening socioeconomic divide between North and South. In 1788 James Winthrop urged rejection of the proposed federal constitution because that stronger national union might force New England—with its "small and nearly equal estates [and] equality of rights"—to become more like the South, with "unequal distribution of property, the toleration of slavery, [and] the ignorance and poverty of the lower classes." Slavery even lay at the root of sectional differences in taxation: northern taxation was traditionally local, democratic, and generally more experienced and competent, whereas southern taxation suffered because the region's culture of "sovereign mastership" made assessments seem unduly intrusive to domineering plantation owners. Some southerners agreed with this critical view: for example, South Carolinian David Ramsay condemned slavery for "producing many baneful consequences" in the South, including "the engrossing of land, in the hands of a few," and Thomas Jefferson in *Notes on the State of Virginia* (1787) wrote that slavery taught the children of slave owners to be tyrants. On the other hand, after 1790 southern slavery rebounded with the development of cotton plantations and played a large role in settling regional and class tensions.[13]

Regardless of how Americans viewed slavery, equality, and the distribution of property, they acknowledged a systemic class structure that could play a powerful political role in the new country. In South Carolina, Aedanus Burke described three distinct classes: the "first class, or leading gentry," the "middling orders of our gentry," and the "lower class, with the city populace." But

Benjamin Lincoln Jr., returning to Massachusetts after serving with distinction as a major general in the Continental Army and US secretary of war, articulated (writing as "Free Republican") the more general view that there were two basic divisions in human society: the many who labored for a living and the few who lived on the labor of others, such as merchants, lawyers, and ministers. As he emphasized in that widely republished series, "the source and effects of the dispute," whether rich and poor, patricians and plebeians, nobility and commons, were inherently contending interests grounded in mankind's nature. Lincoln also felt that *persons* and *property* had inherently distinct rights, so that every republican government had to have a structure that separated and acknowledged each in order to manage the inevitable "contest, abuses, and corruption." Even in the United States, he felt, the natural diversity of men meant that that inevitable inequalities and conflicts between rich and poor would emerge.[14]

In fact, Lincoln, who two years later would command the troops that crushed Shays's Rebellion, was writing largely to applaud the constitution for his state, which—as written primarily by John Adams—featured a bicameral legislature with a House that represented *persons* and a Senate upper house that, through a convoluted process, was supposed to represent *property*. In January 1787, while serving as the first US minister to the Court of St. James, Adams wrote in *Defence of the Constitutions* that America's inevitable "natural aristocracy"—formed by wealth, education, and family position—would become a useful resource if the few with property and power held one branch of the legislature. Adams was shocked when many leading Americans mocked that work. But his idea that the structure of government should somehow mirror America's "natural" socioeconomic division was clearly embraced by many, as evinced by the adoption of the Massachusetts Constitution and the debates over a new federal constitution.[15]

But at the same time, Americans began to question these connections between property and polity. In 1780 many Massachusetts town meetings opposed the second proposed state constitution because its senate represented property. More strikingly, at least 42 of the 188 towns whose comments are extant (22 percent) opposed requiring voters to own property worth 60 pounds, even though such a standard was part of the traditional republican paradigm to trust power only to independent men. Towns instead called for this right to be extended to all men at age twenty-one who demonstrated a clear connection to the community by paying taxes, serving in the militia, or proffering a certificate of good character from local officials. Some towns made the principled argument that property qualifications were "an infringement on the

Natural Rights of the Subject," while others feared that, with the economic problems of the time, they might fall into debt and lose their right to vote. As Mansfield in Bristol County wondered, "[H]ow many sensible, honest, and natur[al]ly Industerouss men, by Numberless Misfortins Never Acquire and possess property of the value of sixty pounds? And how many Thousands of good honest men, and Good members of society who are at this day possessed of a comfortable Interest, which before the publick debts of the common we[a]lth are discharged, will not be possessed of a soficiency [sufficiency] to qualify them to vote for Representatives if this article takes place as it now stands?" Some town meetings also objected to the constitution's additional property requirements for elected officials, with senators and the governor having to own noticeably more than representatives. Such views could have been shaped by memories of how the puritan colonists had linked voting to church membership instead of property; inspired by the Revolution's egalitarian rhetoric; or driven by growing fears of the postwar recession. But regardless of motivations, these towns clearly rejected the old paradigm that only property holders should have a voice in shaping the state's political economy. Their protests and proposals were, however, largely ignored.[16]

Not surprisingly, the most bitter battles during that first decade of peace were over policies that made many fear the creation of an aristocracy of wealth and power. Nationally these issues emerged when Congress finally agreed in the summer of 1783 to provide Continental Army officers with a pension equivalent to five years of pay. Many objected, partly because it meant one more large expense for taxpayers, but more so because enlisted men were given just three months of pay in the form of certificates that could be used to claim land. Moreover, many soldiers had not yet received promised service pay, and many who had been paid found that compensation had lost substantial value due to inflation. In September, "A Querist" in the *New Jersey Journal* raised thirteen questions about American virtues—playing on the already common tradition of offering thirteen toasts at national celebrations—three of which challenged the pension plan: "Is there not an apparent disposition in some leading men in these States to raise some above others, so as to destroy equality, and in the end to destroy freedom and republican government?" The controversy also highlighted American concerns that aristocracy was becoming linked to capital instead of land.[17]

Concerns about this potential threat to republican government intensified when news spread that Continental officers had also formed an exclusive fraternity, the Society of Cincinnati, which was not only the first national organization but (of more concern) one in which membership would be inherited by the sons and grandsons of members—just as the English aristocrats passed their status and privileges to their male descendants. Judge Aedanus Burke rushed out a pamphlet to argue that the society *"creates a race of hereditary patricians, or nobility,"* predicting that "the Cincinnati will soon be corrupted, and the spirit of the people depressed; for in less than a century it will occasion such an inequality in the condition of our inhabitants, that the country will be composed of only two ranks of men; the patrician or nobles, and the rabble."[18]

Many Americans feared a different source of a potential aristocracy of wealth: speculation in war debt. During the war some rang the alarm that rich merchants and farmers were buying up bills of credit at a steep discount and would later demand full face value from laboring taxpayers. Payment of war debt indeed became a major issue in the mid-1780s, and state legislatures whipsawed between investors and taxpayers tried various solutions to reduce the value of the notes so that the payments and taxes would not be so high. In Pennsylvania, a popular proposal called for the old certificates to be replaced by new ones that reflected their market worth instead of face value; the taxpayers who had once held the bills would still benefit because their taxes to repay the new certificates would be much lower. Other egalitarian proposals included taxing income from war debt certificates, bank stocks, and unoccupied acreage. None became law, but elites were alarmed by the egalitarian language and demands. In the summer of 1785, when three-quarters of the New Hampshire towns petitioned the state legislature to issue paper currency that could be used as legal tender, "A Friend to the Rights of Mankind" called the proposal an unconstitutional taking of property and accused one advocate of wanting to "bring on a jubilee and a universal levelizm in respect to property." The conflict pointed not only to the increased role and power of capital in the Revolutionary period but also to the survival in the new republic of radical English religious and political rhetoric.[19]

These tensions exploded in the agrarian uprising known as Shays's Rebellion. Wealthy Boston and Salem merchants who held nearly all the state's war debt had persuaded the state legislature to quickly retire that debt at face value by imposing a high tax that had to be paid in specie—and put directly into their hands. Not only did farmers in "backcountry" Massachusetts and New Hampshire lack the money to pay these taxes, but they were outraged at the prospect of losing their property and right to vote in order to pay a small group of already wealthy individuals, especially since farmers had held much of that debt until circumstances led them to sell to the speculators at greatly reduced prices. At town meetings they passed resolutions for the General Court demanding reform, including paper money, lower legal costs, tax reforms, and the use of personal property to pay debts and fines—and even moving the state capitol to the middle of the state. Finally, in the autumn of 1786, they gathered and closed county courts to stop debt cases and in late January 1787 formed a force of fourteen hundred men (including one group led by Daniel Shays) that marched on the armory at Springfield defended by a company recently raised by Boston merchants and commanded by Benjamin Lincoln. On January 25 Lincoln's men fired artillery into the advancing locals and then chased the shattered remnants around western Massachusetts. This "regulation" was not an isolated movement; such movements began before the war and would erupt again in 1794 in what is called the Whiskey Rebellion.[20]

Concerns about an aristocracy of wealth grew in the 1780s and 1790s as state legislatures began to issue charters to private companies to build roads, construct bridges, and (especially) establish banks. The new state governments lacked the money and bureaucracy to accomplish these public functions and so followed the English tradition of granting specific powers such as eminent

Woodcut of Daniel Shays and Job Shattuck, by an unidentified artist, 1787. Book in the collection of the National Portrait Gallery, acc. no. NPG 75.25; accessed through https://commons.wikimedia.org/wiki/File:Unidentified_Artist_-_Daniel_Shays_and _Job_Shattuck_-_Google_Art_Project.jpg.

domain and charging tolls to private parties in order to meet public needs. The men who formed the companies that sought state charters were generally the "monied gentry" who believed they were acting in the public interest as proper republican gentlemen rather than as self-interested entrepreneurs. But American habits and republican ideology created particular frictions, because a charter moved important social and economic concerns from the public arena to a small private group. In some cases this ideological tension was built into a state's legal framework; for example, North Carolina's Constitution included an article that "perpetuities and monopolies are contrary to the genius of a free State, and ought not to be allowed," which was inevitably trumpeted by opponents to charters in that state. Furthermore, the mismanagement and failure of many of the projects and the clearly self-interested behaviors of their directors dredged up memories of the South Sea Bubble and increased public hostility.[21]

These fears arose first in opposition to the Bank of North America. In 1781 the bank was chartered by Congress and Pennsylvania; it was primarily backed by funds obtained by Congress, and printed currency circulated among wealthy merchants and government contractors. Interest rates on bank notes increased rapidly, making them unaffordable to all but a few. These circumstances generated more wealth for holders of notes and stocks even as Americans generally faced economic troubles; in Pennsylvania's western counties, more than half of all farmers faced foreclosure for inability to pay their debts, and a huge percentage of "middling" men was forced to sell bills of credit at rates that ranged from a sixth to a fortieth of face value. General loathing of the bank intensified when it became clear that its stockholders were the largest speculators in the discounted bills. In 1784 Pennsylvania elections gave reformers control of the assembly, and in September 1785 the assembly revoked the bank's state charter after a committee reported that the institution lacked "that equality which ought ever to prevail between the individuals of a republic." The bank continued operating under a congressional charter, but its stockholders and officers now faced personal liabilities for its debts and closer examination of how it had used its deposits to speculate in war debt.[22]

Six months later, the assembly reconsidered that repeal. Robert Morris defended the bank for bringing capital from Europe and stimulating trade for the farmer, mechanic, and miller, and he insisted that it was not a monopoly because anyone could open another bank or buy the bank's stock and notes. What Morris did not mention was that the bank shares began at $400 each, at a time that a tailor in Philadelphia earned about $215 a year, and that when a group had sought a charter for another bank, he fought hard against it. His opponents focused on broader issues, including questions of economic equality. For example, one assemblyman charged that the bank had "promote[d] the spirit of monopolizing" and so was "inconsistent with not only the frame but the spirit of our government." While the new republic was "too unequal in wealth to render a perfect democracy," Americans were "so equal in wealth, power, &c. that we have no counterpoise sufficient to check or control an institution of such vast influence and magnitude." As the assembly debated, "Atticus" warned that "the possession of property" inevitably brought "the possession of power." Morris finally won this battle after the bank threatened to move to Delaware and new elections swept the reformers from power.[23]

But monopolies and the threat of an aristocracy of wealth remained a sensitive concern. On the first day of 1790, "The Politician" wrote in the *Massachusetts Magazine* that "an unequal distribution of wealth" would cause the "final ruin" of a nation, as it created bitter divisions, discouraged or barred those without property from gaining an education, and created the danger of "a single independent fortune." Because it was "impossible" and "manifestly unjust" to redistribute an individual's property as per agrarian laws, the best way to prevent great inequality would be to refuse to create chartered companies with "exclusive privileges" that would inevitably "enrich a few." Three years later, Pennsylvania petitioners circulated English- and German-language petitions demanding that the state legislature not grant a charter to a company to build roads and canals in the state, expressing "great anxiety" about the power given to corporations to take and control property. "The outrages committed by those privileged orders, have already occasioned several hundred of our fellow citizens to appeal to the legislature for redress. The inequality introduced by such establishments, must destroy the liberties of our country. No observation is better supported than this, that a country cannot long preserve its liberty, where a great inequality of property takes place. Is it not therefore, the most dangerous policy in this infant republic, to combine the wealthy in order to make them powerful?" Doubtless these petitioners and their contemporaries would be astonished at the recent US Supreme Court decisions holding that corporations have "natural" rights and that money in political campaigns is protected speech that cannot be regulated.[24]

The 1793 anti-charter petition acknowledged that socioeconomic differences "in society" would inevitably always develop "according to the physical and acquired abilities of its members," but it rejected both a competitive and a hierarchical society and instead argued that such differences would cause "the members of the same society mutually to assist each other, according to the various abilities." Given this ethos, the signatories held that granting monopolies through charters was "arbitrary" and destructive." Opponents of charters demanded that instead the state government should fill these public needs, as Pennsylvania and other provinces had done with land banks during the colonial period. Six years later, when the bank sought another charter, it similarly encountered passionate opposition. One handwritten petition charged that stockholders received far better interest rates and more favorable treatment than "the husbandman or Mechanic." The petitioners also spoke for small shopkeepers who owed large debts with usurious interest and could be forced into bankruptcy when the economy stalled. Finally, they accused the bank of giving easy loans to "favorites," resulting in an institution that tended to "destroy that equality which ought to take place in a Commercial Country."[25]

Some urged more active measures to maintain the new nation's essential socioeconomic equality. Two sympathetic and prominent English writers urged the United States to pass limits on landholding in order to prevent the concentration of wealth. In 1781 the Scottish philosopher William Ogilvie in *An Essay on the Right of Property in Land* held that America could and should include in its constitutions "well regulated" agrarian measures. Four years later, Richard Price wrote in *Observations on the Importance of the American Revolution*, in the section "The Unequal Distribution of Property," that American equality had greatly helped in forming new constitutions but that, because power was derived from property, the new nation should look at Rome's agrarian laws and Israel's Great Jubilee "to find out means of preventing too great an inequality in the distribution of property." Both English writers were influential in the United States: John Adams owned Ogilvie's *Essay*, Price's *Observations* was reprinted in Hartford and other cities in 1785, and "The Unequal Distribution of Property" was featured in several New England newspapers in early 1785 as the currency and taxation battles began to rage.[26]

Americans made similar calls for limits on individual wealth in the nation. In 1782 a Rhode Island pamphlet criticizing the call by Congress for state payments also added, almost as an aside, that "the powers of an over-grown private purse are well known; the danger of a misapplication of it, politically considered, ought ever to be held up to our view." A year later, the South Carolinian author of *Rudiments of Law and Government* wrote on the need for agrarian laws to preserve the republic. Although he began by noting that laws should never take any part of an individual's property, he put more emphasis on the idea that society owed individuals a "natural right" of "due proportions of common property." Although these ideas seem contradictory, it was apparently not at the time, probably because so much land (taken from Native peoples) still seemed "vacant" and available. *Rudiments* then quoted *Cato's Letters*: "An equality of estate, will give an equality of power," and it went on to condemn "the ill effect of superfluous riches" and to urge that the United States "maintain a mediocrity and equipoise" by keeping individuals from "soaring too high"—that is, gaining excessive wealth and power.[27]

These demands for limits on property and power connected politics and social morality in a manner that was quite common at the time, particularly in New England with its long tradition of election sermons, including Benjamin Trumbull's 1773 New Haven call "to keep property as equally divided among the inhabitants as possible, and not to suffer a few persons to amass all the riches and wealth of a country." Ten years later, on December 11, 1783, the national Day of Thanksgiving to celebrate the Treaty of Paris, the Reverend John Murray, Presbyterian minister of Newburyport, preached a "*discourse on America's duty and danger.*" Among other threats, he warned against a future "when government has lost its energy and the laws their force—when the confederation is weakened or broken—the union dissolved—the constitutions of particular states corrupted . . . when AGRARIAN LAWS cannot be obtained; or must pass unexecuted—when individuals are permitted to purchase or possess such enormous tracts of land as may gradually work them up to an influence, dangerous to the liberty of the state."[28]

A few went further to call for substantive barriers against the perceived threat. In 1779 and 1780, as Massachusetts again sought to write a constitution, writers urged an "Agrarian law" enabling the confiscation of estates with more than a thousand acres in order to "maintain the character of a free Republic, prevent monopolizers of land in their devices, and hinder those who may aim to bring our country into Lordships." A year later, after that constitution had been written and ratified, a correspondent told the *Massachusetts Spy* that the residents of his town were concerned about a speculator obtaining forty-eight thousand acres in Maine and had instructed their representative to press for a measure that would bar ownership of more than a thousand acres. Their resolve opined that Rome was corrupted by its neglect of agrarian laws and that the biblical Great Jubilee was the best way to avoid oppressing their brethren. In 1787 John Welton similarly recommended to his fellow Connecticut assemblymen that the Jubilee as the best way to achieve a rough equality of wealth in the state. Such substantive calls were few and gained little, but it is noteworthy that men urging agrarian laws tended to justify their proposals by holding up biblical and classical precedents, just as the English radicals had during their Civil War.[29]

The demand by "Shaysites" for economic and political reforms, along with the occasional call by others for economic equality, made many merchants and political leaders surmise that the regulators sought the same goals as the dreaded radical Levellers during English Civil Wars: to appropriate the lands of the "better sort" and (apparently) end private property. Of course, that had been the goal of the Diggers, but by this time *Levellers* had become a provocative, conspiratorial reference. In September 1786 William Plumer told a friend that the two hundred farmers confronting New Hampshire's legislature had demanded "equal distribution of property," and five months later the *New Haven Chronicle* report on the state's recent paper money law included a mocking elegy describing the burial of paper money with a drawing of six pallbearing "Levellers" named Dishonesty, Idleness, Bankruptcy, Knavery, Dissipation, and Insolvency. After the uprising had been crushed, Henry Knox told George Washington that the "creed" of the insurgents in his state had been that land "Ought to be the common property of all." Similarly, in October 1787 "Camillus" wrote in a Philadelphia magazine that some Shaysites "aimed at the "abolition of public and private debts," whereas others sought "an equal distribution of property." In fact, the regulators made no explicit calls to redistribute land, although their demands for paper currency and authority to pay debts with crops struck many merchants as having that effect.[30]

The upheaval became notorious in other parts of the United States and influenced the delegates to the Constitutional Convention and the debates that followed. As the convention finished its business, Alexander Hamilton told his fellow delegates that he expected the new US Constitution would earn "the good will of most men of property" since it would "protect them against domestic violence and the depredations which the democratic spirit is apt to make on property." Nicholas Collin's "Foreign Spectator" series frequently condemned Shays's Rebellion and urged a stronger national government as well as other means to prevent the "extreme liberty" that not only violated all "religious and moral principles" but was "the source of agrarian laws, and all the foul monsters of anarchy." James Madison expressed similar concerns when he argued (in Federalist no. 10) that direct democracies "have ever been prey to spectacles of turbulence and contention" and were therefore "incompatible with personal security or the rights of property." Those who favor such government, he wrote with a sneer, "have erroneously supposed that by reducing mankind to a perfect equality in their political rights, they would, at the same time, be perfectly equalized and assimilated in their possessions, their opinions, and their passions." In 1790 John Adams was still thinking of the uprising when he told Richard Price that "too many Americans, pant for equality of persons and property," and later he insisted that he had written *Defence of the Constitutions* "to suppress Shay's Rebellion."[31]

Not surprisingly, those who opposed corporate charters or full-face payment of debt notes felt compelled to insist that they were not Levellers agitating to strip men of their property nor seeking to open the mouth of hell for the foul monsters of anarchy. In March 1786, as the Pennsylvania Assembly debated whether to reconsider issuing a charter to the Bank of North America, Robert Morris accused prominent opponent William Findley of raising the future option of agrarian laws. Findley insisted that he had called such measures "unjust," and later explained that he was arguing against the claim by Morris that repeal of the bank's charter would be an agrarian law. Similarly, seven years later, the writers of the petition opposing a charter for the "wealthy" and "privileged" owners of a Pennsylvania road and canal company, because "a country cannot long preserve its liberty where a great inequality of property takes place," felt compelled to reassure the state legislature that they thought "an equal division of property" to be quite unjust.[32]

Yet there was one significant agrarian measure that *did* gain widespread support at this time and was at least in part made law in every state between 1780 and 1800: the elimination of primogeniture and entail. These were the feudal foundations of English inheritance law: primogeniture meant that a man's houses and lands were always inherited by the eldest son, and entail was a set of limitations placed on an estate so that it could not be divided, sold, or otherwise altered in future generations. The New England colonies had at their beginnings instituted partible inheritance following biblical rules, and a consensus emerged among Americans during the Revolution that such laws were the best way for property to be more evenly distributed in future generations without the need for "Leveller" measures. For example, Noah Webster in 1787 urged states to prohibit entail in order to continue the "general and tolerably equal distribution of landed property" that served as "the whole basis of national freedom." Thomas Jefferson is particularly famous for this movement, introducing in October 1776 a bill that nearly barred entail in Virginia, and nine years later sponsoring the measure that ended primogeniture intestate (when a property owner died without leaving a will). Decades later, Jefferson noted this "best of all Agrarian laws" was directed to replace the state's "aristocracy of wealth" with an "aristocracy of virtue and talent." A recent study of entail in Virginia shows that he was hardly exaggerating, estimating that its prohibition ended restrictions on about three-quarters of privately owned land in the state.[33]

The inheritance reform movement spread throughout the United States, beginning with some of the first state constitutions. North Carolina's condemned the "perpetuities and monopolies" of entails as well as charters, and Georgia's explicitly barred entail and mandated that estates be "divided equally" among children. In debates over the proposed federal constitution, men on both sides voiced their opposition to entail and primogeniture. When Charles Pinckney opened South Carolina's ratification convention, he warned delegates of the potential threat to the republic if a few men gathered "large amounts" of wealth, and to prevent that evil he urged following New England's example and ending primogeniture. North Carolina had already required intestate partible inheritance with a law that declared the state's intention "to promote that equality of property which is of the spirit and principle of a genuine republic." Ten years later, Delaware's repeal of its biblical "double portion" for the eldest declared "it is the duty and policy of every republican government to preserve equality amongst its citizens, by maintaining the balance of property." By the end of the century, nearly every state had intestate laws mandating equal division of estates among daughters as well as sons, with the exceptions of Connecticut (double share for elder son) and New Jersey and North Carolina (limiting such inheritance to male children). But this reform movement had a severe limit: states ended entails, but the bans on primogeniture were limited to intestate cases so men remained free to will their property to one son. The *Aurora* in 1793 mourned that many men were continuing to "give a preference to the elder son," and in the South it became common for a cotton plantation owner to give the buildings and lands to his oldest son and slaves to his daughters as dowry.[34]

Some did urge more active agrarian measures. A few calls were heard for legal limits on the amount of property a person could obtain in the future. Such appeals also echoed American ideals of the sanctity of private property, in contrast to those (like the anonymous Massachusetts town in 1781) which called for reducing *all* holdings and justified such measures with references to the Great Jubilee and Roman agrarian laws. The anonymously penned South Carolina *Rudiments of Law* (1783) urged that if the end of primogeniture failed to "diffuse property," then the "further increase of property must be positively restricted." Similarly, while Robert Yates Jr. of New York began a January 1784 piece by assuring the state's great landowners that he opposed any agrarian laws that would alter their estates, he then called for a law to limit the size of future purchases or grants from the "public realm," no doubt thinking of the vast rich area being pried from the Iroquois.[35]

Others considered taxes or tax reforms to maintain or encourage more egalitarian property ownership, particularly progressive levies on large estates. Thomas Jefferson at least twice during his life considered such measures. In the early 1770s, in his commonplace book, he seemed to endorse Montesquieu's belief that economic equality "should be promoted" by the creation of a progressive tax "laying burthens on the richer classes, & encouraging the poorer ones." Then in 1785, while in France, surrounded by extremes of wealth and poverty, he wrote James Madison not only that the law needed to encourage the division of property among all children but also that property above a certain size should be taxed, with the tax rising "in geometrical progression" with the owner's wealth. In 1784 Yates had similarly suggested laws that would "encourage land-holders to dispose of their lands, instead of keeping them unsettled," apparently thinking of higher property taxes on unimproved lands. Similarly, many Pennsylvanians called for taxing unoccupied lands in order to reduce the burdens faced by farmers and artisans in repaying the war debt held by speculators. In 1789 the Philadelphia *Independent Gazette* insisted that, because society's laws supported private property, property was "subject to the calls of that society whenever its necessities shall require it, even to the last farthing." South Carolina did institute a property tax in 1784 that shifted the burden to the wealthier and more powerful low country; apparently this was part of a political deal that allowed the coastal area to keep its majority in the legislature and helped restore political peace to the state. But, in general, progressive taxes proved elusive.[36]

A clear coda to the 1780s and Confederation period came with the new federal Constitution. Those who dominated the Philadelphia convention and then, calling themselves Federalists, drove the campaign for its ratification wanted a more stable, secure, and powerful national government, with the power to raise taxes and keep state legislatures from infringing on "private" matters of debt and trade. Those who opposed this revolution feared that the new government's structure would allow elites to quickly gain domination, create an aristocratic regime, and monopolize wealth and power. Americans of the middling and lower classes would become the easy prey of merchants, landlords, creditors, and lawyers. Although economic equality was rarely an explicit focus of the fierce debates, broader questions of class relations and sociopolitical hierarchies were implicit in many of the constitutional arguments and more explicit in the alarms about the threats of aristocracy. Perhaps the most important consequence of the ratification battle, besides victory for the Constitution in mid-1788, was that, because of the broad public participation in the debate, often across state lines, Americans began to think and write in more national terms.[37]

Historians generally depict the 1790s as the decade when national ideological and political conflicts emerged in the United States, driven by deep disagreements over economic policies and foreign relations. Even though factions continued to be regarded as enemies of the public interest, the contending parties in the new national government quickly coalesced, as Federalists and Democrat-Republicans established newspapers and popular societies to publicize their concerns and organize supporters. Socioeconomic equality became one of the more significant concerns at the center of the increasingly angry political divide, shredding the Revolutionary consensus that the new republic rested on widespread relatively egalitarian property ownership. One broad egalitarian movement did emerge, in the calls for limits on individual purchases of newly organized federal territories. But by the end of the century, the ideological rift in the country had grown to the point that some prominent Americans openly rejected the very idea of equality.[38]

As the Constitution won passage, spontaneous celebrations were channeled into nationalistic parades and feasts. Some historians see the organized events as the gentry working to broaden its definition of respectable citizenry to include middling artisans, although that picture is complicated by the reality that artisans played a critical role in most of the committees of safety that had governed towns during the war and the fact that parade organizers put farmers at the front of the procession and clergymen, lawyers, and doctors at the rear. A more recent view analyzes the organized events as public rituals that helped Federalists widen their base of support, including forcing those still concerned about the Constitution to publicly celebrate its passage and the Federalist vision of a new stronger nation or to risk alienating what appeared to be community consensus. The celebrations also allowed artisans and tradesmen to link their livelihoods with the new structure and publicly demand protection for domestic manufacturing as part of the optimistic vision that the stronger nation would restore American prosperity. The nation seemed to experience a burst of good feeling and hopes for the future.[39]

The economic plans of the new secretary of the Treasury, Alexander Hamilton, shattered this harmony. On January 9, 1790, in his *First Report on Public Credit,* Hamilton urged Congress to redeem part of the credit notes at face value with new securities that paid a high interest and could be used as legal tender. Many congressmen, particularly Hamilton's former ally James Madison, were outraged at the huge profits this promised to speculators who had purchased about three-quarters of the certificates from farmers and soldiers or their widows at deep discounts, often at 10 cents on the dollar. Still, the measure passed easily, in part because many congressmen were themselves speculators in the debt. More controversial was Hamilton's proposal to have the federal government take responsibility for the states' remaining wartime debts. Southerners in particular were outraged, in part because their states had already paid most of their debts with western lands and in part because the move would give the national government far more influence over the economy and accelerate the dreaded "consolidation." After extensive negotiations, that measure passed on July 26.[40]

But Hamilton's most controversial proposal, on December 15, 1790, was for a Bank of the United States, which would be funded at $10 million, about five times the size of all other American banks combined, to hold government revenues and provide loans for commercial development. Only 20 percent of the funds and a fifth of the board of directors would come from the national government, giving private bankers control of the bank, which would be chartered for twenty years. The measure passed swiftly, but the outcry against this private-public entity grew. After President Washington signed the bill into law on February 25, 1791, Jefferson and Madison began organizing against what they viewed as Hamilton's corrupting influence. Critics of the bank were louder and more widespread than opponents of the smaller, more localized Bank of North America, but their complaints were basically the same. Typical was the charge by George Logan, head of a prominent Pennsylvania family, that the bank was sacrificing "the Farmer, the mechanic, [and] the laborer" in favor of the "rich monied man." Bank critics saw it as another barely cloaked effort to create an aristocracy based on wealth.[41]

Hamilton's opponents saw more evidence of this menace after he persuaded New Jersey to grant a special charter to the Society for Establishing Useful Manufactures (SUM) to fulfill his vision of establishing a major industrial center. In January 1792 Madison in the *National Gazette* pointed at SUM when he condemned excessive political and economic power and urged that the "evil" be combated by barring "*unnecessary* opportunities" that could "increase the inequality of property." In fact, he wrote, laws should, "without violating the rights of property, reduce extreme wealth towards a state of mediocrity, and raise extreme indigence towards a state of comfort"—in this context meaning limits on capital, not land. A few months later, Logan wrote more *Letters* that explicitly condemned SUM's charter as "one of the most unjust and arbitrary laws" because it gave "a few wealthy men" a range of "unconstitutional privileges." Such power was "the perpetual source of oppression," and he feared a replication of the "abject servitude" found in English manufacturing towns.[42]

While Madison and Logan were most concerned about maintaining a nation of farmers, many artisans feared SUM as part of a growing threat to their trades and financial independence. Connecticut shoemaker Walter Brewster wrote a series that in part attacked the society's charter and a similar measure in his state as "exclusive privileges" that impoverished artisans, threatened their political rights, and marked "a very rapid stride towards tyranny." In a thinly veiled condemnation of SUM, New York City artisans and traders in the newly formed Tammany Society closed their celebration of Washington's birthday with the toast "May the love of liberty be ever superior to the love of property." These "middling sorts" were anxious about their future as the economy stagnated and the wealthy seemed to gain ground. One recent study found that in Philadelphia between 1780 and 1795 the bottom 90 percent of property holders saw its share of wealth in the city drop from more than half to 18 percent.[43]

In this increasingly bitter political conflict, the French Revolution served as an ideological dividing line. By early 1789, King Louis XVI faced terrible financial problems after losing the Seven Years' War and then helping the United States win independence. He called the Estates-General to assemble in May (for the first time since 1614) to solve the nation's financial problems, but the Third Estate (commons) insisted on first addressing constitutional issues. The momentum increased with the creation of a National Assembly in mid-June to push for a constitutional monarchy, the storming of the Bastille a month later, and the Assembly's *Declaration of the Rights of Man* in late August. The revolution reverberated around Europe: Austria and Prussia mobilized to crush the beast, while those who hoped for freedom to spread exulted, like America's friend Richard Price in London. Americans were nearly unanimous in their applause. George Logan thought the Declaration of Rights superior to the Constitution in barring privileges, and even dour John Adams remarked, "The great revolution in France is wonderful," although he insisted that it could not eliminate "the great and perpetual distinction" between the few rich and the many poor.[44]

For about four years, public celebrations in the United States inevitably connected the American and French revolutions to the universalistic ideals of equality and liberty—even as the two concepts were increasingly contested and, in the eyes of growing numbers of Americans, somewhat contradictory.

The enthusiasm peaked in early 1793 after news arrived that France had repulsed the invading armies and declared itself a republic. On January 24 Boston held particularly elaborate festivities to celebrate "the SUCCESS of their French brethren, in their glorious enterprise for the establishment of EQUAL LIBERTY." The parade was led by two citizens on horseback with civic flags, followed by a band, several groups without any distinction of social rank, and wagons bearing huge amounts of food: 800 loaves of bread, two hogsheads of rum punch, and a half-ton roasted ox ornamented with ribbons and gilded horns. The ox lay on a wagon displaying the flag of republican France on one side and that of the United States on the other, with a board inscribed "PEACE OFFERING TO LIBERTY AND EQUALITY." The procession traversed the city with cheers for state leaders before everyone gathered to eat. Not all were enthralled: Abigail Adams told John that "to Men of reflection the Cry of *Equality* was not so pleasing, and to Men of Property very alarming," although it was better to "unite with the Mobility in their Feast"—and pay the special 3-dollar tax—in order to ensure order and avoid "being Stiled Aristocrats." No doubt others in the country were similarly secretly resentful.[45]

But most Americans remained strong supporters of the French Revolution even after the execution of Louis XVI in January 1793 and the beginnings of the "Reign of Terror" in April. The international connection intensified the emotional and ideological pitch of the political struggle that had begun over America's economic policies. This conflict increased in 1794 with the eruption of a domestic insurrection that became known as the Whiskey Rebellion. Hamilton's economic plan included an excise tax on that liquor, but almost immediately the men deputized to collect the tax in western Pennsylvania and Virginia faced determined opposition. Scholars have connected this western insurrection to broader socioeconomic fears as foreclosures and bankruptcies multiplied, and the Revolution's egalitarian promise seemed endangered by measures including the new Pennsylvania Constitution of 1790 that reduced democracy and created a strong executive. Western protests focused on Hamilton's economic plans, called for limits on the size of land purchases from the public realm, and targeted federal excise agents as the sole presence of the unpopular programs. In turn, Federalists saw the insurrection as inspired by French radicals, organized by the new Democratic-Republican societies, and a direct threat to the national government in Philadelphia. When President Washington called out the army to put down the "rebellion," the protests shriveled and the zealous moved far away.[46]

America's republican paradigm emphasized a single public interest and condemned political parties; political opponents were therefore regarded more as dangerous conspirators than respectable adversaries. But two distinct parties developed nonetheless, driven and shaped by conflicts over Hamilton's economic programs, the French Revolution, and the Whiskey Rebellion, and then heated to white-hot passions by the hated 1795 Jay Treaty with England and the bitterly contested 1796 election to choose Washington's successor as president of the United States. Questions of socioeconomic equality became a significant focus of the debates as Republicans and Federalists sponsored newspapers to build public support, and the local Republican elites organized broadly based "Democrat" societies. Federalists were likely to envisage a stable social hierarchy even as they lauded a commercial economy that seemed inherently unsettling, while the insurgent Democrat-Republicans were more likely to warn of class conflict and to call for a more egalitarian socioeconomic structure.[47]

Thus, in 1794 New Jersey's Democrat societies insisted that they represented the "mechanics and farmers, the poorer class of people," against "rich influential characters." Two years later, "Back-Woods Man" in the *Aurora* explained that the two distinct parties of "speculation and labour" had existed since American independence, with the former "opposed to every principle of equality and just government" with a "uniform and constant tendency to aristocracy." George Warner told a New York City gathering of artisans, journeymen, and shopkeepers on July 4, 1797, that they guarded America's republican virtues against the threat of rich men controlling elections. South Carolinian Richard Beresford bitterly derided those who had gained "rapid fortunes" through commerce and gloomily noted that "the respect paid in monarchies to nobility is, in free republicks, where no nobility is established, transferred to opulence." In 1798 William Manning, a Massachusetts tavern owner, wrote in *Key of Liberty* that "the Few" (speculators, lawyers, ministers) sought economic policies that made them wealthy and "always bring the Many into distress and compel them into a state of dependence." Before he was arrested and jailed for sedition, David Brown had traveled through at least eighty towns in New England, publicly denouncing governmental officials, clergymen, and lawyers as "enemies of the people" and calling for "a thorough Revolution."[48]

These views of a deep and bitter class conflict were driven by fears that the seeds of commercial capitalism, sown by Robert Morris in the 1780s and fertilized by Alexander Hamilton in the 1790s, threatened the American republic with the aristocratic weeds of wealth. Englishmen who wrote slashing attacks on corruption at the start of the century, such as Trenchard and Gordon in *Cato's Letters*, had focused on Britain's emerging political system and called for a series of reforms, including an expansion of the electorate and a more representative Parliament. American critics in the 1790s focused instead on ways to prevent the Few from controlling the new legal, political, and economic structures in a way that would enlarge and make permanent their share of the nation's wealth at the expense of the Many.[49]

As in the previous decade, some appealed for limits on individual wealth. In May 1795 the Reverend Perez Fobes in Boston repeated the call, first made during the English Civil War, for the biblical Great Jubilee in order to redistribute excessive wealth. With the Massachusetts governor and legislators listening in rapt attention to the Election Day sermon, the minister emphasized the dangers to "human liberty" when "National wealth" became "accumulated in the hands of a few individuals." The resulting "corruption of morals" would lead to "anarchy and despotism." Fobes particularly condemned the ability of the candidate with "the longest purse" to get the most votes and urged his elite audience to follow God's wisdom and establish the Jubilee in order to maintain liberty "among selfish, degenerate beings." While the legislature paid to have the sermon published, no legislator actually proposed such a measure.[50]

Two years later, Philip Freneau published a more modern view "On Some of the Principles of American Republicanism." The writer described the new nation's system as resting on popular representation, a lack of hereditary honors, rotation of men in office, frequent and "uncorrupted" elections, freedom of the press and religion, separation of church and state, and the abolition of entails. But in this republic, he warned, the law should prevent men from becoming "exorbitantly rich" in order to avoid creating "a *natural aristocracy*" that had concerns different from those of "the people" (the Many) and that was "apt to acquire a dangerous influence." Freneau's paper obviously presented a very different view of a natural aristocracy than John Adams had and repeated the call, often made in the 1780s, for republican limits on wealth.[51]

Calls for legal limits on wealth were noticeably fewer in the 1790s than in the 1780s, even though there were similar concerns and controversies: debt speculation, scarce capital, and the danger of losing land along with one's manhood and the right to vote. There were at least two apparent reasons for that decline. First, the ratification of the Constitution and Hamilton's economic program made it much harder (as intended) for states to consider debt reforms or limits on wealth and property. Second, during the Revolution, Americans embraced the paradigm that the individual right to property was a natural liberty. It was not surprising that, in 1795, the writer who called for "equality of circumstances" followed that with the caveat that "an arbitrary leveling of estates to create such equality and mediocrity would be an outrage against the right of property."[52]

Some American writers who wished to promote measures to ensure economic equality yet avoid being labeled a Leveller often reprinted pieces from Europe that made arguments potentially too radical to claim as their own. For example, while Freneau's *National Gazette* insisted in March 1789 that American and French democrats were "*not the levellers of property*," six months later it reprinted a piece from a French paper that began: "In every democratical government the laws ought to destroy, and prevent too great an inequality of condition among the citizen." Two years later, Irish immigrant Mathew Carey published *The Spirit of Despotism*, a radical English book celebrating the middling and lower classes as "bulwarks of liberty" because they lacked corrupting wealth; the *Aurora* proclaimed that, "tho' intended for the meridian of a despotic court, many passages in it apply wonderfully for this country." William Godwin's *Enquiry Concerning Political Justice*, published in the United States in 1796, criticized sources of economic inequality, blasted charters and monopolies, and praised the benefits of laws providing for better health and education for all.[53]

One original idea to enhance economic equality without violating the paradigm of liberty of property came from Thomas Paine, who had returned to England in 1787 and then embraced and barely survived the French Revolution. In *Agrarian Justice*, published in France in late 1795 and in the United States in mid-1797, Paine urged the national government to provide £15 to every man and woman at age twenty-one and annual pensions of £10 to every person aged fifty and older; the payments would be funded by taxing every estate worth more than £500 at 10 percent of its value. He grounded this plan on the paradigm that individual ownership was not an inherent aspect of land, and so only improvement and produce could be owned in absolute terms. This reflected John Locke's century-old theory that a man's labor gave land its value and was therefore the ultimate source of private property. Paine held that because ownership of land was a social right, land could and should be taxed for social needs. But he also sought to distinguish his proposal from what he called "unjust" redistributive agrarian law, and advertisement for his book's sale in American newspapers emphasized it was "Opposed to Agrarian Law and Agrarian Monopoly." *Agrarian Justice* did not match the storm raised by *Common Sense*, but several American papers did publish excerpts.[54]

The marginalization of agrarian laws can perhaps best glimpsed in Robert Coram's *Political Inquiries* (1791). Coram, editor of the *Delaware Gazette*, praised the idea of limits on individual wealth but thought such measures impossible given the consensus that patriarchal property was a sacred right. The first chapter praised Native Americans for being "strangers to all distinction of property" and emphasized that they saw it causing many evils among Europeans, for it was "irrational" that one man should have more than another. His second chapter examined the origins and development of the idea of property while savaging William Blackstone for arguing, in *Commentaries on the Laws of England*, that agriculture, civilization, and morality rested on individual ownership of land. Quite the contrary, argued Coram: land held in common (as Native Americans did) was "the most effectual check" against individual ambition and the ever-increasing desire for wealth that generated "almost all the disorders in the body politic." At the same time, he acknowledged that there was no popular support for "equal division of lands" and promised instead a "highly practicable" substitute.[55]

Coram's substitute was a public system of education, following Noah Webster's call in 1788 for a publicly funded school system throughout America for "every class." Of course, the Connecticut lawyer was not the first prominent American to advocate a school system in the new nation; most felt that a successful republic depended on an informed and economically independent adult male citizenry. In 1783 the South Carolina writer who called for laws limiting wealth had also urged a system of universal education because those born into unfortunate circumstances "must be encouraged to elevate their ideas." Three years later, Benjamin Rush presented *A Plan for the Establishment of Public Schools* throughout Pennsylvania as "Favorable to liberty," necessary in a republic, and useful for social cohesion because people in the state came from so many European countries.[56]

Although these men and many other Americans agreed on the need for universal education, they held different views of its benefits. Some, such as the writer in Philadelphia's *American Museum*, viewed such a system (using New England as an example) as the means for the most talented poor to gain wealth and prestige within the existing socioeconomic system. South Carolinian Richard Beresford similarly envisioned a conservative, though more political purpose, arguing that "the general diffusion of knowledge among the people" would end the "very dangerous ground of dispute" between rich and poor and that if the "deluded multitude" was to be educated then it would perform its *republican* duty and vote for "good and wise" candidates rather than "aristocratick" Federalists. Not surprisingly, Coram had a more radical vision, emphasizing the role of education in facilitating a *democratic* government and ensuring a more egalitarian economy. Similarly, William Manning proposed in 1798 a system that encouraged the Many to learn through participation in local political (Jeffersonian) clubs. Although he failed to publish his plan, one could argue that the growing number of partisan newspapers, political organizations, and voluntary associations did follow that path.[57]

Americans also agreed that a critical aspect of their new republic was its absence of inherited titles and privilege. The traditional honorifics that for centuries had denoted status seemed increasingly inappropriate, and in 1793 a gathering of "magistrates, planters, and merchants" in Charleston condemned the use of titles like excellency and esquire as "conducive not to national dignity or public order, but to the degeneracy of the people." One dark side of this movement was the racialization of social hierarchy in the North as states began to pass gradual emancipation laws in the 1780s and 1790s. For example, Charles Janson, a visitor in 1793, remembered a "servant-maid" in New England who retorted, after he asked whether her "master" was home, that "I have no master. . . . I am no *sarvant*; none but *negers* are *servants*." The Englishman commented "the arrogance of domestics in this land of republican liberty and equality, is particularly calculated to excite the astonishment of strangers."[58]

The most substantive and long-term effort to ensure an egalitarian future in the United States may have been the call, beginning in the 1790s, to limit the size of individual purchases of federal lands. In 1785 Congress created a system to organize, survey, and sell lands that were not part of existing states, including large areas in the fertile Ohio Valley and the old Southwest. The program had two inherently contradictory goals: to help fund the national government, and to facilitate a republican future of independent family farms. Areas were to be surveyed in townships of six square miles, subdivided into thirty-six sections, each consisting of 640 acres (one square mile). The land was to be sold at auction for at least $2 per acre, requiring at least $1,280 in cash—far more than most men could manage. As a result, in the 1790s, as US troops forced Natives to abandon more of their lands—18,500 square miles in all, taken through treaties for less than 2 cents an acre—loud voices demanded that measures be adopted to ensure widespread ownership and prevent its monopolization by wealthy speculators. The vicious irony is that the greatest egalitarian potential in the new country, this land and its resources, depended on dispossessing Native communities that had more egalitarian societies, cultures, and economies than did contemporary Americans.[59]

Fittingly, the first person to call for land limits was Herman Husband, the spokesman and thinker for the North Carolina Regulators before the Revolution, who had settled in the Pennsylvania backcountry—and had coincidentally hosted the German surgeon Johann Schoepf for a night in the mid-1780s. In 1790 Husband published a pamphlet demanding constitutional reforms including a national homestead law to provide every western settler enough land for a farm while forbidding the purchase of larger areas to avoid creating aristocratic and tenant classes. Not surprisingly, no changes were made in the law as Hamilton and his allies not only depended on the monies from land sales to build and maintain the new national government but also preferred to limit the extent and speed of western settlement. In July 1794, an essay in the *Carlisle Gazette* charged that the emerging pattern was a "forestalling" of public lands that would force millions of Americans to become tenants, and its author urged limitations of three thousand acres for each man and one thousand "to each of his family." A month later, men in that town signed a petition holding that the United States as a republic should encourage the "equal division of property."[60]

Many prominent Americans agreed with the call for agrarian reforms. In 1795 St. George Tucker, professor of law at the College of William and Mary, called for land to be sold only to actual settlers in parcels no larger than two hundred acres, and a year later Elhanan Winchester, a New England preacher and one of the founders of American Universalism, taught schoolchildren through his *Plain Political Catechism* that public lands should be sold only to settlers and not to speculators or land companies. More generally, Thomas Jefferson and his allies urged policies that would support a nation of independent, landowning farmers, which they believed essential for a successful, virtuous republic. But no immediate reforms resulted because there was little unity and insufficient pressure to support these proposals, and although over the subsequent half-century the price per acre and the minimum purchase requirement declined, limits were never placed on the amount a person or company could purchase.[61]

All these efforts and appeals for a more egalitarian country seem quite moderate. But the growing public heat produced by the emergence of two political parties—both of which viewed the other as a pack of subversive conspirators rather than a group of respectable opponents—generated a strong anti-egalitarian reaction among more conservative public figures. Federalists began to view America in ways that echoed the way conservative Britons like Edmund Burke were portraying their country, celebrating the stability and order of a hierarchical society headed by an elite wealthy class. In February 1795 the minister in Hanover, Massachusetts, delivering a sermon in response to President Washington's call for a day of Thanksgiving, insisted: "All rule and government supposes subordination and degrees of standing. There must be some to govern, and others to be governed." This reflected the Federalist emphasis on the interconnected nature of social, economic, and political authority. That same year, a Philadelphia printer published William Brown's *An Essay on the Natural Equality of Man*, in which the English minister argued that hierarchical distinctions among people were inherent and that education could have few effects in leveling those differences.[62]

Of course, Federalists as well as Democrat-Republicans drew close connections between foreign and domestic policies. Hamilton, Adams, and other leading Federalists admired England's stability and influence, which they felt rested on a system that connected political and economic power, and feared France's revolutionary rhetoric as an international contagion that threatened the fragile American republic. They viewed the Jay Treaty, despite its continued burden for American traders, as the country's best opportunity for a prosperous, peaceful, and stable future through improved ties with England. Connections with revolutionary France, on the other hand, promised only military defeat and domestic anarchy. In May 1796, after Congress refused to block the treaty, a Virginia Federalist mocked the state's Democratic-Republicans: "It is hoped they will still continue to persevere in the same principles of *Liberty and Equality*" and, "without delay, pass a law, to make an equal distribution of property throughout the United States—and that our black brethren so unjustly held in slavery may be emancipated, and partake with us all in the general distribution—*No Government!—Huzza!*"[63]

As the confusing political maneuverings and fierce ideological conflict continued, Federalist newspapers, politicians, and ministers connected Thomas Jefferson to French Jacobin conspiracies and depicted those radical Enlightenment elements as a threat to the "natural" Christian beliefs and patriarchal affections that formed America's social glue. Such views were particularly prominent in New England, which became the nation's conservative core. In December 1796, Federalist John Adams won the first real presidential contest, while the nation's electoral system gave the vice-presidency to his political and ideological opponent, Thomas Jefferson. This result did not end political conflict. A month after the election, Henry Cumings, minister of Billerica, Massachusetts, William Manning's town, preached the need to defer to those in power and located the greatest threat to the republic as those "under the baneful influence of leveling principles," who "cannot brook any civic distinctions and restraints." More broadly, celebrations of the French Revolution disappeared from feasts and celebrations, and the toasts issued at those fetes rarely raised the specter of equality.[64]

The domestic political conflict and its connection with European developments intensified as the French navy targeted US merchant ships, beginning the "Quasi-War." In mid-1797 Adams sent a commission to Paris to settle disputes and end the attacks, but the commissioners faced a maze of hostile officials, three of whom demanded a sizable bribe prior to negotiations. On March 19, 1798, two weeks after receiving the initial reports, President Adams told Congress that little hope remained for successful talks but refused to release the commissioners' dispatches. After Congress obtained copies, the resulting popular outrage put Republicans on the defensive. While the immediate crisis involved foreign policy, many Federalists saw clear connections between revolutionary France and democratic leveling in America. On May 9, the day of fasting and prayer declared by Adams to contemplate problems with France, Nathaniel Emmons, Newburyport minister, preached that "the lower order ought not to deprive the higher order of their honor, wealth, or influence" and that efforts to "reduce" the better sort to an equal level with others violated natural law.[65]

Such reactionary rhetoric became more prominent after Congress passed the Alien and Sedition Acts in the summer of 1798, allowing the president to expel radical foreigners and prosecute "seditious" publishers. The Connecticut Society of Cincinnati celebrated Independence Day with a speech by Thomas Day, who decried the "anarchy" driven by the "class of people who have neither character, property, nor Religion." One year later in Providence, Jonathan Maxcy, head of Rhode Island College (later Brown University), defended the Alien and Sedition Acts and scorned "the revolutionary demagogues of our country [who] talk much of equality." To the contrary, it was inevitable and welcome that "the industrious, prudent citizen, will gain vast quantities of property, while the negligent and idle will remain in the depths of poverty." Among the latter were the advocates of the "pernicious doctrine" of equality, who in reality wished to spread anarchy and shatter deference for "eminent and dignified men"[66]

By the end of the century, the maturing two-party system embodied foreign and domestic debates. The elections of 1800 made it particularly clear that parties and candidates were absorbing and redirecting long-standing ideological concerns, including the Revolution's egalitarian ideals. As the campaign for the presidency developed, Republicans quickly demonstrated that they had gained strength in northern cities among laborers and journeymen and, most usefully, with the emerging "mechanic's associations" angered by Federalist rhetoric and policies that seemed increasingly elitist, antidemocratic, and pro-British. But they did not call for measures to increase or ensure economic equality. In late April 1800, Aaron Burr's effective organization won a large majority in New York City's state legislative election, surprising Alexander Hamilton and other Federalists, and making it clear that the state's large slate of electoral votes would go to Republican candidates. The rest of the nasty presidential campaign followed this pattern, resulting in a tie for the Republican candidates Jefferson and Burr, which was decided for the Virginian after a long battle in Congress.[67]

During the last two decades of the century, the Revolutionary consensus began to splinter as fissures developed in America's political landscape. One of the most systemic fractures involved wealth, power, and concerns of economic and social equality—in a word, *class*. At the end of the war, all agreed that the new United States enjoyed the smallest gap between rich and poor in the world and that widespread property ownership and voting among adult men provided the essential foundation of the new republic. But because Americans continued to view all power as connected, they also feared the future: many elites defended their traditional authority and complained that subversive democrats wanted to take all property and level all distinctions, whereas many farmers and artisans feared an aristocracy of wealth (which German physician Johann Schoepf apparently found in his postwar tour). Some Americans called for an end to property qualifications for voting rights, limits on wealth, depreciated currency, or more progressive taxation—which would unlink socioeconomic status from political power—especially when the postwar depression and high taxes to repay the war debt threatened many with the loss of property and political citizenship. More broad-based was the strong opposition to state charters with special privileges for banks and turnpike companies. But the only truly successful reform was the effort, pushed by Americans of all classes, to abolish entail and limit primogeniture.

With the establishment of the new Constitution, the economic issues intensified. Alexander Hamilton's policies connected the federal government to men who had made fortunes in the war and made them key players in a national bank to encourage commerce, capital development, and manufacturing. The resulting ideological divisions deepened over the increasingly radical French Revolution, resulting in the first, fierce party system of Federalist and Republican, and the establishment of dueling newspapers and popular societies around the country—including mechanic associations organized by artisans who felt threatened by manufacturing corporations. However, the dynamics of party politics, increased national power, and return of general prosperity curbed calls for limits on wealth; more acceptable were the demands for universal education and federal homestead laws grounded in a call for equal opportunity. In this vein, perhaps the most important development during this period was the broad embrace of a new distinction between *liberty* and *equality*. The Revolution had instilled strong support for individual property rights among American men, and in its wake economic equality became more of an abstract ideal rather than a substantive goal. But that ideal would re-emerge on a strong tide of reform efforts in the 1820s.

CHAPTER FIVE

Raising Republican Children

The American Revolution heralded the development in the United States of new republican norms of raising, socializing, and enlightening boys and girls. The dynamics of wartime life and the widespread embrace of sentimentalism provided women with greater authority within the household and more generally over child-rearing, particularly among the upper and middling classes in towns and cities (who were more likely to embrace new social and cultural mores). Not surprisingly, the Revolution's political changes generated, particularly among white men, anxieties about many of their social, cultural, and economic effects: the expectation of a higher standard of living and the scramble for wealth among even middling men; the apparent decline of deference to the traditional social hierarchy; and an apparent increase in selfishness and "excessive democracy." These concerns grew from fears of the radical aspects of the American and French revolutions and, more generally, the growing importance of the individual during the Enlightenment and Romantic eras.

One significant result was an increasing emphasis on formal education for children that began early and continued into adolescence. The goal became for young Americans to learn, in addition to reading, writing, and math, a strong sense of social duties and republican virtues. In the North, a network of reformers (ministers, artisans, lawyers, and merchants) pushed for the creation of publicly funded schools that would also teach regular habits, group work, and self-discipline. Girls as well as boys attended, although the highest level of school was reserved for the latter, and most local authorities barred the growing population of free blacks who in response established their own schools.[1] In the South, where plantation agriculture based on racial slavery grew in importance and resistance to effective taxation remained high, weak governments lacked the power and money necessary to organize schools. As a result, only the children of planter elite and those living in the few cities in the region regularly received schooling. In the South and West, most families taught children at home, using the schoolbooks printed in northeastern cities.

The lack of organized education made schoolbooks and other literature for children a particularly important element in the effort to forge a new American generation. Indeed, schoolbooks not only served to guard and inculcate republican ideals but also played a critical role in shifting those ideals into more conservative and nationalist channels. Schoolbooks appeared alongside Bibles and almanacs in many American households regardless of region or occupation. This demand was driven by the growing rate of literacy, already high in northern states, and the popular interest in *American* history, geography, and science. In some places, particularly in the North, voluntary organizations sought various ways to encourage and spread knowledge, such as the libraries established in more than five hundred New England towns between 1790 and 1815. The growing demand was stimulated and fulfilled by the declining price of books due to the increasing number of printers, larger runs of particular editions, and the mechanized production of paper after 1817.[2]

Initially much of the children's literature was produced by British authors reprinted (without permission or royalties) by American publishers. A few American writers did publish schoolbooks in the 1780s, but for a half century most popular works were English in origin. Regardless of the writer's nationality, these didactic stories contained the lesson that a strong class structure was natural, inevitable, and beneficial; the wealthy were depicted as having earned their status through hard work, so the poor were responsible for their condition and indeed ought to be grateful that they did not suffer the many responsibilities faced by gentlemen. At the same time, the wealthy "better sort" needed to fulfill their genteel duty to give assistance as well as respect to the poor and unfortunate. About the only difference between the two groups of writers was that American authors included lessons that their new nation was a land of freedom and equality primarily because there was no titled aristocracy so everyone was equal before the law.

In the 1830s a tidal wave of American-authored schoolbooks burst forth, facilitated by the emergence in the North of state-organized public school systems and vastly improved printing technology and distribution networks. These works focused on practical matters, American history, and foreign cultures, while encouraging the "middle class" values seen as necessary to succeed in the industrializing market economy. At the same time, like older works, they urged guarding one's reputation and observing proper manners toward social superiors and inferiors. Indeed, many continued to teach that men (and women) must accept and appreciate inequalities of property and power and that the poor were fortunate to escape the burdens faced by the wealthy. These traditional blessings for a stable class system were sometimes modified with the uniquely American democratic dogma—later encapsulated by the Horatio Alger story—that the poorest boy could rise to wealth and influence through hard work and moral behavior. Yet even those stories taught the virtues of the existing social and economic hierarchy.

In the seventeenth and early eighteenth century, Anglo-American childrearing and education emphasized patriarchal authority, even though women played a critical role in the early socialization of boys as well as girls. A clearly bifurcated notion of gender—women were shaped by "natural" submissiveness and love of luxury, men by inherent ambition, assertiveness, and reason— drove how Americans viewed household, social, and political duties. Those duties shaped a person's character and were imbedded in relationships with relatives and neighbors. Individualism was regarded warily, particularly for women but also for men. Boys and girls were socialized and educated within their households until about age thirteen, at which point many were sent to relatives, neighbors, or (for boys) formal apprenticeships with artisans. All were subject to the absolute authority of the (male) head of the household. During the first half of the eighteenth century, however, the tradition of patriarchal authority eroded as Enlightenment notions of affectionate childrearing became more influential, and economic developments such as declining farm sizes in older areas weakened traditional paternal controls.[3]

As the Revolution erupted, Americans writers generally celebrated the replacement of patriarchal authoritarianism by the republican bonds of affection and patriotism. Masculinity took on more individualist connotations, including assertiveness, ambition, and avarice; in response, many called for the potential harm of these characteristics to be checked by self-control and self-denial. At the same time, the wartime unraveling of hierarchical social bonds along with crowd actions and calls for more democracy made American leaders anxious about the social order and harmony of their new nation. They found one solution in their country's women, viewed increasingly as necessary "custodians of communal virtue," with the "natural" ability and duty to maintain republican values within the household. Virtuous wives would ensure virtuous husbands and inculcate those morals within their sons not just early in life but into young adulthood, which meant that girls as well as boys needed to be trained in the arts and morals. In fact, children and their education be-

"The mother sways the dominion of the heart, the father that of the intellect."

Samuel Goodrich, "The Mother Sways . . . ," frontispiece from *Fireplace Education* (New York: F. J. Huntington, 1838). Courtesy, American Antiquarian Society.

came the primary focus for those seeking ways to maintain a virtuous American republic, particularly since the country's high birth rate meant that half or more of its new citizens were under age sixteen.[4]

Children in all parts of the United States experienced various aspects of the Revolution. During the war they noticed the absence of fathers, uncles, brothers, and cousins; many felt hunger and saw troops or prisoners marching through their towns; some witnessed battles. They also absorbed republican ideas and principles from family discussions or important public events, such as rallies around liberty trees, community readings of the Declaration of Independence, and sermons that touched on political concerns. These common experiences became defining moments in individual lives and important national links that transcended regional differences. The broad political lessons continued after the war: for example, in January 1793, when Boston celebrated the French Revolution, each child attending the festival received a "civic cake" that enabled them to literally imbibe the words "Liberty and Equality." The cakes also provided a lesson in social and economic egalitarianism, because every child regardless of wealth or class received the same cake and witnessed all in the city celebrating together. These widespread personal connections with revolutionary ideas accelerated the erosion of patriarchal authority and its replacement by personal independence and individual autonomy, at least for adult white men. But what would replace king-and-father in the new country's cultural and political bonds, and how would future generations sustain the socioeconomic hierarchy that most American leaders felt was "natural" and necessary for a nation's stability and virtue?[5]

The solution, they agreed, was for young children to be imbued with a strong sense of self-discipline, social duties, and republican virtues. In the seventeenth century, particularly among Calvinists, such a goal would have been deemed impossible if not heretical, but by the mid-eighteenth century Americans generally believed that, as first postulated by John Locke in *An Essay on Human Understanding* (1690), humans were born with a "blank slate" (*tabula rasa*) filled by education and shaped by their environments. Locke advocated three stages of child-rearing: ensure future health by exposing the child to regular discomforts and a simple diet; imbue virtuous character through various measures so the child learns "to *deny himself* his own Desires, cross his own Inclinations, and purely follow what Reason directs as best"; and provide a formal education practically suited to the child's social station and future career. Locke's system was modified slightly by Scottish Enlightenment writers, who stressed affectionate sociability rather than pure reason, and by Jean-Jacques Rousseau, who emphasized developing "natural" abilities and interests, including tutoring in whatever arts seemed interesting. The Americans who wrote on child-rearing and education, like Congregational minister Enos Hitchcock and Philadelphia physician Benjamin Rush, added religion as a source of virtue and harmony. They emphasized using affection and reasoned discipline to instill internalized restraint and obedience in a child and teaching benevolent acts through repetition "fortified" by Bible stories, prayer, and praise.[6]

Americans educators did not agree about everything. Some celebrated the egalitarian opportunities for ambitious young men regardless of class, whereas others emphasized the need for individuals to accept their "proper" social class and responsibilities. They also disagreed about the extent of formal education that was proper for girls. But all agreed that the new Republic needed state or local systems of publicly funded schools. Such a program had its roots in the Protestant emphasis on widespread literacy enabling all to read the Bible, extended by English puritans to support their social ideal of "ordered liberty." For many the model was Massachusetts, where nearly every town supported a school for young boys. In 1765, in an essay published in the *Boston Gazette*, John Adams emphasized the social aspects of education: "The preservation of the means of knowledge among the lowest ranks, is of more importance to the public, than all the property of all the rich men in the country." Two decades later in a July Fourth address, Thomas Dawes connected the Revolution's egalitarian ideals to the Bay Colony's early laws mandating local schools and partible inheritance. "It is easy to see," the jurist told his Boston audience, "that our Agrarian law and the law of education were calculated to make republicans—to make *men*." That history was renowned: for example, in 1792 a writer in Philadelphia's *American Museum* praised New England's public schools for enabling "the poor to become rich, and the humble to raise themselves to eminence."[7]

Like partible inheritance, public education was a markedly egalitarian objective, particularly in terms of class among white Americans, especially south of Pennsylvania where education beyond basic literacy had been limited to the sons of wealthy planters able to hire tutors. As Virginia's governor during the Revolution, Thomas Jefferson urged not only an end to primogeniture and the creation of more egalitarian forms of taxation but also a system of grammar schools for "the More General Diffusion of Knowledge." All free boys and girls would be taught reading, writing, and arithmetic, as well as Greek, Roman, English, and American history. For three years the state would pay tuition; additional years would be paid for privately. After the war Jefferson continued to urge a statewide public education system with several levels, although he succeeded only in establishing the University of Virginia in 1819. Further south, in 1783 the anonymous South Carolinian who called for laws limiting wealth also urged a system of universal education because those born into unfortunate circumstances "must be encouraged to elevate their ideas."[8]

Indeed, all of those calling for new systems of education, North or South, grounded their appeals on the assumption that a successful republic required an informed as well as an economically independent citizenry. In 1782 Governor George Clinton reminded New York's legislature that it was "the peculiar duty" of state government "to diffuse that degree of literature which is necessary to the due discharge of public trusts," and that they needed to close the "chasm of education" created by the war. Two years later, General Benjamin Lincoln of Massachusetts urged universal public education because "in a free republic the people that compose it is the monarch," and therefore should get the same level of education as a monarch. In 1786 Benjamin Rush published his very influential *Plan for the Establishment of Public Schools*, calling for a Pennsylvania system to unite the state's diverse population and serve as "nurseries of virtue and knowledge" to turn youth into "republican machines." These common schools would teach literature and politics alongside farming and mechanical skills, for "free government can only exist in an equal diffusion of literature." Rush also advocated universal schooling for girls "in the principles of liberty and government" so they would be prepared to instruct their republican sons. Connecticut lawyer Noah Webster, in *On the Education of Youth in America* (1788), presented a somewhat different plan, arguing that schools should teach not traditional classical history and Latin, but math and reading and writing in English, as well as American history, government, and "the principles of liberty." For women "a *good* education" included the "*useful*" skills of reading and writing English, some arithmetic and geography, and "a taste for poetry and fine writing."[9]

More importantly, these men agreed that education should serve republican rather than egalitarian purposes. America had rejected a patriarchal monarchy, and in the new nation all power rested with the people. An orderly society and the protection of property depended on these schools to prepare children for public virtue by first teaching them obedience to the "natural" hierarchy of age and eminence. The hope was to prevent selfish ambition and resentful "levellism." Clinton proclaimed that education in the "liberal science" served the public service of "restraining those rude passions which lead to vice and disorder." Rush urged teachers to levy "arbitrary" discipline to "prepare our youth for the subordination of laws" so that they would have "never known or felt their own wills" until they became adults. Webster wanted children to learn "submission to superiors" as part of their "moral or social duties."[10]

In the 1790s these goals almost certainly became more significant as intense conflict over the French Revolution emerged and conservative concerns about social and political stability intensified. In 1797 the American Philosophical Society held a contest "for the best system of liberal Education and literary instruction." The two who divided the $100 prize, Samuel Harrison Smith (a publisher-printer in Philadelphia) and Samuel Knox (Presbyterian minister and head of a Maryland academy), espoused national systems to inculcate common republican values, not individual intellectual growth. Smith extolled the republican instincts of an "enlightened nation" and condemned the selfish "indulgence in luxury"; he called for property taxes to fund the education of boys from age five to eighteen in agriculture and mechanics as well as English, math, history, geography, and "the laws of nature." Knox hoped the system would produce "harmony of sentiments, unity of taste and manners, [and] the patriotic principles of genuine federalism amongst the scattered and variegated citizens of this extensive republic." In 1801 the Reverend Aaron Bancroft in his election sermon told the governor and legislators of Massachusetts that the state's schools helped inoculate the "rising generation" against "that spirit of innovation, and rage for change, which endanger the primary principles of good order."[11]

Some school advocates did see a more egalitarian purpose for education. In 1791 Robert Coram of Delaware advocated democratic equality rather than a republican hierarchy and envisioned "A System of Equal Education" as the only practical means to achieve that goal without property redistribution. After pointing to how nearly all legislators were lawyers and merchants because farmers could not afford college, he noted, "An equal representation is absolutely necessary to the preservation of liberty. But there can never be an equal representation until there is an equal mode of education for all citizens." Six years later, Massachusetts tavern owner William Manning called for a national system of local political clubs to regularly educate and organize "the Many" (farmers, artisans, shopkeepers) to prevent "the Few" (lawyers, ministers, and speculators) from subverting "free government." Judith Sargent Murray urged that all girls be educated to the same level as boys because equality of knowledge was just and necessary for American society. In addition to the "feminine" arts of music, poetry, history, and moral philosophy, generally seen as useful to raise properly republican sons, they should also learn geography, astronomy, philosophy, government, and other subjects regarded by others as unsuitable for the female sex.[12]

None of these grand plans materialized until the late 1830s. Schools continued to be managed and financed on a local basis, although there were occasional efforts by states to provide funds and by larger cities to unify their schools. In rural areas of the North, schools were generally organized locally; funded by property taxes, tuition, contributions, and occasional state aid; and administered by parents. There were also academies that drew scholars from many places regardless of class and incorporated new methods of instruction, including public competitions. In the South, schoolmasters charged tuition or worked as tutors to the children of wealthier planters. In northern cities, very young children attended schools run by women in their homes; middle- and upper-class boys went to "independent pay" schools; and the children of the poor might learn to read and write through their church's charity school or an apprenticeship. In the early nineteenth century, as the system of apprenticeship declined, charity schooling expanded into a wider system to educate the working class, evolving into public schools as a means to ensure social stability and alleviate the harmful influence of a home or neighborhood wracked by poverty and disorder. But in the rural South or "frontier" West, schools rarely if ever met, and parents purchased grammars and readers, mostly published in the Northeast, to educate their children at home. As a result, most Americans through the Civil War developed their social, political, and moral assumptions at least in part from schoolbooks.[13]

Initially most of the publications for children were long-standing favorites like *The New England Primer* (printed first in Boston around 1690), which taught the alphabet alongside truncated theological and moral lessons, such as "In Adam's fall, We sinned all" or "The idle Fool / Is whipt at School." One of the most persistent works, *The School of Good Manners*, published by Boston schoolmaster Eleazar Moody in 1715 (using an English translation of a French work), taught deference to one's "betters." The work was reprinted at least twenty-eight times in many places through 1818; although printers revised particulars, the overall message of understanding, accepting, and acknowledging one's place in the social and economic hierarchy remained strong. An edition published in Boston in 1790 opened with these rules: "1. Fear God and believe in Christ. 2. Honour the President of the United States, the Governour, and all other Rulers of the land. 3. Reverence thy parents. 4. Submit to thy superiors. 5. Despise not thy inferiors. 6. Be courteous with thy equals." Subsequent chapters featured rules for children's behavior at church, at home, at the table, and in public, including walking behind one's "parents, master, or any superior"; doffing your hat and bowing "to persons of worth, quality, or office"; and remaining bareheaded when "a superior speak to thee in the street." Twenty-five years later, a version published in Vermont "Americanized" the spelling and simplified a few rules—for example, no. 2 became "Honor the magistrates"—but delivered the same lesson.[14]

Also popular were many English works (often written for the children of gentry) republished in America with their conservative hierarchical lessons intact, although some printers added references to local places and religious concerns. One of the most famous, *The Friendly Instructor*, first published in England in 1741 and reprinted in various American cities, initially in 1769 and then nine times between 1782 and 1822, was subtitled *A Companion for Young Ladies and Young Gentlemen. The Friendly Instructor* gave social lessons in the form of dialogues between two children. In the chapter providing guidance on the proper "Carriage to Superiors and Inferiors," the "correct" young girl Emilia advises her friend Lemira that, although one should be polite to poor children because illness or death might cast any family into poverty, "tis best" to play with other wealthy children "because we are most likely to learn of them a Behaviour suitable to the Rank in which we are placed."[15]

Rank and privilege also formed the essential background of another popular imported children's book, *The Sister's Gift*. The main characters, Kitty and Billy Courtly, were the only children of Sir William Courtly. She was graceful, gentle, and witty; Billy on the other hand, though smart, was frequently cruel. After their father and mother died of scarlet fever, they were sent to separate boarding schools where Billy continued in his cruel habits and was finally shunned by the other boys. When sister and brother were finally reunited, she rebuked him for his nasty ways; hearing this criticism from his virtuous sister, Billy came to his senses and, weeping, repented of his evils as the story ended. The siblings were depicted as well off and, because of their noble family, went to live in the households of various gentlemen. The title was first published in England in 1769; three years later the title was being sold in Boston, and editions were published in various New England cities through at least 1811.[16]

Some of these works held seemingly egalitarian lessons. "Vanity Punished" in the serial *The Children's Friend* taught that an individual's social class did not define his moral and practical value. In 1790 William Bentley, Salem's prominent Congregational minister (with Jeffersonian political sympathies), noted that this was a "valuable" book in the schools. "Vanity" begins with Valentine, a gentleman's son, scorning Michael, the son of tenants on the family's estate, as a "little fool of a country boy." The father rebukes Valentine, telling his arrogant son that he can learn much from Michael and that "there is more honor and integrity in his father's cottage, than in many palaces." But the son is too proud to listen, until Michael helped him get through a night in the woods, after which Valentine vows, "Henceforth I will not despise those of a lower condition than myself."[17] But the additional lesson that the virtuous poor should not rise above their station was emphasized by two other stories in that collection. In "The Man Who Rose to Sudden Fortune," a middling cloth merchant won the lottery and became even wealthier by expanding his trade and investing well. Initially he continued being generous to the poor, but as his funds shrank, he came to focus on his money, stopped donating, lost touch with his trade, became mired in poverty, and was soon a beggar. At the end, the father telling the story to his son emphasized that its moral is that one should be happy with what one has and not wish to be wealthy. Similarly, the explicit lesson taught by "A Competence Is Best" was that gentlemen find it expensive and troubling to take care of their large estates, so those born with less should be grateful they aren't cursed with wealth and power.[18]

The virtues of social and economic hierarchy and the need to defer to authority were also important lessons taught by the most popular series of

English children's works, Hannah More's *Cheap Repository Tracts*. More was already a noted writer of religious verse in 1793 when, at the request of the bishop of London, she wrote *Village Politics*, a didactic pamphlet to counter the growing popularity of the French Revolution (with its ideas of "Liberty and Equality, and the Rights of Man") among artisans and laborers. Its commercial success and the need for cheap reading material for adults in her school led her to start publishing the *Tracts*; clergymen and social reformers purchased issues in bulk for charity schools and missionaries. Individual pieces and sets (sometimes with different titles, like *The Entertaining, Moral, and Religious Repository*) were quickly reprinted in New England, Philadelphia, and New York and continued to be published after More died in 1833.[19]

While the *Tracts* lacked the reactionary rhetoric of *Village Politics*, various pieces defended a stable conservative hierarchy, assuring the laboring poor that the wealthy and powerful suffered from their responsibilities, which included looking out for the best interests of the lower sorts. In "The Shepherd of Salisbury-Plain," when a visiting "very worthy, charitable Gentleman" asks whether his "laborious life is a happy one," the shepherd enthusiastically responds, "I do, Sir, and more so especially as it exposes a man to fewer sins." He then praises how "poverty is a great sharpener of the wits" and praises his industrious family for working and scrimping in the most virtuous fashion. In "The History of Diligent Dick," day laborer Richard Rogers rescues a gentleman who had fallen off his horse and nearly died in the snow and then refuses a proffered award, saying he'd do the same for anyone and had no desire for wealth "since I have seen how little comfort they often enjoy who possess it." That gentlemen turns out to be the uncle who had cheated Richard out of a fortune promised by his grandfather, who since suffered various evils because of his sinful action. More's works were published as collections and (as in England) individually; "Shepherd" was particularly popular, with eleven different American editions published between 1806 and 1818.[20]

These English stories seem like inappropriate literature for the children of a nation that had just fought a long war for independence and a republican (even democratic) form of government. All of them emphasized the didactic lesson that people should be happy with their fate and status in life and that, although all men share some characteristics and concerns, training and social status as well as ability and aptitude created inequalities in power including wealth that should be embraced, not challenged. They also showed the reader that inequalities formed the very structure of social relations and thus the warp and woof of individual happiness. On the other hand, these stories did highlight values that Americans considered fundamentally republican and necessary for their children and the future of the nation. As already noted, Locke and other Enlightenment writers on child-rearing emphasized the importance of young children learning obedience, discipline, and social obligations. The stories also stressed that, regardless of wealth or social status, people should be valued equally with regards to their virtue, intelligence, and actions. Several also highlighted how individuals could rise or fall in wealth, status, and power, and that such a fate (or luck) did not necessarily degrade *or* enhance their character or abilities.

For Americans today perhaps the most jarring aspect of these stories was the important role played by *gentlemen*. Yet many at the turn of the century embraced the honorific as appropriate for their republic. Before the Revolution, in England and its American colonies, a "gentleman" lacked either a title (nobility) or enough land to live off the rent (gentry) but held a profession (like merchant or banker) and enough wealth so he did not need to work with his hands. It was a designation of wealth, culture, refined behavior, and broad influence, but with little inherent legal power. During the Revolution, democratic passions included hostility to elite titles, including "gentleman," and their use declined notably. But with the creation of a stronger national government in 1790, "gentleman" came back into favor, particularly among the Federalists, who sought to forge an elite class that they saw as necessary to gain deference and thereby stabilize the new republic. They did see this American elite as quite different from that in England or Europe: John Adams wrote that "gentlemen" did not mean those who were rich, "high-born," or the sons of the powerful; instead, it was "all those who have received a liberal education, an ordinary degree of erudition in liberal arts and sciences." This was a republican "natural aristocracy" that Adams, Thomas Jefferson, and other Founding Fathers hoped to maintain through the widespread education of America's best and brightest men. We should not be surprised that they sought stories for their children that featured gentlemen. However, the reality was, particularly as the new country's economy became more complex, that few poor (and "low-born") children would be able to join that natural aristocracy.[21]

Many Americans were also gratified by the explicit defense of organized religion in some of these English works. That is perhaps most notable in Hannah More's "The History of Mr. Fantom, the New Fashioned Philosopher, and His Man William," aimed at Thomas Paine's controversial *The Age of Reason* (1792). Fantom, a London shopkeeper, "got hold of a famous little book written by the NEW PHILOSOPHER, whose pestilent doctrines have gone about seeking whom they may destroy," and he enthusiastically repeated its attacks on the "*narrowness*, and *ignorance*, and *bigotry*, and *prejudice*" of organized religion, thinking he was "set free from the chains of slavery and superstition." But Fantom repented after his butler William, who took those "lessons" seriously, stopped going to church, stole, murdered, and was tried and hung. American conservatives were concerned that the Paine's book would foster a popular religious skepticism undermining the country's moral foundations, social order, and legal protection of property. The Reverend Gideon Hawley groused to Jeremy Belknap, one of the most influential ministers in New England, that *The Age of Reason* "is so very agreeable to common readers that it will have a most pernicious effect in a country like ours." Elhanan Winchester in *Plain Political Catechism* (1796) told American schoolchildren that recent efforts "to introduce deism, infidelity, and atheism into this happy country tend . . . not only to destroy religion and true morality, but also to overthrow all government" and "to destroy the liberties of these states." In fact, Americans became more devout at the turn of the century, and Paine became *persona non grata* in large part because of that book.[22]

Even as Americans reprinted, bought, and read books from England, they sought their own explicitly republican voice. The first wave of domestic literature consisted of schoolbooks that featured an aggressive pride in the moral and political superiority of the United States (with close links between those two elements), in part because of its widespread property ownership and relative social equality, and promised that studying the right incidents and persons from their country's history would improve the student and the nation. Winchester's *Plain Political Catechism* told its young readers why the country's "sons of freedom" were able to win the war: "They had generally property, principle, or public virtue, and knowledge." Noah Webster intended the three volumes of *A Grammatical Institute of the English Language* "to promote the honour and prosperity of the confederated republics of America" and declared at the start, "This country must in some future time, be distinguished by the superiority of her literary improvements, as she is already by the liberality of her civil and ecclesiastical constitutions." Volume 3 in the set, *An American Selection of Lessons in Reading and Speaking*, included snippets from Shakespeare, classical works, and European history, but overwhelmingly featured short biographies and sketches from the country's history along with extensive excerpts from speeches commemorating the Boston Massacre and the Fourth of July.[23]

In 1783 Yale divinity student Jedidiah Morse established a school for young women in New Haven, and one year later published *Geography Made Easy*, featuring descriptions of each state's geography, produce, history, economy, government, population, and character. The book implicitly praised the North by harshly condemning Virginia as a place where "you no longer find that simplicity and uniformity of manners . . . that is peculiar to that people, where property is equally distributed, and a happy mediocrity is uniformly preserved." More generally, Morse noted that the South had only rich and the poor with no middling class (in part because it relied for labor on Africans kidnapped into slavery) and that among the former "pride and ostentation" prevailed. Elijah Parish, Morse's coauthor on another work (*A Compendious History of New England for schools and private families*), was more explicit in *A Compendious System of Universal Geography* (1807). In New England, he noted, "Estates are equally divided among the children of the family; hence a happy equality of circumstances prevails. If a man wishes to be richer than his brethren, he must be more industrious, more economical, more enterprising."[24]

Given New England's tradition of public schooling, it is not surprising that the authors of these early textbooks were natives of that region who praised its history and norms. They shared similar family backgrounds, education, and careers: Morse and Webster were graduates of Yale, the most conservative of the New England colleges, and Morse, Parish, and Winchester were Calvinist ministers. All saw the need for close connections between churches and other institutions and emphasized the organic intimate relationships between "proper" religion and morality, government, and human achievements or failures. All were part of an informal alliance of conservative ministers, lawyers, and merchants in Connecticut and Massachusetts, who in the 1790s developed close connections to the Federalist Party as it supported state funding for churches and schools, encouraged policies to build a strong socioeconomic hierarchy, and fought against the perceived radical threats of atheism and "levellism." Morse highlighted those connections in his 1799 national fast sermon, telling his Charlestown parishioners "the foundations which support the interests of Christianity, are also necessary to support a free and equal government like our own."[25]

While these writers believed in the need for hierarchical social relations, the long-standing "equality of circumstances" described by Parish in the region (and America generally) meant that the norms of social behavior were quite different from those in Europe, particularly with regard to the informal rules that governed how the "lower sort" acted toward those with status, money, and power. European visitors to America before and after the Revolution, like Johann Schoepf, often remarked on the refusal of ordinary inhabitants to doff their hats or bow to those "whose only claim is that of descent and birth." American writers and leaders did consider gentility essential for maintaining a virtuous republic and sought to "improve" their people's notoriously "rough" manners. In that spirit, Webster in *American Selection of Lessons* offered more egalitarian "Rules for Behavior" to replace aristocratic European standards. "Good breeding does not consist in low bows and formal ceremony," he advised children, "but in an easy, civil, and respectful behavior. . . . In mixed companies every person who is admitted, is supposed to be on a footing of equality with the rest." The only salute to social hierarchy was to age: "Be not forward in leading the conversation—this belongs to the oldest person in company."[26]

Yet while Webster's work was certainly popular, many more books were published that called on young Americans to honor the wealthy and obey the powerful. For example, Moody's *School of Good Manners*, which advised children to "Submit to thy superiors" and to doff their hat and bow to governors, legislators, magistrates, and ministers, was printed as late as 1815. *The Economy of Human Life*, an older English work published in the United States beginning in 1801, told young readers, "The man to whom God has given riches, and blessed with a mind to employ them aright, is peculiarly favoured and highly distinguished"; on the other hand, those in "the state of servitude" gained that "appointment" from God with the "advantages" of escaping "the cares and solicitudes of life." Similarly, Lindley Murray's *English Reader*, first published in England and New York in 1799 and used as the main reader in Boston schools and the Northeast generally until the 1830s, repeated in various forms the aphorism that the rich man had worries that the poor escaped. Murray, an American Quaker who had moved to England after the Revolution, also hammered home the lesson that "the order of society requires a distinction of ranks" based on property and social standing. Similarly, while Parish celebrated the "equality of circumstances" in New England and insisted that all were treated equally by the law, "fortune and the nature of professions form different classes. Merchants, lawyers, physicians, and clergymen form the first class; farmers and artisans the second; workmen, *who let themselves by the day or month*, the third." These three classes, he concluded, kept to their own kind at public events.[27]

After 1800, particularly in the wake of the War of 1812, the nation's economy shifted toward more manufacturing; in the North particularly, towns and cities mushroomed in population, size, and complexity. The transportation and manufacturing facilities that shaped and were fostered by the new conditions confronted Revolutionary-era concerns about preventing excessive wealth and poverty. One result was that those who sought charters from the state legislatures faced strong opposition. Another was the increasing importance of transient wage labor and declining opportunities for journeymen. New class conflicts emerged: factory developers faced resistance to their dams that killed fish that generations of farmers had eaten during spring planting; workers grew increasingly aware that mass production was rapidly foreclosing future opportunities to become independent artisans; and owners of shops and factories wanted to set hours, wages, and prices as they felt proper without the interference of laborers or traditional public norms. At the same time, Americans of all classes enjoyed the increasing production, wider distribution, and (especially) decreasing prices of books, newspapers, and other consumer goods.[28]

Schools and schoolbooks were deeply imbedded in these developments. The new middle-class occupations required strong skills in literacy and math; manufacturing and commercial companies demanded that their employees respect the chain of authority in the workplace, practice self-discipline, and obey the new system of working according to the clock instead of the job or the season. At the same time, traditional property limits on voting were dropped from most state constitutions, and laborers and journeymen in northern cities organized workingmen's parties to press for political, social, and economic democracy. The men concerned about the apparent chaos, particularly northern ministers, lawyers, and merchants involved in the emerging Whig Party, pushed for publicly funded schools that would teach important skills and inculcate patriotism, responsible character, and respect for authority. Widespread public schools were also championed by workingmen and Jacksonian Democrats, who felt that *all* children should get a good education in order to manage in the rapidly changing economy and become effective participants in the republic, though they generally distinguished between grammar school (through age fourteen) and high school, believing that the latter's liberal arts focus was unnecessary, beyond the reach of most children, and would only increase inequality.[29]

In 1837 Massachusetts became the first state to establish a board of education, signaling that the education of all children in the commonwealth was a public priority; its superintendent, Horace Mann, used his limited powers to educate, persuade, and organize teachers, local school committees, and school advocates in other states. By the end of the 1840s, most of the New England states required towns to establish school boards and had appointed state-level superintendents following Mann's example. The reformers driving this movement were, like all Americans, aware of the problems and controversies of rising poverty and class inequalities. In its 1847 report, the school committee of Coventry, Rhode Island, noted that, while "the few" had deprived "the many" of various "inalienable rights," the "glorious common school system" promised "to restore the rights of the oppressed" and to "place the children of the poor on an equality . . . with the children of the rich." But it was not yet clear, its members thought, whether "the poorer classes" would choose to ride "the rising wave, that will elevate them and their children to positions of influence in society, by the attainment of knowledge, which is power." The vision of broader public education, shared by Democrats and Whigs alike, was about accommodation and adaptation, not revolution or opposition.[30]

The explosive growth of public schools and state-level coordination of curriculum fueled a massive increase in the publication of educational books for children. After 1820, as Washington Irving and James Fenimore Cooper began to fulfill the desire for a uniquely American literature, writers like John Pierpont, Samuel Goodrich, and Lydia Sigourney sought to fulfill the mushrooming market for republican educational material. In addition to distribution within the North, where public school systems were established before 1850, large numbers of the new publications were shipped (via the many canals and railroads built between 1825 and 1850) to the frontier West and rural South for farmers to buy to educate their children at home.[31] These books were in many ways different from those used since the 1780s. Many of the readers designed to teach literacy and speech had four versions for the different levels of public schools: primary (generally ages four to seven), intermediate (ages six to ten), grammar (ages nine to fourteen), and high schools. Readers included selections on natural science, American and classical history, and colorful scenes from other countries, along with stories emphasizing the virtues of temperance, thrift, education, and the traditional values of a good reputation, formal behavior, and respect for hierarchy.

The genesis of this pattern can be seen in Abner Alden's third *Reader*, Daniel Adams's *The Understanding Reader*, and Titus Strong's *Common Reader*, all published for schools and children generally in various editions between 1802 and the 1820s and circulated widely in the Northeast. Alden and Strong focused on morality, proper behavior, and God and Creation, whereas Adams featured extended accounts of natural history, such as the chapter on "Reindeer" with descriptions of Laplander society and culture, some biblical stories (including the Book of Esther), and a few inspiring anecdotes about Benjamin Franklin. All three urged students to work hard, avoid bad companions, and not waste time. They also gently advised not to envy the rich or otherwise to challenge class boundaries. For example, Alden noted that "the poor man, who envies not the rich, and cheerfully spares something for him that is poorer, is, in the realms of humanity, a king of kings," and Strong told students to "Respect your superiours . . . and be civil to your inferiours." The only passages that pointed toward gaining wealth appeared in Alden's and Adams's assurance that hard work and long hours would result in a good livelihood. None hinted at the democratic message that wealth and power could be achieved by any man.[32]

While Alden's books were adopted by Boston and some rural Massachusetts schools in the 1810s, Murray's *Reader* remained the most popular schoolbook in America for two more decades. Thus, even during the Age of Jackson students throughout the country were taught (by repeating aloud) the following lesson: "Society, when formed, requires distinctions of property . . . [and] subordination of ranks . . . in order to advance the general good." William Herndon later remembered that his law partner Abraham Lincoln had told him that "Murray's English Reader was the best schoolbook ever put into the hands of an American youth." Perhaps Lincoln when young and poor gained solace from the selection which told readers that, although "the poor man" lacks "some of the conveniences and pleasures of the rich," he is fortunate to escape having to worry about "great affairs to manage, intricate plans to pursue, and many enemies, perhaps, to encounter in the pursuit"; he also benefits from a more tranquil domestic life, more satisfying "plain" food, sound sleep, and (because of his hard work) firmer health.[33]

The clear shift toward American themes and topics started with John Pierpont's *American First Class Book* (1823), intended for "*the Highest Class in Publick and Private Schools,*" and *The National Reader* (1827), designed (as the subtitle trumpeted) to replace Murray's *Reader* in American schools. Pierpont worked as a tutor and lawyer before becoming minister of Boston's prominent Hollis Street Church, and his selections reflected his Unitarian preference for rational religion, New England history and culture, and social reforms. The short chapters applauded Indian oratory and culture, described important events in American history, highlighted transcendent landscapes, and, when delving into morality and religion, emphasized reason and science. Pierpont avoided the heavy-handed advice on belief, virtue, and manners so prominent in previous readers, avoided praising social hierarchy, and each work contained just one reference to class. *The American First Class Book*, in "The Contrast: or Peace and War," listed among the virtues of PEACE: "The rich, softened by prosperity, pity the poor; the poor, disciplined into order, respect the rich." *The National Reader* included an essay that insisted that educating the poor would *not* lead them to "forget their station and their duty." Both books were quickly adopted by Boston's school committee—*American First Class* in 1823 and *National Reader* in 1829—and both sold widely and as late as 1848 were still standard in many grammar schools including those in Providence, Rhode Island.[34]

During the 1830s, a new wave of schoolbooks added stories designed to inculcate respect for the wealthy and powerful, while depicting that status as open to all in democratic America. That narrative almost certainly reflected growing middle-class and elite concerns about the increased violence in many northern cities, labor unrest and the Workingmen's Movement, and the rise of the Democratic Party. Noah Webster, bridging the gap from Federalists to Whigs, led the way with one of his last books, *Instructive and Entertaining Lessons for Youth* (1835). Webster insisted that any American boy could become wealthy through hard work, ambition, and moral virtue—a vision later made famous by Horatio Alger's stories. As a result, "the poor have no right to complain, if they do not succeed in business"; poverty resulted from "want of industry, or judgment in the management of their affairs, or for want of prudence and economy." Therefore, ambition and accumulated wealth had to be respected and protected, and the poor "have no more right to invade the property of the rich, than the rich have to invade the rights of the poor."[35]

Webster's *Lessons* represented a republican version of the assumption, common in earlier schoolbooks, that a stable society was stratified along economic lines and reflected in dress, manners, and responsibilities. That concept clearly gained new authority as many Americans became alarmed at the growing calls among labor activists for limits on individual wealth and corporate power. The elderly author and educator also added a uniquely American twist to the older conservatism: "The greatest hereditary estates in this country are usually dissipated by the second or third generation." During the Revolution, Jefferson, Madison, and other "Founding Fathers" had promoted partible inheritance as the optimum solution to the threat of property and power accumulating over the generations and creating an aristocracy in the United States. But those reformers viewed the matter entirely in political terms, not as a matter of generational moral decline. Webster was apparently the first to introduce the notion into children's literature, along with the accompanying vision of social and economic democracy: "The sons and grandsons of the richest men, are often hewers of wood and drawers of water to the sons and grandsons of their father's and grandfather's servants."[36]

The tenor of the time was similarly reflected in Rufus Claggett's *The American Expositor, or Intellectual Definer* (1836) designed to teach complex words to beginning readers. The lawyer and high school principal in Providence, Rhode Island, disliked the standard practice of having students memorize definitions, so wrote his book "to render the study of words in our language subservient to the general discipline of the mind." The result was a series of sentences, each with an italicized word to learn along with its didactic moral lesson. Claggett placed a heavy emphasis on religion, unlike Webster or Pierpont; many sentences were selections from the Bible or statements such as "True Christianity depends on fact. Religion is not a *theory*, but fact" and "The skeptical system subverts the whole foundation of morals." But he echoed (in simpler form) Webster's defense of wealth, for example, noting that students should "Be not *envious* of the prosperity of others," and that "Few need be poor, if they would practice *economy*." Claggett also added an explicitly hostile view of the egalitarian movements bubbling in Jacksonian America, having students repeat lessons such as "I would *premise* that I am no friend to the kind of liberty which consists in leveling all distinctions in society" and "Demagogues *ingratiate* themselves with the people by a pretended attachment to liberty." These perceptions were widespread among educators and other elites, and *The American Expositor* was reprinted many times in New York and Boston through the mid-1840s.[37]

Similar ideas without Clagget's hostility appeared in Lydia Sigourney's *The Boy's Reading Book* (1839). Sigourney was one of the most influential women in antebellum America, perhaps the first to make a living by writing, and her schoolbook continued to be printed into the mid-1840s for wide distribution by the American Common School Depository in New York. Her chapter on the "Privileges of the Poor" echoed Murray's view that the poor benefited morally and intellectually from the need to practice "industry" and "exertion." Like other New England intellectuals at the time, Sigourney was skeptical of the American passion to become rich: she advised students to seek instead "virtue and learning" and avoid the "reverence to the rich" that would (as Jefferson and others had believed) ultimately corrupt our republican government. At the same time, she agreed with Webster's view of the democratic nature of wealth, quoting Massachusetts governor Edward Everett on how the path to wealth through "industry and frugality" was "open to all" and how our laws and customs caused "the wheel of fortune" to turn constantly so "the poor in one generation, furnish the rich of the next." Therefore, Everett had noted, not only should the rich treat the poor with respect, since their grandfathers shared that condition, but "the poor man who nourishes feelings of unkindness and bitterness against wealth, makes war with the prospects of his children, and the order of things in which he lives." By the end of the 1830s these ideas had become gospel among many Americans; all appeared, for example, in Daniel Adams's *The Monitorial Reader,* published at least five times in two New Hampshire towns between 1839 and 1845.[38]

Not all children's books during this period moralized about class. Samuel Goodrich, perhaps the best-selling antebellum children's author, wrote and published an extraordinarily popular series narrated by a fictional old man, Peter Parley, that ignored the topic altogether. His first book, *The Tales of Peter Parley,* published initially in 1827 and still occasionally reprinted, opened with a colorful narrative of the indigenous and colonial cultures in South America, before turning to Columbus, skipping to the Seven Years' War, and then describing the American Revolution solely as a movement for independence from England. The last section of the book described the structure of federal and state governments. A decade later, Goodrich published a slightly different version, *Peter Parley's Common School History,* adding the popular Pocahontas story, which was revised at least once and reprinted nearly every year until the Civil War. Neither book mentioned slavery, social structure, wealth, or voting eligibility; Goodrich wrote them in a highly visual, concrete fashion with little moral commentary other than condemning how we treated the Indians and celebrating our war for independence.[39]

Peter Parley's cool neutrality was striking considering that Goodrich was inspired by Hannah More's *Moral Repository,* even seeking her out during his first visit to England in 1824, and that his autobiography frequently expressed hostility to "demagogism and democracy" and the "Destructives" who "make war on property, and those who possess it." True, he wrote that autobiography (with its nostalgia for New England's "old federalism") three decades after the first Peter Parley story. But Goodrich continued for years to be relatively muted on issues of class, and his elitism was perhaps most manifest in his dislike of the contemporary American passion for becoming rich regardless of the means. For example, his *Fireside Education* (1838) emphasized "every individual" should be educated "to reason wisely upon the social, political, moral and religious questions which are agitated in the community," and its only comment on property was to advise that young men "be warned against that greedy appetite for wealth" which caused so many Americans to "engage in flattering speculations."[40]

Only in *The Fourth Reader, For the Use of Schools* (1839), did Goodrich offer (in addition to the standard chapters on science, nature, and history) his conservative vision of America. In the fable of "The Discontented Mole," he told students that it was "folly" to envy the wealthy, that instead "we should endeavor to fulfill the duties of that situation in which we are placed." His essay on "The Duty of Industry" lamented "how unjust that poisonous envy, with which the laborer sometimes regards the other classes of society," and echoed Murray's *English Reader* in assuring children (and their parents) that "those who occupy what are often called, often falsely, the highest stations in life, pay dearly for their giddy elevation. The rich have sorrows, which the poor know not." On the other hand, in "Wealth and Fashion," eighteen-year-old Caroline appears arrogant when she declared American republican equality "odious," after the new chambermaid spoke with insufficient respect, and argues that "wealth constitutes our nobility." Her bemused older brother Horace retorted that the best government had "neither extreme of high or low," and that "talent, health, and unwavering principle" were better than money. In the end, his way led to prosperity and hers to "mortification." Ultimately Goodrich's message was that one should neither envy nor emulate the wealthy and powerful but work hard and keep one's nose clean.[41]

While Goodrich's works sold well, the schoolbook with the greatest long-term impact on American culture was clearly William McGuffey's *Eclectic Readers*, which was part of a series first published in 1836. McGuffey participated in the rapid colonization and transformation of the Ohio Valley during the early Republic: he was born, raised, attended college, and taught and ran a college in that region as he worked on the *Readers*, which was eventually purchased by one of the largest publishers in Cincinnati. That origin and distribution network helped the *Eclectic Readers* quickly become the dominant primer west of the Appalachians, and the series remained a mainstay in American education circles into the late twentieth century. Many prominent Americans noted the significant role that the *Readers* played in their education, including Henry Ford and Robert LaFollette.[42]

The *Second Reader*, probably the most widely read McGuffey, included short chapters about good animals, bad and reformed children, diligent scholars, whaling, the peacock, gypsies, Washington cutting down the cherry tree, and various Bible stories including Jonah. One chapter, "The Good Boy whose Parents are Poor," was clearly meant to teach children to respect the wealthy and powerful. The good boy sought every scrap of education his parents could afford and then hurried home to care for siblings and the garden. But when he saw other children riding on horses or in coaches, or wearing fine clothes, he neither envied them nor wanted to be like them; after all, God had determined who was to be rich and who poor, and "the rich have many troubles which we know nothing of, and that the poor, if they are but good, may be very happy." In this fashion American children continued learning conservative lessons about social hierarchy and wealth, lessons first featured in the schoolbooks written by Hannah More and Lindsey Murray for English children.[43]

The American tradition of structured education as the best route to social stability and individual improvement emerged after the Revolution. Education promised to quiet the leveling ideas encouraged by the French Revolution, tame the desire of Americans for speculation and quick riches, and facilitate a natural aristocracy open to talent and virtue instead of a corrupting one limited to the very wealthy. A properly educated citizenry would choose the most virtuous leaders, follow the steadiest course, and guard the fragile nation's Revolutionary inheritance. During the 1820s and 1830s, the need for such schooling seemed to increase as northern cities mushroomed, mob violence increased, the tide of Irish Catholic immigration grew, and frustrated workingmen organized political parties and pushed for measures to limit wealth and power.

Schoolbooks played a critical role in American education; they became the sole curriculum for scattered farm households, aided overworked masters of rural schools, and served as the foundations for the publicly funded and organized schools that emerged in the Northeast. Schoolbooks also became a critical element in the effort to inculcate in future generations a conservative and nationalist republican worldview. Through the 1820s, most of these works came from England, written for the children of gentry or potentially rebellious laborers, and republished in America with their conservative hierarchical lessons intact. These stories reinforced the long-standing tradition that all power was connected while teaching the blessings of hierarchy: that birth, training, ability, and aptitude created inequalities in power and wealth that should be *embraced*, and that all people should be happy with their fate and status.

The Americans who began to write schoolbooks, a few in the 1780s and many more in the 1830s, were overwhelmingly Federalists and Whigs anxious to smother radical ideas of economic equality and forestall the social and political chaos of a fully democratic United States. They emphasized practical science, nature, and history more than the earlier English books but presented a similarly conservative vision. The readers in particular depicted the United States as a land of freedom primarily because there was no titled aristocracy and everyone was equal before the law; that quick riches were corrupting but hard-earned wealth (achievable regardless of class) was a sign of respectable virtue; and that the poor were lucky not to have the responsibilities and cares of the wealthy. These schoolbooks were meant to forestall class conflict, teach children to accept America's "natural" hierarchy, and ensure that future generations would maintain the republican values of self-discipline and social obligations. Through such lessons, the country would thread the difficult channel between the Scylla of aristocratic wealth and authority and the Charybdis of anarchy and disdain for property. To an amazing extent, these goals were realized.

CHAPTER SIX

Clashes over America's Political Economy

In the summer of 1832, after striking ship carpenters in Boston were forced to return to work without concessions, Seth Luther, a thirty-seven-year old "practical mechanic," traveled through New England sounding the alarm that "our rights are not only *endangered*, but some of them already wrested from us, by the powerful and inhuman grasp of monopolized wealth." This "spirit of monopoly . . . produced and sustained by *Avarice*" was responsible for "sapping and mining the VERY FOUNDATIONS of our free institutions." Such dire warnings had not been unusual during the early Republic and were often directed at men like Robert Morris who were suspected of using their public power for private gain and venal purposes. But Luther and his audience had different concerns about a very different America. His book cataloged the horrid conditions and severe poverty in Britain's manufacturing districts, particularly for child laborers, before turning to show America's "HIGHER ORDERS" had the same plan. New England's mills had become cruel jails for thousands of children—abusing them, denying them schooling, and driving them for longer hours than the dreaded English factories—and the owners had become "aristocrats" who "talk about mercy to mechanics and laborers." Six months later, Luther focused even more on class conflict in America, between laborers and mechanics who "produce all the real wealth" and the "monied aristocracy" who accumulated the riches and oppressed the poor. This worsening plague was entirely due to *avarice*, for which men sacrifice everything "on the bloody altar of Mammon."[1]

During the first few decades of the nineteenth century, particularly with the Panic of 1819, Americans began to reconsider the current and future condition of their country's economy, society, and polity. Political economics, the forerunner of the field of economics, had developed during the Enlightenment and involved studying the relationships between a nation's polity, production, and consumption; the sources and effects of wealth and poverty were particular concerns. At the turn of the century, Americans of all occupations and classes avidly read and argued about their nation's political economy; that was particularly true of artisans, also known as mechanics, who formed the fulcrum point of the country's rapidly shifting economy. As manufacturing grew in the North, feeding on the developing cotton agriculture in the South, Americans could no longer ignore the growing gap between rich and poor and were forced to bitterly accept the reality that their country was developing a strong class structure with a few extremely wealthy elites at one end and a huge cluster of unskilled wage laborers at the other. The adult literature about the country's political economy was thus far more realistic than the children's literature published during the same period.

Americans like Luther who produced and consumed this literature increasingly saw the economy instead of government as the main source of inequality and oppression and advocated various ways to overcome the rising tide of economic inequality that they viewed as an existential danger to the republic. Some embraced collective enterprise as the best way to make real the tradition of economic equality, whereas others sought political and legal reforms to improve the lives of laborers. But there were also many Americans, particularly merchants, entrepreneurs, and rural adolescents, who accepted or even embraced mass production and unregulated capitalism; they largely abandoned the classical fears of luxury and greed and became far more willing to leave property ownership and market behavior to the conscience of individuals. They also tended to embrace a dark vision of the poor as a morally dangerous group, in a noticeable shift away from the more optimistic egalitarian ideals that had marked the American republic in the wake of its Revolution. Strikingly, both sides of this debate made increasingly secular arguments, mirroring the widening split between church and state. As few called for Christian redistribution of property, the idea of the Great Jubilee disappeared; indeed, most appeals to religious morality did so to justify poverty.[2]

The first political economists were French physiocrats such as Jacques Turgot, who argued that a nation's wealth was derived primarily from agriculture and that self-interest was a necessary element in making the various segments of a nation's economy operate properly. They were followed by the leading figures in the Scottish Enlightenment, who connected the study of political economy to the larger field of moral philosophy. David Hume's *Essays Moral,*

Political, and Literary (1758) was largely about the interplay between Britain's state and economy, and Adam Smith wrote *The Theory of Moral Sentiments* (1759) and then *An Inquiry into the Nature and Causes of the Wealth of Nations* (1776). The last is probably most famous for describing the "invisible hand" of the marketplace, but it also extended John Locke's argument about work and property rights (that "Labour . . . Puts the greatest part of Value upon Land") to *all* of the wealth generated by a nation, manufacturing as well as agriculture. This *labor theory of value* quickly became gospel in political economics, particularly in the United States where *The Wealth of Nations* became popular in the mid-1780s. Smith also noted that the industrial revolution created mind-numbing labor for poor workers even as it improved the lives of the wealthy, and he proposed giving laboring-class children a "practical education" at public expense.[3]

Not surprisingly, the leaders of the new United States considered these issues, as they commonly used the Scottish Enlightenment scale of social development to measure the future viability of republicanism in their new country. Thomas Jefferson, for example, sought to protect the primacy of agriculture because he believed that was necessary for republican government, whereas Alexander Hamilton saw commerce and manufacturing as the country's necessary future. Because these visions involved very different national policies and priorities, a political and ideological divide rapidly formed between Jeffersonians and Federalists. Conflicts focused on Hamilton's Bank of the United States and Society for Establishing Useful Manufactures as well as efforts by state legislatures to charter corporations with unique privileges and public powers. While most opponents focused on the threat that "monopoly privilege" posed to republican virtue and equal opportunity, some called for egalitarian taxation and a jubilee redistribution of property, and a few even sought "a thorough Revolution" against elite "enemies of the people."[4]

At the same time, Americans agreed that their country was distinguished by the highest level of socioeconomic equality in the world, with high levels of property ownership and low levels of poverty. They also agreed on a few measures to maintain economic equality, particularly the expansion of primary education and the end of entail and primogeniture in order to prevent the accumulation of land and power (measures also urged by Smith and other English political economists). Most saw economic inequality as a threat to the moral and political order of the United States but believed that future opportunities—including land taken from Native Americans—along with economic growth and the right political framework would prevent the worst outcomes and would also relieve social strains. The calls to regulate property were relatively weak and marginalized as most Americans embraced the liberal assumption that the individual's right to manage possessions without interference was a natural law. These rights were limited to white men and excluded women (common-law rules of *femme covert* prevented women from owning property) and the growing number of free African Americans in the North, who faced increasing prejudice. True, conflicts over national economic policies as well as international politics played a significant role in the 1800 election, but Jefferson and his Republicans won in large part because they trumpeted a vision of classlessness that attracted white men from all backgrounds.[5]

Also at the turn of the century, English political economists began to analyze their country's emerging industrial and commercial revolution. The most prominent voices thought it inevitable and necessary that poor laborers would suffer and the wealthy become richer. Thomas Malthus wrote *An Essay on the Principle of Population* (1798) to refute William Godwin's *Essay Concerning Political Justice* (1793), which envisioned the "perfectibility of society" and equality of property; Malthus argued to the contrary that poverty was inevitable because human population multiplied geometrically while food production could rise only arithmetically. David Ricardo's *On the Principles of Political Economy and Taxation* (1817) introduced the idea that rent (payment for using a scarce or monopolized productive resource) would increase as the price of food increased along with population, thereby enriching landlords and the nation even as wages shrank to a barely subsistence level. These men were eager to advocate for national policies that seemed to best meet the challenges they posed in their studies. In 1821 Malthus and Ricardo along with a handful of others helped create the Political Economy Club in London, partly to provide a place to discuss their ideas, partly to lobby for laws including measures to protect private ownership of land and capital, to make contracts sacred, and to end financial assistance to the poor because (they thought) need and misery served a necessary social and economic function. Even before their books were republished in the United States—Malthus in 1809 (in Washington) and Ricardo in 1819 (in New York)—their ideas circulated widely and were immediately influential among Americans.[6]

One of the more intriguing sources of their ideas on both sides of the Atlantic was a book supposedly for children, *Conversations on Political Economy*, published in London in 1816. The writer, Jane Marcet, daughter of a wealthy London banker and wife of a Swiss-born physician, hoped to popularize Smith, Malthus, and Ricardo and thereby correct the "uninformed benevolence" of young people. The *Conversations* took place between a young girl, Caroline, and her teacher, Mrs. B.—a didactic formula common at the time. Caroline initially challenges but ultimately embraces the "scientific" tenets laid out by Mrs. B: that people were poor because they were indolent, that great wealth inevitably created more employment, that destroying weaving machines would create poverty rather than jobs, and that calling for wages to be set by law so that the poor could afford bread was irrational and destructive. This pedestrian and overly long book proved popular in the United States: it was printed in Philadelphia just one year after its London debut and was republished in New York in 1820 and Boston in 1828.[7]

Americans drew heavily on this literature and added distinctive elements as they sought to understand and to shape their country's rapidly changing economy. The most significant concept they adopted was, not surprisingly, the labor theory of value. The English colonists had embraced the idea that agriculture provided a right to land and the social independence necessary to participate in politics, and the widespread ownership of land before the Revolution shaped their distinctive level of economic equality. Farming continued to dominate the US economy as the United States expanded west; it included family-based subsistence in the backcountry and isolated valleys; grain, livestock, and fruit production for booming urban markets; and export crops including wheat and (increasingly) cotton. The desire of farmers for more land and the hopes of laborers and immigrants to join their ranks would for the rest of the century shape federal land policies. Those developments pushed the United States in the opposite direction from that predicted by Malthus and Ricardo; indeed, as noted by Loammi Baldwin in 1809, the availability of more fertile land west of the Ohio along with the increasing prices obtained overseas for wheat and cotton stabilized farmland prices in the East and (he thought) would prevent more dependence on wage labor.[8]

The labor theory of value was perhaps even more important for the master and journeymen mechanics, who at the turn of the century embraced the ideology of artisan republicanism. By the mid-1790s, as the percentage of landowning farmers declined and the number of artisans increased, they gained support for the argument that labor and trades held the same republican virtue as farming. Prominent men like Paul Revere established mechanic societies that organized, regulated, and educated their members about politics and economics, linking the artisan class to debates over the health and welfare of the American republican. Such efforts facilitated and reflected the emergence of a clear artisan interest and their influence in politics and policy; for example, in 1794 a group of master artisans formed the Democratic Society of New York to organize journeymen and laborers with the goal of reforming city, state, and national politics in line with Thomas Paine's democratic vision in *The Rights of Man*. In 1796 a guest lecturer told the Providence Association of Mechanics and Manufactures that, although agriculture had "precedence" because it was "the oldest and most productive Employment," mechanics were a close second and part of the class "who in the Hour of Danger" would serve as the "Champions and Defenders" of their nation. When William Duane, publisher of the *Philadelphia Aurora*, assembled his collection of anti-Federalist pieces titled *Politics for American Farmers*, it was in the "Politics for Mechanics" section that he quoted Adam Smith as to how a nation's labor was the source of "all the necessities and conveniences of life."[9]

The artisans' embrace of republican labor led many to join with western farmers and southern plantation owners in opposing the Bank of the United States and other special charters that seemed designed to increase the wealth and power of merchants and bankers. One of the prominent toasts at the 1795 Fourth of July celebration of New York's Juvenile Republican Society acclaimed, "Less respect to the consuming speculator, who wallows in luxury, than to the productive mechanic, who struggles with indigence." By 1800, as the region's economy shifted toward manufacturing as well as commerce, the fear of excessive capital accumulation became more apparent. That year Tristam Burges warned the Providence Association of Mechanics and Manufacturers about the dangers of "dependency" posed by the "birth of aristocracies" in the country, fed by the gathering of "the wealth of a nation into the hands of a few." That monster grew at the end of the Revolution, when a relatively few bought up most of the war debt from needy workers, farmers, and widows. "This began the first act in the great farce of American speculation," followed by the inevitable bursting of the financial bubble that left behind many poor men and a wealthy few who wielded influence "hostile to the first principles of our government." Nevertheless, Burges reassured his audience of masters and journeymen that their "noble spirit of independence" would play a critical role in the maintaining the country's republican virtue.[10]

That angry rhetoric was aimed at speculators in capital rather than the speculation in land. Speculation in western lands had long been a quintessential American pursuit, marking a strong continuity between colonial British America and the early Republic, conducted by large land companies, middling merchants, and individual farmers. Similarly, colonial contempt for Native Americans, which sometimes found an outlet in the pretense that they were savage hunter-gatherers who lacked the right to land, would be repeated into the nineteenth century by squatters, surveyors, speculators, and senators. While those parties often quarreled over their "rights," all embraced the assumption that land was a properly republican investment; that "developing" and "improving" the land was virtuous labor adding value to property to be sold for profit; and that Native Americans lacked any legal or moral right to the land. Labor, conquest, and commerce were all part of the settler enterprise to push out Native peoples, take their lands, and impose American law and culture. That was the "dark side" to the labor theory of value in America: it justified or even inspired the theft of Native lands. In the new cotton-growing region from Georgia to Louisiana, there was the added blasphemy that somehow the immense fortunes created by the enslaved laborers were viewed as properly belonging to the enslaver.[11]

Not all Americans agreed with the labor theory of value. Perhaps the most famous dissident, John Taylor of Caroline, is today regarded as one of the first political economists in the United States. Taylor owned a large plantation in northeast Virginia and, not surprisingly, became the foremost voice of Jeffersonian ideas about political economy. He wrote a series of essays in 1803, followed by three books between 1813 and 1820, that stressed the intrinsic value of land and the owner's "natural right" to control its use and inheritance. More generally, Taylor was suspicious of liberalism, capitalism, and progress. He did embrace some of the ideas identified with liberalism: he regarded luxury as enriching rather than corrupting and rejected limits on individual property ownership. But Taylor also feared wage workers as dependent servants and thought factory workers were treated worse than slaves, a notion that decades later would become part of the southern gospel. For Taylor, while capital was necessary and "authentic property" when obtained by talent or industry, its value fluctuated too widely to be the result of labor and was too often "artificial property" obtained by special interest legislation or fraud. He therefore believed that the greatest threats to the republic were chartered banks, incorporated manufacturers, and the protective tariffs desired by northern politicians and entrepreneurs.[12]

A somewhat different critique came from those who argued that expanding the nation's capital and commerce was essential for the development of farming. Perhaps the most widely read advocate was Samuel Blodget, who started life in a New Hampshire village; after the Revolution he made a fortune in the East India trade and then became director of the first insurance company in the United States. In 1806, he wrote *Economica*, apparently the first book on political economy written by an American, arguing that commerce and capital were necessary "social stimuli" for agriculture. Blodget thus praised Jefferson while advocating a number of Hamiltonian policies: more borrowing from Europe to benefit the nation; increasing the number of branches of the Bank of the United States; incorporating many more public projects and businesses of various types in order to "preserve order, amity, and peace"; and stopping the sale of public lands until the increase in American population raised their value. He also criticized the Congress of 1801 (newly dominated by Jefferson's allies) for voting to redeem the debt without first studying how much specie remained in the treasury or was needed for operations of the government. At the same time, Blodget had significant differences with Hamilton: he envisioned a far more democratic infusion of capital, widespread development, and laws to ensure more egalitarian landholding by barring the ownership of excessive acreage in any county or state.[13]

After 1800 and particularly after 1811, economic development as espoused by Blodget proved more popular than the purist agrarian notions defended by Taylor. The nasty political battles at the end of the century seemed to absorb the nascent class conflicts glimpsed during the Revolution and early Republic, and the victory of Jefferson and his allies over the Federalists eased fears of an aristocracy of wealth. Even as the new president celebrated returning to the republican principal of small government, growing numbers of American farmers and artisans embraced increasing the stream of capital and funding for infrastructure. Federalists had defined their party in large part by support for banks and internal projects like canals, but Democrat-Republicans increasingly felt that transportation projects and the circulation of more money would help temper the threat of economic inequality by driving dynamic development and providing new opportunities. Of course, there was one thing on which all Americans could agree, whether Jeffersonians or Federalists, and including most political economists from Burges to Taylor to Blodget: the central and "virtuous" role of western expansion that (acknowledged or not) required taking land from Native peoples.

Jefferson's cabinet members and congressional allies quickly came to favor an active program of roads and other improvements, inspired in part by the growing flood of constituent letters and in part by Federalist opposition to the measures. The subsequent failure of those proposals, as congressmen fought each other over funds, and Federalists along with "Old Republicans" (purists such as Taylor and John Randolph) stood against them, did not end their popularity. Americans generally sought easier credit and access to capital, particularly as western migration and international trade expanded after the War of 1812. As a result, state-chartered banks multiplied from 114 in 1811 to 256 in 1816, issuing currency that pumped up lines of local and long-distance credit and exchange.[14]

The Democrat-Republican alliance soon splintered into "radical" and "liberal" factions with noticeably different views of the correct political economy. In Pennsylvania, a sizable Jeffersonian "radical" faction led by William Duane, publisher of the *Philadelphia Aurora*, insisted that private property rights had to give way to the public good in order to maintain the "happy mediocrity of condition" that best protected the country against "arbitrary power." The conservative "Quids" faction rejected greater democracy as threatening stability and property rights and promoted unregulated rapid economic development as the best means to overcome economic inequality. A third group, the "Snyderites," gained a majority in 1805 (roundly defeating the radicals) and sought to shape a dynamic and open marketplace by working with entrepreneurs to build transportation, offering bounties to useful trades, chartering more banks, and seeking a protective tariff to help local artisans. Neither Quids nor Synderites thought the state (or "the people") should have the power to regulate property and instead agreed that a growing economy would prevent unequal economic conditions, shaping the modern American political economy that fused liberal and capitalist values. Similar factions developed in New York, shaped in part by personal rivalries focused on Aaron Burr. In 1800, James Cheetham, a recently arrived English radical about to take control of the anti-Burr *New York American Citizen*, wrote in *A Dissertation Concerning Political Equality* that the right of the people to wield political power had the same source as the right of every man to "dispose of his property" as he wished, which meant that democratic governments had the fundamental authority to closely regulate property ownership.[15]

At the same time, a dramatic fundamental shift in the structure of manufacturing caused a new class structure to emerge in the country's rapidly growing cities and raised the menace that "wage slavery" would supplant artisanal independence and that class conflicts would roil American shops. While in 1800 traditional shop organization dominated cities like New York and Philadelphia, toward the end of the 1810s the division of labor for mass production became increasingly common, particularly in the shoe and clothing trades. Manufacturers became able to hire more unskilled men, women, and children, pay them far less than journeymen, and then dismiss them easily when forced to cease production due to weather or plunging prices. The situation was made worse by the rising tide of emigration from England and Ireland and by the movement of young men from the countryside seeking opportunities in the expanding urban economies. Journeymen and apprentices were confronted by the threat of a life of unskilled labor—intermittent and low-paid—instead of the promise of the independence and prestige of "owning" one's trade as a master artisan. Mechanic associations were faced with the choice of becoming class-based craft unions or social welfare organizations embracing employers and laborers. The emerging conflicts were highlighted in the strikes by journeymen shoemaker societies in Philadelphia (in 1805) and New York City (in 1809); the efforts by master shoemakers in both cities to have the journeymen arrested and tried for conspiracy; and the use of egalitarian republican language in speeches, articles, and petitions published by all sides. But the meaning of that language was shifting, as the master shoemakers (like the liberal Quids and Snyderites) referred to equality in terms of *opportunity*, not *condition*.[16]

This shift in language and the emerging labor conflicts did not mark an end to the older republican paradigm that artisans and laborers should avoid selfish ambition and work cooperatively for the good of the community. Even in the late 1830s and beyond, some reformers (including Whigs like Tristam Burges) continued to argue that employer and employee, labor and capital, shared common interests. But the traditional communitarian standards that had served to limit excessive wealth and economic inequality were undermined by the increasing embrace of liberal individualism that accompanied new opportunities. An anonymous writer in a Charleston newspaper in 1789 celebrated ambition as the means "by which we have been wafted from a barbarous, to an enlightened age." Twenty years later, New England engineering entrepreneur Loammi Baldwin noted, "Nothing can more effectually contribute to the general improvement of the country, than . . . leaving every department of industry free, and open to the pursuits of individual exertion, unshackled by the restraint of law." Baldwin and others felt that, while wage labor should not be considered disgraceful, it would certainly be merely temporary if a young man was properly ambitious.[17]

The waning of a moralistic political economy that decried ambition and competition was aided by two distinct trends. First, particularly in northern states, there was growing enthusiasm for ambitious individuals with the "enterprise" and "public spirit" (and desire for wealth) to build turnpikes, bridges, canals, and other internal improvements. Their efforts were facilitated by the changing legal climate that, despite intermittent public anger, gave greater political support and powers to corporations and made them increasingly common—further undermining opposition. Second, particularly after 1815, the risks of investment and entrepreneurship became much easier as credit and circulating currency mushroomed. This was particularly true in the West, where the US Land Office sold plots on credit and accepted dubious bank notes at face value. And it was especially true in the cotton Southwest, where beginning in 1816 the Second Bank of the United States (along with other lenders) provided easy credit for land, slaves, and manufactured goods; by 1819 about 93 percent of the value of land in the Mississippi Valley had been obtained by credit.[18]

Anxieties about the seeming decline of a moral political economy increased as the nation's rising wealth allowed many more Americans to purchase and flaunt luxury goods. Cotton plantation owners sought to live like English aristocrats and were aided in that pursuit by a growing corps of merchants who specialized in extending credit to planters and selling the mortgaged crop in England. Their *un*republican luxury, like that of many of their English counterparts, was based on the vicious abuse of laborers (e.g., slaves) as well as massive debt. Wealthy merchants and bankers in the booming port cities similarly sought luxury goods like carriages, silks, and paintings in part because the quickening pace of commerce and production had turned the growing trickle of consumer goods once considered luxuries—books, paintings, furniture, clocks, ceramics—into a virtual flood available to the middling as well as the "better sort," farming households as well as urban dwellers. Many Americans feared that the easy availability of luxury endangered their republic. In 1815 Robert Walsh of Philadelphia told his friend Robert Wickliffe of Lexington, Kentucky, that the furniture, clothing, and "exotic delicacies" that have flooded into cities and were "purchased at enormous prices by persons of every profession and class" made him "tremble for the national morals." More significantly, a growing number of northerners connected southern slavery to the threat of aristocratic luxury, pride, and power.[19]

At the other end of the widening economic gap, the rising tide of poverty raised an even more fundamental challenge to how Americans viewed their political economy. Traditionally, Anglo-American communities had cared for their own: local officials judged the needs and worthiness of the poor and then imposed local taxes to pay for assistance or care; outsiders could be "warned out" and denied relief. In mid-eighteenth-century America, as transiency increased along with periodic waves of poverty in some cities (like Boston), this traditional system floundered, so local elites created organizations to build and manage almshouses where the poor could be gathered, monitored, and put to work in order to make the enterprise self-supporting and save taxes (which rarely happened). By the turn of the century, as poverty rose and became a permanent feature of towns and cities, poor relief was handled haphazardly by a patchwork of those different methods. At the same time, the Second Great Awakening, the first national religious surge, fundamentally reshaped the way that Americans viewed the poor and poor relief. The long-lasting broadly based "revival" shaped and spread the new paradigm that humans could gain salvation through their own efforts and, thus, could control all aspects of their destiny, including wealth or poverty. The movement also provided new opportunities for upper- and middle-class women to engage in public service, working with ministers, lawyers, and merchants to reform social and economic evils. But while the movement fostered ideals of "self-improvement," it marked the general abandonment of the perception that the United States was distinguished by a relatively egalitarian socioeconomic structure and widespread ownership of property.[20]

As conditions worsened in the rapidly growing cities, organizations like New York's Society for the Prevention of Pauperism (NYSPP) took on the task of reforming the poor and turning them into virtuous workers, while protecting the community's economic and social structure. Most of these reformers viewed poverty as a personal moral failure that could be "cured" by temperance, hard work, and virtuous behavior. Some groups, like the Pennsylvania Society for the Promotion of Public Economy (SPPE), officially acknowledged cyclical or seasonal employment and extremely low wages as significant causes of poverty. But the overwhelming emphasis was on the evils of liquor and the need to compel the lazy and improvident not only to work—but to become more virtuous individuals. "Habitual drunkards, if unrepentant," could even be stripped of their civil rights. Some occasionally pointed at the growing prominence of wealth and luxury as a bad example for others. Mordecai Noah, a columnist for the *New-York National Advocate*, wrote in October 1818: "Mankind is the same all over the world, and the same remedies may be safely applied in like cases. *The want of industry is the foundation of the evil*, and industry in the poorer order of the community can only be promoted by example among the better educated and refined." The poor were thus increasingly viewed not as an inevitable aspect of human sin but as a morally and socially dangerous multitude.[21]

In fact, many reformers embraced the view of Malthus and Ricardo that financial assistance to the poor should be cut or eliminated because need and misery served a necessary social and economic function. The SPPE reported in 1817 that "the multiplication of charitable institutions" made far too many dependent on the dole; such societies should instead unite, establish workhouses, and deny assistance to the "indolent and worthless" who took the lion's share of assistance. The NYSPP, perhaps the most prominent reform organization in the country, began its 1818 *Report* by emphasizing that poverty and vice resulted from "misguided benevolence, and imprudent systems of relief," and pointed to how efforts "to provide for the sufferings of the poor, by high and even enormous taxation," had actually "augmented" the problems by "diminish[ing], in the minds of the laboring classes, that wholesome anxiety to provide for the wants of a distant day, which alone can save them from a state of absolute dependence." Even in rural western Massachusetts, the Reverend Herman Humphrey warned in his April 1818 sermon, soup kitchens had become "efficient recruiting post[s] for pauperism," and charity served only to reward "improvidence and vice" and amounted to "throwing oil upon the fire" of poverty. These critiques resulted from the ideology of self-improvement and perfection imbedded in the Second Great Awakening. But perhaps almost as significant was the fear among of influential Americans that their country was no longer the beacon of republican equality for the world.[22]

These views were part of the growing acceptance among white Americans of the widening gap between rich and poor in their country, although they still generally believed, as Connecticut senator Samuel Dana wrote, that this was a result of "industry and talent" rather than privilege and family. Europeans had a different view of the situation, often complaining that Americans "pay little attention to merit" but instead classified "every man without distinction by the same scale, viz. by that of fortune." French ambassador Louis Felix de Beaujour also noted scornfully that the primary virtue among Americans was the "unbounded love of money," because the country's "political equality" made wealth the only source of prestige and honor. Some American conservatives had similar concerns: John Watson complained that by 1810 Philadelphia's genteel social structure had broken down, with artisans dressing like gentlemen as they hired others to do the hard labor. The infection of "republican principles of equality" had even resulted, he bemoaned, in servants refusing to accept that designation and dressing and acting like "genteeler people." Beaujour thought on the other hand that the vaunted equality was in fact "less real than apparent" because the varying manners of different classes had created very clear distinctions in social status and power. Children's literature at this time depicted an essential harmony between different classes. But in reality an increasing number of Americans, like Senator Dana, saw "the RICH and the POOR" as separated by very different interests, character, and conduct and "disposed to unite for their own advantage" against the other, in dangerous conflict rather than blissful harmony.[23]

Systemic inequality and class conflict were fostered by the Panic of 1819, which resulted from several nearly simultaneous developments. Britain closed Caribbean ports to American flour in retaliation for US tariffs on manufactured British goods, causing the price of flour to crash; the new director of the Bank of the United States sought to discipline western branches and state-chartered banks that had flooded the country with dubious credit and currency. For years the US Land Office had sold federal acreage for a small down payment and accepted often risky state bank notes at *full value*; in addition, the western branches of the bank usually offered such land as collateral for the notes they issued, which meant that much of the circulating currency was built on a very weak foundation. When the prices of farm commodities plunged, farmers could not afford to pay interest on the notes, and the land that backed many of the loans was suddenly almost worthless. The crash began in major trading ports, quickly affected eastern farmers, and moved slowly westward; by 1821 many Ohio towns starved for trustworthy currency had turned to barter. Between 1820 and 1824, nearly 20 percent of the land purchased on mortgages from the Land Office was forfeited. But perhaps hardest hit was Philadelphia, the national center for flour exports: housing values dropped 40 percent and unemployment in manufacturing may have reached 78 percent.[24]

The Panic of 1819, which Americans called simply "hard times," had significant long-term national effects. Congress stopped selling public land on credit and lowered the basic price from $2.00 to $1.25 per acre in order to encourage settlers. This first depression generated new uncertainty about currency, banking, and more generally the moral and financial greatness of the American republic. Slavery and tariffs became increasingly occasions of sectional political differences rather than shared political debates. Cotton rocketed past foodstuffs as the export product driving the American economy. As power looms begin to dominate English mills, southwestern plantation owners were encouraged to focus on the crop, which increased the market price for and abuse of enslaved laborers. A growing number of northerners opposed slavery as the source of an abusive aristocracy of wealth that sought control of the national government, while southerners increasingly supported slavery as a foundation of the "white man's republic."[25]

Debates over the solutions to the depression raged at the state and national levels. State legislatures considered measures that would compel banks to revive lending and offer some relief to debtors by postponing or regulating the seizure of property. Such proposals were particularly popular in western states as well as hard-hit Pennsylvania but faced criticism that immoral men— bankrupt speculators and spendthrifts—would be the main beneficiaries and that debt relief would violate the sanctity of the contracts clause in the Constitution. The most significant issue nationally was whether to raise tariffs on imported manufactured goods in order to protect American producers. Opponents, mostly southerners, including John Taylor, touted the benefits of international trade, the threat that taxing consumption posed to production, and the dangers of providing particular individuals and groups with benefits and privileges; some noted the potential moral threat of factory labor and argued that, because the United States was "underpopulated," the high unemployment was temporary. Protectionists such as Philadelphia publisher Matthew Carey and American Temperance Society leader Rev. Lyman Beecher rejected laissez faire economics and argued that high tariffs would, by fostering domestic manufacturing, provide employment for the idle and increase the home market for agricultural products.[26]

Until the late 1820s, few challenged the long-standing belief among white Americans that success could be gained by working hard and practicing good morals and careful household management. Mordechai Noah echoed children's literature when he told members of the New York Society of Mechanics and Tradesmen in 1821 that they should avoid idleness, rise early, live frugally, not drink too much, and not get into debt. "Be not envious of others possessions, sigh not for the splendid habitations of the rich, or their luxurious fare; remember that when fatigued with labour, you repose upon your hard pallet, with a pure conscience and a healthy frame, you enjoy a more soft and sweet repose, than the votaries of wealth, upon their downy pillows." Such rosy assertions were increasingly challenged in the wake of the Panic of 1819 as large-scale manufacturers seemed to gain more of the market and wealth, factories started popping up in New England, and laborers including women and journeymen continued to suffer from very low wages, seasonal employment, and limited opportunities. In 1831 Mathew Carey marshaled data on wages, employment, and living costs to attack the assertions that anyone willing to work hard could "support themselves comfortably" and that the "sufferings and distresses" of the poor "arise from their idleness, their dissipation, and their extravagance." Carey pointed to unskilled laborers and women seamstresses as particularly handicapped by the emerging economy. Yet the image of the self-made man remained dominant even as such criticisms became common and inheritance played an ever-greater role in determining wealth and power in the United States.[27]

The one notable challenge to the entire system came from Daniel Raymond's *Thoughts on Political Economy* (1820). Raymond, a Connecticut lawyer who had recently moved to Baltimore and gained Carey's support, made the protectionist argument for a high tariff to help manufacturing gain its potential—which he saw as equal to commerce and farming—and to fund internal improvements and other needs. In the larger view, he wrote that the economy should work for the community rather than for individuals and that the accumulation of wealth or land was far less important than putting those resources to work for the good of society. Raymond thought that the wealthy "miser" who thought himself virtuous for saving should instead think of "how many laboring poor his avarice has kept out of employment." Contrary to Taylor, Raymond saw landownership not as a natural right but a lifetime privilege open to regulation or even redistribution for the common good. Any legal measure such as entail, primogeniture, or corporate charter that produced inequality was "a direct and unnecessary violation of the laws of nature" that tended to encourage "overgrown wealth, idleness, luxury and effeminacy" among the fortunate and "wretchedness, poverty, pauperism, and moral degradation" in those lacking privilege. At the same time, he condemned the "forcible equalization of property" as similarly unnatural. For Raymond, government's duty was to preserve the highest equality of rights and property consistent with the "natural inequality" of abilities among men. In some ways his arguments echoed classical republicanism, with its dislike of the idle rich as well as the dependent poor, but contained notions of class that anticipated Thomas Skidmore and other radicals a decade later.[28]

Another significant result of this first Panic was the emergence of the workingmen's movement, whose spokesmen revitalized and modernized the American tradition of economic equality. The goals and rhetoric of one branch of that movement echoed those of the agrarians and artisans during the early Republic. That branch continued to celebrate patriarchal republican independence, condemn chartered privileges and selfish excessive profits, and call for a publicly funded system of education for all children together, rich and poor. But it also advocated ideas and innovations that began to reshape the American landscape in the 1830s, including a ten-hour workday, an end to debtor's prison, and political parties pledged to elect men who would answer to laborers instead of merchants. Another branch embraced the call for those reforms but went much further to challenge the norms of private property and to welcome either collective enterprise or democratic socialism and the redistribution of land and wealth as the best way to fulfill the American promise of equality. Regardless of their disagreements, all in the movement spoke with an intensified anger that went far beyond older republican concerns, spoke increasingly about class conflict and the interests of labor opposed to employer, and saw economic power instead of governmental authority as the source of oppression.

The initial signs of this movement appeared just before the Panic. In mid-June 1816, the final issue of William Leete Stone's literary periodical *The Lounger*, published in Hudson, New York, included a satirical column bemoaning "the progress of luxury" in America and urging as a solution "a LEVELLING SYSTEM" that would equalize rich and poor and thus benefit artisans like cobblers because now new shoes (and other consumer goods) would cost more. That piece may have been in part a commentary on recent tenant uprisings in the county. A year later, Pennsylvania's Democratic Republicans denied a story, possibly spread by the fading Federalists, that someone at a dinner supporting William Findlay, their candidate for governor, had toasted the "Equal Distribution of Property." More significantly, at about the same time, Cornelius Blatchly, a New York City doctor raised in a middling rural New Jersey family, put forth his vision of a Christian socialist commonwealth in *Some Causes of Popular Poverty*. Blatchly insisted that God gave man the right to own land solely "in his aggregate capacity." Only those who used or lived on land should own it; banks, speculators, and other investors living elsewhere had no right to rent, and when a person died, his property should be redistributed in equal shares to "every child" in the nation—an idea that reflected Thomas Paine's *Agrarian Justice*. He depicted rent as the moral equivalent of usury and called for progressive taxation of wealth rather than duties or other retail taxes.[29]

In the wake of the Panic, the use of unskilled labor and mass production rapidly increased, as improving transportation and recovering demand allowed manufacturers, particularly in New York, Philadelphia, and Boston, to sell more and more ready-made shoes, clothing, and other consumer goods to increasingly distant markets. Wages and opportunity remained low, and more factories were being built that resembled their dreaded English counterparts. In response, intellectuals and artisans became more willing to advocate radical economic reform and to draw on the new socialist ideas from England. In 1822 Blatchly joined with eighteen others (mostly physicians and ministers) to organize the New York Society for Promoting Communities. Blatchly wrote the society's constitution, which pointed to the "system of *exclusive* rights to *property, power,* and *respect*" as "the cause of all social evil," and was also the author of its manifesto *An Essay on Common Wealths*. While the *Essay* (like *Causes of Popular Poverty*) assumed that men were generally farmers and said little about the emergence of mass production and factories in cities like his own Philadelphia, it was a milestone in highlighting and condemning economic inequality in the United States and in pinpointing its causes as the profit motive and exploitative capitalism rather than political corruption.[30]

The *Essay* also contained selections from Robert Owen, the industrial reformer who had gained fame in Britain. After imbibing progressive social ideas at the Manchester Philosophy Society, Owen bought a factory in New Lanark,

Scotland, and endeavored to change the conditions that he believed were responsible for the evils of factory work: child labor, alcoholism, bad health, high mortality, violence, and ignorance. He provided unadulterated food to the workers at cost, education for the children, a savings bank, a free medical clinic, community gardens, an insurance fund, and modern plumbing. By 1817, after a growing stream of prominent visitors praised the results, Owens wrote *A New View of Society*, calling for enlightened elites to establish small villages to farm, run factories, and share the proceeds in common. These socialist utopias would end rent, profits, and other aspects of economic inequality. Owen's ideas sparked a strong interest in the United States, and in the fall of 1824 he crossed the Atlantic to create his utopia in Indiana. After arriving in New York, he visited Blatchly's organization and made the rounds of the best and the brightest in that city, before heading off to Philadelphia, where he received a thunderous reception. After several days there, he went to Washington City where the agnostic socialist was feted by the nation's leaders. Henry Clay invited him to speak to a special joint session of Congress on February 25, 1825, and the new president John Quincy Adams had him address Congress again on March 7. As Owen left for New Harmony, a New York publisher issued the first American edition of *New View*.[31]

Owen's socialist ideas had even greater impact through the writings of others, beginning with John Gray's *A Lecture on Human Happiness*. Gray, who had helped establish an Owenite community near London, directly attacked the republican assumption that corrupt government caused human misery and inequality, pointing instead to economic power. He held that the most effective way to "abolish the cause of misery" was to redistribute property on an equal basis; charitable societies were helpless in the face of immense and growing poverty; rent and interest were immoral demands imposed by "UNPRODUCTIVE member[s] of society"; and the only moral property right was the labor involved in making land productive. That last point added a Ricardian emphasis to socialism, as Gray noted that "the foundation of all property is LABOUR, and there is no other just foundation for it." Moreover, the demands and nature of labor made unity and cooperation far more efficient than competition and individualism. Gray's short pamphlet ran through several editions in New York and Philadelphia in 1825 and 1826, and in 1828 it was serialized in the *Mechanics Free Press*.[32]

It may seem strange today that English socialism appealed to American white men in the Jacksonian period, particularly with the apparent dominance of liberalism and the common assumption that the ownership and free use of private property was a natural right won in the Revolution. But traditions of

guild and corporate identity along with republican ideals of virtue and commonwealth remained strong among American artisans. Many still preferred
small shop production rather than faceless and risky mass production. The
journeymen who learned these traditions along with their craft had every reason to embrace communitarian socialism when faced with the disruptive
transformation of their work as well as a lifetime of dependent and undepend-
able wage labor. In addition, British immigrants brought to America not
only their labor and skills but the identities and tactics fostered in the textile
mills. In 1828, for example, New York City weavers sought to systematically
destroy looms as part of their strike, and striking Hamilton textile workers in
Patterson, New Jersey, led by British immigrants from Manchester, adopted
the symbols of that city's radical labor movement, which authorities tried to
crush in the "Peterloo Massacre" of 1819. On the other hand, Americans farmers, who were by far the majority in every state and territory, were far less
enthusiastic about labor socialism, having happily embraced the gospel of
landownership in severalty along with the promise of western lands taken from
Indians. Few joined Owenite or other communes. Southerners were particularly dubious: the region had a deeply rooted tradition of masculine autonomy
that lacked the communitarian values of New England, and the cotton slave
plantations fostered a culture of patriarchal authority and luxury dependent
on borrowed capital.[33]

Owens's fame and Gray's writings opened the gates to publications that expressed the anger and alienation of wage laborers that had grown since the
Panic of 1819. In early 1826, Langdon Byllesby, a journeyman proofreader in
New York City, raised in Philadelphia by English parents, wrote *Observations
on the Sources and Effects of Unequal Wealth*, the first American condemnation
of mass production and emerging class inequalities. Byllesby began by echoing the ideas of earlier political economists: that labor was the only source of
just wealth, that men should not own more land than necessary to earn a living, that it was essentially slavery for a person to be compelled to labor for
wages, and that the political power held by the wealthy meant that most laws
and all wars were designed to help *the few* at the expense of *the many*. He even
repeated the Enlightenment trope that "savage nations" deserved praise
because among them "the means of subsistence are equal and open to all.[34]

But Byllesby then broke new ground by analyzing how "the Inequality of
Wealth, and its attendant Evils" had increased terribly with "the introduction
of Labour-saving Machinery, and improved Processes in the Arts." Factory
machines were affordable by only a few and guaranteed overproduction that
would drive down prices and "overwhelm a large portion of the labouring

classes with resourceless distress, and intense misery" with low wages and frequent unemployment. The results included the recent rise in alcohol abuse, imprisonment, and other social problems, and the only "Remedies" were to create communal settlements like New Harmony or, in cities like New York, for mechanics and laborers (including mariners) to form cooperative associations. Byllesby's fiery *Observations* expressed the feelings bubbling among small artisans, journeymen, and laborers and would guide New York's most active and radical workingmen's writers and activists through the 1830s.[35]

At the same time, in the Philadelphia suburb of Southwark, William Heighton, a middle-aged cordwainer (shoemaker) who had immigrated from England in 1812, was spending many of his evenings with other journeymen and friends discussing their problems in light of Gray's *Lecture* and the writings of other political economists, particularly Ricardo. By early 1827, he had developed a plan for a mechanic's association to push for systemic reforms and made two speeches that were published to gain wider support. Heighton reiterated Gray's point that, even though labor was the source of all wealth, those who produced that abundance "receive nothing but the crumbs." This exploitive state of affairs had developed because, after American independence had been achieved, "our predecessors for want of information" had surrendered their "rights" to the "non-productive and accumulating class." While the efforts of mechanic and craft societies to strike for hours and wages may serve a momentary "good purpose," that was at best "poor patch work." What was necessary, he emphasized, was to join together and elect "friends to our interest." He also noted that "we shall be denounced as a band of '*levellers*'"—showing that the term retained its potency.[36]

Heighton envisioned the association as uniting skilled journeymen and unskilled day laborers in "a band of brothers" who could claim "our equal rights" and make "oppression begin to totter on its throne." Workers from throughout the city should meet to create the organization and establish a newspaper, library (with courses in political economy), and welfare and strike funds. Perhaps most importantly, the association needed to become politically powerful by backing candidates for public office. These goals were a notable departure from the tradition of artisan republicanism that privileged skills and patriarchal independence and were obviously far from the Owenite efforts to create socialist utopias in remote areas. In September 1827, the Mechanic's Library opened in North Alley and soon had more than sixty members and a hundred books, with Wednesday night debates on public topics. In December, Philadelphia workingmen met at Tyler's Tavern and created the Mechanics' Union of Trade Associations, adopted a constitution written by Heighton that condemned the "unequal and very excessive accumulation of wealth and power into the hands of a few," and promised to seek "a just balance of power" in the city by running candidates for public office. About a month later, Heighton began editing the *Mechanic's Free Press*, the first labor newspaper in the United States. The union's initial effort in October 1828 to elect candidates for local and county offices met with little success, as only those connected with Andrew Jackson or John Quincy Adams won election. The "Workie" ticket one year later gained better results, but the union was increasingly torn by conflict over whether to join forces with more electable but less "pure" politicians. While the organization remained active, it failed to get any candidates elected in 1830.[37]

The workingmen's movement in New York City, the nation's center of finance and manufacturing, emerged about a year after its counterpart in Philadelphia and initially pursued the more drastic agenda set by its sparkplug and organizer Thomas Skidmore. Skidmore was born in 1790 in Connecticut, during the 1810s worked as an itinerant tutor as far south as North Carolina, and finally moved to New York City in 1819, where he established a machinist shop and read political economists from Locke to Byllesby. In 1829 he published *The Rights of Man to Property!*, one of the most radical visions of the country's political economy. Instead of calling for universal education and other reforms, he ridiculed the sanctity of private property and the labor theory of value; pointed to community consent as the true source of property rights; and called for limits on landholding enforced by a more democratic government, which would include blacks and women. Many of his ideas reflected traditional republican hostility to great wealth and held that access to property was essential to life, liberty, and happiness. But he celebrated a strong state and pushed the emerging socialism to new ground, calling for New York to redistribute all property and end inheritance so that a person's property would at death be taken by the government and annually distributed on a relatively equal basis to men and women reaching age eighteen.[38]

Skidmore provided, in addition to a glimpse of emerging socialist ideas, the initial blueprint for New York's workingmen's movement. In late April 1829, journeymen in the city considered striking if manufacturers carried out their rumored increased workday, from ten to eleven hours; instead, urged by Skidmore, they met and adopted a resolution (that he probably wrote) insisting on a ten-hour workday regardless of craft or class and warning employers that, because "all men hold their property by the consent of the great mass of the community," those who demanded "excessive toil" or paid only starvation wages would face "the displeasure of a just community." Five days later, a huge

THE

RIGHTS OF MAN

TO PROPERTY!

BEING A PROPOSITION

TO MAKE IT EQUAL AMONG THE ADULTS

OF THE

PRESENT GENERATION:

AND TO PROVIDE FOR ITS EQUAL TRANSMISSION TO EVERY
INDIVIDUAL OF EACH SUCCEEDING GENERATION, ON
ARRIVING AT THE AGE OF MATURITY.

ADDRESSED TO THE

CITIZENS OF THE STATE OF NEW-YORK, PARTICULARLY, AND TO

the people of other States and Nations, generally.

"I hold these truths to be self-evident; that all men are created equal; that
they are endowed, by their Creator, with certain unalienable rights; and that
among these are life, liberty and *property*.'—Altered from Mr. Jefferson's
Declaration of American Independence.

BY THOMAS SKIDMORE.

New-York:

PRINTED FOR THE AUTHOR BY ALEXANDER MING, JR.
106 Beekman-street.

1829.

Title page to Thomas Skidmore's *The Rights of Man to Property!* (New York: printed for
the author by Alexander Ming, 1829). Courtesy, American Antiquarian Society.

gathering in the Bowery passed a resolve that insisted every worker who left "his original right of soil" had a natural right to a "comfortable" living and angrily condemned any employer who sought more than ten hours of labor a day. They also elected a committee of fifty men, mostly journeymen and including Skidmore, to meet regularly; during the summer that committee worked on a slate of candidates (journeymen and poor masters) for public office and a set of resolves. Those resolves, adopted by another public meeting on October 19, began by calling for "a civil revolution" to create a government to guarantee every person "an equal amount of property" upon adulthood, along with various moderate reforms: a mechanics' lien, no imprisonment for debt, the abolition of private banks, and the taxation of clergymen and churches. But that language alarmed the charismatic English feminist Fanny Wright and Robert Owens's son Robert Jr., who organized a competing faction that took control at the end of December, adopted a platform that proclaimed the individual right to property "sacred" while endorsing the reforms advocated by their Philadelphia counterparts, and ran their own ticket in the 1830 election. The result in New York City was a workingmen's movement weakened by factionalism.[39]

Between 1828 and 1834, workingmen's parties mushroomed throughout the United States, publishing nearly fifty newspapers in places like Tuscaloosa (Alabama), Wilmington (Delaware), New Orleans, Woodstock (Vermont), Gardiner (Maine), Ravenna (Ohio), Charlestown (Indiana), Boston, and Albany, Buffalo, and Rochester in upstate New York. All condemned the "monied aristocracy" created by chartered banks and wealthy elites and called for a specific set of social and economic reforms. They were most passionate in demanding tax-funded school systems to educate all children instead of the inadequate and demeaning "charity" schools. The *Connecticut Sentinel* of New London, announcing a Mechanic's Association in that town, mourned that the lack of "a general system of education" was the primary reason that "the wealthy and powerful" had created a high level of inequality in America. To the south, in Baltimore, the *Mechanics' Banner*, in a long piece condemning the rise of inequality in the United States, made one demand: "a liberal education" for all. Seth Luther, who lectured, organized, and helped run a newspaper for the workingmen's movement in New England, concluded his long jeremiad on *The Origin and Progress of Avarice* by listing these remedies: "A system of universal equal education by means of manual labor schools, supported at the public expense, open alike to the children of the poor as well as the rich—abolition of all licensed monopolies,—abolition of capital

punishment,—abolition of imprisonment for debt,—an entire revision, or total abolition of the militia system,—a less expensive law system,—equal
taxation on property; and an effective *lien* law on building of all kinds." Labor
papers also frequently called for the elimination of property qualifications for
office; direct election of all public officials; and the right of urban mechanics
to claim and work family farms on federal lands—what later became known
as a homestead law. Brief calls to organize separate political parties were dis-
carded to embrace Andrew Jackson's Democratic Party, and rarely did any
discuss a desire for a fundamental restructuring of the American economy.[40]

Given the power of religion in American life, the overwhelmingly secular
focus of the workingmen's movement and the body of work on America's political economy is surprising. But concerns about the country's increasing gap
between rich and poor did find religious expression. The most overt connections came from Christian socialists like Cornelius Blatchly and his New York
Society for Promoting Communities, which declared private property a violation of God's law. Christian communitarians, most notably the Shakers, who
lived in large villages with all property held in common, made even more em-
phatic the vision that all men *and women* should be equal in terms of property and wealth. More widely, artisans and laborers feeling threatened by the
rise of mass production and ambitious capitalism found support and fellowship in the insurgent evangelical movement, particularly Methodism, which
embraced a moral economy and rejected luxury as sin. The wealthy and bour-
geoisie, on the other hand, preferred the denominations that emphasized intellect, ritual, and order: Presbyterian, Congregational (including the new Uni-
tarians), Episcopal, and "respectable" Baptist. At the same time, artisans and
Methodist leaders displayed some ambivalence about the potential for more
radical elements in their congregations, because as producers they adjusted to
the shifting economic system and continued to favor individual enterprise and
property ownership even as they cursed the seeming loss of communitarian
harmony, traditional socioeconomic relationships, and the patriarchal authority that had linked master, journeyman, and apprentice—and their patrons
and customers.[41]

These men who spoke, wrote, and organized for economic equality at the
turn of the century often used terms of defending traditions of artisan republicanism, patriarchal independence, and the communitarian ethos that rejected the selfish pursuit of excessive profits. Long-standing anger at the para-
sitic wealthy increased as the upper class grew in power, social distance, and
willingness to flaunt luxury. But in the wake of the Panic of 1819, there were

fundamental shifts in their language and concerns. Most importantly, they increasingly expressed their anger in terms of *class*, reflecting a new concept of the social structure instead of the older view of human orders that had categorized men as artisans, farmers, merchants, or ministers. In addition, they had an increasing tendency to equate rather than contrast the social, economic, and political situations in England and the United States. As before, English radicals like Robert Owens and William Heighton played a significant role in this American development, this time shaped by their own country's industrial transformation at the turn of the century, although more prominent were the native-born radicals like Thomas Skidmore and Seth Luther.[42]

On the other side of this widening conceptual and policy divide, more "respectable" men sought to maintain many of the assumptions from the turn of the century. In October 1830, for example, Joseph Buckingham, master printer and state representative for Boston and Cambridge, gave a major address to the Massachusetts Charitable Mechanic Association (which he had led for many years). He condemned recent efforts to organize workingmen's parties and insisted that "inequality in personal affairs" was the natural result of differences in "industry and intelligence and economy." Buckingham insisted that the wealthy were "the architects of their own fortune" and individuals rather than a distinct and powerful class, scoffing at the "derogatory" idea that "our free institutions" could allow "the fostering of a monied aristocracy." All Americans sought to acquire property, which formed "the great lever of society" and inspired "industry and enterprise" along with other virtues. The interests and obligations of employer and worker were "reciprocal" and did not conflict. While he granted that there were different classes, all had equal civil and political rights, and their true interests harmonized in cooperation and order.[43]

As the Whig Party emerged after 1835, the essential harmony among classes became one of its key tenets. Henry Carey, son of Philadelphia publisher Mathew Carey and one of the leading political economists at midcentury, emphasized in his first major work, *Principles of Political Economy* (1837), that "the interests of the capitalist and the labourer are . . . in perfect harmony with each other, as each derives advantage from every measure that tends to facilitate the growth of capital, and to render labour productive, while every measure that tends to produce the opposite effect is injurious to both." Tristam Burges joined the Whig Party in its infancy and lectured widely on the common interests of employer and employee, labor and capital, and the unlimited opportunities for individual advancement. This was the mirror image of the workingmen's yearning for a return to social harmony and the moral economy that attracted them to evangelicalism and to oppose liberal economics and industrial capitalism. The men on the other side of that mirror, like Buckingham and Burges, tended to separate commerce from personal morality and to see the relationship between employer and employee not as social and paternalistic but primarily as a paycheck from one and hard work from the other.[44]

Starker views about class were broadcast by influential conservative clergymen. In January 1835, Jonathan Mayhew Wainwright, the English-born Harvard graduate (1812) who was ordained an Episcopal priest in 1817 and bounced between pulpits in New York City and Boston, delivered the annual Massachusetts election sermon that he published as *Inequality of Individual Wealth the Ordinance of Providence, and Essential to Civilization*. Wainwright began with the reminder from Deuteronomy that "the poor shall never cease out of the land" and then went on to argue that "the inequality of condition, which it implies, is essential to the political, the intellectual, and the moral and religious improvement of the human race." Although men like Godwin or Rousseau, "under the influence of wild romance" might argue for economic equality, doing away with distinctions of wealth was ultimately destructive. For the best example, he pointed to the same group that had often served that purpose: Native Americans. They not only lived in a state of savagery but were rapidly dwindling to extinction because they lacked "that industry, enterprise, forecast, self-denial, which the great principle of holding property in severally always produces in a community of men."[45]

An even more extreme reflection came from Francis Wayland, president of Brown University and pastor of the First Baptist Church in America, in an annual series of lectures to the senior class, published in 1837 as *Elements of Political Economy*. In the third chapter, "Of the Laws Which Govern the Application of Labor to Capital," he explained how the Creator made Man inherently desirous of labor, and that those who disobeyed that natural law paid the penalties of ignorance, hunger, poverty, and nakedness. On the other hand, riches, capital, convenience, and intelligence "is the work of industry, and is the reward which God has bestowed upon us, for obedience to the law of our being." Want or wealth was therefore a reflection of a person's sins or virtues, reflecting ideas long held by conservatives. But Wayland went much further, reflecting Malthus rather than traditional norms about the moral economy by insisting, *"It is necessary that every man be allowed to gain all that he can."* Indeed, if property was held in common, the professor of moral philosophy told his audience, there would be "a premium for indolence" rather than industry. Also, like Malthus, he condemned public support for the poor as removing "the fear of want" that served as one of the "universal stimulants to labor," and which therefore served to encourage pauperism, undermine property rights, and foster "insubordination."[46]

Most of those with a conservative view of the American political economy insisted, like Buckingham, that wealth and poverty resulted from differences in character and abilities rather than class or circumstances. Typical was Samuel DeFord's assurance to a group of firefighters in Massachusetts that, although "all men were born free and equal," they were born with different talents and "advantages" and so "ought not to aspire to equally exalted stations in society." In that vein, demands to restore America's relative economic equality were scorned as efforts to violate natural law. One writer in a literary journal published by Amherst College students argued that since "distinctions have been made by Nature," calls for the "leveling of distinctions" were at best silly and at worst "a wild frenzy for reformation" that "would demolish institutions which are the result of the wisdom of the ages." A phrenologist even argued that limits on "the free accumulation of wealth . . . would impose an arbitrary restraint on *Acquisitiveness, Love of Approbation*" and various other innate aspects of the human mind.[47]

Reforms were not entirely scorned, at least in order to restore peace and maintain order in the United States. Some asked employers to pay their workers more. Rev. Wainwright argued that "the working classes" should be "stimulated to industry" with "all measures that are calculated to secure to them high and certain wages." Willard Phillips in *A Manual of Political Economy* (1828), one of the earliest American textbooks in the field, held that high wages that enabled men to save money were not only important to laborers but "of vital importance" in fulfilling the primary purpose of government and social institutions to ensure the "well-being" of Americans; also, if workers were denied the hope that they could rise through the system, they would be more likely to join rebellions and uprisings. Nearly all urged publicly funded universal education for children, at least in part to teach republican civics and the norms of hard work, cleanliness, and respect. Wainwright even argued that "improving and diffusing education" should be provided free to workers with "ample time . . . for the cultivation of their minds." But not all agreed. An anonymous writer in South Carolina scorned the idea that "the poor, the ignorant, the idle and dissipated" were capable of learning philosophy or science. And the *Philadelphia National Gazette* in 1830 condemned publicly funded education as "virtually 'Agrarianism,'" because it would require the rich to give to the poor and distract "peasants" from focusing on their fields and mechanics on their trades; the result would be "languor, decay, poverty, [and] discontent . . . among all classes."[48]

At the turn of the century, as mass production grew in the North and cotton agriculture emerged in the South, Americans could no longer ignore the growing gap between rich and poor, between those who could live on capital and those who had to labor for wages. Particularly after the Panic of 1819, the bitter reality of a large permanent population of wage laborers shattered the Revolutionary consensus that the United States was blessed by a wide distribution of property. Political economists sought to understand the problem and prescribe solutions. Those who focused on economic inequality increasingly saw business and wealth instead of government as the main source of inequality and sought deep structural reforms in the property laws and arrangements. Journeymen and laborers angered by their increasing insecurity, poverty, and loss of mastery, as well as the increasingly ostentatious display of luxury by the very wealthy, organized to push for public education and a wide range of social and legal reforms, although most soon left the nascent political efforts for Jackson's Democratic Party. Their adversaries embraced the unfettered expanding economy, largely abandoned classical fears of luxury and greed, and urged government to promote and finance but not regulate. This view was clearly more successful by midcentury, embraced by first the Whig Party and then Republicans. But regardless, a new focus on class *structure* and *conflict* became a critical, prominent, and permanent element in America's public discourse on the state and the economy.

CHAPTER SEVEN

Separating Property and Polity

On November 15, 1820, nearly five hundred delegates elected by towns gathered in the Massachusetts State House in Boston to consider a host of revisions to the state's constitution, adopted forty years earlier during the Revolution. Several of the more contentious proposals involved extending the right to vote and hold office to men who did not own property. Those who favored the reforms, probably in the majority, were led by Jeffersonian Republican leaders Samuel Dana, Henry Dearborn, Levi Lincoln, and James Austin. Several noted that "honest laboring men" had and would again be called upon to fight for the state and so should be able to shape that state and its policies by voting; the property requirement to vote they condemned as "an aristocratical and anti-republican principle." In various ways they argued that patriotism and republican virtue rested not on property ownership but on "institutions, laws, habits, and association" and that by paying taxes or serving in the military men established sufficient connections to the state and community to participate in elections and serve in public office.[1]

Their Federalist opponents may have been fewer but were better organized and led by political giants like Daniel Webster, Supreme Court justice Joseph Story, Josiah Quincy, and Samuel Hoar. They argued that the right to vote was a privilege, earned by personal virtues that formed an important source of social stability. The state's sliding scale of the amount of property required to vote and hold office at different levels served as useful "incentives to industry and community," and the lowest barrier was so easy to clear (they thought) that those who failed must be "indolent and vicious." Although men with property might gain extra protections from the current system, they did not gain extra power, and any aristocratic "distinction of families" would be prevented by partible inheritance: the division of an estate among all sons. Moreover, it was properly republican that those who add more to the "common stock of the community" should have more of a voice in the government, and that those without property should not be able to shape a government that could harm men with property. The proposed changes would replace the republic with a democracy, greatly increasing the number of voters who would "improperly influence" or even "corrupt" men of character; it would be but a short step to despotism.[2]

The differences in how the conservatives and reformers in the 1820 Massachusetts convention viewed the right of factory workers to vote was particularly revealing. At that time, the many water-powered spinning mills scattered around the region and the sole factory (in Waltham) employed young women and some children, none of whom were eligible to vote or hold office because of their sex or age. But everyone was aware that large-scale mechanized manufacturing facilities would soon become common. The conservatives who wished to maintain property requirements emphasized the long-standing fear that those factories would employ large numbers of laboring *men* who, lacking property, would be completely dependent on their employers, thus becoming an army of voters directed by the factory owner. The reformers retorted that education, virtue, and attachment to home and country were open to all; thus, if factories were established in the state ("God forbid"), those laboring men *should* have the vote and thus a stake in a stable government in order to avoid creating a "Lazaroni"—the homeless, jobless, dangerous Naples mob-for-rent feared as a threat to property and order.[3]

These arguments were not new: in fact, most had been wielded forty years earlier when the same state debated its first constitution. But the subsequent economic and social changes had dramatically reshaped the political environment and made democratic reforms seem more necessary than dangerous. During the 1780s and 1790s, Americans concerned about republican equality in their country focused on preserving widespread property ownership and preventing monopolistic corporations. But by the turn of the century, as increasing economic inequality and a permanent growing class of laborers and poorer farmers became more apparent, a consensus emerged that limits on landownership or redistribution laws were impossible. Even before the Panic of 1819 shocked the country, Americans had stopped boasting that property ownership in their republic was widespread and roughly equal, and a growing number argued that the long-standing link between property and polity was no longer appropriate. Between 1815 and 1840, most of the original thirteen states held constitutional conventions and enacted reforms that connected the increasingly democratic polity to masculinity and race. Those changes snapped the traditional connections between political and economic equality.

Anglo-Americans during the early Republic almost universally thought that widespread property ownership provided the critical social and political foundation for the independent voters and competent officeholders necessary for a healthy republic. They also believed their new country was blessed to experience that fortunate condition. This republican paradigm meshed with the English norm that voting had to be limited to those who owned a farm or a business, and more property would be necessary if one wanted to run for a higher public office. Such limitations were based on timeworn European assumptions that men with property had a unique stake in society; that property alone provided sufficient independence to give them a voice; that government's power to take property through taxation should be controlled by those who owned property; that the poor should not vote because they had no will of their own; and that the poor should not vote because they could over time threaten the interests of property.[4]

Political participation marked membership in a community, and formal participation in the form of voting or officeholding was linked to one's status, including wealth. Men of "good breeding" served in higher local or state office; those of average or "middling" status voted and occasionally filled minor local posts such as fence viewer or juror. Voting was commonly done in public by voice or literally standing behind one's candidate. Barely considered and thus unresolved was the question of whether voting was a right or a privilege. Clearly those without property, including women and servants, were not able to have the vote or hold office. Building on Reformation ideas that *understanding* was necessary to embrace God's grace, Enlightenment writers viewed reason and informed consent as critical elements in political participation. This did not shatter the connection between polity and property: for example, John Adams continued to believe that only those able to act independently were truly able to refuse as well as consent and that property ownership marked the boundary between dependence and independence. But new ideas of intellectual development, beginning with John Locke's *Essay Concerning Human Understanding*, increasingly emphasized age and maturity as critical to reason and therefore informed consent.[5]

By the mid-eighteenth century, in most British colonies, men had to own land of sufficient acreage or value in order to vote, and in the others the limitation was personal property of a set value. Many who lacked sufficient property to vote were young men who worked farms belonging to their fathers in the expectation that they would inherit some or all of the estate in the future. In some colonies, particularly Massachusetts and New York, widows who had legal control of sufficient property voted. Property was not the sole hurdle, of course: religious dissidents were not allowed to vote, a barrier that could be as narrow as to affect only Catholics and as wide as to include all those who were not members of a colony's established church. For various reasons, the barriers to vote in local elections were usually fewer and more porous than for provincial officials. For example, in New England town meetings, a man who owned no land but whose father had land in the community was allowed to speak and vote, probably because he labored for his father and was expected to inherit the farm. Generally voting percentages varied from 80–90 percent of all adult white males in rural villages to 40–50 percent in coastal shipping ports like Ipswich, Massachusetts, and larger cities like Philadelphia and Boston. On the eve of the Revolution, particularly in southern New England, generations of rapid population growth and recent economic problems were driving a decline in the rate of property ownership and the proportion of men eligible to vote.[6]

These conditions at the outbreak of the war gave special urgency to the Revolutionary rhetoric of popular consent that developed in tension with English common-law traditions and the republican connection between economic independence and political virtue. The result was intense debates over state laws and constitutions regarding property requirements for voting and officeholding. In Connecticut a petition to the assembly in May 1776 sought an end to such barriers, arguing that it should not be "the Want of *Fifty Shillings*" that "distinguisheth a Bondman from a Son of Liberty." Five years later that assembly considered extending the vote to all taxpayers. In spring 1776, the Philadelphia militia's Committee of Privates published notices urging the provincial assembly to open the vote to all who served in the military or paid taxes. That summer the Maryland militia marched on the polls to demand the right to vote and in some counties to choose election judges. In both Massachusetts and New York, debates over proposed constitutions highlighted strong support for extending suffrage to all men who demonstrated a clear connection to the community: some specified taxpayers, others added militia service, and still others called for only a certificate from the local selectmen attesting to good character. Some made principled arguments against property qualifications, whereas others expressed more practical fears that the economic problems of the time would cause them to fall into debt and lose their right to vote along with their farms.[7]

Despite such democratic sentiment, political leaders throughout the newly independent states continued to insist on the need for property restrictions on voting, and most state constitutions contained such limitations. John Adams, who drafted the Massachusetts document, wrote that a system without such limits would "confound and destroy all distinctions, and prostrate all ranks to one common level." There were some notable exceptions: Pennsylvania and North Carolina enfranchised men who paid taxes as well as adult untaxed sons; New Hampshire allowed men to vote who paid their poll tax; Georgia's 1789 constitution specified men who paid taxes; and Vermont went the furthest by giving the vote to all adult men. But elsewhere voters had to own property. New Jersey required a freehold (real estate not encumbered by a mortgage) worth £50 "proclamation money." Connecticut and Rhode Island maintained pre-Revolutionary requirements for property worth £4 or producing 40 shillings per year, and Massachusetts insisted that voters for House delegates own land earning £3 per year. Freehold requirements were standard in Delaware (fifty acres), Virginia (twenty-five acres with a home, fifty acres without), South Carolina (fifty acres), and Maryland (fifty acres or land worth £30). New York required a freehold worth £20 or—with widespread tenancy in the Hudson River Valley—a leasehold worth 40 shillings per year. Three states set higher restrictions for senate and gubernatorial elections: New York required a freehold worth £100, which barred tenants; North Carolina mandated a freehold of fifty acres; and Massachusetts required a freehold worth at least £60. The Massachusetts constitutional convention warned that extending suffrage to all men would make the government "liable to the control of Men, who will pay less regard to the Rights of Property because they have nothing to lose."[8]

Men seeking office were generally expected (and in most states required) to have more wealth than was necessary to vote, probably because of the tradition that only the wealthy had the leisure time necessary to gain the knowledge and skills required for proper governance. In the states with constitutions that specified minimum estates for officials, the requirements were higher for senators (usually twice that of representatives) and governors. In New Hampshire, for example, members of the House of Representatives had to own at least £100 worth of personal estate including a freehold valued at £50; senators needed a freehold worth at least £200; and governors needed property worth £500 including a freehold worth half that amount. Similarly, in New Jersey and Maryland, senators had to own property worth twice as much as that held by representatives. Massachusetts and North Carolina required their senators to own three times as much as representatives. South Carolina set the bar for House members at the same level as voters—a freehold of fifty acres or a town lot, or payment of taxes the previous year—but senators had to own a freehold worth £2,000, and a governor's freehold had to be worth at least £10,000. By comparison, farmers and artisans in 1774 made about £30 per year profit, and the median personal estate of all men was about £150. For obvious reasons, artisans owned far less land than farmers. Although the state legislatures after the Revolution did contain increasing percentages of "middling" farmers and artisans, particularly in the North, these constitutions still created floors that ensured representatives would be wealthier than the average voter and reserved the upper house for the "better sort."[9]

A recent study of voting rights concluded that the result of the Revolutionary struggles over suffrage "was a mixed bag of substantive changes, cosmetic alterations, and preservation of the status quo." Residence requirements became more important and religious qualifications less so, although most states limited officeholders to Protestants. Only three states—Georgia, Virginia, and South Carolina—included explicit racial (white) limits, while Massachusetts towns rejected the proposal to put that limitation in their constitution. With regard to class and wealth, the reforms generally expanded the range of who could vote and hold office without severing connections between property and polity. Indeed, in southern states the continued property restrictions provided a bulwark for powerful coastal elites. Most states reduced the amount of property or wealth required to vote (e.g., New York's freehold qualifications were reduced by half), with the exception of Massachusetts, but the scattered data indicate that the percentages of men voting did not change by much. Suffrage may have actually declined toward the end of the eighteenth century, as in Connecticut, perhaps because property holding became more concentrated and land more expensive.[10]

At the same time, the distinctions between municipal and state levels of voting rights widened after the war, with urban residents increasingly given the right to vote in municipal elections if they paid taxes or owned enough personal property. In addition, the popular passion for democratic politics became palatable along with strong support for widening the formal polity to most if not all adult men. Perhaps as a result, the limits of that polity were woven into written constitutions instead of legislative action. It is also important to remember that imbedded in that passion for popular politics was the hope and even the assumption that a rough economic equality, without extremes of poverty or wealth, would remain a fundamental aspect of the new United States.[11]

In fact, economic equality became the focus of fierce political battles in many states over who would pay the costs of the war. One of the most contentious issues was the debt from state bonds and other notes, much of which had been obtained by speculators from veterans and farmers at huge discounts. When the state assemblies sought to pay those legal obligations by levying heavy taxes, taxpayers demanded paper money (to make the taxes easier to pay) and other forms of relief; their demands were often granted because the more democratic constitutions allowed them to exert more political pressure. Similarly, the legislatures in Connecticut, Pennsylvania, New Jersey, New York, and other states sought to avoid paying their share of the interest on federal bonds that Congress issued to pay pensions to Continental officers. This became an explosive issue of class and democracy because common soldiers had to pay most of the taxes to fund the bonds but were not provided federal pensions. Rural residents and town laborers wanted relief from their legislatures and worried that the combination of tight money and higher taxes—three to four times what they had been before the war—was not only rapidly eroding their country's roughly equal distribution of property but would also force them into bankruptcy and end their right to vote. Creditors and national elites, on the other hand, including many of those today considered Founding Fathers, thought that the state legislatures' granting so much popular relief would threaten the virtue and stability of the new nation and endanger its already-precarious international standing.[12]

Indeed, in 1787 one of James Madison's primary goals in creating a more powerful federal government was to rein in the power of overly democratic state assemblies, and he pushed hard to give Congress a veto over state laws. During the convention in Philadelphia, in a speech that (unusually) took up the entire day on June 18, Alexander Hamilton noted the fundamental divide between "the mass of the people" and "the rich and well born"—connecting wealth and social status—and suggested giving the senate and presidency life terms because the people seldom judged correctly and therefore needed to be kept in check. Subsequent discussions about the structure of the senate focused on making that body represent the propertied "better sort," and several men, including George Mason, suggested that could be done by not paying senators a salary.[13]

Many delegates, including Gouverneur Morris and James Madison, would have liked to restrict voting in national elections to freeholders, those who owned property free of debt; some, like Mason, wanted higher property standards, whereas others, including Benjamin Franklin, rejected the idea of disenfranchising so many men who had fought for the new country. In the end, the proposed constitution imposed no property requirements to hold office or to vote except those imposed within each state for "the most numerous Branch of the state legislature," and of course state legislatures retained the power to elect senators. When the proposed constitution went to state ratification conventions, the widespread and often bitter opposition often focused on the concern that practically only rich merchants and lawyers would have wide enough reputations to be elected and the financial wherewithal to serve in national office.[14]

Even as the Constitutional Convention was meeting in Philadelphia, the Northwest Ordinance enacted by Continental Congress in New York demonstrated a similar conservative concern to connect political authority to landownership. The ordinance laid out the mileposts and procedures required for a territory to become a state equal to others in the union. The journey to statehood began with Congress choosing a governor, secretary, and three judges for a particular "district." When the district achieved "five thousand free male inhabitants" (no racial designation) at least twenty-one years old, the governor would call an election of a "representative assembly" that would help choose five councilors to assist the governor, together forming the territorial legislature. The ordinance required governors to own at least 1,000 acres; secretaries, judges, and counselors to own 500 acres; representatives to own 200 acres, and electors to own 50 acres. All of the land had to be held in the district (territory) where they lived, voted, and governed. These standards in theory ensured strong republican links between the people and officials. But considering that the land in the territories was being sold for a minimum of about 2 dollars per acre, even 50 acres represented a considerable sum. These standards were higher than those in many of the existing states and remained in place until 1811, even as states replaced property ownership with tax payment or eliminated economic requirements.[15]

In 1792 the *American Museum,* one of the first national periodicals, published by Mathew Carey in Philadelphia, ran a brief article that lovingly described New England's "pure republican equality" in economic as well as political terms: suffrage not limited to landholders, partible inheritance laws, and public provision of schools for all children including the poor.[16] But during the next half century, the intimate connection between property and politics almost completely disappeared as part of a monumental shift with fundamental social, economic, and political causes. New states entered the union with constitutions that contained no economic barriers to vote or required only the payment of taxes. Existing states followed, initially with some tentative reforms, followed by a wave of constitutional conventions between 1815 and 1840. In this atmosphere, Americans became increasingly likely to debate the question of expanding the right of (white) men to vote and hold office but less likely to raise any question of maintaining or expanding access to property as an essential part of republican government. The clear majority pushing to expand voting rights rarely addressed questions of economic equality because its goal was to end political distinctions of wealth or income. Those opposing democratic reforms, on the other hand, highlighted the protection of property rights as the main reason to continue such limitations. These debates highlighted an emerging consensus that men did not need to own property or pay taxes in order to demonstrate industry and virtue or to participate in the increasingly democratic political arena.

The hot presidential contest of 1796, followed by the election of Thomas Jefferson to the presidency in 1800 and James Madison and James Monroe during the following quarter century (forming the "Virginia Dynasty"), drove the formation of national broad-based political parties and, in the process, undermined the traditional connections between property and politics. The Democrat-Republicans and Federalists competed for voters not only to win elections but also because their organizers and newspaper editors benefited from widening their pools of supporters. Already enfranchised Americans increasingly believed that their interests and those of the republic would be served by the addition of more of the right kind of voters and that property was or should not be a factor. State legislatures had to define what counted for personal estate or freehold values, particularly as the economy became more commercialized and complex, and within each state the application of those rules probably varied widely between different locales. Incorporated towns and cities began to allow men who owned house lots or a set amount of personal property to vote. Severe inflation played havoc with suffrage requirements that specified values rather than acreage, essentially nullifying those barriers in several states. Increasingly, the lines that separated those allowed to participate in politics and those barred from voting and officeholding seemed arbitrary and unrepublican. One New Jersey newspaper noted in 1798 that state property qualifications were no longer enforced "from a conviction of its repentance to the principles of republicanism, and from the impracticability of its observance."[17]

This democratic tide was amplified by the increasing numbers of Americans who owned little if any land. Along with rising class tensions, seemingly every state with property qualifications, even those suffering from depreciating currency, experienced an apparent increase in the number and percentage of men who failed to meet the property requirements to vote. Shrinking farm sizes, urban growth, and mass production led to an increasing body of artisans and laborers unable to afford homes or land. Tenancy increased in the Hudson River Valley and western New York, and settlers in western Maryland, Virginia, the Carolinas, and northern Louisiana felt their state constitutions gave all the power to wealthy coastal elites.[18]

Men lacking the sufficient freehold or personal wealth, joined by sympathetic or ambitious elites, began to demand an end to property qualifications along with other reforms to create more democratic local and state governments. This movement was widespread: in 1794 Baltimore mechanics insisted that "wealth ought not to be made a qualification to office," and ten years later a meeting of delegates from ninety-seven towns in Connecticut demanded a new state constitution that would enshrine the right to vote for all taxpayers. In 1806 Franklin Burgess in the *Impartial Observer* of Richmond, Virginia, called for the "industrious labour, and ingenious mechanic or artist" to be "restore[d] . . . to their rights" to participate in politics, in place of that state's current freehold mandate that had established "a landed aristocracy, ugly and deformed, in the sacred temple dedicated to freedom and the rights of man." In 1811 another (anonymous) Virginian complained that, although the state's government was supposedly republican, "a vast majority" of white men lacked enough land to vote, and those with the power sought laws to "bind" not only "the honest industrious poor" but also " *the worthy mechanic and the useful manufacturer*"—men who still had to pay their taxes and, in the case of invasion, would be "the greater part" of those called upon to take up arms.[19]

The democratic pressure grew with the War of 1812. A huge percentage of the men who fought for the vulnerable United States against the British were poor farmers or laborers without property, and the country's condition and culture encouraged them to demand a voice in the governments they had defended. Landless men had similarly filled the ranks of colonial militia and, during the Revolutionary War, the Continental Army. Those soldiers were paid in part with promises of land taken from Native peoples, which of course included the assumed right of the freeholder to vote. This American "tradition" incorporated ideas from classical history that soldiers who had risked their lives and fought for the republican government should be rewarded with land and regarded as freemen with the right to a voice in that government. But after 1800 few states had much surplus land and the established federal land system left little opportunity to make new grants to soldiers. After the War of 1812, the shift was particularly noticeable in states like Virginia, with high freehold requirements to vote, and many men like Thomas Jefferson became acutely aware of how "a very great majority of the militia were men unrepresented in the legislation which imposed this burthen on them." One newspaper reported that, in a company of seventy-eight that went from Culpepper County in 1814 to repel the British invasion of Tidewater Virginia, only four had the right to vote.[20]

Conservatives feared that removing the connection between landholding and political power would endanger property rights and social order. Like English critics of the Levellers, American elites feared that ending freehold requirement would allow radicals and ne'er-do-wells to outvote and control the "better sort" who owned land, ruthlessly raising taxes and even seizing property in the name of the people. That paradigm could be used to justify reactionary opposition to reforms, as when South Carolina conservatives opposed calls to give more representation to backcountry counties because it would lead to a tyranny of the lazy majority over the industrious wealthy minority. Initially, such concerns about broadened suffrage were secondary to the intense paranoia about agrarian measures designed to widen property holding and prevent individual accumulation of wealth. But as the calls for economic equality grew fainter and more marginalized, holding the line on property qualifications for suffrage became a conservative focus.[21]

Fears of greater democracy intensified at the turn of the century as the United States became more entangled with the French Revolution and other European radical movements. In 1798 a screed published in Baltimore and two Federalist New York papers, the *New York Gazette* and *Albany Centinel*, condemned the easy access to citizenship that encouraged "foreigners" (French and Irish radicals) to reject "the most wholesome subordination" and to consider every protection of their neighbors' property "as encroachments upon their natural rights—as a prostration of Liberty and Equality." At New Haven's Independence Day celebration in 1802, the famed political writer Noah Webster told the gathering that, because property was inevitably unequally divided, allowing all men to vote regardless of property would create an "inequality of power" resulting in "a monstrous inversion of the natural order of society." Some protested that their governments were already close to perfection. In August 1805, one year after a large convention of Connecticut town delegates called for democratic reforms, the leading newspaper in the state boasted that the state's constitution was more republican than most because its property threshold was so low, and a man could never lose the right to vote. Besides, the state had "as great a degree of republican equality" as anywhere else, including the right to a basic education for the poor. Indeed, only "a few intriguers" kept the people from being happy "in the present state of things."[22]

But these conservative voices were increasingly isolated as the pressure to expand suffrage grew. The formal barriers fell first in the West. Many settlers who had been unable to afford farmland in the East lacked the capital or credit to buy title; they (correctly) gambled that they could without interference "squat" on the fertile lands in the West and, in the long run, gain at least compensation for their "improvements." Settlers wanting to establish clear title often faced great difficulty and expense because of the extensive and often conflicting land speculation that began during the late colonial period and continued during the early Republic. The situation also offered opportunities for merchants and artisans unable to gain a solid footing in the East. The democratic course was carved by Virginia's western "county" of Kentucky in 1784, when leading men called a convention to discuss separate statehood with delegates elected by militia companies, thereby ignoring Virginia's freehold requirement. In the subsequent annual conventions, until Kentucky statehood was achieved, delegates were elected by all free white men. When a constitutional convention was finally held in April 1792 with the approval of Congress, it created a government with suffrage and officeholding open to all free men without any property or taxpaying requirements.[23]

This democratic pattern would be magnified in the federal territories even though (or perhaps because) Congress had established in the Northwest Ordinance high freehold requirements for voting and officeholding. From the beginning, territorial governance and landholding were shaped by bitter ideological conflicts reflected in the emergence of national parties. The appointed governor of the territory, Arthur St. Clair, struggled to maintain Federalist dominance of the territory and future state. He clashed with squatter settlers and the local leaders who supported Democrat-Republicans, particularly when that party's leaders in Congress, like James Madison, sought to authorize the purchase of smaller lots in the territory but were outvoted by Federalists. Perhaps more importantly, the new nation's weak bureaucracy and expansive ambition was unable to shape or control western settlement. The effects became clear in 1798, after the territory's population of American citizens had clearly gone beyond the point empowered to elect a legislature, and St. Clair reported that so many men had yet to obtain title that most freeholders owned only small lots in towns. At the governor's reluctant request, Congress modified the fifty-acre freehold requirement and opened the suffrage to men owning town lots worth at least the market value of fifty acres—about $100.[24]

After 1800, as the Democrat-Republicans gained control of the national government, Congress took a series of measures that liberalized voting in the territories and, in the process, knowingly or not, largely separated political participation from property ownership. While the Northwest Ordinance had mandated standards for the territorial governments, its description of the process whereby a territory became a state was very short and vague: after its population exceeded sixty thousand "free inhabitants," it could become a state if Congress found its constitution and government "properly republican." But nothing was said about the procedure for writing the constitution. That made it simple for Congress in 1802 and 1816, when it separated sections to become the Ohio and Indiana territories, to authorize all resident men who paid taxes to elect delegates to constitutional conventions. In 1805 Congress similarly opened Mississippi territorial elections—a region not covered by the Northwest Ordinance—to all tax-paying men, and in 1811 extended that policy to all territories. In the wake of the War of 1812, Congress became more liberal, removing the taxpaying requirement: its enabling acts for Illinois in 1818 and Alabama in 1819 authorized all men aged twenty-one and older to vote for territorial constitutional convention delegates.[25]

Not surprisingly, nearly all of the resulting state constitutions similarly separated political participation from the ownership of property. Ohio in 1802 required voters to pay taxes but did not require them to own property, although, as in most states at the time, representatives, senators, and governors were required to own property. Indiana (1816), Illinois (1818), and Missouri (1820) required neither property ownership nor tax payments for voting—following the standards for voting in the constitutional convention elections—and lowered the requirements for officeholders to simply paying state taxes. Alabama's constitution (1819) eliminated tax payment and property ownership requirements for holding office as well as voting. At the same time, many Americans, particularly elites, were concerned about this democratic tendency. That anxiety was reflected in the first constitutions of the two most southwestern states, Louisiana (1812) and Mississippi (1817), both of which featured deeply embedded slave plantation cultures that connected market capitalism and a mythical aristocracy. While both states gave suffrage to any white man who paid taxes, they raised high barriers to holding office: Louisiana required ownership of freeholds worth $500 for representatives, $1,000 for senators, and $5,000 for governors; Mississippi required 150 acres or $500 worth of real estate for representatives, 300 acres or $1,000 for senators, and 600 acres or $2,000 for governors.[26]

When this democratic tide hit eastern states during the Era of Good Feelings, the very public arguments over whether or how to extend political rights re-

vealed a great deal about the changes in how Americans viewed the connections between property and voting, economic and political equality. In October 1820, a writer in *Niles Weekly Register*, a national magazine published in
Baltimore, wished success to the efforts in "several" states to expand the right
to vote and wondered why "in this enlightened day" there were "so many barriers . . . placed between the people at large and their local governments."
Regardless of the particular state, *Niles* insisted that "every man, liable to fight
the battles of his country, or to pay taxes to support its government, should
be a qualified voter." These suffrage standards were, of course, already common in western constitutions, and they became the goals of those seeking
democratic reforms in the older states. The writer then contended that requiring property ownership for suffrage—even a house or shop in a city—had
little validity because property was worth nothing unless made productive by
labor and defended by arms. On the other hand, he thought suffrage should
not be "cheap" and suggested that those wishing to vote should be required
to register and prove their citizenship.[27]

Between 1800 and 1820, a few of the original states did relax their property
restrictions on voting. Maryland in 1801 ended its property ownership requirement to vote in state elections and in 1810 amended its constitution to end it
for all elections. South Carolina in 1810 dropped the requirement that voters
pay taxes. The push for reforms increased in the wake of the War of 1812, when
word spread that many militia members lacked sufficient property to vote despite their sacrifice for the state, and mushroomed during the Panic of 1819,
as every state with property qualifications experienced a decline in the number and proportion of adult males who met those standards. Petitions demanding the right to vote became more common, and such efforts not only echoed
ideas hallowed by the American Revolution, including natural rights and no
taxation without direct representation, but also revealed a rapidly shifting
sense of what created a voter's "stake" in government. These demands and the
responses they provoked found their clearest forum in the state conventions
called by legislatures, in which delegates elected under distinctly liberalized
suffrage standards were tasked to rewrite the constitutions that (mostly) dated
from the beginning of the Revolution. The resulting reforms followed the
paths blazed by western states and weakened the traditional links between political and economic equality.[28]

Connecticut became one of the first of the original thirteen states to completely rewrite its constitution during this period. As already noted, the state
made few changes in its colonial charter, and when (in 1804) ninety-seven
towns demanded a new constitution, they met with a blizzard of scorn from

the elite, and the effort froze. Indeed, nine years later the legislature passed rules that, among other things, allowed only unmortgaged property to count toward freehold voting standards and required men to vote publicly by standing. One writer complained in the *Hartford Times* that these "reforms" had been designed "to overawe the poor man and make him silent," creating "an important link in the chain . . . to fetter the poor and build up a monied aristocracy in the State." In response, Jeffersonians and evangelicals together created the Toleration Party, held a convention in 1816, and in 1817 took control of the executive branch and lower house. That victory inspired a deluge of town petitions supporting a call for a constitutional convention.[29]

In early June 1818, the Connecticut legislature considered a measure that would have changed the qualifications for freemen—the basic right to participate in *state* elections—to any white man aged twenty-one who paid taxes or performed military duty. The debate focused briefly on whether to require "a good moral character" but then turned to the ultimate question of whether to eliminate property requirements. Federalists, including Shubael Griswold, who scorned the measure as creating universal suffrage and had opposed the constitutional convention, emphasized that voting was not a natural right but one conferred by the community. Griswold wondered about "the security of real property, when the poor and destitute can vote it away" and were "liable to be controuled by the wealthy and influential." He also noted that many "accomplished females" were far better suited to vote than the poor white men who would get it under the proposed measure. On the other side, Toleration Party members like Nathan Pendleton from North Stonington, which was rapidly becoming a mill town, scorned the idea of a factory owner bringing "regiments" of wage workers to vote because they would gladly come on their own if the bill was made law. Orange Merwin noted that it was often said that "the poor may oppress the rich, but this never *has* happened and never *will*." Henry Channing from New London added that the bill met "the fundamental principle, that taxation and representation go together." After another short debate, a large majority voted the measure into law.[30]

On the same day, the legislature approved a constitutional convention, to be elected by freemen on July 4 and to meet beginning in late August. Over the next few months, writers in the *Times* and the *Connecticut Courant* considered the question of suffrage. The *Courant* presented a restrained discussion of possible changes in the new constitution. Regarding voting, the paper began by noting that, while all agreed on the need to require "*good moral* character and a *proper age,*" there was still conflict over whether to require ownership of property. Those in favor argued that such limits would provide more protection for property, and that while poverty generally indicated "*incapacity* and *bad character*," a requirement to own property "encourages *industry*, and . . . *respectability*." Those opposed insisted that "the *poor*" had "*rights* and *interests* to be consulted," that property requirements tempted dishonest measures such as candidates arranging "temporary transfers of property" to poor supporters, and that high standards tended "to *discourage* industry, and to *depress* the hopes of rising to respectability." These arguments would generally mark the two sides in the constitutional conventions in other states. Two months later, "Judd" in the *Times* argued that voting should rest on "*personal considerations*" instead of property standards because all men were "by nature equal." Those who condemned the poor for accepting money to vote a certain way should instead consider the real criminal to be the rich person "disposed to abuse their wealth" in that fashion. In fact, he argued, should property be a factor in suffrage, the "correct" measure would bar men who had accumulated "an unwieldy mass of wealth" as "*dangerous to the public security.*"[31]

The convention began on August 26 and three weeks later approved and submitted to the voters a constitution that gave the vote to men who either owned a freehold worth 7 dollars, had paid state taxes in the last year, or had served in the militia. It also laid no additional property requirements on elected officials. Six days later, "A Freeman" in the *Connecticut Courant* thundered against the broader suffrage because past republics that had taken similar measures soon after became monarchies. Besides, in Connecticut "every person possessing honesty, prudence, and industry, the principle qualities of good character"—the main standard for voting—could easily obtain sufficient property to vote under the existing constitution. The following week, "Freeman" sniffed that the new constitution might as well go completely democratic and end all property requirements thereby, for the proposed document would give the state into "the hands and power of such men as throng the cities for day labor, or with other less meritorious views." Again, these arguments would be repeated in other states by opponents of proposals to eliminate property requirements for voters and officeholders. But Freeman's points gained little traction, and the proposed constitution passed by a majority and remained the state's structure until the 1860s.[32]

When Massachusetts held its constitutional convention two years later, delegates made similar arguments regarding the proposal to eliminate property requirements for state elections. The delegates opposing the reforms insisted that the property limits on voting were important incentives for young men to work and save, served as a critical bulwark of deference, and should remain as "the reward for good conduct." Supreme Court justice Joseph Story insisted that property should get special protection since that was a primary purpose for government, and he repeated the rapidly vanishing myth that in America wealth did not "form a permanent distinction of families" because the ban on entail and primogeniture—"the only true and legitimate agrarian law"—meant that estates were divided among all children. Those embracing the changes argued that men born with property should not be given special rights, that the laborers without property who might be asked to fight for the state should be able to vote, and that morality was shaped not by property ownership but by education. Many reformers also attacked as unrepublican the property basis for the state senate that John Adams had designed in 1780, and they pushed for that to be abolished. In the end, a majority of delegates, reformers and conservatives, agreed to open the vote to all men who paid taxes and their sons, while maintaining the existing rationale that the state senate would represent property.[33]

New York became the next state to revise its constitution, which, like that of Massachusetts before the reforms, set a higher restriction to vote in elections for senators and the governor. But while the conventions in both states were driven in part by the challenge of accommodating a rapidly growing urban population of laboring men, many of whom were recent immigrants, New York also had a unique history of violent conflicts over land rights and tenancy. The sizable population of tenants in the Hudson River Valley, and those in the rapidly developing west (formerly Iroquoia) unable to gain title until completing payments, were barred from voting in senatorial or gubernatorial elections and were increasingly alienated by the controls exerted by western land companies and Hudson River landlords. For decades the swirl of New York politics and influence of powerful families prevented reforms, but in the winter of 1820–21 a new reform-minded "Bucktail" alliance led by the young Martin Van Buren took control of the legislature and rammed through a measure allowing all men to vote on whether to call a constitutional convention in late summer 1821; not surprisingly, it passed by a huge majority. Given the existing constitution, and concerns of urban laborers and rural residents without freeholds, arguments over extending the vote inevitably involved long-standing concerns of landownership and republican virtue.[34]

In late September 1821, the convention's suffrage committee proposed extending the right to vote for *all* offices to every white adult male who paid any tax, worked on a public road, or served in the militia. Immediately, Chief Justice Ambrose Spencer rose and proposed an amendment restoring the landholding requirement ($250 value) to vote for senators, in order to prevent landless urban laborers from dominating the government. That was supported by

Chancellor James Kent, who scorned "the idol of universal suffrage" and praised "property distinctions" for ensuring the stability and wisdom of the state and its government. Kent warned that allowing "men of no property" and laborers working for manufacturers to vote for the senate would "jeopardize the rights of property, and the principles of liberty" because "there is a tendency in the poor to covet and share the plunder of the rich." Elisha Williams argued that the settlers who held purchase contracts to their farms rather than deeds *were* qualified to vote under freehold rules and thus had no need for the proposed reforms, and he warned that the "streaked and speckled population of our large towns and cities" were (quoting Jefferson) "upon the body politic great sores." Conservatives also echoed the arguments common in Massachusetts and Connecticut, that with the end of entail and primogeniture large estates were being rapidly divided and that the property threshold created "a strong inducement to that industry and economy which are the life of society." Williams charged that giving the vote to "the idle and profligate" meant they would never try to "*earn* those privileges" but would instead (like peasants during the French Revolution) simply demand property.[35]

The radicals (who wanted universal suffrage) joined with moderates (who formed the majority) to oppose the amendment and support the initial proposal. Peter R. Livingston told the convention that "the poor and hardy soldier" in the recent war deserved the right to vote and that property "will always carry with it an influence sufficient for its own protection." John Cramer went further, insisting that "life and liberty" were "dearer than property" and that the valor of the militia showed that "the laboring class" had "more integrity and more patriotism" than "the higher orders." Next, moderate David Buel highlighted the trend to eliminate property qualifications and pointed out that the more open assembly had not suffered radical movements so there was no danger having the same rules for senatorial elections. But regardless of such practical considerations, noted the young lawyer, "our community is an association of persons" rather than property, and while property should be protected, it need not be woven into the structure of government. Martin Van Buren was one of the last to speak, and his political clout gave his words special emphasis. The fundamental point of the reforms, he argued, was that the many "mechanics, professional men, and small landholders" who formed "the bone, pith, and muscle" of the state but failed to meet the $250 barrier, should be allowed to vote in senatorial elections. In fact, the convention was called in large part "to relieve them of this injustice, and this oppression." Later that day, the amendment to restore the freehold requirement was overwhelmingly defeated, 19-100. The only question became whether men who paid no taxes but served in the militia would be able to vote, and in the end that detail was approved and became part of article II of the new constitution.[36]

The debates in Virginia similarly reflected arguments between protecting property and widening or revitalizing democratic representation. The arguments in this state were particularly long and bitter in part because its property requirements remained among the highest in the nation and in part because slavery ensured the wealth and power of the elites who mostly lived in the eastern tidewater region. The Commonwealth's 1776 constitution required white men wishing to vote to possess a freehold at least fifty acres in size, or twenty-five acres if the land included a house measuring at least twelve feet square. Calls to end this requirement began in the early 1800s, as tenant farmers and mechanics gained political prominence, and in 1811 a writer in the *Alexandria Herald* angrily compared the political condition of most white men in the state to that of slaves. In July 1816 a prominent Virginia lawyer sent petitions for a constitutional convention to Thomas Jefferson. While Jefferson's reply is most famous for asserting that every generation had the right to create government anew, he also opined that "every man who fights or pays [taxes]" should be able to vote for members of the legislature. A month after that, *Niles Weekly Register* noted that the state was "in a great bustle to reform the constitution" because suffrage restrictions drove white men to western states and territories where they could participate as full citizens. Two weeks later, delegates from ninety-seven towns gathered in Staunton, in the western part of the state, to petition the legislature for a convention to write a more representative constitution.[37]

When the Virginia legislature debated the question in January 1817, Smyth of Wythe rose to condemn the freehold requirement as a "feudal principle" because, despite the new rules of partible inheritance, the increasing shortage of land had created an "oligarchy" that wielded power over the majority. The freehold rule originated in times when the commonwealth had only freemen and slaves, but now those who owned sufficient land were a small minority. Smyth emphasized, "It is men who constitute the state; and it is men who should be represented in the legislature; not the earth on which we tread." But even as he suggested extending suffrage to long-term leases (as in New York) or ownership of public stock, he did not mention payment of taxes as a qualification and assured his colleagues that he agreed with them that "the pauper, the vagrant, the stranger, should be excluded—and perhaps some others." While "moderate" reformers in the state wanted to accommodate the changing economic situation, they still thought that a republic rested on stable independent farmers.[38]

Although the legislature tried to still the uproar by increasing the proportion of senators elected from western counties from four to nine of the twenty-four members, powerful voices continued to press for reforms. Advocates demanded the right of suffrage for men who paid taxes or served in the militia, and one of Jefferson's last published pieces mourned how few of the militiamen who had risked their lives for the Commonwealth during the War of 1812 had been able to vote. In 1824 and 1825, community meetings to rally support for a constitutional convention were again held throughout Virginia and expressed the hope that suffrage would be opened to all free men who paid taxes or served in the militia. In June 1825 *Niles Weekly* condemned Maryland and Virginia for having "the most *aristocratic* constitutions of any in the union," and the *Richmond Whig* complained that the state's freehold mandate had established "a landed aristocracy." But the conservatives in the legislature continued to defeat bills calling for a convention, until the 1827–28 session when the body agreed to ask the voters, who in turn approved the meeting. *Niles* predicted that the convention would ultimately "please the poor, but laboring, arms-bearing freemen of Virginia, the very muscle and sinew of her population, in the full enjoyment of political rights."[39]

The convention gathered in Richmond in early October 1829; the attendees included Chief Justice John Marshall and former president James Madison, and President James Monroe presided. Almost immediately, "non-freeholders" in that city and in rural communities on both sides of the Blue Ridge Mountains submitted petitions insisting that they had the same "natural right" to the vote as did freeholders, especially with the clause in the constitution that "all men are by nature equally free and independent," and that defending the state in war demonstrated just as much devotion to the commonwealth as owning a farm. After some initial discussions, a subcommittee recommended extending the vote to men with long-term leaseholds or heads of households who paid taxes, while a more radical dissenter filed a resolution insisting that "suffrage, without regard to birth or condition of estate" was the absolute right of every free white man "proving permanent common interest with, and attachment to, the community" through residence and paying public taxes. Clearly most preferred modest reforms that would stretch the definition of property to include long-term leases and city householders while maintaining the traditional connection between property and political power.[40]

An opponent immediately challenged the reformers to justify the change that he and other conservatives compared to the folly of the French Revolution in delivering control of the state's wealth into the hands of those who owned little. The reformers responded by depicting the freehold requirement as an aristocratic innovation imposed by King Charles II in the wake of Bacon's Rebellion and asserting that Virginian leaders at the start of the Revolution had reluctantly kept the restriction to avoid chaos during that tumultuous period. At the same time, noted John Cooke, the Virginia Declaration of Rights included the principle that "*a majority of the community* possess, by the law of nature and necessity, a right to control its concerns" including rules of property ownership. By contrast, he noted, the conservatives who wanted representation figured by property as well as population would give wealthy eastern plantation owners even more power. Another reformer, Philip Doddridge, from the western edge of the state, scorned property representation as an aristocratic innovation, whereas the proposals to expand the suffrage continued (he said) the Virginian republican tradition of "equal political rights."[41]

The conservative opponents wielded Locke to argue that, since men formed a social compact to protect property, it was far more important for political systems to account for property than to seek an impossible equality of persons. Abel Upshur insisted that it was most important for government to be structured to protect property and prevent chaos. Benjamin Leigh sternly lectured westerners that the attempt to separate property and political power would end in a disaster, for either "property will purchase power, or power will take property. . . . If property buy power, the very process is corruption. If power ravish property, the sword must be drawn." Either would end free government in America. As in New York, those who wanted to maintain the property restrictions argued that the need to protect property and social stability was far more fundamental than the abstract and dangerous principle of universal suffrage. But slavery was deeply imbedded in Virginia's debate because eastern plantation owners wanted to maintain their political weight vis-à-vis the western side of the state, where (they believed) the non-slaveholding white population was increasing rapidly and—especially with the proposed reforms— could soon take control of the legislature and end much of the legal scaffold that protected slavery. Upshar concluded, quite honestly, that defending "*our* property" (i.e., enslaved people) required "*that kind of protection* which flows from the possession of power." In the end, the convention passed, and voters approved, a constitution that gave the vote to every citizen owning or renting property worth 25 dollars or who had paid taxes to the state in the previous year.[42]

Similar pressures from western counties pushed neighboring North Carolina to hold a constitutional convention in 1835, but its authorized scope did not include the long-standing requirements that senators be substantial property holders and that voters for senators own at least fifty acres—and those restrictions remained law. Thirteen years later, when David Reid, a powerful Democrat, ran for governor on a platform of unrestricted white suffrage, Whigs labeled that goal "a system of communism unjust and Jacobism." Whig newspapers claimed that those calling for unrestricted suffrage hoped to include women and, with it, "desecration of the Bible and the abolition of Matrimony." In turn, Reid in June 1850 accused his Whig opponent, Governor Manly, of opposing "Equal Suffrage" as "too 'levelling' and too 'Agrarian.'" On the contrary, held the Democrat, many "enterprising young men" and "industrious farmers and mechanics" lacked the fifty acres necessary to vote for senators but would never "impose on the landed interest" because they intended as soon as possible to join the landowning class "with the proceeds of their honest industry." Four years later, the state finally abolished all property ownership requirements.[43]

The fiercest contest came in Rhode Island, which still used its colonial charter and restricted suffrage to owners of freeholds worth $134 or renting for $7 per year, about 40 to 60 percent of the state's white male adults, and retained a structure of representation dominated by rural towns, neglecting the booming industrial and commercial cities. In June 1829, nearly two thousand men petitioned for widened suffrage, noting that Virginia required less than their state. But conservatives insisted such reforms would allow factory owners and merchants to run the state and impose outrageous land taxes. In April 1833 workingman organizer Seth Luther came to Providence to support the call for reform, telling the audience of laborers that the state's "aristocrats" feared the "*poor mechanic*" and believed that "'*good society*' ought not to be disturbed by the unlearned rabble." Luther was not exaggerating, as the Brown College president Francis Wayland told the senior class that "probably, the right of suffrage should be restricted to those who are able to read and write." Those who wanted constitutional reforms were also deeply divided over how far to extend the vote given Rhode Island's increasing diversity; Democrats generally urged extending the vote to immigrants, many of whom were Catholics, but not blacks; Whigs called for the opposite.[44]

For the 1834 elections, Thomas Dorr, a Rhode Island assemblyman and a Whig, formed a Suffrage party and called for a new constitution with voting rights given to all men, but when the party finished a distant third, the Whigs expelled Dorr. The call for democracy faded until 1841, when the failure of the state to deal with the lingering severe depression revived support for Dorr and his Suffrage Association. That October the Association held a huge extralegal convention and drew up a "People's Constitution" giving the vote to all white men with one year's residence. It is noteworthy that Dorr initially wanted to extend suffrage to black men, but most of the association as well as his Democrat allies were opposed, so he dropped the idea. The state allowed an informal referendum on the People's Constitution in which all white men could vote, but afterward it declared the results meaningless. Two parallel elections were held in April 1842 and chose different governments, including governors Dorr and Samuel King, a Whig. The "People's Legislature" adjourned shortly after meeting in an abandoned factory, while Dorr led a small group in an effort to seize the state arsenal—and was easily repelled by a force that included a large group of black volunteers. Dorr fled but was quickly arrested and sentenced to life for treason (though he served only a year). The legislature called for another convention, with African Americans also allowed to vote for delegates, resulting in a constitution that resembled the "People's Constitution" in giving the vote to any native-born man who paid at least 1 dollar per year in taxes or performed military service but was unique in including black men and requiring immigrants to meet the older property requirements.[45]

The imbroglio in Rhode Island highlighted how, even as democrats sought to separate political rights from economic concerns and to make American equality about the right to vote, political rights and equality in America were increasingly connected to *masculinity* and *race*. Through the early Republic, ownership of land was the ultimate source of masculine authority. Ministers and writers emphasized how God had appointed Adam and his male offspring as patriarchs to "subdue the land" as well as their dependents. One of the few widely shared paradigms in early America was that everyone had to live within and contribute to the well-being of a household and that the head of that household could only be a man. Only men had the strength of body and mind to supervise and support the household, and politics and public life were considered extensions of the household. The most extreme version of this paradigm was the old monarchist argument, as exemplified by Robert Filmer's *Patriarcha* (ca. 1640), that a king served as father of the nation and therefore the ultimate source of authority. But even in the acutely republican United States, the independence of mature masculine power was economic as well as political: the two elements were closely linked.[46]

But after 1800, and particularly after the War of 1812, more and more mature men were unable to own land or even homes and found themselves doing lifelong wage labor. At the same time, America's dynamic market economy seemed to offer limitless opportunities to ambitious individuals, and its increasingly democratic culture pushed aside older norms of household and community interdependence. The right of an individual to participate in politics and related activities was increasingly associated with manhood and masculine independence, and the phrase "all men are created equal" became rooted in democratic political activities.[47] Masculinity and democracy became closely connected in the urban firefighting societies, which served to organize and mobilize men of various occupations, often played a significant role in city politics, and occasionally joyfully participated in election day riots that shook major cities in the second quarter of the nineteenth century. The Democratic Party also worked to provide jobs and other assistance to working and middle-class men.[48]

Unfortunately, these new democratic, individualistic, masculine norms were tightly attached to the scourge of racism, as racial inequality became part of the new political equality. White Americans increasingly viewed race as a fundamental and necessary "scientific" hierarchy. In the North, even as states passed gradual emancipation laws and slavery dragged toward extinction, whites scorned and abused the growing free population of African Americans, who were forced into menial jobs and separate neighborhoods. This racism was nearly universal, although it was noticeably more vicious and violent among urban working-class Jeffersonians (then Democrats) than among elite Federalists (then Whigs), who tended to emphasize distinctions among classes. As a result, there was only occasional and slight opposition when states added racial suffrage restrictions even as they removed property qualifications.[49]

It is not surprising to see these measures in southern states where race-based slavery was increasingly defended as a beneficial foundation of civilized society. The first constitutions adopted by Georgia (1777), South Carolina (1778), and Virginia (1776) explicitly limited suffrage to white men. Maryland in 1810 adopted amendments that eliminated property requirements for elected officials and extended suffrage to all free white men; North Carolina followed in 1835. When southwestern territories applied for statehood—Louisiana in 1812, Mississippi in 1817, Alabama in 1819, Arkansas in 1836—their constitutions invariably provided for liberal or even universal suffrage as long as you were a white man. In the older states, racial masculine concerns drove subsequent debates over expanding the suffrage. For example, in the 1810s and 1820s, those pushing to broaden voting in Virginia insisted the state's property restrictions were causing large numbers of young white men to move west. Three decades later, constitutional conventions in that state and in neighboring Maryland, in response to hundreds of petitions, included measures to keep employers from hiring or working black laborers alongside white men, thus "protecting" the "respected laborers" from "wire drawing politicians" and leaving "the old aristocracy" in the dust.[50]

But western and northern states also created racial barriers even as they dropped property restrictions. The first constitutions of Ohio (1803) Indiana (1816), Illinois (1818), Michigan (1835), Iowa (1846), and Wisconsin (1848) restricted the right to vote to white men, and only a few required payment of taxes or militia service. In 1807 New Jersey's legislature ignored the explicit standards in its state constitution and barred blacks as well as women from voting, thereby linking voting with white masculinity. Seven years later, Connecticut restricted suffrage to white men, and the June 1818 bill that ended property requirements for freemen would have likewise limited that privilege to white men. Largely ignored was the argument made by Federalist Aaron Austin that blacks should be included "if they had property sufficient and a good moral character." When that state's constitutional convention met in September, it considered a bill that would have limited suffrage to white males aged twenty-one and older. That designation was split in half, with the majority voting to keep "white," while dropping the explicit limit of "men."[51]

New York's constitutional convention explicitly connected widening the vote for white men with restricting it for blacks. The state had the largest population of African Americans in the North, and the concentration around New York City created a potentially important swing bloc generally regarded as favoring city over rural interests. That connection was highlighted by an Ithaca meeting in 1818 that demanded that all white men who paid taxes be given the right to vote for state senate candidates, ending the existing $250 property qualification but adding restrictions of race. That would also be the proposal reported to the convention in September 1821. For the committee, John Ross of rural Genesee County explained the new racial restriction by insisting that blacks rarely if ever shared "the common burdens or defense of the state" and had "no just concepts of civil liberty"—although, of course, they had struggled for freedom, paid taxes, and fought for the state. Chief Justice Spencer then proposed his amendment restoring the $250 qualification without reference to race, immediately followed by the Bucktail Samuel Young of rural Saratoga County moving to add the "white" restriction. In that way the debate on suffrage rules first focused on whether to disenfranchise African Americans, which was linked to the parallel issue of property restrictions. Several delegates argued the blacks were able and entitled to vote, while Young insisted that they were "not competent to vote" and that the state's constitution should reflect social prejudice and reserve political equality for white men. In the end, Van Buren arranged a "compromise" that ended the $250 freehold requirement for white men while extending it for blacks wishing to vote in *any* state election.[52]

Sixteen years later, when Pennsylvania held a special convention to reform aspects of its 1790 constitution, including possibly expanding suffrage by eliminating the requirement to have paid state and county taxes, Democrats used similar racist language to push for black disfranchisement. While the first effort barely failed, during the subsequent six months newspapers throughout the country and especially in the South connected African American suffrage to the larger controversy over slavery and abolition, making the issue a national concern. Pennsylvania political leaders and delegates increasingly spoke of disfranchisement in terms of mollifying the South, supporting the Union, and maintaining national peace. Of course, the all-white delegates also continued to argue over whether blacks were innately inferior and subservient (implicitly comparing the race to white women), and whether political equality should be reserved for white men. In the end, "white" was added to the suffrage qualification in the Pennsylvania Constitution, although the property (tax-paying) restriction remained the same. By the start of the Civil War, only Massachusetts, Rhode Island, Vermont, Maine, and New Hampshire allowed black men to vote.[53]

The standard narrative of this period in the United States is the widening victory of democracy. Although that was certainly the pattern in politics, it was not completely or comfortably embraced by Americans. Many continued to believe that disconnecting suffrage from property posed a danger to the republic. Federalists in particular continued to believe that better "breeding" and sensible independent farmers and artisans should control the country's political helm. Later, Whigs were far less likely to use that kind of language to justify restrictions but still retained a basic belief that politics should reflect social and economic hierarchies. Whigs continued to believe in republican virtue and the idea that widespread property ownership was connected to polity, but this was clearly an increasingly minority position. Given the drastic change in the country's economic, social, and political conditions, these conservatives were certainly not going to argue that the republic should facilitate widespread property ownership. As a result, Whigs as well as Democrats generally separated discussions of political equality from considerations of economic equality. The contrast with the arguments over equality during the Revolution and early Republic is quite striking.

These constitutional debates highlighted the increasingly powerful paradigm that political participation should not be connected to an individual's economic independence. On the losing side, conservatives wanted to maintain the traditional connection between economic, political, and social power. They insisted that any man who worked hard and limited expenses could meet the property requirements to vote, and that extending suffrage to the idle and profligate endangered the Republic. This was closely connected to the presumption that the poor deserved their fate because they refused to work or save, that poverty was as much a moral as an economic condition. Thus, one of the leading conservatives at New York's 1821 convention directly compared ending property limits on suffrage to "indiscriminate and misguided charity."[54] Of course, this position ignored the reality that increasing numbers of American heads-of-households lacked land or economic autonomy.

The reformers who increasingly dominated politics sought to maintain a broad republican polity without reshaping the economy by separating the vote from other aspects of power. They scorned conservatives who saw universal suffrage as the means for democratic demagogues to gain power and take property from the virtuous. Congressman Ely Moore of New York City, speaking in the House on May 5, 1836, decried how his southern colleagues had recently characterized laborers "as agrarians, levellers, and anarchists, and their *unions* as unlawful and mischievous." Rather, he insisted that America's "unadulterated democracy" was "founded on *persons*, and *not* on *property*; on equal rights, and not on exclusive privileges." Whereas few were now willing to argue that "political equality" meant "sedition" or "pillage," he noted, more were happy to block democracy by raising the specter of "agrarianism" and dangers to "the rights of property." In 1839 James Leib, a Philadelphia lawyer, praised the broad electorate in the United States and insisted that the requirement to own property or pay taxes in order to vote or hold office was the vestige of the old notion that a citizen was required to support "good order and tranquility." Instead, he argued, universal suffrage had the unique virtue of creating "the most effectual balance" by giving the poor equal political power and civil rights with the rich. Indeed, the very "spirit of our Constitution" was hostile to any voting restrictions "founded upon wealth."[55]

The often-heated discussions about "free white man suffrage" did occasionally grapple with the question of how this change might affect the traditional republican connection between a "rough" economic equality and broad participation in a virtuous polity. But the debate usually focused on the somewhat related question of whether men lacking property would have the ability and desire to use their democratic political power to take or control what belonged to others. Not surprisingly, neither the advocates nor the opponents of opening the franchise to all white men explicitly addressed whether this change would undercut efforts to maintain economic equality in the United States. But this passionate focus on democracy, separating voting and officeholding from the wider spectrum of republican equality, clearly had the effect of inoculating public life and politics against efforts to mitigate the rapidly widening divide between rich and poor. In this fashion, the American tradition of economic equality became marginalized and political life became racialized. This movement during the first half of the nineteenth century would shape the future of the United States in many ways. In particular, Congress during Reconstruction was willing to federalize civil and political rights but resisted republican land reforms, refusing to redistribute southern plantation lands to the freedmen who had for generations worked the soil.

CHAPTER EIGHT

Reviving the Tradition

In February 1844, George Henry Evans called a meeting in New York City to forge a new effort for agrarian equality in the United States. Fifteen years earlier, Evans had gained fame by spearheading the city's workingmen's movement as editor of the *Working Man's Advocate*, organizing events and election efforts with Robert Owen, and publishing works like Seth Luther's *Address to the Working Men of New England* (1833). Initially he like others embraced Thomas Skidmore's view (in *Rights of Man to Property!*) that inequality began with the unequal division of landed property, although he was soon persuaded to focus on calls for public education and the end of monopolies and imprisonment for debt. When the Working Man's Party fizzled, he moved to a small farm in Rahway, New Jersey. Beginning in mid-1841, Evans started publishing the monthly *Radical*: he admitted that it had been wrong to have settled for "an equivalent" of economic equality instead of "the natural right of soil" and urged that uncultivated lands be reserved for workingmen as a safety valve to relieve urban misery and low wages. His insistent goal became the "Abolition of the Land Monopoly": ending all future sales of public lands, allowing any citizen to stake a lifetime claim to any vacant 160-acre farm or 5-acre town lot, with the right to sell improvements along with that right, and barring anyone from holding more than 160 acres.[1]

The five friends who met Evans in the back room of John Windt's printing shop were older artisans who had also been involved in labor and agrarian issues, so they were not surprised by his proposal to organize the National Reform Association (NRA). The NRA would have three primary goals: free homesteads for actual settlers, the exemption of a family's home from seizure for debt, and a limitation on the amount of public land any person could claim *and own.* Embracing the idea, the group quickly adopted a pledge to vote only for candidates who promised "to restore to the people, in some equitable manner, the Equal Right to Land"; wrote a manifesto that filled in the details; began holding weekly "Working Men's Meetings" and rallies on street corners; wrote a constitution that emphasized outreach to other organizations; and published a stream of articles that emphasized the connection between needy urban laborers and a basic American right to land.[2]

In the middle of the nineteenth century, some Americans agonized over the rising tide of excessive wealth flaunted by an elite class that, along with the increasingly obvious poverty suffered by many, mocked the country's tradition of economic equality. A growing number again embraced the egalitarian agrarian vision that had inspired the Diggers and James Harrington's *Oceana*. That ideal found its initial expression in communitarian religious movements like the Shakers and, in the 1840s, gained further momentum and strength in its secular counterpart Fourierism. But it was the NRA that would be the country's most significant movement for economic equality during the first half of the nineteenth century. Although Evans's ideas were not new, his organization renewed the American vision of economic equality by, first, tying the liberal ethos of family-held farms to the republican ideal that landownership and sustenance were basic human rights and then strongly connecting that agrarian goal to the problems faced by urban workers. The NRA grew rapidly, forging connections with the anti-rent movement, Fourierist communes, "Workie" remnants, and even the international communist movement; it would play a role in the Free Soil and Republican parties and spawn the 1862 Homestead Act. Yet the primary reforms sought by the NRA of lifetime usufruct instead of fee simple ownership and a limit on the acreage held by individuals would be spurned by Congress.

America's first communal movement, during the second quarter of the nineteenth century, had two parallel prongs: a religious effort connected to the Second Great Awakening and a secular effort connected to the early international socialist movement and broader American social reform concerns. At the same time, these groups and communities shared the goal of planting the seeds of a more consensual and peaceful society that would replace one they saw as increasingly corrupted by a competitive culture that allowed a greedy and ambitious few to dominate wealth and power. In order to nurture a healthy replacement, members of these communities focused on the spiritual growth of individuals and the welfare of the whole. Religious groups saw individual ownership of property as a selfish impediment to such fulfillment. Secular ones pursued a vision of social consensus, condemning selfish capitalists *and* "labor anarchy," as the best solution to the very new problems of economic power and mass manufacturing. These concepts of economic equality seem very different from the older American ideal of a republic of independent artisans and farmers. Yet, at their roots, all shared the goal of relative economic equality among all people, avoiding excessive wealth and poverty.

Religious communalism in American began with radical evangelical groups from northern Europe. In 1659 Netherlander Pieter Plockhoy, inspired in part by the Diggers, published *A Way Propounded to Make the Poor in These and Other Nations Happy, by Bringing Together a . . . Little-Common-Wealth*; four years later he sought to make that plan a reality with a settlement of Dutch Mennonites in New Amsterdam—and almost immediately fell victim to the English conquest. In 1683 another group of Dutch radicals, inspired by the Geneva mystic Jean de Labadie, established a short-lived commune in Maryland. Subsequent efforts by German pietists in Pennsylvania were more successful. The first group came in 1694, inspired in part by the Labadists. That settlement did not survive the 1708 death of its founder but influenced subsequent efforts, including Ephrata in 1732 in Lancaster County. More influential were the Moravians, founded in the 1720s by a Saxony nobleman, Count Nicolaus von Zinzendorf; members gave their time and labor, and the church provided food, clothing, and shelter (a system they called the General Economy) and sent missionaries to create sister communities overseas, including Bethlehem (near Ephrata) in Pennsylvania in 1741.[3]

Another group came a half-century later, led by the dynamic millennial "prophet" George Rapp; in 1805, about five hundred members established Harmony north of Pittsburgh and adopted Articles of Association committing them to surrender all of their property to the community that would provide food, clothing, medicine, and access to all available educational and religious benefits. Nine years later, the group moved west to the Wabash River, and New Harmony grew in size and influence as the Indiana territory became a state. The community served farmers in the region as a marketplace for crops and supplies, although members preferred to work with other religious communal groups in the region, including the Shaker village with which they considered merging in 1816. But for a variety of reasons, in 1824 Rapp decided to move back to western Pennsylvania and sold the Indiana property to Robert Owen, where the British industrial reformer established a communal industrial village. That final Rappite community, Economy, continued to prosper and draw considerable attention even after it suffered from a deep schism in 1832 and the death of George Rapp's brother and assistant Frederick in 1834.[4]

The Shakers were the probably most influential, widespread, and longest-lived spiritual communal effort in America. In the mid-eighteenth century, some radical Quakers in northwest England insisted on following millennialist visions and ecstatic ("shaking") worship instead of their brethren's more quietist path, calling their church the United Society of Believers in Christ's Second Appearing. In 1774 a small group led by "Mother" Ann Lee followed a divine vision to America. For more than a decade it traveled around southern New England and eastern New York, dealing with anti-English prejudice while looking for place to settle and follow the voice of God. In 1780 the small band gained many Believers when a New Light Baptist church in New Lebanon, New York, decided that the Shakers had found the Truth. After Lee's death in 1784, her successor, James Whittaker, emphasized the principle of communal property. When he died three years later, the society gathered at New Lebanon and adopted a covenant that emphasized (in addition to millennialism and salvation for all) a communitarian economy, a celibate society led jointly by Joseph Meacham and Lucy Wright, and an insular orientation. In that form, noted an official history, "the strength of the whole body becomes the strength of the member; and being united in the one Spirit of Christ, they have a greater privilege to serve God than they possibly could have in a separate capacity, and are better able to be mutual helps to each other; and they also find a greater degree of protection from the snares of a selfish and worldly nature."[5]

The Shakers gained immense success with the Second Great Awakening, which was particularly strong in that region at the turn of the century. "Father" Meacham directed Believers to live in separate enclaves instead of simply forming congregations, and by the time of his death in 1796 ten additional Shaker communities formed between Maine and eastern Massachusetts. He also separated spiritual and temporal leadership and instructed the latter—at New Lebanon, his brother David—to "give all members of the Church an equal privilege, according to their abilities, to do good, as well as an equal privilege to receive according to their needs." (Karl Marx became famous for writing nearly the same words about eight decades later.) Prospective members signed all their property over to the Brethren and received food, clothing, medicine, companionship, and spiritual fulfillment. The growth continued into the nineteenth century, fed by the Awakening's continued enthusiasm and the Brethren's increasingly well-known success. Between 1800 and 1830, the number of adult members rose from 1,373 to 2,316, and seven new communities were established in Ohio, Kentucky, and Indiana.

But Shaker growth and prosperity also created problems. "Winter Shakers" became notorious, as individuals and families joined when conditions became dire and then left when spring arrived. Shaker communities were happy to adopt orphaned children, but many of those adoptees decided at adulthood that they would rather seek their individual fortunes in the outside world. Community leaders worried that the national passion for individual fortune was undermining the Brethren; in 1815 Mother Lucy worried that "the sense seems so drowned in temporal things that there can be but little desire for the gifts of God," and she wished that "the sense was so that it could be satisfied with less . . . of this world's treasures." In the 1830s the villages became agitated by disagreements over whether to embrace Sylvester Graham's dietary reforms, even as they experienced a revival of enthusiasm replete with visions of the spirit world.[6]

At the same time, the Shakers and Rappites were increasingly viewed with respect, particularly by those non-Believers concerned about swelling individual avarice. British industrial reformer Robert Owen by 1817 showed a strong interest in both groups, by 1820 was corresponding with George Rapp, and in late 1824 traveled to both the recently founded Economy and the Shaker village of Niskayuna (near Albany) before heading to his planned socialist settlement in Indiana. In 1838 journalist Horace Greeley, who a few years later became deeply involved with Albert Brisbane and the Fourierist movement, visited the Shakers and praised the community as peaceful and happy. Shortly after, Transcendentalists and social reformers George and Sophia Ripley spent time at a few Shaker villages and were impressed by their communitarian values; two years later, the Ripleys with Ralph Waldo Emerson and other prominent intellectuals began to plan the egalitarian secular commune of Brook Farm.[7]

Far more controversial was the communitarian Church of Latter-Day Saints established by Joseph Smith after his visions of the angel Moroni and translation of gold plates—all in the area of western New York "burned over" by a wave of enthusiastic evangelical revivals at the time, including the Shakers. The resulting Book of Mormon, published in 1830, contained not only an America-centered history involving ancient Christianity but also the promise of city of Zion in which all would live on same-sized lots and none would be poor. As the church grew and gradually shifted west from Ohio to western Missouri and then (driven by hostile mobs) back across the Mississippi to western Illinois, it was occasionally roiled by the question of whether loyal Mormons could retain their property or, as an act of consecration, should give everything to the church. That question was somewhat resolved by Smith's 1838 vision that church members would give an initial sizable "consecration" of their property and thereafter pay an annual tithe of a tenth of their income.

Although Smith sometimes condemned socialism, he built cooperative institutions to manage assistance for the poor, missionaries, and building projects. These communitarian efforts did not anger nonbelievers; what did generate that fury, triggering the 1844 lynching of Joseph Smith and his brother Hiram, was the church's autocratic leadership and aggressive control of local government and militia, and stories that the Mormons embraced polytheism and polygamy. After Brigham Young led the believers west to Utah, much of the work needed to fence, irrigate, and manage resettlement was handled communally, and in the 1860s church leadership established a series of manufacturing, herding, and retail cooperatives.[8]

During the first half of the nineteenth century, the belief that Americans could and should create economic equality was, in fact, a prominent aspect of the increasing popularity of postmillennial Christianity—the idea that Jesus would come *after* humans had created utopian conditions. Nevertheless, that belief was not embraced by all American evangelicals, including the Mormons, nor was it necessarily an aspect of the broader eruption of the Second Great Awakening that also drove nonsectarian reform movements such as temperance and abolitionism. But there was a long-standing connection between postmillennialism and democratic socioeconomic ideas: Gerrard Winstanley and the other English Diggers had been postmillennialists, believing only that returning to the Edenic condition in which the Earth was "a Common Treasury" and that ending the private ownership of property that fostered "Honor, Dominion and Riches" would lift Adam's Curse and open the way to Christ's return.[9]

In 1817 New York Quaker physician Cornelius Blatchly followed Winstanley in arguing (in *Some Causes of Popular Poverty*) for a Christian socialist commonwealth; householders should pay no rent on their land, and when they died, their property would go back to the nation to be redistributed to young children. Although Blatchly's ideas seem radical, unlike the Shakers and Rappites he embraced the American norm that households should be the centers of production and reproduction. Five years later, Blatchly formed the New York Society for Promoting Communities and wrote *An Essay on Common Wealths*, a constitution and manifesto that condemned private property as a social evil and argued that, because Christian history and beliefs dictated communism, successful communism required a Christian foundation.[10]

Blatchly's *Essay* also introduced Americans to the writings of Robert Owen, who had already established progressive factory communities in Scotland and urged the creation of socialist villages that would transcend the inequalities of the past. In fall 1824, when Owen brought his vision to the United States, to be set up on the site that he had recently purchased from the Rappites, he first visited Blatchly and other society leaders before heading to Philadelphia and Washington City. Historians of the Owenite and Fourierist communities tend to distinguish those from the overtly religious Shaker and Rappite efforts. Owen and other collectivist leaders certainly scorned organized churches as drags on human development, yet elements of radical postmillennial Protestantism can be glimpsed in the socialist movements, and American reformers moved back and forth during their lifetimes between the two outwardly distinct efforts. Langdon Byllesby in his 1826 *Observations on the Sources and Effects of Unequal Wealth* praised both the Owenite and the Harmonist communities. With such connections and shared values, the boundary between religious and secular communitarian efforts seems forced and artificial.[11]

Owen took title to the land on January 3, 1825, and on April 27 opened New Harmony. But the wealthy reformer's welcoming speech promised his paternalistic elite leadership rather than democratic socialism. Residents could keep their possessions, but they had to live in community housing and obtain tools, furniture, food, and clothing from a community store; at the end of the year, the profits would be divided on the basis of the amount of work done, after deducting the individual's purchases. By January 1826, eastern newspaper editors were denouncing the endeavor, and the community suffered from battling cliques, insufficient workers to grow food and produce goods, and the resentment of married women at having to do all the domestic labor. Owen offered a new constitution that promised a "Community of Equality," with every adult member holding an equal right to vote and draw on the company store, but without details on Owen's power or how community profits (or losses) would be handled. The village continued to be burdened by members who refused to labor, conflicts over political authority, and the dislike among devout Christian members (especially Methodists) of Owen's agnostic attitudes. New Harmony split into several factions. Owen made several more efforts to rescue the community, all of which failed, and on May 6, 1827, he announced that he would sell the village in pieces to its residents and return to England. Some tried organizing other communities on the basis of Owen's ideas; perhaps the most interesting was in Nashoba, Tennessee, started by Fanny Wright as a place where slaves could work toward buying their freedom. All failed by 1828.[12]

For more than a decade, American interest in communes seemed to languish as other matters dominated public attention, particularly among reformers. As the United States emerged from the crash of 1819, the promise of prosperity and individual advancement seemed renewed, particularly in farming areas. Yet even as a new middle class became a prominent part of the country's socioeconomic and cultural fabric, concerns grew about the dangers of growing economic inequality, driven by the Workingmen's movement and wider concerns of social reforms. Many were angered by the increasing opulence and apparent arrogance of the urban wealthy classes who built their fortunes in trade, manufacturing, and finance. "Distinctions of rank," according to a Viennese visitor to Philadelphia, "have their defenders in America, as zealous as in the Old World. The only difference is the necessity here of concealing the tendency."[13] But when it came to elections, Americans were confronted by the Democratic Party's embrace of laissez-faire economics, presented as a means to counteract elite power, or the newly formed Whig Party's preference for expanding the role of government (and investors) to increase access to transportation and capital. Neither offered an effective means to control or counter the growing urban poverty and excessive wealth that seemed so contrary to the American tradition of republican equality.

These tensions and contradictions intensified with the second national crash in 1837. Again, farmers faced the loss of their lands, and laborers (a much greater percentage of the northeastern population than in 1819) were confronted by infrequent work at very low wages and little social assistance. By 1840, as Orestes Brownson noted, "death by actual starvation in this country . . . is no uncommon occurrence." The depression lasted five years and highlighted the long-term transformations and resulting vulnerabilities of the US economy, particularly the shift from small-scale artisanal workshops and farms to the capital-dependent mass production of goods and agricultural products. Ministers, writers, and newspaper publishers like Horace Greeley sought solutions to the problems of social instability and alienation, poverty-level wages, underemployment, the shift from cooperation to cut-throat competition, and the rapidly widening gap between the increasingly opulent wealthy and the desperate working poor. It was during this period that new traditions of celebrating Christmas and America's past were embraced as a means to domesticate and unify the country. It was also when secular communes became an apparent alternative instrument to implement social reform and renew the tradition of economic equality.[14]

In 1840, as the depression deepened, Albert Brisbane published *The Social Destiny of Man*, his translation of the writings of the French socialist Charles Fourier. In late 1831, while living in Europe, Brisbane had encountered and embraced Fourier's vision to replace human avarice and corruption with communal associations (called phalanxes) and free love. He spent the next year and a half in Paris, studying with the elderly man and his associates, then returned to America with the intention of obtaining land for phalanxes and winning the country to Fourierism. The 1837 crash made the first goal impossible, so Brisbane wrote *Social Destiny* to accomplish the latter. For American preferences, he left out Fourier's ideas about sex and emphasized a practical plan of action to combine private property and productive cooperation and to ensure that every person would have the right to the produce of his labor by ending the destructive individual concentration of capital. As detailed by Brisbane, Fourierist associationism promised the elevation of workers to manufacturing partners, cooperation rather than conflict, and a healthy return to the land for underemployed laborers.[15]

Brisbane toured eastern cities to publicize Fourier's ideas, met elites like Ralph Waldo Emerson and John C. Calhoun, got various journals to review his book, and persuaded the *Boston Quarterly*, the *Democratic Review*, and the Transcendentalist's *Dial* to publish reviews and articles on Fourierism. Most importantly, he gained the ear and growing support of Horace Greeley, who saw in Brisbane's ideas an extension of his own beliefs. Greeley bankrolled the periodical *The Future*, along with a series of meetings and lectures, and then beginning in March 1842 let Brisbane write a front-page column regularly for the *New York Tribune*. That fall, Brisbane announced plans for the first American phalanx, and in 1843 he collected many of his columns into a pamphlet that sold ten thousand copies and, along with a successful lecture tour, spread the enthusiasm for Fourierism through the northeast and upper Ohio Valley. The Fourier Association soon included prominent liberal New Englanders like Charles Dana and William Henry Channing, as well as New Yorkers like Greeley and Park Godwin and westerners like Henry Van Amringe of Pittsburgh.[16]

Fourierism gained popularity because it provided explanations for and solutions to the nation's socioeconomic problems. It explained poverty generally and the crash in particular as the results of systematic forces, including the competitive free-market economy and power exerted by the wealthy, rather than (as ministers and moralists generally held) the poor person's laziness, wastefulness, or intemperance. American Fourierists feared that the country's trend toward avarice and cutthroat competition was threatening its egalitarian republican foundations. Amringe in *Association and Christianity* (1845) condemned the "capitalists and manufacturers" who pushed for lower wages, "even bringing it down to the starving point," giving workers no incentives to do more than the minimum necessary" and generally fostering a culture of "selfishness." He believed (like most) that the United States faced a lower level of these problems than England but that "the same results are flowing in upon the workingmen here, with a gradual, but very fast increasing progress," and that "the very principle of antagonistic selfish society, connects the fate of the American mechanic with the English pauper."[17]

Phalanxes offered modern, egalitarian communities to replace the households, shops, churches, and villages shattered by the accelerating market and industrial revolutions. The movement would cure that selfishness and all the resulting social and economic conflicts, thereby rejuvenating the country's republican values and institutions. It appealed to Whigs like Horace Greeley who feared radical change and class conflict and wanted cooperation between labor and capital and to Democrats like Parke Goodwin who saw in the collectivist effort a means of reviving the Jacksonian vision of democracy, which he thought was endangered by the increasingly competitive capitalist economy. Unskilled laborers saw phalanxes as a way to become partners in manufacturing enterprises; artisans saw them as a way to limit competition and reduce their vulnerability to mass production; farmers saw them as a way to end their dependence on markets, mortgages, and wage labor; and middle-class urban Americans saw them as deliverance from salaried bondage. By 1846, twenty-six phalanxes had been established from Massachusetts to Iowa and around twenty-four Fourier groups were meeting in various cities.[18]

Other communal efforts also gained traction. Shakers and Rappites continued to draw new members, and enthusiasts established religious and secular communes, totaling at least fifty-nine founded in the 1840s, more than in any other decade in American history. Brook Farm was probably the most famous because it was driven by leading Transcendentalists. In October 1840, about a year after visiting several Shaker villages, George Ripley proposed to a Transcendentalist meeting in Ralph Waldo Emerson's parlor that those assembled should pool their money, buy a farm he had visited in West Roxbury, and—by farming cooperatively and living simply—"return to the soil" while keeping the time to write and think. Six months later, the Ripleys, Nathaniel Hawthorne, and a small group of other middle-class intellectuals organized a joint-stock company to buy the farm, about eight miles from Boston. By 1843, more than a hundred lived in the commune, and prominent writers and reformers (including Emerson and Thoreau) occasionally visited. Their social and economic goals were vague but generally sought to end competition and unrestrained ambition, while encouraging individual development and reducing the divide between the educated and the laboring classes. Time spent laboring or writing were compensated equally.[19]

As Brook Farm grew and developed, it rapidly moved toward a focus on social and economic reforms. Shoemaker Lewis Ryckman had joined in early

1843 and pursued that trade rather than farming. The community embraced Fourierism with a new constitution in mid-January 1844; workers were welcomed and encouraged to organize into production groups, and twice as much of the community profits were credited to labor as to capital invested. Members became involved in the resurgent labor movement: Ryckman was elected president of the New England Workingmen's Association in March 1845 and proposed an industrial congress to organize workers to win power through elections. Unfortunately, disaster struck on March 3, 1846, when fire gutted the nearly completed Phalanstery, the massive building planned to house all of the members. The community never recovered, and by the fall most residents left.[20]

Fruitlands was similarly a Transcendentalist effort, although significantly different in its utopian mission, transatlantic foundation, and rapid failure. It was the product of the idealistic imagination of Amos Bronson Alcott, pioneering educator and father of the more famous Louisa May Alcott, whose novel *Little Women* reflected her family's life. After Alcott's schools failed in the late 1830s, he tried to work as a farm laborer largely to avoid the market economy, "whose root is selfishness, whose trunk is property, whose fruit is gold." He echoed the Diggers, insisting that "to property man has no moral claim whatsoever; use, not ownership of the planet and parts thereof, constitutes his sole inheritance." In 1842 Alcott went to England to meet with that country's Transcendentalist group, which had more interest in radical economic ideas than its American counterparts, and returned with Charles Lane, who bought a ninety-acre farm in Harvard for the commune while insisting that "we do not recognize the purchase of land; but its redemption from the debase state of *proprium*, or property, to divine uses." Alcott, Lane, and the handful of others who moved there initially refused to use (or eat) animals, although they soon (reluctantly) jettisoned their purism. But even so, Fruitlands dissolved in just seven months.[21]

The Northampton Association of Education and Industry (NAEI) also incorporated Transcendentalist ideas of moral reform and social equality but from the beginning focused on manufacturing. NAEI members produced silk cloth and tried to raise the worms; made and sold knives, tools, and machines; grew some crops needed by the community; and worked outside on lumber and carpentry jobs. Most came from either the top or the bottom of the manufacturing and commercial trades, and they joined in order to live in a moral cooperative community free of the evils of competition, conflict, and hierarchy. The founders envisioned a joint-stock company that would pay equal wages while fostering a community of equality, cooperation, and harmony, but in mid-January 1843 members voted to scrap the wages and instead receive their regular needs for working (if able) ten hours a day; at the end of the year a quarter of any surplus would be divided equally among adult members. But the NAEI was not a Fourierist effort: many members criticized that movement for its emphasis on class conflicts and economic motivations instead of morality and benevolence. They were also dedicated abolitionists, and Sojourner Truth and Fredrick Douglass joined. The NAEI lasted four and a half years as an egalitarian community and for much longer as a manufacturing center.[22]

The short lives of these secular communitarian efforts despite initial enthusiasm raises the question of why such efforts were at best marginal in the United States, whereas others, particularly the devout Shakers, survived and even thrived. Clearly certain deep social and cultural norms made Americans reluctant to join communes even when facing poverty. Probably the most obvious was a strong preference for the patriarchal household as the social and economic center of life. It is noteworthy that there were no efforts to establish communes in the South, where the patriarchal household paradigm was particularly strong.[23] Of course, the first British American colonies featured the opportunity for householders to own sufficient property to support the family and provide future farms for sons. That arrangement, as well as being symbolic of masculinity and economic independence, was the requirement for access to political and social power, including the right to vote and hold office. Those ideals fed the individualistic liberal values that emerged during the Revolution and quickly dominated American culture.

In fact, given these norms, the number of Americans interested in communes points to significant social, economic, and cultural developments in the country. Religious passion was certainly a critical motivation, which explains the success of the Shaker and Rappite efforts and the failure of the Owenite movement in the 1820s. The passion for social and economic reforms found a more secular outlet in the 1840s with the international socialist movement, and the crashes of 1819 and 1837 made many more Americans, especially in areas with stronger commonwealth traditions, more interested in socialist alternatives to the capitalist household economy. Indeed, the Panic of 1837 renewed fears about economic injustice, corruption, and the future of the American republic; increased support for measures to solve the threat of concentrated wealth; and pulled that movement (perhaps unconsciously) back to the fertile mixture of religion and politics in the English Digger effort. Thus, the American experience with communal efforts highlighted the continued connections between the United States and Europe, with the German and

English radical evangelicals (Rappites and Shakers), English socioeconomic reformers (Owen and Chartists), and French socialists (Fourier). Of course, there were also significant differences, which is why Robert Owen's autocratic management proved unacceptable in America and why Brisbane carefully eliminated Fourier's "pioneering" ideas about sex and marriage out of his translation.

Many communitarian villages were located in the fertile region around the Hudson River Valley, at the center of Mahican territory and the eastern edge of Iroquoia and one of the earliest centers of Dutch settlement in New Netherlands. That area was also an agrarian powder keg. After England seized the colony in 1664 and renamed it New York, several royal governors seeking to increase their influence granted huge tracts along the river to powerful men in the province. A prominent few had the power to hold courts and issue laws and rules covering their lands. Such medieval manorial powers were unique in British colonial America. New York manor lords sought to lease rather than sell tracts in order to maintain their power and increase their wealth as decent available farmland east of the Appalachians became more difficult and expensive to purchase. After 1750, even as those leases began to provide revenue, a series of uprisings erupted as many farmers (especially recent arrivals from western Massachusetts) refused to recognize manor titles and insisted that only their labor made the land valuable. Landlords were able to regain authority by rewarding loyalty, using state power to squash revolts, and granting rights, on an individual "ad hoc" basis, to improvements and resources.[24]

By 1800 the hierarchical landlord-tenant relations had shaped Hudson River hillside communities distinguished by "rough economic equality, household autonomy, and widespread access to natural resources"—nearly the goals that in 1842 would be envisioned by the NRA. But this rough equilibrium was already weakening, paradoxically, as manor lords embraced partible inheritance—the one agrarian ideal embraced during the Revolution—and their sons facing huge debts and smaller estates felt compelled to abandon "patrician benevolence" and chase after every dollar owed by tenants. The crash of 1819, along with the tenants' more extensive and exhaustive use of the commons, intensified the developing socioeconomic conflict, pushed tenants toward a view of property rights grounded in individual legal title instead of community membership, and put the conflicts between tenants and landlords at the center of New York's politics just as Martin Van Buren (from the area) began organizing the Democratic Party.[25]

The tensions exploded after residents of the Helderberg area west of Albany petitioned their "manor lord" Stephen Van Rensselaer in late 1839 for more affordable leases and the right to purchase their farms, but they were rejected as the landlord insisted on his patrician privileges and the sanctity of contract. The anti-rent effort spread rapidly through other manors where landlords spurned tenant demands and took two forms: first, associations that circulated petitions and held public meeting to rally support, much like contemporary temperance organizations, and taxed members to fund legal cases; and, second, armed "Indian bands" that intimidated sheriffs trying to collect rents and ensure local support for the resistance. These "White Indians" appealed to agrarian traditions and proved popular: by 1845 about ten thousand men had joined a neighborhood "tribe" after participating in an elaborate ritual in which each created a unique "Indian" identity. The fraternal secrecy and disguises allowed the anti-renters to avoid responsibility for breaking the law, use the racist imagery of bloodthirsty savages to terrify dissenters, and (as in an Anti-Rent song) connect their demands to the older claims by aboriginal inhabitants to their land rights. Ironically, the earlier anti-manor resistance had included Wappingers and Mahicans, actual Indians living in the area, but by the 1830s most members of those tribes had moved west of the Ohio or to the few reserves left at the other end of the state, and the few who remained probably tried to avoid public notice.[26]

The anti-rent movement quickly gained the attention of Whigs and Democrats in the state government. Liberal Whigs including Governor William Seward saw the tenants' demands as linked to their campaign to end ancient limits on individual mobility and economic development; consequently, they proposed giving the legislature the power to seize an individual's property for public purpose. While the measure passed, the subsequent 1841 election brought the Democrats to power, and the judiciary committee threw out the measure as an unconstitutional interference with private property. The tenants renewed their campaigns with dances, meetings, parades, and feasts: by early 1845 the movement had enlisted 25,000 to 600,000 supporters and in several counties held conventions to nominate anti-rent candidates for state offices. Movement leaders and participants saw the people's will as sovereign and thus able to change or ignore laws that seemed to frustrate that will; their opponents saw contracts and property rights as sacred. While some anti-renters hoped to elect independent legislators dedicated to that cause, most were also members of an established party and sought to join their cause to the larger organization—even as party leaders saw the activists as important supporters

ANTI-RENT LYRICS.

A CORRECT LIKENESS OF

AN ANTI-RENTER LECTURING.

LYRIC No. 1.

Tune.——

Ye sons of Tuscarora, to arms! to arms! advance;
'Tis time to take your guns in hand, and make landholders prance;
  For sixty years our Rents we've paid,
  And not a word against it said,
  Now it's time a settlement's made
    With brave Indian Boys.

We have a gallant chieftain, Tecumseh is his name,
If you are not acquainted you will know him by his fame;
  He is the Indian's joy and pride,
  They'll never be severed from his side,
  But by his fate they will abide
    Like brave Indian Boys.

We never knew the reason these lands could not be sold,
'Till late we found it out, the story soon is told,
  The Deeds they had was to deceive,
  No signer's name could you perceive;
  When this you know you will believe
    The brave Indian Boys.

We advise these British Barons to leave republic land
Before they are surrounded by an angry Indian band,
  For if we get them in our hands
  So closely we will draw their bands
  That they'l be glad to leave their lands
    To brave Indian Boys.

They call us poor rag-muffins, and each disgraceful name;
If we are poor by their oppression I'm sure we're not to blame.
  Our fathers paid their Rents, you see,
  And left their sons in beggary,
  But now we've sworn we will be free,
    Like brave Indian Boys.

We want no treacherous murderers joined to our Indian band,
They always bring destruction when e'er they raise their hand.
  We want brave hearts, that when we try,
  They from our cause will never fly,
  Souls that are not afraid to die,
    Like brave Indian Boys.

LYRIC No. 2.

Tune.—"With a helmet on his brow," &c.

With his mask upon his brow, and his rifle in his hand,
The Indian marches forth to drive oppression from the land;
All English Laws he hates, their tyranny disdains,
Against their never-ending Tax most loudly he exclaims.
  Then let the Tin Horn sound 'till hills and vales reply,
  The Indian must for freedom live, or else for freedom die.

Old Johnny Bull it seems gave his favourites much ground,
But for them a right and title has never yet been found;
Likewise he'd ought to know, this generous hearted King,
Should not have given lands away that ne'er belong'd to him.
  Then let the Tin Horn sound 'till the hills give back reply,
  The Indian must be free from Tax or boldly he must die.

Our Country we adore, her Laws are Just and Good,
These would-be-lords of America must cross the raging flood.
Our Freedom, sure it is, the bone and sinew of our hand;
With them we mean to drive these false pretenders from our
    land.
  Then let the Tin Horn sound, till it reaches o'er the main,
  To tell that monarch we have sent his lordlings home again.

At Boston, we have heard, it was the self-same thing,
That there a few brave Indians dare resist the British King;
Oh! the Taxes came so hard that the Tea went overboard,
From the ships into the ocean, where it had long been stored.
  Then let the Tin Horn sound till it reaches rock and glen,
  The Indian must be free from Tax, or bravely die like them.

Rhode Island too, e'er long, must join the Freedom song,
To break the chain of monarchy that's kept her bound so long,
She has brave hearts and true ones, that e'er long will try
To burst the bands assunder, sworn to conquer or to die.
  Then let the Tin Horn sound till it reaches every brave;
  For Freemen must be free indeed, or find a bloody grave.

America is our boast, and the pretty Squaws our toast,
For their sakes we'd dare to fight a numerous British host.
We cannot marry yet, but if any should survive,
We pray these pretty Squaws to keep a hand for every brave.
  Then let the Old Horn sound till it makes the welkin ring,
  The Indian he is free from Tax, and now he'll shout and
    sing.

> We advise these British Barons to leave republic land
> Before they are surrounded by an angry Indian band,
>   For if we get them in our hands
>   So closely we will draw their bands
>   That they'l be glad to leave their lands
>   To brave Indian Boys.
>
> They call us poor rag-muffins, and each disgraceful name;
> If we are poor by their oppression I'm sure we're not to blame.
>   Our fathers paid their Rents, you see,
>   And left their sons in beggary,
>   But now we've sworn we will be free,
>   Like brave Indian Boys.

OPPOSITE AND ABOVE: *Anti-rent lyrics: A correct likeness of an anti-renter lecturing* (New York?, circa 1839–46). Courtesy, American Antiquarian Society.

in critical elections. One result was that in New York the Democrats split into factions: Hunkers, Barnburners, and Loco-Focos. Another was that the tenants' movement became part of the NRA.[27]

Those Evans invited to that initial meeting to form the NRA, on February 8, 1844, included John Windt, a printer who had worked closely with Evans in the 1830s and had continued organizing labor in the city, at whose shop they met that cold Sunday; Lewis Masquerier, who had learned the printing trade in Kentucky, practiced law in Quincy, Illinois, and moved to New York City in 1835, where he spearheaded the local communitarian-socialist Owenite group; and Thomas Devyr, an Irish radical who led the 1840 Newcastle Chartist uprising and was forced to flee to the United States, where he settled in the village of Williamsburg in Brooklyn, at the western tip of Long Island, and published a Democratic paper. A few weeks later, Evans and Windt began publishing the tri-weekly *People's Rights*, which they used to publicize the NRA's first public meeting for Friday, March 8, in Croton Hall at Bowery and Division streets near the infamous Five Points. Their first issue of a new series of *Working Man's Advocate* on March 16 reported speeches and results from the meeting along with the NRA pledge to endorse only those public officials who would support laws to reserve land for actual settlers.[28]

The first *Advocate* also featured the NRA's platform, "Equal Right to Land," which would remain the organization's focus. While no land should be taken from those who currently owned a "superfluity," all lands currently owned by states and the federal government should become free and open to claims only by actual settlers. The entire public realm should be laid out in townships six

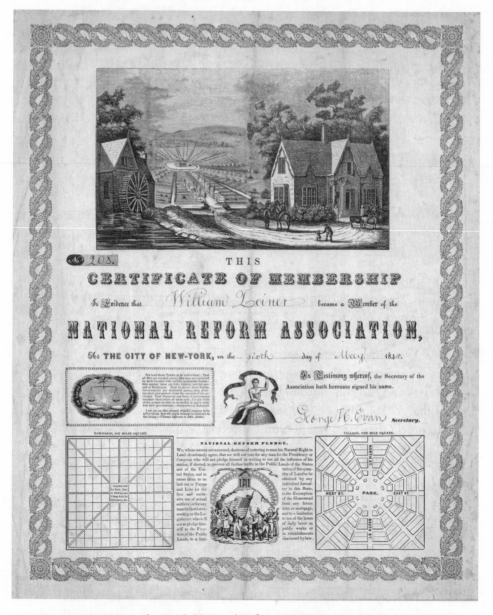

ABOVE AND OPPOSITE (DETAIL): National Reform Association membership certificate signed by George Evans, 1846. Courtesy, American Antiquarian Society.

miles on a side, each divided further into 160-acre farms surrounding a public square made up of smaller lots (about 5 acres each) including a townhouse where all public business would be transacted. Each town would contain 160 farming families and about 40 nonfarming households. The lands would

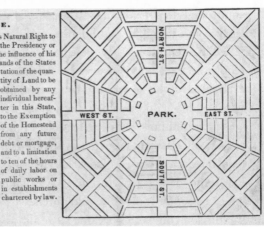

NATIONAL REFORM PLEDGE.

We, whose names are annexed, desirous of restoring to man his Natural Right to Land, do solemnly agree, that we will not vote for any man for the Presidency or Congress who will not pledge himself in writing to use all the influence of his station, if elected, to prevent all further traffic in the Public Lands of the States and of the United States, and to cause them to be laid out in Farms and Lots for the free and exclusive use of actual settlers; or for any man for the Governorship or the Legislature who will not so pledge himself to the Freedom of the Public Lands, to a limitation of the quantity of Land to be obtained by any individual hereafter in this State, to the Exemption of the Homestead from any future debt or mortgage, and to a limitation to ten of the hours of daily labor on public works or in establishments chartered by law.

never be sold; instead, "Any man, *not possessed of other land*, may take possession and keep the same during his life or pleasure, and with the right to sell his *improvements*, at any time, to any one *not possessed of other land*." The land needed to begin and remain free so that the actual settlers, who would hopefully be mostly "surplus laborers" from the overcrowded cities, would be able to afford the expenses of moving there and obtaining stock, tools, and provisions. These goals and the organization's vision of the resulting egalitarian towns became a feature of NRA publications, including its ornate membership certificate.[29]

Evans and other NRA leaders closely linked improving conditions of workingmen to agrarian reforms of federal land policies. Such reforms would not have been a revolution. Indeed, even during its formative stages, US land policy had been shaped by a range of often-conflicting purposes and interests. The egalitarian ideals that had emerged during the Revolution envisioned that the Ohio and Mississippi valleys "won" in the war would serve the republican goal of fostering a nation of free and independent farmers. At the same time, the new national government hoped to finance a large part of its operation through the sale of its lands, including providing payment to soldiers who had fought, bled, and died for American independence. The sale of large areas at market value would draw the interest and energy of men with substantial resources and experience, who would then use their capital and abilities to further develop the region to shape an orderly, republican society. By contrast, an uncontrolled flood of settlers could foster anarchy and trigger devastating wars with the indigenous people who lived there. In addition, many "Founding Fathers" (such as George Washington) were investors in large western land companies; they therefore saw the postwar influx of squatters as threats to the legal, political, moral, and financial stability of the new country.[30]

The first effort to satisfy these needs was the Land Ordinance of 1785, which required the rectangular survey of federal land into 6-mile square townships, each divided into 36 sections of 1 square mile (640 acres). After an area was surveyed it would be sold at auction for a minimum price of $1.00 per acre with a minimum size of one section. Even though purchasers could use depreciated Continental currency, the minimum requirement of $640 to buy federal land meant that eastern speculators rather than western settlers dominated the market. In addition, the Ordinance placed no limit on how much land a person or company could purchase. The preference for large-scale land speculation companies became clear almost immediately. In 1787, Congress passed a special act selling 1.5 million acres of prime Ohio Valley land to the Ohio Company for $1 million, a joint-stock operation of former Continental Army officers, with a provision that the connected Scioto Company could seek another 4.5 million acres. Another speculator obtained a 1-million-acre grant in southwest Ohio, later to include the city of Cincinnati, and the Connecticut Land Company purchased (cheaply) 3 million more acres claimed by that state in the area that would include Cleveland.[31]

Initially, the Federalists led by Alexander Hamilton shaped policies designed to sell large blocks of land to speculators in order to maintain social order and maximize national revenue. By the turn of the century, however, western agrarian interests gradually gained influence. In 1796 the House passed a bill reducing salable areas to 160 acres to encourage "real" settlers, but Federalists in the Senate rejected the change and raised the price to $2.00 per acre with one year of credit. Four years later, Congress did reduce the minimum area by half and allowed four years of credit. In 1804, with Thomas Jefferson as President and agrarian Republicans dominating Congress, the minimum acreage was slashed to 160 acres and the price to $1.64 per acre. Particularly after the War of 1812, the easier terms joined with the sudden availability of credit to trigger a boom of land speculation. It became apparent that the line between speculator and actual settler was a mirage and that land speculation had become as American as apple pie. Settlers would buy large tracts using credit, then sell sections that they did not need in order to finance the part where they lived and farmed. But the Crash of 1819 put an end to this short boom and renewed the traditional moral lesson that speculation was wicked as well as risky. In 1820 Congress's response to the situation was reduce the minimum price to $1.25 per acre in 1820 while requiring all purchases to be made in cash.[32]

In 1828 the victory of Andrew Jackson and his Democrats heralded the victory of agrarian interests. Beginning in 1830, Congress regularly enacted preemption acts allowing squatters farming on federal lands to purchase, prior to public auction, up to 160 acres at the minimum price of $1.25 per acre, and two years later it reduced the minimum sale size to 40 acres. Yet, as the NRA charged, the reality of federal land sales remained far from the Jeffersonian vision of a nation of freehold farmers. Speculators continued to purchase huge areas, often wielding political connections, fraudulent means, and borrowed funds (which led to the 1819 and 1837 crashes). Especially in the South, squatters sought homes and subsistence livings on lands either not yet sold by Indian tribes or the federal government or owned by speculators or large planters. Settlers who did seek title, especially in the South where the main crop was cotton for market, were often forced by circumstances to obtain mortgages and ended up losing their land to large banks in London or New York.[33]

These deeply rooted tensions mushroomed in significance in the 1840s as US interests began to move with American settlers into Mexico (Texas and California) and the Oregon territory. NRA leaders proclaimed that their organization and goals were meant to renew American equality and the republican vision of America's founders, particularly Thomas Jefferson. Evans, in his very first column in the *Working Men's Advocate*, announced that he would focus on shaping "the condition of society more in accordance with our national professions, as set forth by Jefferson's immortal pen." In many ways their view of those "professions" was quite correct. The NRA vision of neat geometric townships six miles square with 160-acre farms echoed Jefferson's plan in the 1785 Ordinance, modeled in turn on the New England archetype; its passionate belief that public lands should be used to promote a republican nation of independent farmers had been Jefferson's vision in the Northwest Ordinance of 1787 and was also reflected in many of his writings; and the Sage of Monticello frequently condemned the accumulation of excessive wealth and suggested various ways to prevent it, from ending entail and primogeniture to a progressive tax falling heavily on the "richer classes" while "encouraging the poorer ones." Such ideas were widespread during the early Republic.[34]

The NRA's platform was also clearly a product of the Jacksonian era. NRA speakers frequently repeated the idea, common in the workingmen's movement and the Democratic Party, that low-wage factory labor was just as much a form of slavery (if not worse) than that suffered by African Americans on cotton plantations (the same line trumpeted by proslavery ideologues like George Fitzhugh in *Cannibals All*), although NRA speakers inevitably added that they condemned southern slavery. NRA literature depicted the colonial period as a time when the land "was parceled out to a few in immense tracts, at the whim or caprice of a foreign power," so everyone else had to purchase from a favored few. This was certainly the case in upstate New York, but otherwise even the proprietary "owners" of the Restoration colonies made little effort to control and profit from land sales. Yet it was true that companies had emerged in the mid-eighteenth century to control and profit from the Ohio Valley, and such speculative efforts continued to shape settlement in the western parts of the country. As a result of this "land monopoly," proclaimed the NRA, workers were forced to stay in cities and compete for jobs, depressing wages.[35]

Not surprisingly, the NRA platform contained notable contradictions. On the one hand, the organization's view on the cause of and solution for low wages seemed to embrace the paradigm of supply and demand rather than that of a moral economy or collective production. The NRA also insisted that it rejected the idea of redistributing property, thereby accepting existing extremes of wealth and poverty even as it imagined that free land would end the problem. It also kept the patriarchal household as the center of production, thereby rejecting socialist collectivism. Yet while it denied the inevitable accusations of agrarian "levelism," the association's vision featured the explicit goal of removing public land completely from the private marketplace: it could not be bought nor sold, ever, and a man could not accumulate more than was necessary to support his family and produce a small surplus.

The NRA would also completely ignore the indigenous peoples who lived where it wanted landless laborers to settle. One of the few manifestos to mention Native Americans trumpeted, in July 1844, that "*the Public Domain*, in all its boundless wealth and infinite variety" belonged not to "the Aristocracy" but the people. "Have they not been redeemed from the aboriginal tribes by monies paid into the Treasury by the productive classes of the whole United States? Are they not ours, therefore, by every just right, natural and acquired?" Indians also occasionally appeared as stereotyped foils for industrial "savagery." One such story tells how a man blundered into a group of fearsome Seminole warriors, initially mollifies them with liquor, but fears the worst when the scariest-looking one takes him alone into the woods. To his surprise, the fellow told him in Gaelic that he had been a journeyman who fell in with the Indians; he liked his new life much better than his old one as a mill operative, he confided, because the "savages" truly fulfilled the principles of liberty and equality. The NRA clearly embraced the ethos of western expansionism (though without the jingoism of Manifest Destiny) that required ignoring the existence and land rights of Native Americans. Moreover, Americans had never embraced the European image of the Edenic Indian, and during the nineteenth century their views of Natives shifted even further toward the "Nasty Savage."[36]

The NRA's second public meeting on March 18 elected a special committee to write its constitution; it was read and approved at the third meeting ten days later and printed in the second *Advocate* on March 30. It began with the organization's platform and the promise to consider "other remedies for the distresses and embarrassments of the productive or working classes. as may appear likely to be practically useful." Between meetings, the NRA would be governed by an elected Central Committee, whose main duty was (judging from the bulk of the constitution) to create alliances with a long list of potential allies. It was to prepare and circulate petitions to Congress and state legislatures, meet candidates for offices, assist journalists, circulate tracts and newspapers, and hire traveling lecturers in what it called "the Missionary system." It was also to correspond with a wide range of groups: clergymen (arguing that the land system violated Christian principles), settlers in new states and territories, city officials outside New York City (particularly Albany, Lowell, Philadelphia, and Boston), merchant and laborers organizations, and temperance and other benevolent societies. All those organizations would also be invited to send delegates to the NRA.[37]

Evans and his associates initially reached out to "Workie" veterans and laborers in New York City. John Commerford, one of the most important trade union leaders in the 1830s, joined by mid-March and gave the main speech at the third public meeting on March 20. He began by condemning factory machinery as the "most dangerous of our foes," particularly given the example of the English "oligarchy" that had "confined the great mass to the drudgery of manufactures." The horrors of that system, Commerford insisted, was worse than southern slavery. "Shall I say, and speak the truth, that by choice I would rather change my skin and become obedient to the will of the Planter at the South, than be the walking free born, free starving machine of the British aristocracy!" Such a horrid regime, he went on to say, would be the future of American working men forced by poverty to enter "these principalities of *low wages*, the Eastern Factories." The only solution was to persuade the government to give laborers "free access to the lands which the blood and creatures of their ancestors acquired." Commerford's speech highlighted the bridges that the NRA built with labor leaders and their radical Democrat allies who were attempting to renew the workingmen's movement after the disastrous crash of 1837. When the weather warmed, the NRA held street rallies where Evans and others spoke from a cart festooned with banners (made by the Ladies Auxiliary), condemning the growing power of landlords and factory bosses and blaming poverty and hard circumstances on the land monopoly.[38]

The NRA's effort to create alliances with other organizations gained traction that summer. In June the Cordwainers Union endorsed the NRA, and both organizations added their voices to the call by mechanics in Fall River, Massachusetts, for a national trade union convention. By August, so many groups had responded that the meeting was moved to Boston. The convention welcomed NRA delegates, founded the New England Workingmen's Association (NEWA), and passed resolves calling for a ten-hour workday, Fourierist cooperative labor, and abolishing "the shameful and sacrilegious Monopoly of the Soil." The NRA also quickly formed alliances with Fourierist organizations: several Brook Farm leaders including Parke Godwin regularly attended NRA meetings, Lewis Ryckman went on speaking tours for the cause, and in February 1845 Albert Brisbane loudly joined the association. By that time, the NRA and its call for land reform had gained the endorsement of labor papers and a growing chorus of local groups in Illinois, Ohio, Pennsylvania, Virginia, and elsewhere around the country. These local organizations, largely organized and led by craftsmen, often added their own concerns to the general NRA call to reserve public lands for "actual settlers" and bar land speculation. In late March 1845, Evans changed the title of the NRA paper to *Young America*; over the subsequent decade, that name became synonymous with a reform-minded expansionist faction of the Democratic Party led by Stephen Douglas.[39]

Not surprisingly, the anti-rent resistance up the Hudson River also immediately drew the focus of the NRA, led by Thomas Devyr, who had already agitated for the beleaguered tenants drawing from his experience in Ireland and England. In 1835 in Belfast he had published *On Natural Rights*, slamming the British constitution (like Thomas Paine's *Common Sense*), decrying the laws that gave abusive landlords an unjust "Absolute Ownership of the Soil," and warning Americans that if they failed to stop the "conscienceless rapacity of landlords," their "freedom and happiness" would disappear. After escaping to Williamsburg in 1842, he was hired to edit and publish a newspaper and reprinted that pamphlet with a long appendix that warned Europe's tyranny was inevitable unless America changed the laws that "permit unprincipled and ambitious men to monopolize the soil." Devyr also attacked Stephen Van Rensselaer and other New York patroons, insisting that the "Law of Nature and Nature's God" overruled their title and that "every man who comes into this world has an equal right in the soil." He rejected making "an equal division of the soil," because many people pursued other trades, but he insisted that all should have an "EQUAL RIGHT" to claim a tract of land in order to make a living. At about the same time, Devyr published columns supporting the anti-rent protesters, and wrote letters to a pro-tenant newspaper in Helderberg that (among other things) equated the patroons with "Dukes, Earls, aristocrats and Highwaymen." It is not surprising that he helped form the NRA, became one of its leaders, and served as its primary connection to the anti-rent effort.[40]

In 1845 Devyr became the foremost advocate for the upstate agrarian movement. At an NRA meeting on January 3, he asked for the group's approval of an anti-rent convention that he was calling to meet in five days. After he spoke for nearly two hours, describing the history of the patroonships, the meeting authorized delegates to the convention and called for a state law limiting the quantity of land any one person could own to "a reasonable sized Farm." Devyr attended the convention, held in Berne in the center of Helderberg and, upon returning to New York City, reported that about two thousand delegates attended from eleven counties. He was struck most by the need for a strong anti-rent newspaper in the area and offered to take his paper, the *National Reformer*, to Albany to create "a comprehensive and efficient organ of the movement." Instead, in spring the owner of the *Albany Freeholder* offered its editorship to Devyr, and in April he moved upriver to devote his energy to the anti-rent movement. He filled the paper with reports on peasants of Europe, articles from English Chartists, and reports from Evans's papers, striving to forge the NRA alliance of tenants, urban workers, western farmers, and social reformers into a powerful force for egalitarian land and labor laws.[41]

Devyr and his NRA comrades supported the more egalitarian elements in the movement. That was perhaps most clear in a series of articles appearing first in *Young America* and then in the pamphlet *The Jubilee*. It began by noting the potential "cure" in the call to amend the New York Constitution and then laid out a Declaration of Rights that insisted all men had "a natural and inalienable right" to land and that government existed "to effect such a guarantee." Unfortunately, the current "Land Monopoly" not only caused poverty, low wages, and other vices but drove "aggressions on the rights of the Indian tribes" (perhaps the only defense in NRA literature of Native rights) and undermined the republic. Finally, Devyr called for New Yorkers to reclaim their "indisputable right and title to land enough to live upon" and to ensure that "no one has a just title to a foot more than is necessary for the subsistence of his family while another is without Land." That meant barring anyone from holding more than 160 acres or one lot in a city or village, creating a special commission to judge and settle claims by tenants wishing to own lands leased for twenty years or longer, and requiring corporations with land to transfer those holdings to the landless within five years. A person's homestead or farm could not be seized for debt (as sought by the workingmen's movement), and the law would support landholding in common or joint occupancy.[42]

But as Devyr quickly discovered, the NRA and its egalitarian agrarian agenda would be embraced only by those willing to demand ownership of leased land and to denounce patroon restrictions in the name of natural rights and traditional neighborly exchanges. Many farmers feared that any alliance with the NRA would endanger reforms promised by the major parties, and some embraced the liberal view that unregulated market forces would lead to widespread landownership. In late May 1845, the *Freeholder* called for voters to elect NRA delegates to anti-rent gatherings. The major parties combined to stop the effort and proposed moderate bans on exploitive long leases, but anti-renters in five counties chose agrarian delegates and called for strict limits on landholding.[43]

By August the conflict intensified: Albany's Democratic leader warned against "agrarian, leveling doctrines," and a few weeks later Devyr was fired by the conservative owner of *Freeholder*; he moved down the street and opened the *Anti-Renter*. While some in the national parties began to embrace the NRA's call for egalitarian federal land laws, including the Whig congressman Richard Herrick from Rensselaer, in New York the liberals who rejected agrarian reforms proved victorious. The state constitutional convention, held between June and October 1846, adopted measures encouraging short leases and an open market for land, and that fall when an anti-rent convention nominated a Whig for governor, the few NRA and radical Democratic (Barnburner) delegates walked out. Ten days later they gathered, established the Free Soil Party, called for land and labor reforms, and nominated NRA leader Lewis Masquerier for governor. But with the election less than two weeks away, the Free Soilers won few votes. Although the election did boost the anti-rent cause, including Whig endorsement of a homestead law, the agrarian wing had been marginalized and subsequent reform efforts largely fizzled. Devyr was forced to close his newspaper and return to New York City.[44]

In the meantime, the NRA had extended its connections and alliances to become *the* national movement for economic equality, linking communal efforts and workingmen's groups from Maine to Virginia and Kentucky to Wisconsin, joining socialist and agrarian goals. Activists established NRA groups in cities like Lynn, Pittsburgh, and Cincinnati and in communes like

New Harmony and Brook Farm, but probably the greatest growth came from existing labor organizations and Fourier phalanxes around the country that embraced the NRA. Of course, the NRA's leaders had deep roots in the labor movement and embraced trade union demands, and associationists proclaimed that land reforms that democratized property ownership would generate a growing range of cooperative enterprises. In mid-October 1845, the NRA hosted a National Industrial Convention of reformers including "Anti-slavery men, Associationists, Communitists [*sic*], Temperance men, Peace men, Free Trade men, and Free Land men." The meeting established an Industrial Congress to work for guaranteed "Rights of Men" and "Redeem the Industrial Classes from [their] condition of Inferiority," to meet each year in early June in a different city; it also passed resolutions calling for the NRA's land reforms plus a mandated ten-hour workday, regulation of child labor, and various communitarian measures.[45]

Over the next few years the NRA continued to enjoy growth and success. Its annual Industrial Congress drew delegates from various reform organizations. More prominent men joined, including the abolitionist philanthropist Gerrit Smith from Syracuse, New York, organizer of the Liberty Party and its presidential candidate in 1848; the Philadelphia novelist and journalist George Lippard, organizer of the fraternal order Brotherhood of the Union; the Pittsburgh mystic and Ohio Fourierist organizer Henry Van Amringe; and, perhaps most noteworthy, Horace Greeley, whose influential *New York Tribune* in June 1846 began echoing the NRA's call for free public land. The NRA's influence on electoral politics was quickly noticed in Congress. On March 9, 1846, Richard Herrick from Rensselaer presented to the House an NRA memorial calling for a law allowing any person without land "to take and use a small quantity" of public land, with the right to sell improvements to anyone else without land in order to avoid "creating a great landed aristocracy." On the same day, Felix McConnell, Democrat from Georgia, introduced a bill to grant a homestead of up to 160 acres to any head of a family, "man, maid, or widow." Four months later, Andrew Johnson, Democrat from Tennessee, later to gain infamy as US president combating Congress over Reconstruction, proposed allowing any head of household, without sufficient resources to purchase public lands, to claim up to 160 acres, of which he would obtain formal ownership after four years of residence and cultivation. All three measures, though rejected, would open the gates for additional land reform proposals.[46]

In 1847 and 1848 the NRA's political effort gained traction. Growing numbers of newspapers throughout the country endorsed land reform, including the idea that the federal government should prevent "land monopoly" by limiting the amount of land a person could hold and ensuring that only actual settlers could hold it. Those papers were joined by NRA-related groups, and together they organized petition drives to Congress. As a result, a *Young America* call to end the sale of public lands and allow Americans without land to claim farms and house lots attracted the signatures of more than four thousand New Yorkers, and similar petitions came from rural New York, Indiana, Illinois, Ohio (especially Cincinnati), New Jersey, Wisconsin, and Pennsylvania. Not surprisingly some congressmen responded. On March 20, 1848, John Slingerland, Whig from upstate New York, called for public lands to be sold for at most 50 cents an acre, "only in limited quantities to actual settlers, so as to exclude the grasping and oppressive speculation"; on the same day, John C. Murphy, Brooklyn Democrat, proposed dedicating the public lands entirely "for the free use" of settlers without land. Neither bill got out of committee. Nine months later, Horace Greeley, chosen by New York City's Whigs to fill the Sixth District's seat in the House for three months, introduced a bill in the House giving landless settlers the right to preempt up to 160 acres for seven years and, after proven occupancy and improvement, to keep free 40 acres if single or 80 acres if married. As before, the reform measure was tabled and ignored. Yet it was clear that the two national parties were competing to capture the votes of NRA supporters.[47]

As the NRA gained influence and created alliances with many other organizations, its agenda began to expand. A stoutly radical stream emerged out of the labor and associationist wings. Groups connected through the Industrial Congress began to discuss a national general strike "to enforce the popular will on recalcitrant elites and institutions." Also, the NRA communitarian vision included a strong preference for direct instead of representative government, so it was not surprising when members began to call for replacing the country's "*Republican rubbish*" with a "superstructure of Pure Democracy." Several speakers at the 1847 Industrial Congress urged the body to declare the abolition of government the main goal, and only one vote prevented the adoption of a measure "to legitimize an agrarian seizure of land." While the NRA had initially stoutly avoided embracing the growing (but still marginalized) abolitionist movement, perhaps in part to avoid alienating southern allies, the involvement of Gerrit Smith and the noticeable antislavery presence in the initial Congress emphasized the rapid mingling of the free soil and free labor movements. That marriage was sealed by the eruption of war with Mexico in April 1846; for example, when the New England Workingmen's Association met in Boston on May 27, it passed resolutions that included opposition to the

Mexican War, a petition drive for ten-hour day, and cheers for the success of "National Reform." But the core of the NRA agenda remained economic equality through free homesteads and explicit limits on public landownership.[48]

Beginning in 1848, the gradual disintegration of the second party system offered promise and peril for the NRA. During the presidential campaign, both Whig and Democratic leaders sought the endorsement of the Industrial Congress and pledged support for more egalitarian land distribution, but most National Reformers went with Van Buren's radical Democrat Barnburner faction, which supported the Wilmot Proviso. In early August 1848, when the Barnburners and antislavery Whigs met in Buffalo to form the Free Soil Party, NRA representatives from several states attended but found that the major parties already dominated the key posts and platform. After the new party nominated Van Buren for president, he barely mentioned the land issue. His defeat and the political chaos that followed, as Barnburners returned to the Democratic fold, antislavery Whigs searched for a new home, and the national conflict over the extension of slavery swelled, exhausted the NRA leaders and left the organization largely moribund. At the end of 1849, faced by growing personal and financial difficulties, George Henry Evans moved back to his New Jersey farm and only occasionally published *Young America*; the last extant issue is dated November 2, 1850. The Industrial Congress also faced internal conflicts over the embrace of racial equality by the majority, which came to a head when those attending the June 1851 meeting in Albany (chaired by Evans) battled over whether to allow African American John Bowers from Philadelphia to participate.[49]

Yet although the NRA was splintered and distracted, members and allies continued to push for making public land free to settlers and to limit the amount any one person could hold. In April 1849, gatherings of Democrats and Free Soilers in Wisconsin and in Worcester, Massachusetts, called for limits on landholding and free farms for settlers; two months later, a similar meeting in Michigan called for public lands to be "gratuitously distributed in limited quantities to actual settlers and to them only." That spring various NRA-affiliated newspapers published petitions for their readers to send to Congress, charging that the current "system of Land Traffic," imported to this country from Europe, is wrong in principle," and in practice is causing "rapid increase of inequality, misery, vice and crime." Congress should bar "traffic in the Public Lands" and instead provide "Farms and Lots, for the free use of such citizens (not possessed of other land) as will occupy them." *Young America* repeatedly published a "boilerplate" state law to limit individuals to 160 acres and give those with more land one year to sell the surplus, along with a proposed federal law that would bar the future sale of public lands and instead make 160 acre farms available for free to settlers. From 1849 through 1851 at least a hundred separate petitions were submitted to Congress, most calling for limits on landholding as well as inexpensive if not free farms and lots for actual settlers.[50]

After 1850, more congressmen responded to the call for land reform, but only by making it easier and cheaper if not free to claim farms on the public domain. In the Senate, in late December 1849, Stephen Douglass introduced a bill allowing anyone to preempt up to 160 acres, and to establish ownership after four years of residence and improvement, and a month later Daniel Webster introduced a similar bill but with just three years of residence necessary before full ownership. Senators Sam Houston of Texas, Henry Dodge and Isaac Walker of Wisconsin, and William Seward of New York endorsed the measures. In the House, in late February and again in June, Andrew Johnson introduced bills requiring occupancy and cultivation for five years as condition of title. Even these measures, however, failed to pass, largely due to southern opposition. More importantly, from the viewpoint of land reformers, none imposed any limits on landownership. Johnson himself noted, in a speech on the floor of the House on July 25, that he "wished to be distinctly understood that he was no agrarian, no leveller, as they were termed in modern times," but wanted only to "take the man who was unfortunate in society, and elevate him to the condition of those who had been more favored." He offered a helping hand up but placed no ceiling on the amount of land or wealth one could hold.[51]

Land reform became a secondary concern to limits on the expansion of slavery as new national parties formed in the 1850s. The Free Democracy Party, which formed in Pennsylvania in August 1852, came closest to fulfilling NRA desires: its platform included a call to reserve the public domain for landless settlers. Yet NRA groups still pushed for the Whigs in that presidential election, probably in an effort to defeat the southern-dominated Democrats. When the Republican Party was formed by Free Soil, Whig, Liberty, and radical Democrat remnants, it initially ignored land reform, and its first national platform in 1856 approved government aid to the Pacific Railroad (opposed by the NRA as an expansion of the land monopoly), though the party would include a homestead proposal in its 1860 platform. Beginning in May 1852, Congress began to seriously consider homestead measures. The initial restriction to men owning less than $500 was quickly dropped, followed by the ban on the subsequent sale of claimed land. Over the next decade, the House would frequently pass a homestead act making it easier and nearly free for men to settle and claim up to 160 acres, and the bill would die in the Senate largely as a result of conservative charges of socialism and southern opposition due to its feared dampening effect on slavery.[52]

Finally, in May 1862, after the southern states and their senators left the Union, Congress enacted a Homestead law, signed by President Abraham Lincoln. That measure allowed any head of family, or male twenty-one years old, to obtain for a 10-dollar fee entry to 160 acres that was priced at the minimum cost or 80 acres that was double the minimum price. If the claimant remained there for five years, the US Land Office would issue a patent granting that land. The only limitation was that no individual could acquire more than 160 acres under the terms of the law. Congress did not seek to prevent the new owner from selling the land to someone else, nor did it consider limiting the amount of national land a person or company could buy or own. Of course, during this same period, Congress gave away millions of acres of the public realm to transcontinental railroad corporations. To the NRA and its allies, national limits on "Land Monopoly" were as or possibly even more important than opening the public realm to actual settlers, because such wealth allowed individuals to corrupt and control legislatures and the courts. George Henry Evans is sometimes called the "Father of the Homestead Act," but had he not died in 1855, he would have opposed the measure passed by Congress. He and his agrarian allies also wanted land to remain free, with settlers allowed to sell or will improvements but not the soil, which should remain public property. As in the past, an American movement for economic equality gained only enough traction to create a shadow of the original goal. That ultimate failure resulted at least in part from the persistent paradigm that all wealth came from land and from the assumption that the increasing gap between the few wealthy and the many poor could be overcome if independent property ownership and production could be protected and promoted.[53]

In the middle of the nineteenth century, even as the industrial revolution and urban growth transformed the United States, the National Reform Association drove the first great agrarian movement for economic equality in America. The ideals in that movement were not new; as Thomas Devyr and other reformers noted, they were inspired by the Diggers who during the English Civil War had insisted that the land belonged to God and that it was violation of basic rights for anyone to hold large areas and excessive wealth when others went hungry. The revival of agrarian egalitarian goals began with the Rappite and Shaker religious communitarian settlements early in the century, and in the 1820s the Quaker surgeon Cornelius Blatchly organized friends to advocate for Christian socialist villages and then embraced the secular Owenite effort. While the 1837 crash seemed to destroy the infant workingmen's movement, it made many Americans reconsider the rush for wealth and laid the groundwork for Albert Brisbane's popular Fourierist movement in the 1840s, although ultimately that movement fizzled due to the strong American preference for individual property ownership and household production. When George Evans and his friends launched the NRA in 1844, they were able to rapidly gain prominence by connecting English Digger and Chartist ideals to American social and cultural norms, building bridges with the lagging Fourierist effort, and, most importantly, creating a strong alliance with nascent trade unions and farming associations across the country. The NRA renewed and popularized an American individualist form of socialism even as the international collectivist socialist movement emerged.

CHAPTER NINE

Reconstruction and the Rejection of Economic Equality

As the war for the Union became a campaign to end slavery in the South, the religious and secular traditions of economic equality together drove a strong call to confiscate plantation lands and redistribute it to freedmen. On the religious side, abolitionists first touted the Great Jubilee's promise of freedom and during the war added land rights for freedmen. On February 24, 1863, Laura Towne of Philadelphia, sent with her Quaker friend Ellen Murray to help the newly freed residents of Helena Island, on the coast of South Carolina, recorded in her diary: "Hurrah! Jubilee! Lands are to be set apart for the people so they cannot be oppressed, or driven to work for speculators, or ejected from their homesteads." As the war ended, the Jubilee promise of full freedom tinged the belief widespread among freedmen that the lands once held by their former owners would be at the end of the year given to them for homesteads. But when divine redistribution failed to transpire, freedmen readily turned to the more widely accepted secular language of republican equality as well as national loyalty, insisting that they were due land as well as freedom.[1]

Congress, in fact, considered land confiscation and slave emancipation as two aspects of the same goal. The initial proposals envisioned "confiscating the property of Rebels and setting their Slaves free," and by mid-1863 Republicans like Thaddeus Stevens and Charles Sumner were urging the redistribution of plantation lands to those formerly forced to work it. In January 1865, General William Tecumseh Sherman's Field Order 15 confiscated huge swaths along the southeast coast and redistributed it to freed families in forty-acre allotments, and about a month later Congress created the Freedman's Bureau with the duty to rent up to forty acres of abandoned or confiscated land to freedman at low rates. But after Lincoln was assassinated in April, President Andrew Johnson ordered the return of confiscated land to the former rebels. While some bureau and army officials sought to slow restoration, and "squatting" freedmen often resisted eviction, Congress rejected proposals to break up large plantations and redistribute land to former slaves and loyal whites. Some congressmen argued, accurately, that freedmen could like other Americans go west and take up land under the Homestead Act or could use army or labor wages to buy land in the South, as indeed about 20 percent of black farmers in the region did by 1880. But although Republicans acknowledged that freedmen faced systemic barriers to obtaining land, including agreements by southern whites not to sell to blacks, their consensus was that a free labor market and the right to vote should be sufficient for freedmen to protect their interests.

Congress's myopic focus on the transcendent power of the vote is particularly puzzling. Anglo-American traditions envisioned widespread property ownership as a foundational element in a republican polity; in the 1840s the NRA had renewed that agrarian ideology, and its influence in the Republican Party was demonstrated by the 1862 Homestead Act. The labor theory of value, which had long been an article of faith among Americans, also strongly supported the freedmen's right to the lands from which their labor, for generations without compensation, had brought forth great wealth for others. In fact, Congress's desire to extend the franchise while refusing to eliminate those barriers highlighted how fundamental changes in the nation since 1800 had marginalized the tradition of economic equality. While racism was a factor, the debates over confiscation and redistribution demonstrated that the ideology of sacred private property had largely supplanted the Revolution's ideal that a republic had the responsibility to prevent concentrations of great wealth or grinding poverty.

Although the Great Jubilee largely faded after 1800 from demands for economic equality, it was increasingly embraced by the growing effort to end slavery. The trope may have first appeared in June 1787 with a missive in a Philadelphia newspaper, widely reprinted elsewhere, that called for the Pennsylvania legislature to "break off every chain of slavery, and let the oppressed go free" and concluded with Leviticus 25:9–10, "Blow the glad trumpet of Jubilee throughout your land, and proclaim LIBERTY to all the inhabitants thereof." That reference became a common touchstone as slavery became controversial; for example, in August 1820, during the debates over Missouri statehood, Senator Jonathan Roberts of Pennsylvania quoted the passage when he condemned the proslavery state constitution and denied the morality or constitutionality of establishing slavery. A few years later, some ministers and writers marking America's jubilee, the fiftieth anniversary of the Declaration of Independence, similarly quoted Leviticus in calling for an end to slavery. That was the chapter and verse cited by an article in the *Boston Recorder and Telegraph* on June 2, 1826, which called for a day of manumission on the fiftieth Fourth as "an offering most acceptable to that God, who gave us our freedom and independence." Of course, as most Americans knew then, and as radical Englishmen discussed at the beginning of the seventeenth century, that the same chapter in Leviticus called for all land to be returned to its original owners.[2]

It was in this context that American abolitionists "created" the Liberty Bell. Philadelphia's bell, cast in the mid-eighteenth century with the verse "Proclaim LIBERTY Throughout all the Land unto all the Inhabitants Thereof," had by the mid-1820s become famed as the "Independence Bell" rung to announce the first public reading of the Declaration in July 1776. But beginning in February 1835, a growing avalanche of articles in abolitionist and children's publications dubbed it the "Liberty Bell" and mourned that so many Americans with dark skin were still denied the liberty that the cast passage promised. In 1837 it became the featured graphic on the cover of *Liberty*, the magazine of the New York Anti-Slavery Society; two years later the Boston Friends of Liberty did the same on its (retitled) periodical the *Liberty Bell*; and William Lloyd Garrison's *Liberator* published a poem "The Liberty Bell" that decried celebrating freedom in America as "base hypocrisy." By the 1840s it was widely known as the Liberty Bell, and its Leviticus passage was frequently quoted to condemn slavery in the United States and call for its abolition.[3]

In the 1850s, calls for more egalitarian land policies began to again spotlight the Great Jubilee while noting its connection to the abolition of slavery. In early 1850, Boston's *Puritan Recorder*, a newspaper connected to the Congregational Church, noted that Leviticus, chapter 25, "one of the most remarkable features of Mosaic legislation," was designed "to train up the Hebrew people to become a nation of 'free-soilers.'" That year marked the zenith of the national Free Soil Party, whose platform called for Congress to bar slavery from the territories and enact a homestead law that would provide free land to settlers. The article went on to praise the jubilee because it "tended to prevent the undue impoverishment of the many, and the dangerous accumulation of wealth in the hands of a few; and also cherished the spirit of liberty and self-respect even in the bond servant."[4]

Those who fought for egalitarian economics generally sought, like the NRA, to brush aside the divisive issue of slavery. In September 1855 the "Jubilee

Catechism" of the Associated Working Men and Women, a utopian union of carpet workers in Philadelphia, scorned abolitionists as "straining at a gnat and swallowing a camel," because until the concept of "Land Monopoly and Land Limitation" was abolished, along with "its greater evils," it would be "impossible to secure human freedom." Indeed, the Catechism actually blamed Africans for having "tempt[ed] the cupidity and avarice of the children of higher latitudes [Europeans] to enslave them." Two years later, *Vanguard*, the Ohio spiritualist newspaper, noted the "hand-in-glove" connection of "the monster evils of Land-Monopoly and Slavery," but insisted that the former should end first. "Chattel slavery will receive its death blow about the time that practical measures are taken to extinguish the monopoly of the soil." In November 1860, the abolitionist newspaper *National Principia* declared firmly that "land speculation and monopoly" were the greatest causes of poverty and that "the cure of poverty must include a return to the divine law" of the Great Jubilee, which prohibited those sins.[5]

One question that the reformers failed to address was whether the formerly enslaved would have access to the land liberated by these agrarian measures. Long-standing racist paradigms included the strange assumption that blacks were unable to manage on their own, and such presumptions limited the civil and political rights of African Americans as emancipation spread in the North. As Congress began to seriously consider reserving public lands for settlers at little to no cost, the 1857 Dred Scott decision implied that blacks would be denied that republican opportunity because (as Chief Justice Roger Taney opined) African descendants could never be US citizens. But some did recognize that freedmen, most of whom would be skilled only in agriculture, would need land. Perhaps the first prominent American abolitionist, the Quaker Anthony Benezet, in his 1762 and 1771 works advocating programs to free slaves, also called for those freed to be given land along the western edges of Georgia and South Carolina.[6]

As the conflict between North and South widened, some envisioning the immediate end of slavery recognized the need to give land to those freed. One was, not surprisingly, John Brown. As the fiery prophet of war began enlisting support for a slave uprising in Virginia, he held a meeting at Chatham, in Canada across Lake Erie from Cleveland, to make plans for the (hopefully) liberated territory. The resulting constitution mandated that "all captured or confiscated property, and all property the product of the labor of those belonging to this organization and of their families, shall be held as the property of the whole, equally, without distinction." That communist egalitarian vision may have had its roots in the connections between abolitionists and Fourier phalanxes like Brook Farm. More significantly, after war erupted some black leaders called for the confiscation and redistribution of southern plantations. In November 1861, New York's *Weekly Anglo-African* foresaw that the war, only three months old, would in the end create "four million of free men and women and children" and extensive vacant lands that the government would confiscate from the "extravagant aristocracy." The writer noted that such lands would be "subject to preemption rights, or if [NRA leader] Gerrit Smith gets again into Congress, turned into 'free land for the landless.'" The best course in terms of justice, politics, and the national interest would be to "bestow these lands upon these freed men who know best how to cultivate them, and will joyfully bring their brawny arms, their willing hearts, and their skilled hands to the glorious labor of cultivating as their OWN, the lands which they have bought and paid for by their sweat and blood."[7]

Even as both sections mobilized for total war, Congress and President Lincoln hesitated to free the enslaved and blanched at the idea of imposing democratic economic reforms on the South through confiscation and redistribution. Shortly after the first Battle of Bull Run, Secretary of War Simon Cameron told Lincoln that he had the right under the Constitution's war powers to emancipate slaves in the rebellious states, but Lincoln balked at this seemingly excessive exercise of executive power. In August 1861, Congress passed the first Confiscation Act, aimed specifically at property "used in promoting the insurrection," which could be (and was) construed by some to mean escaping slaves, since their labor was needed to produce goods and income for the rebellion. By the end of the year, Republican pressure grew for broader confiscation, and several congressmen introduced bills that directed the president to confiscate rebel-owned land and free the slaves in order to deny the enemy critical resources for its war effort. But those bills stalled.[8]

This hesitancy appalled Adam Gurowski, a Polish exile working in the State Department, who wrote with disgust in his diary in December that "the emancipation of slaves is spoken of as an expedient [of war], but not as a sacred duty"; even "leading emancipationists" still seemed wedded to sending free blacks to Liberia or elsewhere, and "not one thinks to give freeholds to the emancipated." Gurowski grumbled, "Freedom without land is humbug," and he foresaw the advantages of giving "small freeholds" to freedmen "cut out of the plantations of rebels, or out of the public lands of each State—lands forfeited by the rebellion."[9] Indeed, only in late 1863, months after President Lincoln issued the Emancipation Proclamation, did Congress discuss redistributing confiscated land to freedmen.

In the early spring of 1862, even as Gurowski continued to complain to his diary, bills emerged in Congress to confiscate the land and slaves of rebels. Democrats like Senator James McDougall of California and border state Unionists like Congressman Aaron Harding of Kentucky opposed the bills for punishing all southerners, seeing it as a destructive and unnecessary exercise of war powers, and a punishment like one of the penalties for treason but without the due process of a trial. More conservative Republicans like Senators John Doolittle of Wisconsin and Daniel Clark of New Hampshire portrayed the measure to confiscate rebel-owned land as a violation of the Constitution's ban on bills of attainder (Article I, Section 10)—acts of Parliament that sentenced individuals to death for treason without trial and confiscated the traitor's lands so his heirs could not inherit—and sought amendments to allow the president to pardon offenders. Republican supporters like Representative Elbridge G. Spaulding of New York and Senator Lot Morrill of Maine insisted that confiscation and emancipation were necessary to cut away at the "material bases of the rebellion" and were clearly allowed by the Constitution's war-making powers; Morrill also noted that international law, as first laid out by the famed early-seventeenth-century Dutch jurist Grotius, supported "the right to deprive the enemy of his possessions—of anything which may augment his strength, and enable him to make war."[10]

At this point, only a few congressmen connected confiscation to egalitarian land reforms and the needs of the many future freedmen. Senator Charles Sumner of Massachusetts called for the "extensive plantations" of rebel leaders to "be broken up, so that they can never again be the nurseries of conspiracy or disaffection. Partitioned into small estates, they will afford homes to many who are now homeless, while their peculiar and overbearing social influence will be destroyed." Poorer neighbors, so long dupes and victims of the rich rebels, would become independent landowners, along with northern soldiers who would take up the plough and "fill the land with Northern industry and Northern principles." While he noted that freeing enslaved persons would serve the useful purposes of pacifying, punishing, and ending the rebellion, he did not call for the plantation lands to be redistributed to the freemen. Representative George Washington Julian of Indiana, who decades later remembered that in 1862 he was among "the few" congressmen with strong antislavery convictions, celebrated "confiscation and liberation" as the best means to end southern secessionist slave power but said nothing about redistribution. Representative Francis Blair of Missouri applauded confiscation but opposed emancipation, reiterating old beliefs about racial conflicts and warning New England colleagues that the freedmen would flock there and become burdens unless Congress added a measure to encourage them to re-settle elsewhere—implicitly linking emancipation with the need for those freed to be given land.[11]

On July 17, Congress passed the second Confiscation Act. The measure freed people owned by anyone either found guilty of treason or assisting the rebellion or named on a long list of Confederate officials; similarly, any enslaved person owned by rebels who reached US Army lines would be free. At some point in the process, Blair's call for colonization was added to the measure, giving the president the power to facilitate *voluntary* settlement of freedmen in a "tropical country beyond the limits of the United States"—a clause that would be ignored. Those who participated in or abetted the rebellion would have their property confiscated by the national government after proceedings in federal district or territorial courts. Both houses agreed to amendments that gave the president the power to pardon rebels and (as proposed by Senator Clark) limited land forfeiture to the lifetime of the offender; these additions, as President Lincoln noted in a subsequent message to Congress, made the bill acceptable to him so that he signed the measure into law. Years later, looking back, George Julian reflected his disappoint in the "anti-republican discrimination between real and personal property" that seemed to envision a South that retained "a rebellious aristocracy founded on the monopoly of land and the ownership of negroes."[12]

After the passage of that Confiscation Act, federal officials in the occupied South began to see the need for the freedmen to obtain and work confiscated or abandoned land. After Union troops took New Bern along the middle coast of North Carolina in March 1862, a settlement on the other side of the Trent River became a magnet for "contraband," and by the end of the war became a full-fledged city with three thousand residents who ran local businesses and raised crops in adjoining farmland, and around nine thousand more freedmen living in small hamlets and farms within a six-mile radius. In May, General Benjamin Butler became military governor of New Orleans and, among other measures for black refugees, leased land from nearby plantations whose owners had fled the Union advance. Later that year General Rufus Saxton was given the quartermaster position in occupied South Carolina and began to offer freedmen farms on abandoned plantations along the coast. Saxton, a devout reformer and believer in human equality, also recruited women teachers to help those newly freed; one of those earnest volunteers was Laura Towne, who rejoiced when those on Helena Island began to gain formal recognition of their homesteads "so they cannot be oppressed." Eight months later, the New York antislavery newspaper *Principia* reported that the federal Court of Internal

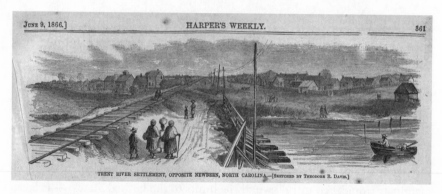

JUNE 9, 1866.]   HARPER'S WEEKLY.   361

TRENT RIVER SETTLEMENT, OPPOSITE NEWBERN, NORTH CAROLINA.—[Sketched by Theodore R. Davis.]

View of Trent River Settlement, later known as James City, North Carolina. *Harper's Weekly*, June 9, 1866, 361. Courtesy of HathiTrust, accessed through https://babel .hathitrust.org/cgi/pt?id=mdp.39015024571229&view=1up&seq=298.

Revenue had ordered the Tax Commissioners for South Carolina to sell "unredeemed land"—land on which federal tax was not paid—to freed slaves for a pittance and commented, "This is a grand beginning of the work of regenerating the South and elevating the enslaved."[13]

In January 1863, Lincoln's Emancipation Proclamation took effect, and Union forces became forces of liberation. In addition to ending slavery, the national government began to move toward providing land to the freedmen who (like their ancestors) had worked throughout their lives without compensation. In late December, Lincoln issued an order allowing freedmen to claim up to forty acres of land that was either abandoned or confiscated when the former owner failed to pay taxes due; the cost to the freedman would be $1.25 an acre with a 40 percent down payment. The political significance of such a policy was clear. As abolitionist leader Wendell Phillips told an enthusiastic Cooper Union crowd, "land dictates government. If the people own the land, it is a democracy; if a few men own it, it is an oligarchy. . . . Confiscate the land of the South and put it into the hands of the negroes and white men who fought for it, and you may go to sleep with your parchments." The orator noted that since independence the United States had "robbed" four million men of their lives and labor, and therefore "owes to the negro not merely freedom—it owes to him land, and owes him education." Segments of the speech were reprinted in Democratic newspapers to show that "the next step in the abolition program" was "the confiscation of the Southern lands and their division among the blacks." In early January 1864, the cofounder of the National Freedmen's Relief Association asked Secretary of the Treasury Salmon Chase to sell plantation land to freedmen for the amount of taxes owed on the site, and a month later the first national meeting of the state associations asked Lincoln for measures to give freedmen "a legal and quiet possession of adequate land."[14]

As the tide of the war shifted and Union troops gained firm control of larger areas, Republican leaders began to consider fundamental reforms in the South. They pushed what would become the Thirteenth Amendment, ending slavery throughout the United States, and looked at extending the Homestead Act to occupied territory. In early January 1864, the House Committee on Public Lands reported a bill allowing free blacks and loyal whites to claim 160-acre homesteads in forfeited or confiscated lands by paying a filing fee, with full title bestowed after five years of "improving" the land. Committee chair George Julian argued passionately that "without a home no man can have, absolutely, any rights," so that if the government seized the "vast estates" of "leading rebels . . . and allot them in small homesteads, you destroy this monopoly and establish independence, liberty, and equality on the ruins of the system which has ripened into this war." Democrats from New York condemned the "socialistic, Fourieristic, Owenistic" proposal, and a Kentucky representative charged that it was intended to "extend to the black population who settle on these lands the right of suffrage and to hold office," highlighting the traditional republican connection between property and polity. In mid-May, the House passed the bill on a party-line vote, and Julian hoped that the Republican national convention on June 7 would, by endorsing the measure, gain the support of more conservative senators. But Lincoln continued to oppose full confiscation and redistribution, dooming the bill that Julian considered "one of the most potent means of putting down the Rebellion."[15]

Although the bill failed, its agrarian goal was gaining traction among those seeking to reconstruct the South in ways more modern. Like the Emancipation Proclamation, land reform fulfilled important military, political, and moral needs. The *New Orleans Tribune* (the first black-owned newspaper in the South) insisted in a series that "no true republican government" could exist "unless the land and wealth in general, are distributed among the great mass of the inhabitants." It claimed, "No more room [exists] in our society for an oligarch of slaveholders or property holders." Freedmen gained the virtuous mantle of laborers whose unpaid sufferings had created the South's immense wealth and should now receive pieces of rebel plantations as reparations. In June 1864, Boston's Methodist periodical, *Zion's Herald*, noted that now "confiscation is the law" and called for freedmen to be given "the land upon which they were born, which they had tilled with their unrequited sweat." Is it not "natural," the journal emphasized, to accept their claims "to the soil which held their sweat and had drank up the blood of their slave fathers and mothers?—aye, the soil which had been enriched by blood drawn from their own backs." Such an application of John Locke's labor theory of value appealed to Republicans, who became increasingly serious about measures that would help freedmen obtain homesteads on the lands that they had worked as slaves.[16]

But at this point it was the US Army rather than Congress that took the next step on the agrarian path of confiscation and redistribution. In the winter of 1864–65, as General Sherman's army cut its devastating swath through the Confederate Southeast, that commander found himself uncertain how to deal with the "vast multitude" who sought freedom with his forces but lacked capital, land, or other means to make a living. On January 12, 1865, after taking Savannah, Georgia, he arranged with Secretary of War Edwin Stanton to meet with twenty leaders of the city's African American community to ask what they needed. Their spokesman, the Reverend Garrison Frazier, told the visitors that their primary desire was "to have land, and turn it and till it. . . . We want to be placed on land until we are able to buy it and make it our own." Education and family rights were also important; less significant was the right to vote. Four days later, more for practical than ideological reasons, Sherman issued Special Field Order 15, confiscating about 400,000 acres of fertile land along the coast from Charleston to Florida and redistributing it to black families in 40-acre allotments under US Army protection, along with army mules to help them plow. The same order added the reserve to General Rufus Saxton's administration, including the responsibility to issue to each head of household "a possessory title in writing." This was not unique: by early 1865, abandoned plantations and farms throughout the South were being leased or held by freedmen; in many cases the owner had died in the war, although widows and heirs could and did press their claims to the estate—as with the Trent River settlement.[17]

At the same time, Congress was considering creating an administrative entity to help freedmen with schools, legal assistance, and other needs—including land. The initial version introduced in the House in the winter of 1863–64 proposed permitting freedmen to occupy, cultivate, and improve abandoned land in rebel states, while saying nothing about permanent homesteads. The Senate's bill, on the other hand, seemed to conceive of freedmen as wage workers rather than farm operators. A joint committee then rewrote the bill to give the bureau the responsibility of renting to freedmen abandoned or confiscated lands for no longer than one year. But at the very last minute, someone added the goal of helping freedmen *and white refugees* to buy small homesteads, a motion probably inspired by Julian's southern homestead bill, previous confiscation measures, and the desire to reform the South by destroying its plantation society built on huge estates, excessive wealth, and slave labor. On March 3, 1865, Congress established the Bureau of Refugees, Freedmen, and Abandoned Lands (the Freedmen's Bureau) within the War Department and gave its agents the power to rent up to forty acres of "abandoned or confiscated land" to any "male citizen, whether refugee or freedmen" (thus white or black) for a small annual rent, after which the renter could buy the land at the value set by the state in 1860.[18]

The Thirty-eighth Congress adjourned shortly after establishing the bureau; the Thirty-ninth would not meet until December 4. Between those two dates, the nation and its reconstruction policy were shattered by Lincoln's assassination on April 14, five days after Lee's surrender at Appomattox marked the essential end of the Confederacy and the southern rebellion. Lincoln's successor, Andrew Johnson of Tennessee, had been born poor in North Carolina and worked for years as a tailor, developing a strong hatred of planter gentry that persisted as he worked his way up through the political ranks. While serving as a congressman in the 1850s Johnson had been a strong advocate for homestead bills, and in 1861 he became the only senator refusing to recognize his state's secession. He was appointed military governor of Tennessee, where he pleased Republicans by endorsing the Emancipation Proclamation and insisting that "traitors must be punished." The party expected the new president to push for reforms in the South; one newspaper hailed one of his first orders, on April 16, as demonstrating that he and Secretary of War Edwin Stanton "agree as to the importance of breaking up the landed aristocracy of the South by parceling out the vast estate of traitors and rebels."[19]

But Johnson instead embraced the southern states, spurned reforms aside from the end of legal slavery, and on May 29 offered amnesty with property restoration (except slaves) to all Confederates who swore allegiance to the United States. He made his personal pique national policy by requiring plantation elites as well as Confederate leaders to individually beg his forgiveness—but when asked, he granted pardons with gusto. Quartermaster General M. C. Miegs urged him to condition those pardons on the grant of small homesteads to the formerly enslaved families, with the men forming a free quasi-independent labor force for the plantation owner. But Johnson was deeply racist, had no objections to the severe "Black Codes" enacted by southern states seeking to recreate racial servitude, and certainly had no interest in land redistribution. In fact, on the same day he granted broad amnesty, he also set up a provisional government for North Carolina that essentially allowed that state to return to its prewar polity, with the power to do anything to freedmen other than declare them slaves. Johnson's use of presidential powers to prevent redistribution, aided by southern white resistance (including violence) and continued racism among northerners, would doom egalitarian land reform in the South.[20]

While Republicans were initially reluctant to criticize the new president, resistance quickly emerged among the "Radicals" who believed in full civil and political rights for freedmen, enforced by the newly powerful national government, and the need to crush all secessionist remnants in the South. Not surprisingly, the Freedmen's Bureau became the focal point of this resistance. In mid-May, General Oliver O. Howard was appointed commissioner of the bureau and began to forge its bureaucracy, including field agents who fostered connections with the army units that would enforce its measures. Perhaps his most strategic appointment was General Saxton as head of the bureau in Georgia; whereas Howard was primarily concerned with civil equality and "moral uplift" for freedmen rather than political and economic equality, Saxton's experience had made him a champion for land redistribution as well as the vote. Howard also received a stream of correspondence from Union officials elsewhere complaining about the efforts of white landowners to reimpose their abusive authority, taking possession of crops planted by freedmen and driving them away. In response, on July 28, Howard issued Circular No. 13, directing that abandoned and confiscated land throughout the South "be set apart for the use of loyal refugees and freedmen" in forty-acre lots. While the commissioner met Johnson's demands by setting up procedures for restoring land to owners, he also mandated that presidential pardons would not extend to land already held and worked by freedmen.[21]

In early September, Thaddeus Stevens, leader of the Radical caucus in the House, delivered a widely reprinted speech in his hometown of Lancaster, Pennsylvania, that announced Congress's intention to fight Johnson's reconstruction policies. He proposed the confiscation of "the estates of every rebel belligerent whose estate was worth $10,000, or whose land exceeded two hundred acres"; that would, he thought, affect only a tenth of all the landowners in the region. Congress would award each adult male freedman forty acres and sell the remainder at auction to help pay the North's war debt. Stevens insisted, "The whole fabric of southern society *must* be changed" in order to eliminate its "features of aristocracy" and make it a "true republic." It was "impossible that any practical equality of rights can exist where a few thousand men monopolize the whole landed property. The larger the number of small proprietors, the more safe and stable the government. As the landed interest must govern, the more it is subdivided and held by independent owners, the better." The congressman intended to make freedmen part of Jefferson's vision of the United States as a nation of freeholder farmers and, in the process, to turn the South into an egalitarian republic.[22]

The Great Jubilee must have seemed imminent to southern blacks as the US Army brought emancipation to growing swaths of the region and their former owners abandoned plantations and fled to Confederate lines. Freedmen began to insist on their right to farm where they had worked and been tormented for generations without pay. In 1864 a black church elder in Port Royal, one of the islands along the coast of South Carolina, told a visiting white northerner: "Tell Lincoln we want land, this very land that is rich with the sweat of we face and the blood of we back. We born here, we parents' graves here; this here our home." African Americans throughout the South who had remained on plantations claimed the freedom from dependency as well as slavery, planting food crops and sometimes a little cotton, some as households and some communally. They created governing councils, churches, and schools, and in various ways sought to control their land. Some took more drastic action. When groups of northern investors sought to buy plantations and reestablish the cotton system with wage labor, freedmen living on those lands drove them off. Similarly, when plantation heirs sought to impose their claims, freedmen forced their representatives to flee and, when ordered by authorities to vacate their former owner's mansion, burned it to the ground. One explained to his former owner, "All de land belongs to de Yankees now, and dey gwine to divide it out 'mong de colored people."[23]

Black refugee settlements like the one at Trent River opposite New Bern similarly established their own governing structures, schools, churches, hospitals, businesses, and farms and, after the war, sought to resist renewed white domination. The Trent River settlers named their community James City, for their minister and chief administrator, and with the support of the Freedmen's Bureau sought to buy the area, including 180 acres of adjoining farmland. As in many similar situations elsewhere in the South, the heirs of the prewar owner (who had been killed in the war) refused to accept the offer and in early 1867 regained formal possession from the federal government. But most of the residents refused to leave and told the Freedmen's Bureau commissioner, "We ar not willing to go and work the land for the Rebs as we did in former days and do in Every Shape like thy say and if we do not aggree in every thing lik the rebs say thy will be come displeased withe us and turn us out doors so we ar not satisfid to live with them." They grudgingly paid rent and two-thirds

Detailed views of Trent River Settlement, *Harper's Weekly*, June 9, 1866, 361. Courtesy of HathiTrust, accessed through https://babel.hathitrust.org/cgi/pt?id=mdp .39015024571229&view=1up&seq=298.

of their harvests to the landowners, and in the 1880s they would form a union, strike for better wages from local white employers, and file suit against the landowners.[24]

Those problems lay in the future. During the summer of 1865, freedmen throughout the South strongly believed that they would soon benefit from a larger redistribution of wealth and power. The army commander in west Tennessee noted people in the area thought "that the Government will expatriate the rebel Southerner and partition all this goodly heritage of lands among the colored race." The bureau's assistant commissioner testified to the congressional Joint Committee on Reconstruction that a majority of blacks in Mississippi, Arkansas, Tennessee, and Alabama believed that the national government would confiscate rebel-owned plantations and give each of them a forty-acre parcel. Not lend, lease, or sell, but *give*. This would have indeed been "the Agrarian idea," as noted by that army commander: a revolutionary redistribution of landed wealth from the top southern white gentry to recently enslaved African Americans. Why did freedmen believe this? Certainly the 1862 Confiscation Act and the 1865 Freedman's Bureau Act, with the other bills and supporting speeches by various congressmen, gave a strong impression that the national government intended to take land from wealthy traitors and redistribute it to those who had suffered under their tyranny. They might have also gotten that message during the war from whites, who publicly declaimed angry fears that the Yankees planned to confiscate and redistribute plantations.[25]

As the Union occupation solidified, freedmen heard similar news from confident African American troops and sympathetic officers. A South Carolina planter complained that black soldiers had told his former slaves that "the whole property of the country, land included, is theirs—and soon to be divided among them." In Tennessee, Captain James Rexford told a July Fourth gathering that "they had made the property and was entitled to it, And, should have it; even at the point of the bayonet." In Mississippi, the commander of an African American company told Howard that freedmen in the area were "oppressed and suffering," and that if he had the power, he "would seize the largest rebel plantation in this and every other county in this State, partition it in lots, of suitable size for the support of a family," and distribute the land to the former slaves. Some Bureau officials had similar views; the commissioner in Virginia, for example, reacting to a newspaper report on local landowners setting outrageously low wage rates, urged Howard "to take possession of all the confiscated lands we require, and permit the Negros to work them on their own account." It is no wonder that General Grant, returning from a fall tour of the Southeast, blamed bureau agents and "colored troops" for convincing freedmen "that the property of his late master should by right belong to him."[26]

African American soldiers may have also spread the promise that the federal government would, between Christmas 1865 and New Year 1866, divide the plantations among freedmen. By fall 1865, that promise had been embraced by freedmen throughout the South. This was reported by the grand jury of Wilkes County, Georgia; the provisional governor of Mississippi; white plantation owners in South Carolina, Louisiana, Tennessee, and Arkansas; General Carl Schurz (to President Johnson); and Freedmen Bureau officials throughout the South. Southern whites, already edgy at challenges to their racist rule, became more fearful at the rumors. First, the former slaves refused to sign work contracts for the coming year because they anticipated getting their own land, so plantation owners lacked needed labor. Second, whites worried about violence if freedmen did *not* get land, especially now that blacks had firearms. Bureau officials scrambled to deny the stories and urged freedmen to sign labor contracts in speeches and circulars, sometimes threatening that those who did not might face local vagrancy charges. But because African Americans had for generations believed in the future Great Jubilee and viewed recent events in light of the Exodus promise of land as well as the end of enslavement, they clung to the hope of economic as well as legal liberation. In southern Georgia, freedmen insisted the president would, by Christmas, make them "more free" by giving them the right to lands. Mississippi freedmen shared the belief that the Freedmen's Bureau had received "a great Document" with four seals that would be broken on January 1 and reveal the government's "final orders." Such mystical perceptions of the promised egalitarian re-distribution were seemingly widespread.[27]

Because the biblical Great Jubilee meant not only civil but also economic liberation, the people who had been so recently tormented as slaves viewed wage labor for the same planter as neither. Like Anglo-American colonists, they linked freedom with landholding. A bureau officer in eastern Texas en-countered blacks who, while seemingly unaware that they were legally free, told him that they had heard that they would be freed on Christmas and shortly after on New Year's Day would get land in a "grand division"; they clearly connected the two forms of liberation. It is not surprising that recently enslaved African Americans in the mid-nineteenth century and the hungry marginalized subaltern Englishmen two centuries earlier drew from the same biblical well of physical, social, and economic liberation. The Great Jubilee was a powerful symbol of restorative justice and human equality, especially in the face of overwhelming authoritarianism, brutality, and poverty. In revolution-ary times, it offered a useful religious touchstone for marking and maintain-ing republican ideals of virtue and relative equality. By the time that the Civil War erupted, it was not the only intellectual and cultural thread of economic egalitarianism in the United States. But for the most marginalized people in America, it remained a very real and powerful promise of justice and redemption.[28]

President Johnson's zealous enforcement of his Amnesty Proclamation soon shattered those anticipations of an imminent Jubilee. He issued an order on August 16 to restore land to a pardoned Confederate from his home state and for the bureau to do the same "in all similar cases"; Howard was away from Washington, so his adjutant informed the state commissioners that Circular No. 13 was suspended. Freedmen on rebel-claimed land would be allowed to harvest their crops but then would have to abandon their farms. When How-ard returned, he tried to get Johnson to force elite rebels to give freedmen small homesteads in exchange for pardons, but the president ignored the idea and instead had his own staff prepare a new policy, Circular No. 15, which made it even easier for former Confederates to regain their plantations. The bureau head considered resigning but instead sought to delay restorations while hop-ing Congress (still in recess) would override the new policy. On October 12, the *New York Independent* decried the policy change and warned that "if . . . the confiscation act is to be completely nullified, the cause of the black man is hopeless." Johnson pushed harder, extending Circular No. 15 to the lands promised to freedmen by Sherman in Special Field Order 15 and ordering Howard to visit the region to announce the new policy.[29]

On October 19, Howard, with General Saxton, went to Edisto Island for his first visit in the painful journey. The two Yankee generals and their accompanying party, which included the two pardoned rebels who had owned the largest plantations on the island, were greeted at the landing by a committee and escorted to the crowded church. Howard told the meeting that President Johnson had ordered him to bring word that the freedmen would have to return the land to their former masters, now pardoned, and would have to seek wage labor instead. One of the teachers from New England wrote that, as his message sank home, "there was a general murmur of dissatisfaction" and calls of "No, never." After further discussions, he asked the islanders to choose a committee to deal with the demands of the landowners and left. A few days later, the committee wrote to Howard that the islanders insisted on homesteads, mourned the government's determination "to befriend its late enemies," and would not work for men who had whipped them mercilessly, stripped and flogged their mothers and sisters, and now took what should be their land. Howard gave little encouragement, so they petitioned President Johnson. In that place "where secession was born and Nurtured," until the war, they had toiled as slaves to make the lands so valuable. Should they, "the only true and Loyal people," be again subject to those "rebellious Spirits" who had "cheated and Oppressed us for many years"? Moreover, "Land monopoly is injurious to the advancement of the course of freedom," they told the president, echoing the NRA language that Johnson had embraced as a congressman, and "if the government Does not make some provision by which we as Freedmen can obtain a Homestead, we have Not bettered our condition."[30]

That petition demonstrated that, while freedmen hoped for the Great Jubilee, they also embraced the Lockean labor theory of value along with the Jeffersonian tradition that owning land was the hallmark of independence and equality. Observers throughout the South reported, like the Freedmen's Bureau official in South Carolina, the "wide spread opinion amongst these people that the land of their former masters belongs to them, that they have worked on it all of their lives without pay and it is now theirs as a compensation for such work." Peter Johnson of North Carolina told President Johnson in November 1865 that more than five hundred fellow freedmen were living on plantations totaling thousands of acres, asked that each adult man receive five acres of land, and told him that the land should belong to "those who have tilled this soil and raised corn and cotton by the sweat of their brow."

In March 1866, at a meeting in Yorktown, Virginia, Bailey Wyatt spoke about their hard life under slavery and sacrifices for the Union—whose officials were moving to evict them from a "redeemed" plantation. "I may state to all our friends, and to all our enemies, that we has a right to the land where we are located. For why? I tell you. Our wives, our children, our husbands, has been sold over and over again to purchase the lands we now locate upon; for that reason we have a divine right to the land." Moreover, he went on to emphasize, it was their labor that provided the rich crops of cotton, tobacco, rice, and sugar that had enriched the "large cities" in the North.[31]

The freedmen's embrace of these agrarian ideas and their horror at the notion of laboring for their former owners drove widespread resistance. That effort was challenged not only by the pardoned plantation owners but also by the Freedmen's Bureau and US Army officers who saw redistribution as impossible. Some officials sought to help negotiate compromises that allowed both the once-enslaved farmers and the pardoned proprietor to hold distinct sections of the plantation, although in most causes that meant that the freedmen would rent, not own. Circular No. 13 mandated that black squatters could stay until they harvested their existing crops, but by the fall it was becoming clear that white landowners were refusing to sell or lease land to blacks and sought ways to force them into near-servile labor. Southern whites took that route, of course, largely because their deep-seated racism was laced with the gall of defeat, but also because (ironically) the republican ideology that reified landowning remained deeply rooted, and they believed that a social and political revolution would accompany black landholding. The *New York Independent* feared that this nullification of the Confiscation Act meant that "the cause of the black man is hopeless." Such opposition soon had its effect: by the end of November 1865 bureau officials estimated that in eastern Virginia at least seventy thousand freedmen had been forced out by plantation owners.[32]

Republicans were increasingly concerned about these developments in the South, especially with President Johnson's support for white resistance, and they pushed legislation to make deeper reforms and provide more help for freedmen. One bill introduced in the Senate in early 1866 by Lyman Trumbull and Charles Sumner proposed reauthorizing the bureau with more powers, including the ability to rent or sell confiscated land at low rates in forty-acre lots to "loyal refugees and freedmen." Johnson vetoed the measure with an angry note that appealed to southern whites and northern Democrats. Congress tried to override the veto but failed. On May 29, House Republicans passed a more limited version, which the Senate approved on June 26. When the president vetoed that bill as well, on July 16, angry Republicans voted overwhelmingly to override his obstruction and make it law. But that version did little to forestall Johnson's effort to restore former Confederates; it simply confirmed titles held by former slaves in the South Sea islands and set fairly easy terms for freedmen to obtain other pieces of coastal land confiscated for unpaid taxes.[33]

Also, in early 1866 the House considered a bill opening public lands in Alabama, Mississippi, Louisiana, Arkansas, and Florida to "actual settlers" under the terms of the 1862 Homestead Act—but with a ceiling of eighty acres. Because the Homestead Act barred rebels (pardoned or not) from its provisions, that meant the southern lands could be claimed only by freedmen and loyal whites. In the initial debates, John Rice of Maine told his colleagues that they should have confiscated and redistributed plantation lands but that this bill would help fend off "the rapacious talons of the monopolist and the speculator" and ensure farms for "the oppressed, wronged, and suffering poor." The final version of the Southern Homestead Act, signed by President Johnson on June 21, gave freedmen and loyal whites until January 1, 1867, to stake claims before the area was open to all. Individuals and groups of all sizes investigated the prospects of obtaining land under its provisions, sometimes sending delegates to look for good settlement locations. Unfortunately, a range of problems doomed the success of most efforts: freedmen lacked the resources to obtain draft animals, tools, and seed; most of the available acreage was of poor quality for agriculture; white residents obstructed black settlers, sometimes with violence; and freedmen had to fulfill their contractual labor obligations before they could settle and file.[34]

In the run-up to the elections of fall 1866, Johnson made his infamous "swing around circle," traveling around the North by train to rally opposition to his Republican antagonists and the Fourteenth Amendment, passed in June and now before the state legislatures. He was sorely disappointed: Republicans swept the elections to dominate the Fortieth Congress as it began its first session in early March 1867, allowing it to pass and then override Johnson's veto of the Military Reconstruction Act: all of the former Confederate states except Tennessee were put under martial law until they ratified the Fourteenth Amendment. At the same time, Charles Sumner in the Senate and Thaddeus Stevens in the House renewed their land reform efforts to confiscate large plantations and divide them into small homesteads to be distributed to freedmen.[35]

On March 7, Sumner introduced a resolution that began by declaring Congress had "paramount authority over the Rebel States" and then listing five goals, including taking extraordinary steps to create republican governments, keeping those states free of rebel influence, creating public schools throughout the South, and distributing homesteads to freedmen "so that at least every head of a family may have a piece of land." Congress clearly has the power; "now as you have already given the ballot, you must go further, and give not only education but the homestead." The resolution was set aside for several days; when it was brought back for discussion, the last measure proved particularly controversial. William Fessenden of Maine asked whether "possession by every man of a piece of land" was necessary for a republican government; Sumner said that it was not, but that in this case homesteads were necessary "to complete the work of the ballot." The Massachusetts senator reminded his colleagues that the national government already held land in the South due to the owners' failure to pay wartime taxes, that the president could and should make rebel pardons conditional on providing land to freedmen, and that more should be obtained through confiscation; indeed, he held, the country would be in much better shape "had the great landed estates of the South been divided and subdivided among the loyal colored population."[36]

On March 11, as the Senate debated Sumner's bill, Stevens in the House proposed a more focused and substantive measure that created a streamlined confiscation process and that allotted to each adult male freedmen or head of family a homestead of forty acres plus $100 to build a home. This was necessary, he told his colleagues, to ensure "not only the happiness and respectability of the colored race, but their very existence. Homesteads to them are far more valuable than the immediate right of suffrage, though both are their due." The millions of southern freedmen, lacking education, land, and capital, were terribly vulnerable to becoming servants and victims unless they could become "independent of their old masters," and he urged the House to prevent this evil by giving them "a small tract of land." This measure would also build a more virtuous and wealthier South: "Nothing is so likely to make a man a good citizen as to make him a freeholder. Nothing will so multiply the productions of the South as to divide it into small farms." After noting the success of Russia's recent land reforms and emphasizing that the freedmen had earned land by their generations of toil without compensation, he concluded, "No people will ever be republican in spirit and practice where a few own immense manors and the masses are landless. Small independent landholders are the support and guardians of republican liberty."[37]

Although both measures were tabled, with the House bill put off until December, they encouraged southern blacks to push for land redistribution. In the spring and summer, when African Americans gathered in state conventions, they embraced a wide menu of social and political reforms. In April those attending the Virginia Republican convention largely supported confiscation: they enthusiastically applauded a speaker who insisted that "if Congress did not give the negroes land, they should be taken by violence," and adopted a platform that "threatens the land monopolists of the State with confiscation if they oppress the laborers and attempt to control his vote." The Charleston Republican gathering in March and the South Carolina convention in July both called for heavy taxes on uncultivated land to force the breakup of "large land monopolies" and to promote "the division and sale of unoccupied lands among the poorer classes." By mid-June, as noted by the *Boston Daily Advertiser,* confiscation and redistribution dominated "the mind of the loyal population of the South—the poor whites and land-lack negroes" and "meanders through the letters and speeches of its advocates in the North." But there was strong opposition within the Republican Party to land reform, at least in part because of its strong belief in the free market and the virtue of wage labor. Gerrit Smith, one of the NRA survivors in the party, told an audience of blacks and whites in Richmond in May that freedmen should not ask for land but instead "seek homes by their honest earnings," and indeed many black Union veterans were pooling their wages to buy land where possible. At the party's Louisiana state convention, held in New Orleans in June, rural freedmen overwhelmingly supported confiscation and redistribution, but "the energetic exertions of the white and free born colored members" managed to limit the party platform to a call to divide rural lands in the state into small farms "as far as practical." Elsewhere a similar divide over the question of land reforms developed between rural and urban freedmen.[38]

The Republican opposition to confiscation and redistribution became particularly clear at the national level. During the Senate debates on Sumner's resolutions in March, Republicans James Dixon of Connecticut, John Sherman of Ohio (brother of William Tecumseh), and Frederick Frelinghuysen of New Jersey had all opposed Sumner's proposal as too extreme and unfair to the South and Congress (which would need to find ways to enforce the measure). Most Republicans and all of the Democrats voted to table the bill, and it was never brought up again for consideration. In early July, Sumner introduced a new resolution mandating that the president, before issuing future pardons to rebel landowners, first require the conveyance to "his former slaves, a certain portion of the land on which they have worked, so that they may have a homestead in which their own labor has mingled." But the Senate similarly tabled that proposal.[39]

By the time the House again considered confiscation, on December 10, the political climate seems to have clearly turned against land reform. Its chances were not helped by the declining health of the once-powerful Stevens, who whispered that he was "too feeble" to stay and asked that the bill be referred to a joint committee where it probably would have received support. Instead, the Democrats, sensing victory, used the bill to attack Republican reconstruction policies. John Chanler of New York called confiscation "intolerant, unjust, unwise, and despotic," and "not only unnecessary, but impossible" to accomplish. The war was over, he scornfully told the Republicans, the time has passed for such laws, and "if [the freedman] has not manhood enough to thrive by his own industry let him quit the soil and make room for his betters." Charles Eldridge of Wisconsin then spoke in similar terms for about an hour. At the end of the day, the House voted to leave the measure on the table. It was never reconsidered. The death of Thaddeus Stevens, on August 11, 1868, marked the end of efforts to confiscate and redistribute plantation lands. Two years later, in the 1870 elections, the few remaining supporters of land reform, including George Washington Julian, were defeated.[40]

As African Americans in the South gained freedom, they embraced two traditions of economic equality: the biblical Jubilee and the republican freeholder, the sacred and the secular. For a shining moment, with Sherman's Special Order and the Freedmen's Bureau, as rural blacks established family and communal farms on the plantations where they had slaved for generations, it looked like that this egalitarian vision could be achieved. Even as the new president pushed to reverse those gains and restore the plantations to their former owners, federal officials reported the continued widespread belief among freedmen that the "Head man" would soon come and make them "more free" and "distribute the lands" to them. Savannah's black leaders had told Sherman and Stanton that their primary desire was for land that would provide critical autonomy because they feared they would remain a detested subaltern people in the South; the vote they ranked fourth, after education and family rights. The Founders would have understood. Yet at the end, except for the largely ineffective Southern Homestead Law, Congress insisted that freedmen needed only the vote.

Congress's refusal to confiscate large plantations from Confederate leaders and redistribute homesteads to freedmen may seem surprising, considering the deep American attachment to Jeffersonian agrarianism and the labor theory of value, and their fierce anger at the South's initial responses to defeat. Congress did take aggressive actions in 1866 and 1867, imposing military rule, the Freedmen's Bureau, and the Fourteenth and Fifteenth amendments on the South. But powerful Radical Republicans like Stevens, Washington, and Sumner were not able to persuade their more moderate or liberal colleagues to enact substantive land reforms, and federal officials in the South largely went along with President Johnson's policy of rapid restoration without considerations for the formerly enslaved whose sufferings had built that wealth. There were many reasons for that failure: the racism that had become deeply woven into the national culture; the North's embrace in the 1800s of free-labor republicanism and democracy without property barriers, which together shaped the paradigm that the vote was more important than land for freedom; and, perhaps most important, the increasingly powerful view that property rights were sacred, and the fear among many national leaders that the confiscation and redistribution of southern lands could ripple through and even shatter the country's economic, social, and legal systems.

Racism had become increasingly powerful in the United States after 1790, even in the northern states that gradually abolished slavery. Most Americans of European origin viewed those of African origin as *inherently* physically stronger but intellectually and morally weaker. Some northern states passed or considered laws that would bar the immigration of free blacks. It should not be very surprising that, even as the Union by 1863 largely embraced the goal of ending slavery, and the Freedmen's Bureau was established to assist blacks in the wake of the war, racism colored the words and deeds of many northerners. Most obviously, Democrats opposed Republican policies for reasons that were often bitterly racist. For example, when Congressman Chanler of New York spoke against Thaddeus Stevens's confiscation bill in December 1867, he scorned extending the vote to freedmen, insisting that "the African" was ignorant of democracy and individual liberty, and concluded that "the dominion of this continent belongs to the white man."[41]

While Republicans had moved far from such virulent racism, many continued to hold racialist assumptions about African Americans. That clearly included some of those who went to work for the Freedmen's Bureau. For example, in October 1865, General Davis Tillson, head of the bureau in Georgia, proclaimed that freedmen were "great liars and most skillful thieves" and "are stealing and killing animals to an extent that jeopardizes the future prosperity of the State." Those in other states were shocked that "ignorant" freedmen might anticipate obtaining land as compensation and worked hard to get them to sign contracts to work for their former masters; Tillson's counterpart in Mississippi even issued a stern warning: "Idleness and vagrancy will not be allowed among the Freedmen," and they "must not expect peculiar immunities." Such paternalistic racism among bureau officials increased over time because, as the organization expanded, it hired more local agents; they were often Unionists with wealth and status, which may have helped legitimize the bureau, but many had held slaves, favored other white elites (who were often plantation owners), and treated freedmen "with undisguised contempt."[42]

Bureau officials pushed hard to get freedmen to sign labor contracts with white plantation owners because they had embraced the mission of replacing the southern system of racial slavery with a northern-style free wage labor system. That mission was shaped by the Republicans' embrace (like their Whig predecessors) of the free wage labor ideology that rejected class conflict and instead embraced a vision of harmony between different economic interests. It was a moral as well as political and economic vision, according to the bureau commissioner, who told the midwestern freedmen's assistance organization in August 1865 that he preferred not to confiscate rebel lands because it was better for the freedman "to begin at the bottom and work up, that he may learn how to preserve the property he acquires." For these reformers, the massive economic and social differences between the agricultural North and the plantation South presented no obstacle.[43]

Southerners on the other hand saw blacks as inherently different, unable to achieve the self-discipline ("mastery") of a white worker and requiring a white master to plan and punish in order to get things done. They gained the sympathy of some northerners, partly for racist reasons, but also because the freedmen who had farms seemed to prefer subsistence crops instead of the cotton needed by manufacturers. As Reconstruction waned, these interests ended the more communal aspects of the South's agricultural economy, where before the war cattle had ranged freely, and put in its place more rigid modern systems of ownership and use of the land. Moreover, while bureau officials sought from the beginning to ensure fair wages for black farm laborers, setting up courts to negotiate contracts and adjudicate conflicts, plantation owners met to set low wages and maneuvered to reimpose their prewar authority, as freedmen sought to maximize their autonomy. The result was a "battle over wages" in the southern countryside that was largely won by plantation owners. One reason they won was because Republicans deeply believed that labor agreements were sacred contracts between employer and employee and avoided challenging them unless they were obviously unfair. More important was the violence and intimidation against freedmen that proved effective because, with the war officially won, the Union Army rapidly demobilized; not only did the United States have a deep prejudice against a large standing army, but the men wanted to go home, and keeping a huge army in occupation duty was terribly expensive.[44]

Another significant element undermining Republican support for confiscation and redistribution was, ironically, the elimination after 1800 of property requirements for voting—a change that, while benefiting white men, came alongside higher political barriers for blacks and women. The widely embraced expansion of the franchise valorized the vote as the ultimate symbol of the increasingly democratic United States and marked the marginalization of the paradigm that widespread landownership was necessary for a stable, virtuous republic. Though initially master artisans claimed the republican mantle, soon it was donned by all wage laborers. Thus, the Virginia Convention of Colored People, held in Alexandria (alongside Washington, DC) in early August 1865, adopted resolutions insisting on "equal protection of the laws" and "the elective franchise, which we believe to be our inalienable right as freemen" and the only "safe-guard for our protection," but the convention gave only a bare nod to redistribution and ignored the question of confiscation. Reports from some of the southern Republican conventions in 1866 and 1867 indicated that urban free blacks opposed calls for land redistribution and emphasized instead civil and political equality.[45]

In fact, the strongest advocate in Congress for confiscation and redistribution, Thaddeus Stevens, urged that policy at least in part because he clung to the older views of republican landownership. In January 1866, in debates over the apportionment section of the Fourteenth Amendment, he suggested restricting black suffrage for a few years so that the freedmen could establish their independence from economic coercion. Otherwise, southern whites "will give the suffrage to their menials, their house servants, those that they can control, and elect whom they please to make our laws." Wendell Phillips had become famous for similarly advocating confiscation and redistribution, and the *Boston Daily Advertiser* cheered Phillip's vigorous argument: "There can be no greater security for republican institutions than legions of small farms, each owned by the tiller of the soil, who, independent in his condition and interested in the prosperity of the country, must necessarily take a lively interest in the general welfare." But most Republicans emphasized the ballot because, as the editor of the *Nation* argued in May 1867, "the distribution of other people's land to the negroes is not necessary to complete the work of emancipation." While farmers might make the best citizens in a republic, possession of railroad stock or good clothes served the same purpose, and there was "no mysterious virtue in land." If the black man is fit to vote, the writer argued, he is also fit to win a farm for himself just like the white man. Subsequent events proved Stevens and the many vocal freedmen correct: without the autonomy offered by landownership, southern blacks were unable to resist the coercive economic and legal power wielded by white "redeemer" elites.[46]

Finally, most Republicans shied away from including substantive land reforms in their Reconstruction laws because they loved property rights more than they hated rebels. The belief that government had the duty to protect individual property rights had emerged during the Revolution, and by the mid-nineteenth century it had become a deeply rooted ideology among Americans. Many Republicans saw their 1862 Homestead Act as making confiscation and redistribution unnecessary for freedmen, as it made public lands available to *anyone* settling in the West. They also thought that the vote, supposedly guaranteed by the Fifteenth Amendment, would allow blacks (like whites) to defend their civil and legal rights at the ballot box. Finally, they also feared that such a fundamental challenge to existing property rights would ripple through the entire country and endanger its economic, social, and political, and legal systems. That May 1867 *Nation* column also argued that "a division of rich men's land amongst the landless, as the result of a triumph at the polls, would give a shock to our whole social and political system from which it would hardly recover without the loss of property," in a notable contrast to the frequent denunciations during the late eighteenth century of the corrupting effects of concentrated wealth. Two months later, the *New York Times* similarly condemned Sumner's call for pardons to be linked to homesteads for freedmen as akin to confiscation, reshaping "the fundamental relation of industry to capital" in a way that would inevitably "find its way into the cities of the North" and provide fuel for the dreaded socialist agitators. Thus the newspaper insisted that Sumner's proposal "strikes at the root of all property rights in both sections" and "concerns Massachusetts quite as seriously as Mississippi."[47]

As a result of these factors, the Republicans willing to push for land reform were increasingly on shaky ground. A congressional committee charged with overseeing Reconstruction declared that the rights of property would not be infringed, and more northerners echoed the reluctant admission of the *Boston Daily Advertiser* that it was too late: "Confiscation, which would have been a war measure" right after Lee's surrender, would be "malicious revenge today" and impossible to enforce. In the fall elections, Thaddeus Stevens failed to win election to the Senate as his health failed, and the party suffered such noticeable losses that the *New York Independent* thought it had "frustrated all schemes of confiscation." At least some Republican leaders were convinced that white northerners were tending to vote racist and were increasingly opposed to measures that would require more of southern whites. At the end of the year, the southern periodical *DeBow's Review* noted the arguments among Republicans over the "monstrous proposition" of confiscation and redistribution, with many "fearful that the spirit of agrarianism thus evoked, will not be appeased by anything less than a general division of spoils, involving the whole country in one common vortex of anarchy and lawlessness."[48]

The struggles over southern land reforms during Reconstruction highlight changes and continuities in the American tradition of economic equality. The calls for a Great Jubilee, which were first heard in English during the radical Reformation and occasionally appeared during the early Republic, inspired many African Americans as they won freedom in the South, but they were largely dismissed by whites and quickly evaporated. The classical vision of a republic, on the other hand, with widespread landownership supporting virtue and preventing the corrupting concentration of wealth, clearly continued to resonate among Anglo-American elites as well as among those without land and power, including rural freedmen. Similarly, the Enlightenment theory that labor gave land its value retained noticeable influence, providing moral weight to the freedmen's claims that they should get freeholds as compensation for the generations of unpaid and abusive labor that had made the plantations fruitful.

But the lack of support for the confiscation and redistribution of rebel-owned plantation lands, even among northern Republicans angered by southern resistance, demonstrated that the liberal ideal of sacred private property had become dominant in the United States. After 1800, the shift to wage labor in the North and the separation of property from polity throughout the country had marginalized the communitarian, republican ideals that seemed so strong during the Revolution and early Republic. Americans increasingly accepted the justifications for the country's growing concentrations of wealth and rigid social stratification, and they blamed the poor for moral failings as their numbers grew. Occasionally calls for fundamental changes to property holding in America gained traction, especially in the wake of the crashes of 1819 and 1837, with labor radicals urging limits on wealth and Fourierists establishing communes for those wishing to live as examples for the rest of the country. But the only meaningful reform effort used the nation's vast public lands to revive the Jeffersonian vision of a republic of patriarchal, independent homesteads; it made no changes in existing property arrangements and proved ineffective in the South after the war. Thus, although the failure to redistribute plantation lands to freedmen was not the death knell of American ideals of economic equality, it confirmed that the tradition had been marginalized.

Epilogue

The American tradition of economic equality persisted between the War for Independence and Reconstruction even as some its core concepts shifted. The most consistent element was the strong belief that the republic would be endangered if close connections developed between individual wealth and political power. As a result, Americans throughout this period generally detested the public flaunting of opulence and feared corporations. Most efforts to prevent an "aristocracy of wealth" focused on limiting or dividing inheritances, making public education available to all boys (and many girls), and helping white tenants, poorer farmers, and wage workers to gain influence and autonomy. There were also occasional calls for progressive taxation on property, income, and inheritances and the democratic redistribution of resources. In addition, despite strong tendencies toward patriarchal individualism and household autonomy, a noticeable number of Americans became interested in communitarian efforts, including religious movements like the Shakers, who echoed the Diggers' denunciation of private property, and secular movements like Fourierism that sought to put proto-socialist ideals into practice. Finally, there was the occasional call for the Great Jubilee, although after 1800 that vanished with the exception of the title of an NRA pamphlet and its short-lived embrace by southern blacks at the end of the Civil War.

This evolving tradition was fertilized and shaped throughout the century by cross-Atlantic currents, with English and European writings and immigrants bringing ideas and controversies to America. To begin with, the rich vein of English egalitarianism that developed during the seventeenth century, from the Great Sabbath to Harrington's *Oceana* to Locke's labor theory of value, fundamentally shaped American ideas of economic equality through the nineteenth century. The French Revolution and its call for liberty, equality, and fraternity triggered new enthusiasm but also a fearful and angry conservative reaction. At the turn of the century, British children's literature and works on political economy were widely reprinted (without royalties) in the United States and deeply influenced subsequent writings by Americans as well as culture and politics more broadly. During the first two decades of the nineteenth century, Britain was shaken by a wave of labor unrest and political radicalism, and new political economists emerged including prominent proto-socialists like Robert Owens and John Gray; not only would their writings inspire Americans, but immigrant laborers like William Heighton and George Henry Evans would help create and shape the Workingmen's Movement. Owens himself came to the United States in 1824 to great acclaim and established one of his patented factory towns, although the ideas of French utopian socialist Charles Fourier as translated by Albert Brisbane would be far more successful. Britain's labor unrest was followed in the late 1830s by the Chartist reform movement, and the resulting violence and repression drove political radicals to America including Thomas Devyr, who reprinted some of his Chartist works for the NRA. Finally, European refugees from the repression of the 1848 revolutions, particularly German socialists, would influence egalitarian ideas in the United States before and after the Civil War.[1]

Egalitarian ideas and policies in the United States were also deeply affected by more distantly related developments. During the Revolution, Americans began to embrace the liberal assumption of individual property rights; that paradigm could clash with republican communitarian concerns, as it clearly did during wartime efforts to regulate prices, but at other times people managed both concepts simultaneously without noticing the latent conflicts. Before the Revolution, landownership was understood to be the primary if not only source of wealth and power, but afterward capital became increasingly significant (and obvious) for riches and influence. After 1800, the rise of mass production in the northeast, although meeting the country's appetite for cheap textiles and other goods, generated a growing body of white unskilled wage laborers who increasingly compared their dependence with that of enslaved African Americans in the South. While class conflict intensified with mass production and industrial capitalism, the worst effects were defused by the rising educational system that taught respect for the social hierarchy and by a broader cultural emphasis on individual opportunity and competition as republican *and* liberal.[2] An even more significant "relief" was the elimination of property requirements from state constitutions, causing economic and political power to be regarded as separate and distinct elements. Americans noticed the marginalization of their tradition of economic equality, but the few ante-bellum efforts to reverse course by establishing communal phalanxes or villages of settlers on free federal lands had little success. Indeed, the country's continued norms of individual autonomy, household independence, and limited government probably doomed the NRA and the efforts during Reconstruction to redistribute land to those formerly enslaved in the South.

In the wake of Reconstruction's failure, the tradition of economic equality would seem increasingly besieged and archaic as industrial corporations grew in size and power, supported by state and national courts and executives, and owners and financiers like Andrew Carnegie, Henry Frick, J. P. Morgan, and others gained and flaunted stunning levels of wealth. These captains of industry believed that they deserved their wealth and were entitled to the resulting power; as Jay Gould told the Senate, "*We* have made the country rich, *we* have developed the country," and John Rockefeller claimed that "the good Lord gave me my money."[3] These perceptions were supported by scholars who justified wealth and privilege with new scientific ideas. Oxford professor Herbert Spencer applied Darwin's biological theories to social conditions, coining the phrase "survival of the fittest" and popularizing the laissez-faire gospel that state intervention in the economy was fundamentally destructive of individual liberty. Yale sociologist William Graham Sumner, a Spencer disciple, taught that efforts to reduce poverty and inequality, including taxing property, were futile because extreme wealth and economic privilege resulted from natural processes. It is noteworthy that the study of "political economy" was replaced by "economics," with a focus on data increasingly divorced from the stories of people's lives and experiences. By the end of the century, Americans seemed to generally believe that economic inequality and privileged wealth was a natural result of the country's founding principle of liberty, and efficiency replaced fairness as a cardinal virtue. At the same time, they also continued to believe the gospel of American opportunity, that the poorest man could become rich through individual effort.[4]

Yet the tradition remained potent. Henry George's *Progress and Poverty* (1879) revived the call for government to encourage household independence with wider ownership of land by imposing high taxes on large estates. Edward Bellamy's novel *Looking Backward* (1887) became a best seller with its vision of a future (in 2000) where equality, abundance, and harmony had replaced greed, poverty, and social conflict. These moral visions gained power as violent class conflict became very real with the first general strike in America. In 1877 railroad laborers struck against wage cuts and new rules reducing their autonomy, triggering the "Great Uprising" as workers throughout the country rose against the poverty and dependence created by the "aristocracy of wealth." The outbreak was doomed by internal divisions and squashed by police, including (for the first time) federal troops, representing a new level of support for corporate power. Still, everyone knew its causes remained, and in the wake of the strike the Knights of Labor became the first national labor organization, featuring fraternal trappings with calls for a "cooperative commonwealth" (in which workers would own and run companies) and demands for wide-ranging reforms from an eight-hour workday to health and safety regulations. The Knights of Labor and other unions led (and usually lost) major strikes throughout the 1880s against efforts by industrialists like Frick and George Pullman to absolutely control workplaces.[5]

A parallel movement emerged at the same time among farmers who formed regional alliances to create purchasing and marketing cooperatives and to press for railroad regulation and a range of other antimonopoly measures. The farmers and laborers came together to form the People's (Populist) Party, which met in 1892 in Omaha to enact a platform calling for the nationalization of railroads and utilities, an eight-hour workday, a graduated income tax, and political reforms including term limits. Two years later, Henry Demarest Lloyd published the widely read *Wealth against Commonwealth*, condemning corporate industrial capitalism as destructive of democracy and calling for a political campaign for economic equality to restore America's republican virtue. That same year, Populist Milford Howard was elected to Congress from Alabama and soon after wrote *The American Plutocracy*, which not only condemned concentrated wealth but also proposed amending the Constitution to limit individual ownership of "all kinds of property" to $1 million "aggregate value." Any "excess" would be "condemned as a public nuisance and a public peril and be accordingly forfeited into the United States Treasury." Howard gave no indication that he was aware that, with the exceptions of the stated limit and the national jurisdiction, this is precisely what was proposed in 1776 for Pennsylvania's constitution and in 1656 by James Harrington for *Oceana*.[6]

In the first quarter of the twentieth century, even as the contest over economic values continued, there was a noticeable shift as those who sought to help workers, solve poverty, and improve the republic embraced a strong and professional state as the best counterweight to corporate wealth and power. Congress finally passed two measures to prevent monopolies, the Sherman Anti-Trust and Clayton acts, but those were designed to limit threats to competition rather than the wealth and power of corporate executives and stockholders. Similarly, President Theodore Roosevelt thundered against trusts and corruption but was fine with wealth piled up by individuals that seemed beneficial to the nation and its economy. Unions wielded growing power even as the courts and governments inevitably supported business owners, and the conservative American Federation of Labor faced hostile competition from the radical Industrial Workers of the World and the Women's Trade Union League.[7]

While many Americans saw economic inequality and great wealth as threats, they also increasingly believed that excessive individualism helped create the problem and saw big government as the necessary solution. Progressive writers like Herbert Croly and Walter Weyl saw an enlarged professional state funded by a tax on wealth as the best entity to care for people's needs, help children and public health, and balance the power of big business. In 1913 the United States finally instituted a national income tax by ratifying the Sixteenth Amendment, firmly establishing a critical tool to redistribute wealth and reduce economic inequality. Immigrants added their voices to native-born socialists and communists, and these communitarian movements gained increasing support for their candidates for public office. But in the 1920s, following World War I, US attorney general A. Mitchell Palmer led the first Red Scare, jailing and deporting thousands of leftists to effectively suppress calls for economic equality, and national leaders like Henry Ford and Calvin Coolidge encouraged American workers to identify their interests with big business and prosperity.[8]

Prosperity widened the gap between the rich and poor, and inequality peaked just before the stock market crashed in 1929 and ushered in the Great Depression. That catastrophe, which traditional national policies could not even slow, resulted in the huge expansion of the national government with substantive efforts to reduce poverty. President Franklin Roosevelt took office in early 1933 and immediately launched a slate of New Deal programs that would not only aid economic recovery but also reduce the yawning chasm between rich and poor. Federal assistance to businesses was tied to their recognizing and bargaining with unions. The government regulated prices and wages and gave direct relief to the poor, supported desperate farmers, spent $10 billion to employ eight million workers and construct a universe of public works projects, and employed about three million young men on national park projects. These programs were financed by progressive taxation, further aiding the trend toward greater economic equality. The New Deal did little to address racial economic inequalities, at least in part because FDR depended on the votes of racist southern Democrats, and in fact some programs made things worse for black farmers and workers. Prominent Americans, such as Upton Sinclair and John Dewey, were disappointed in the New Deal's more moderate reforms and pushed for stronger measures like the nationalization of industries, old-age pensions (later enacted as the Social Security Act), a guaranteed annual income, and steeper inheritance and property taxes. Later, FDR considered but failed to get stronger minimum measures, a national health insurance system, and even guaranteed full employment.[9]

A significant New Deal legacy was the increasing reliance on the national government to reduce poverty, redistribute wealth, and monitor and improve economic equality. The need for a larger more active government developed in part because corporations were becoming huge and powerful (as the Progressives argued), in part because the economy increasingly operated at the national and even international level, and in part because Native American lands and resources were no longer available to maintain the promise of economic equality for white settlers. Ironically, at the same time, influential intellectuals and artists alienated by the increasingly urban, industrial, atomistic national culture were drawn to Indian societies, particularly in the Southwest. Their depictions of egalitarian and deeply spiritual Native societies appealed to Americans and for the first time added that element to the public discourse concerning economic equality. Of course, a powerful national government that could actually *do* something about economic equality seems a substantive improvement over simply talking about it, as had been the norm since the antebellum period when Americans became concerned about the decline but insisted on inadequate public institutions unable to change that pattern. As Michael Thompson noted in *The Politics of Inequality*, the era of the New Deal became "the first time in American political history and thought [when] it became imperative for the state to enter into economic affairs for the purpose of redistribution." While in theory politics and property remained distinct, the New Deal began to again link the two by claiming for the state the power to regulate wealth.[10]

But the Cold War's conservative tide almost immediately created a new and growing disillusionment with federal programs, even as the general prosperity, flourishing unions, and high taxes on the wealthy continued to shrink the distance between rich and poor. The conflict with the Soviet Union moved Americans to identify government intervention in the economy with totalitarian communism and to closely connect political and economic freedom. Proposals for national health insurance were buried as unions focused on gaining employer-provided benefits. In the 1960s that conservative tide was temporarily reversed by Kennedy's War on Poverty and Johnson's Great Society programs, particularly efforts to deal with hunger (food stamps), poverty in rural Appalachia, and racial economic disparities that appeared in declining urban neighborhoods. Many of these programs were continued by President Nixon. By the mid-1970s, however, accelerating inflation and growing unemployment rates undermined political support for the antipoverty programs in particular and federal agencies in general. As a result, Ronald Reagan won the presidency in 1980 and immediately announced that "government is not the solution to our problem, government *is* the problem." Then in the 1990s, Democratic Party leaders embraced neoliberalism, with the gospel that corporate efficiency and size was more important than economic democracy. The agreement by both parties to eagerly pursue global free-trade agreements, allow virtually unlimited corporate mergers, and deregulate the financial industry highlighted how America's tradition of economic equality seemed largely forgotten.[11]

As the twenty-first century began, American became increasingly concerned about the rising tide of economic inequality. Economic surveys reported a wide and increasing gap between the very wealthy and everyone else, with America's vaunted middle class dwindling and struggling. People began to notice that, as state governments embraced the Reaganite dogma of tax cuts and privatization, parents and teachers were increasingly forced to buy school supplies, and college student debt soared as public university budgets were slashed and wages stagnated. The issue became a focus for writers in academic journals, popular periodicals, and even daily newspapers, the most notable being a series in the *New York Times* in 2005 that resulted in the book *Class Matters*. The 2007 crash dramatically underscored the problem, particularly because, as the economy began to slowly recover, it became increasingly clear that *all* the gains were going to those with the most wealth. As Chris Hayes argued in *Twilight of the Elites* (2012), the American "success" of great wealth (for some) was undermining the long-standing American value of meritocracy, and equality of condition and equality of opportunity were actually closely linked. Public anger drove the Occupy movement that targeted Wall Street and wealthy elites and called for the jailing of greedy bank management and tighter government controls. At least one writer called for the "profit motive" to be replaced by "a Sabbatarian economy," even including the Great Sabbath, in order to restore sacred human values and relationships.[12]

But few remembered the long history and development of these concerns in America. Conservative commentators scorned such criticisms of capitalism and inequality as contrary to the individual freedoms and "natural rights," including absolute control of property and laissez-faire economics, that (they argued) the Founders had embraced and embedded in its Constitution and laws. Nearly all the books that described the rising economic equality and decried its effects on American culture and politics, including the *New York Times* series, began (at best) with the Gilded Age. But Chris Hayes's connection between condition and opportunity would have been embraced by many if not most of America's Founding Fathers as well as subsequent generations of writers and political activists. The Occupy movement's hostility to corporate power and greed was more than matched by the fierce opposition during the country's first half-century to corporate monopolies and the great fear that men with excessive wealth would corrupt the country. My hope is that this book will remind Americans that economic equality was a major foundational concern for this country, shed new light on how it became contested by economic liberalism, and help explain why it has persisted as a significant value.[13]

Introduction

1. Quotation from Alan Dawley, *Class and Community: The Industrial Revolution in Lynn* (Cambridge, MA: Harvard University Press, 1976), 70.

Chapter 1. · English Origins

1. Holly Brewer, *By Birth or Consent: Children, Law, and the Anglo-American Revolution in Authority* (Chapel Hill: University of North Carolina Press, 2005), 18–22; Arthur Lovejoy, *The Great Chain of Being: A Study of the History of an Idea* (Cambridge, MA: Harvard University Press, 1936); John Winthrop, "Model of Christian Charity," *Winthrop Papers*, 6 vols. (Boston: Massachusetts Historical Society, 1929–), 2:282–95.

2. Geoffrey Robertson, *The Tyrannicide Brief: The Story of the Man Who Sent Charles I to the Scaffold* (New York: Vintage, 2006); Derek Hirst, *England in Conflict, 1603–1660: Kingdom, Community, Commonwealth* (London: Arnold, 1999), 22; Brewer, *By Birth or Consent*, esp. 18–22; John Locke, *Two Treatises of Government: In the Former, The False Principles and Foundation of Sir Robert Filmer, And His Followers, are Detected and Overthrown* (1689), bk. 1, chap. 4.

3. Hirst, *England in Conflict*, 9–13; Christopher Hill, *The Century of Revolution, 1603–1714* (New York: Norton, 1961), 43–44. While recent scholarship has found slightly higher levels of voter participation, particularly in towns, the franchise was still small; see Derek Hirst, *The Representatives of the People? Voters and Voting in England under the Early Stuarts* (New York: Cambridge University Press, 1975).

4. Hill, *Century of Revolution*, 32–33.

5. Joyce Appleby, *Economic Thought and Ideology in Seventeenth-Century England* (Princeton, NJ: Princeton University Press, 1978), 28–31; Roger B. Manning, *Village Revolts: Social Protest and Popular Disturbances in England, 1509–1640* (Oxford: Clarendon Press, 1988), 159–65; Hill, *Century of Revolution*, 44–45.

6. Peter Laslett, *The World We Have Lost* (New York: Scribner's Sons, 1965), 32–33, 245n27.

7. Lynn Hunt, *Inventing Human Rights: A History* (New York: Norton, 2007), 27–33; Alan Macfarlane, *The Origins of English Individualism: The Family, Property, and Social*

Transition (Oxford: Basil Blackwell, 1978; New York: Cambridge University Press, 1979); Eric Nelson, *The Hebrew Republic: Jewish Sources and the Transformation of European Political Thought* (Cambridge, MA: Harvard University Press, 2010), 57–65. The first published use of *commonwealth* as synonymous with a republic was in Walter Raleigh's *Maxims of State* (1618): "the swerving or depravation of a Free, or popular State, or the Government of the whole Multitude of the base and poorer Sort, without respect of the other Orders"; *Oxford English Dictionary*, cf. "commonwealth."

8. Andy Wood, *Riot, Rebellion and Popular Politics in Early Modern England* (New York: Palgrave, 2002), 1–111 (on use of term "Digger," see p. 109); Manning, *Village Revolts*, 25, 27, 83, 99, 221–24.

9. Michael Winship, *Godly Republicanism: Puritanism, Pilgrims, and a City upon a Hill* (Cambridge, MA: Harvard University Press, 2012), 24–34; Macfarlane, *Origins of English Individualism*, 176–79; Edward Coke, *Institutes of the Lawes of England* (1628).

10. Winship, *Godly Republicanism*, 24–34; Robertson, *Tyrannicide Brief*, 26–29; Hirst, *England in Conflict*, 22–23, 37–49; J. R. Pole, *The Pursuit of Equality in American History*, 2nd ed. (Berkeley: University of California Press, 1993), 11. Puritanism was a wide-ranging movement to eliminate Roman Catholic remnants from the Church of England and generally reform English society and culture. Patrick Collinson, one of the foremost scholars of puritanism, argues persuasively that because it was a very diverse movement, with those involved agreeing about little, including precisely what reforms were needed, its name should be kept lower case rather than capitalized as if it were an organized church; Collinson, *The Religion of Protestants: The Church in English Society, 1559–1625* (Oxford: Oxford University Press, 1982), 114–21.

11. Christopher W. Marsh, *The Family of Love in English Society, 1550–1630* (New York: Cambridge University Press, 1994); T. Wilson Hayes, "John Everard and the Familist Tradition," in *The Origins of Anglo-American Radicalism*, ed. Margaret Jacob and James Jacob (London: George Allen and Unwin, 1984), 60–67.

12. Robertson, *Tyrannicide Brief*, 28–36; Hill, *Century of Revolution*, 46–90; David Como, "Predestination and Political Conflict in Laud's London," *Historical Journal* 46 (2003): 263–94.

13. Hirst, *England in Conflict*, 130–201; Hill, *Century of Revolution*, 46–90.

14. David Como, "Secret Printing, the Crisis of 1640, and the Origins of Civil War Radicalism," *Past and Present* 196 (2007): 37–82; Rachel Foxley, *The Levellers: Radical Political Thought in the English Revolution* (Manchester: Manchester University Press, 2013), esp. 4–13; F. D. Dow, *Radicalism in the English Revolution 1640–1660* (New York: Basil Blackwell, 1985), 30–40; John Lilburne, *The Free Man's Freedom Vindicated* (1646), postscript.

15. Hirst, *England in Conflict*, 222–23, 251, 266; Christopher Hill, *The World Turned Upside Down: Radical Ideas during the English Revolution* (New York: Viking Press, 1972; New York: Viking Penguin, 1975), 58–60, 115–16; but see also Mark A. Kishlansky, *The Rise of the New Model Army* (New York: Cambridge University Press, 1979).

16. Foxley, *The Levellers*, 150–93.

17. Foxley, *The Levellers*, 151–59; Mark A. Kishlansky, "Consensus Politics and the Structure of Debate at Putney," in Jacob and Jacob, *Origins of Anglo-American Radicalism*, 72–79.

18. William Clarke, *Puritanism and Liberty, being the Army Debates (1647–9) from the Clarke Manuscripts with Supplementary Documents*, ed. A. S. P. Woodhouse (Chicago: University of Chicago Press, 1951), http://oll.libertyfund.org/index.php?option=com _content&task=view&id=1322&Itemid=264#lf1346_footnote 132; Samuel A. Gardiner, *History of the Great Civil War*, 4 vols., rev. ed. (London: Longmans, Green, 1893), 3:370.

19. *Light Shining in Buckinghamshire* (1648), large portions reprinted in Louis Henry Berens, *The Digger Movement in the Days of the Commonwealth* (London: Simpkin, Marshall, Hamilton, Kent, 1906), 79–80; *More Light Shining* (1649), in Berens, *The Digger Movement*, 83; Wood, *Riot, Rebellion and Popular Politics*, 153–54; Geoff Kennedy, *Diggers, Levellers, and Agrarian Capitalism: Radical Political Thought in Seventeenth Century England* (Lanham, MD: Lexington Books, 2008); Dow, *Radicalism in the English Revolution*, 74–80.

20. Gerrard Winstanley et al., *The True Levellers Standard Advanced; Or, The State of Community Opened, and Presented to the Sons of Men* (London, 1649).

21. Anon., *The Declaration and Standard of the Levellers of England* (London, 1649), 3; Gerrard Winstanley, "England's Spirit Unfoulded; Or, an Incouragement to The *Engagement*" (1650), ed. G. E. Aylmer, *Past and Present* 40 (1968): 10; Wood, *Riot, Rebellion and Popular Politics*, 160; on the Digger settlements and their ideas generally, see Wood, 155–63.

22. Samuel D. Glover, "The Putney Debates: Popular versus Élitist Republicanism," *Past and Present* 164 (1999): 47, citing *Colonel John Lilburne Revived* [Mar. 23, 1653], 6–23: British Library, London, Thomason Tracts, E. 689 (32); *The Upright Mans Vindication* [Aug. 5, 1653], 6–22: British Library, London, Thomason Tracts, E. 689 (32) 708 (22); Gerrard Winstanley, *The Law of Freedom in a Platform* (1652), in *"The Law of Freedom" and Other Writings*, ed. Christopher Hill (New York: Cambridge University Press, 2003), 295.

23. Eric Nelson, *The Hebrew Republic: Jewish Sources and the Transformation of European Political Thought* (Cambridge, MA: Harvard University Press, 2010), 65–79; Richard Tuck, *Philosophy and Government, 1572–1651* (New York: Cambridge University Press, 1993), 167. This wording of Lev. 25:10 is Everett Fox's translation of *The Five Books of Moses* (New York: Schocken Books, 1995).

24. James Harrington, *The Oceana and Other Works*, ed. John Toland, 3rd ed. (London: A. Millar, 1747), 45, 70, 102. Nelson, *Hebrew Republic*, identifies Harrington's *Oceana* as the first English work to build on the Dutch biblical scholarship.

25. J. R. Pole, *Political Representation in England and the Origins of the American Republic* (New York: Macmillan, 1966), 8–11; Bernard Bailyn, *Ideological Origins of the American Revolution* (Cambridge, MA: Harvard University Press, 1965), 36–54; John Adams to James Sullivan, May 26, 1776, *Papers of John Adams*, 15 vols. (Cambridge, MA: Harvard University Press, 1977-), 4:208–12; Ganesh Sitaraman, *The Crisis of the Middle-Class Constitution: Why Economic Inequality Threatens Our Republic* (New York: Knopf, 2017), 67–72, on Harrington's broader influence in Revolutionary America.

26. Richard Hakluyt, *A Discourse Concerning Western Planting* (1584), in *Envisioning America: English Plans for the Colonization of North America, 1580–1640*, ed. Peter C. Mancall (Boston: Bedford St. Martin's, 1995), 46–54.

27. Karen O. Kupperman, *The Jamestown Project* (Cambridge, MA: Harvard University Press, 2007), 247–50.

28. Kupperman, *Jamestown Project*, 210–60; Warren Billings, ed., *The Old Dominion in the Seventeenth Century* (Chapel Hill: University of North Carolina Press, 1973), 5–8.

29. Kupperman, *Jamestown Project*, 284–87; Allan Kulikoff, *From British Peasants to Colonial American Farmers* (Chapel Hill: University of North Carolina Press, 2000), 109.

30. James Horn, *Adapting to a New World: English Society in the Seventeenth-Century Chesapeake* (Chapel Hill: University of North Carolina Press, 1994), 26–53, 137–56; Christopher Tomlins, *Freedom Bound: Law, Labor, and Civil Identity in Colonizing English America, 1580–1865* (New York: Cambridge University Press, 2010), 25–32, 36–42; Jack Greene, *Pursuits of Happiness: The Social Development of Early Modern British Colonies and the Formation of American Culture* (Chapel Hill: University of North Carolina Press, 1988), 12–18.

31. Alexander B. Haskell, "Deference, Defiance, and the Language of Office in Seventeenth-Century Virginia," in *Early Modern Virginia: Reconsidering the Old Dominion*, ed. Douglas Bradburn and John C. Coombs (Charlottesville: University of Virginia Press, 2011), 158–78; Horn, *Adapting to a New World*, 154–87; Russell Menard, "From Servant to Freehold: Status Mobility and Property Accumulation in Seventeenth-Century Maryland," *William and Mary Quarterly*, 3rd ser., 30 (1973): 37–64.

32. Kulikoff, *From British Peasants*, 113–14; Philip J. Greven Jr., "Family Structure in Andover, Massachusetts," *William and Mary Quarterly*, 3rd ser., 23 (1966): 235.

33. Governor Alexander Spotswood to Board of Trade, Oct. 15, 1712, in *The Official Letters of Alexander Spotswood*, ed. R. A. Brock (Richmond: Virginia Historical Society, 1885), 2:1–2; Spotswood to Secretary of State James Stonhope, July 15, 1715, in Brock, *Official Letters*, 124; Rhys Isaac, *The Transformation of Virginia, 1740–1790* (Chapel Hill: University of North Carolina Press, 1982), 61–113.

34. Winthrop, "Model of Christian Charity"; Stephen Foster, *The Long Argument: English Puritanism and the Shaping of New England Culture, 1570–1700* (Chapel Hill: University of North Carolina Press, 1996), 138–40; Winship, *Godly Republicanism*, 168–72.

35. William E. Nelson, *The Common Law in Colonial America*, vol. 1, *The Chesapeake and New England, 1607–1660* (New York: Oxford University Press, 2008), 50–57; David Hackett Fischer, *Albion's Seed: Four British Folkways in America* (New York: Oxford University Press, 1989), 18–24; Lawrence A. Cremin, *American Education: The Colonial Experience, 1607–1783* (New York: Harper and Row, 1970), 180–82; Pole, *Political Representation in England*, 34–36.

36. John J. McCusker and Russell L. Menard, *The Economy of British America, 1607–1789* (Chapel Hill: University of North Carolina Press, 1985), 103; Tomlins, *Freedom Bound*, 23, 54–55; Fischer, *Albion's Seed*, 14–17, 25–27, 52–54, 71–77; "Judith Coffin/Somersby," http://www.geni.com/people/Judith-Coffyn-Somerby/6000000001713337400.

37. Fischer, *Albion's Seed*, 166–71, 174–80; James Henretta, "The Morphology of New England Society in the Colonial Period," *Journal of Interdisciplinary History* 2 (1971): 379–98; David Cannadine, *The Rise and Fall of Class in Britain* (New York: Columbia University Press, 1999), 38n43.

38. Barry Levy, *Town Born: The Political Economy of New England from Its Founding to the Revolution* (Philadelphia: University of Pennsylvania Press, 2009), 34–40; Nelson, *Common Law*, 57–58; Kulikoff, *From British Peasants*, 113.

39. Brian Donahue, *The Great Meadow: Farmers and the Land in Colonial Concord* (New Haven, CT: Yale University Press, 2004), 41–110; John Frederick Martin, *Profits in the Wilderness: Entrepreneurship and the Founding of New England Towns in the Seventeenth Century* (Chapel Hill: University of North Carolina Press, 1991), 1–45.

40. Greven, "Family Structure in Seventeenth-Century Andover," 235; Nelson, *Common Law,* 57–58; Stephen Innes, *Labor in a New Land: Economy and Society in Seventeenth-Century Springfield* (Princeton, NJ: Princeton University Press, 1983); Fischer, *Albion's Seed,* 166–68.

41. John Winthrop, *The Journal of John Winthrop, 1630–1649,* ed. Richard S. Dunn, James Savage, and Laetitia Yeandle (Cambridge, MA: Harvard University Press, 1996), 137–38.

42. Edward Winslow, *Hypocrisie Unmasked: A True Relation of the Proceedings of the Governor and Company of the Massachusetts Against Samuel Gorton of Rhode Island* (London, 1646), reissued as *The Danger of Tolerating Levellers in a Civil State* (1649); Philip Gura, "The Radical Ideology of Samuel Gorton: New Light on the Relation of English to American Puritanism," *William and Mary Quarterly,* 3rd ser., 36 (1979): 78–100.

43. John Norton, *Heart of N[ew]-England Rent at the Blasphemies of the Present Genera-tion* (Cambridge, MA, 1659), 40, 41, 58; Thomas Ingersoll, "'Riches and Honour Were Rejected by Them as Loathsome Vomit': The Fear of Leveling in New England," in *Inequality in Early America,* ed. Carla Gardina Pestana and Sharon V. Salinger (Hanover, NH: University Press of New England, 1999).

44. Caroline Robbins, *The Eighteenth-Century Commonwealthman: Studies in the Transmission, Development, and Circumstance of English Liberal Thought from the Restoration of Charles II until the War with the Thirteen Colonies* (Cambridge, MA: Harvard University Press, 1959), 25–26; Hill, *World Turned Upside Down,* 344–58; Daniel Richter, *Before the Revolution: America's Ancient Pasts* (Cambridge, MA: Harvard University Press, 2011), 232–41.

45. Richter, *Before the Revolution,* 208–9.

46. Richard Ashcraft, *Revolutionary Politics and Locke's Two Treatises of Government* (Princeton, NJ: Princeton University Press, 1998), 74, 143, 247–50 (quotation, p. 250); Robbins, *Eighteenth-Century Commonwealthman,* 27–30.

47. Robbins, *Eighteenth-Century Commonwealthman,* 27–30; Richter, *Before the Revolution,* 291–94.

48. Peter Laslett, "The English Revolution and Locke's 'Two Treatises of Govern-ment,'" *Cambridge Historical Journal* 12, no. 1 (1956): 40–55; Ashcraft, *Revolutionary Politics,* 154–61; Locke, *Two Treatises of Government,* bk. 2, chap. 6, secs. 54 and 59, and chap. 16, "Of Conquest." *Patriarcha* was published in 1680 but was probably completed before the English Civil War erupted, since Filmer died in 1653.

49. Brewer, *By Birth or Consent,* 46–49, 105–7; Locke, *Two Treatises of Government,* bk. 2, chap.6, sec. 54.

50. Locke, *Two Treatises of Government,* bk. 2, chap. 5, secs. 40–41 and 48–49; chap. 9; Holly Brewer, "Slavery, Sovereignty, and 'Inheritable Blood': Reconsidering John Locke and the Origins of American Slavery," *American Historical Review* 122 (2017): 1065–66; Herman Lebovics, "The Uses of America in Locke's Second Treatise of Government," *Journal of the History of Ideas,* 47 (1986): esp. 575.

Chapter 2. · Indians and Anglo-American Egalitarianism

1. Alexander Moore, ed., *Nairne's Muskhogean Journals: The 1708 Expedition to the Mississippi River* (Jackson: University Press of Mississippi, 1998), 64–65.

2. J. Hector St. John de Crèvecoeur, *Letters from an American Farmer* (1782; New York: Viking Penguin, 1981), 54.

3. Frederick Jackson Turner, "The Significance of the Frontier in American History" (1893), reprinted in *The Frontier in American History* (New York: Henry Holt, 1920), 1, 38. The "germ theory" of American politics was popularized by Herbert Baxter Adams, who obtained his PhD from a German university in 1876 and then returned to teach at Johns Hopkins, where he started the first graduate program in US history; in many ways that idea was closely bound to the broader ideas of "scientific" racism that dominated the country during that century. See Peter Novick, *That Noble Dream: The "Objectivity Question" and the American Historical Profession* (New York: Cambridge University Press, 1988), 74–88.

4. Olive P. Dickason, *The Myth of the Savage, and the Beginnings of French Colonialism in the Americas* (Edmonton: University of Alberta, 1984), 72–81; Susi Coilin, "The Wild Man and the Indian in Early Sixteenth-Century Book Illustration," in *Indians and Europe: An Interdisciplinary Collection of Essays*, ed. Christian Feest (Lincoln: University of Nebraska Press, 1989), 6–29.

5. Dickason, *Myth of the Savage*, 50–51.

6. Quoted in John F. Moffitt and Santiago Sebastian, *O Brave New People: The European Invention of the American Indian* (Albuquerque: University of New Mexico Press, 1996), 254–56. See also Stephen Greenblatt, *Marvelous Possessions: The Wonder of the New World* (Chicago: University of Chicago Press, 1991), 64.

7. Columbus letter of 1493, quoted in Robert F. Berkhofer Jr., *The White Man's Indian: Images of the American Indian from Columbus to the Present* (New York: Random House, 1978), 6; Martyr quoted in Moffitt and Sebastian, *O Brave New People*, 69–70; Michel de Montaigne, "Of Cannibals," chap. 30 in *The Essays of Michel de Montaigne* (1580), vol. 6, Project Gutenberg, http://www.gutenberg.org/cache/epub/3586/pg3586-images.html; Barlow quoted in Berkhofer, *White Man's Indian*, 73.

8. Columbus quoted in Berkhofer, *White Man's Indian*, 7; Montaigne, "Of Cannibals"; Nicholas P. Canny, "The Ideology of English Colonization: From Ireland to America," *William and Mary Quarterly*, 3rd ser., 30 (1973): 582; Berkhofer, *White Man's Indian*, 81–83. Many officers involved in the effort to conquer Ireland, such as Humphrey Gilbert, would later lead the effort to explore and colonize eastern North America, and their perceptions of the peoples of that region were shaped at least in part by their experiences in Ireland; Canny, "Ideology of English Colonization."

9. Philip Barbour, ed., *The Complete Works of Captain John Smith in Three Volumes* (Chapel Hill: University of North Carolina Press, 1986), 1:173–75.

10. Thomas Hobbes, *Hobbe's Leviathan, Reprinted from the Edition of 1651* (1651; Oxford: Oxford University Press, 1929), 94–95; John Locke, *Two Treatises of Government: In the Former, The False Principles and Foundation of Sir Robert Filmer, And His Followers, are Detected and Overthrown* (1689), bk. 2, chap. 5, secs. 41, 49.

11. Herman Lebovics, "The Uses of America in Locke's Second Treatise of Government," *Journal of the History of Ideas* 47 (1986): 567–81.

12. Montaigne, "Of Cannibals"; Baron Lahonton, *New Voyages to North-America*, 2 vols. (London: H. Bonwicke et al., 1703), 2:7–8.

13. Kate Fullagar, *The Savage Visit: New World People and Popular Imperial Culture in Britain, 1710–1795* (Berkeley: University of California Press, 2012), 1–125; Coll Thrush, *Indigenous London: Native Travelers at the Heart of Empire* (New Haven, CT: Yale University Press, 2016), 68–98; Alden Vaughan, *Transatlantic Encounters: American Indians in Britain, 1500–1776* (New York: Cambridge University Press, 2006).

14. Fullagar, *Savage Visit*, 37–64; Thrush, *Indigenous London*, 68–82; Vaughan, *Transatlantic Encounters*, 115–36; Donald F. Bond, ed., *The Spectator*, 5 vols. (Oxford: Oxford University Press, 1965), 1:211–15; Benjamin Carp, *Defiance of the Patriots: The Boston Tea Party and the Making of America* (New Haven, CT: Yale University Press, 2010), 153; "Drama," *Observator* 22 (Mar. 15, 1712).

15. Fullagar, *Savage Visit*, 65–76; Thrush, *Indigenous London*, 82–98; Vaughan, *Transatlantic Encounters*, 137–50; James Adair, *The History of the American Indians* (London: Edward and Charles Dilly, 1775), 418.

16. Fullagar, *Savage Visit*, 77–87; Thrush, *Indigenous London*, 82–98; Vaughan, *Transatlantic Encounters*, 150–60; Nancy Shoemaker, *A Strange Likeness: Becoming Red and White in Eighteenth-Century North America* (New York: Oxford University Press, 2004), 37–38, 50–60.

17. Joanne Brooks, ed., *The Collected Writings of Samson Occom, Mohegan* (New York: Oxford University Press, 2006), 268; Thrush, *Indigenous London*, 107–14, 129–30; see generally Shoemaker, *Strange Likeness*, 53–58.

18. Jean-Jacques Rousseau, *Discourse on the Origin and Foundations of Inequality among Men* (1754), trans. Helena Rosenblatt (Boston: Bedford-St. Martins, 2011), 76, 80; Joseph S. Lucas, "The Course of Empire and the Long Road to Civilization: North American Indians and Scottish Enlightenment Historians," *Explorations in Early American Culture* 4 (2000): 166–90.

19. John Winthrop, "Reasons to Be Considered for Justifying the Undertakers of the Intended Plantation in New England," in *Envisioning America: English Plans for the Colonization of North America, 1580–1640*, ed. Peter C. Mancall (Boston: Bedford-St. Martins, 1995), 136–37; Stuart Banner, *How the Indians Lost Their Land: Law and Power on the Frontier* (Cambridge, MA: Harvard University Press, 2005), 11–43; Daniel Richter, *Trade, Land, Power: The Struggle for Eastern North America* (Philadelphia: University of Pennsylvania Press, 2013), 147–53; Francis Jennings, *The Invasion of America: Indians, Colonialism, and the Cant of Conquest* (Chapel Hill: University of North Carolina Press, 1975), 134–40.

20. Allan Kulikoff, *From British Peasants to Colonial American Farmers* (Chapel Hill: University of North Carolina Press, 2000), 76–77 (Winslow quoted); Brian Donohue, *The Great Meadow: Farmers and the Land in Colonial Concord* (New Haven, CT: Yale University Press, 2004), 1–5; Richard I. Melvin, *New England Outpost: War and Society in Colonial Deerfield* (New York: Norton, 1989), 26–58.

21. Kulikoff, *From British Peasants*, 78–103; William Cronon, *Changes in the Land: Indians, Colonists, and the Ecology of New England* (New York: Hill and Wang, 1983).

22. Lion Gardiner, "Lieft Lion Gardener His Relation of the Pequot Warres" (1637), reprinted in *Early American Indian Documents: Treaties and Laws, 1607–1789*, vol. 3,

New York and New Jersey Treaties, 1609–1682, ed. Barbara Graymont (Frederick, MD: University Publications of America, 1985), 49–51.

23. Helen Rountree, *Pocahontas's People: The Powhatan Indians of Virginia through Four Centuries* (Norman: University of Oklahoma Press, 1990); Cronon, *Changes in the Land*.

24. Kulikoff, *From British Peasants*, 102–6; Rountree, *Pocahontas's People*, 140–52, 180, 182–83; Daniel Mandell, *King Philip's War: Colonial Expansion, Native Resistance, and the End of Indian Sovereignty* (Baltimore: Johns Hopkins University Press, 2010); Mandell, *Behind the Frontier: Indians in Eighteenth-Century Southern New England* (Lincoln: University of Nebraska Press, 1996).

25. Cronin, *Changes in the Land*, 91–126; Kulikoff, *From British Peasants*, 78–80; Peter Mancall, *Deadly Medicine: Indians and Alcohol in Early America* (Ithaca, NY: Cornell University Press, 1995).

26. Cronin, *Changes in the Land*, 91–126; John J. McCusker and Russell R. Menard, *The Economy of British America, 1607–1789* (Chapel Hill: University of North Carolina Press, 1985), 108–9, 113, 129–32, 174, 313; Kulikoff, *From British Peasants*, 78–80.

27. Kulikoff, *From British Peasants*, 90–91.

28. McCusker and Menard, *Economy of British America*, 318–21.

29. David Ramsey, *History of the American Revolution* (1789), ed. Lester H. Cohen, 2 vols. (Indianapolis: Liberty Fund, 1990), 1:30–31. On the ideas and the mechanics of taking the land from Natives, see Banner, *How the Indians Lost Their Land*.

30. Jack Greene, *Pursuits of Happiness: The Social Development of Early Modern British Colonies and the Formation of American Culture* (Chapel Hill: University of North Carolina Press, 1988), 167–69.

31. Greene, *Pursuits of Happiness*, 70; Jon Butler, *Becoming America: The Revolution before 1776* (Cambridge, MA: Harvard University Press, 2000), 50–55; T. H. Breen, *The Marketplace of Revolution: How Consumer Politics Shaped American Independence* (New York: Oxford University Press, 2004); Cornelia Dayton, *Women before the Bar: Gender, Law, and Society in Connecticut, 1639–1789* (Chapel Hill: University of North Carolina Press, 1995); Gary Nash, *Urban Crucible: Social Change, Political Consciousness, and the Origins of the American Revolution* (Cambridge, MA: Harvard University Press, 1979); David Conroy, *In Public Houses: Drink and the Revolution of Authority in Colonial Massachusetts* (Chapel Hill: University of North Carolina Press, 1995).

32. Greene, *Pursuits of Happiness*, 92–99; Butler, *Becoming America*, 50–55.

33. Rhys Isaac, *The Transformation of Virginia, 1740–1790* (Chapel Hill: University of North Carolina Press, 1982); Charles Moore, ed., *George Washington's Rules of Civility and Decent Behaviour in Company and Conversation* (Boston: Houghton Mifflin, 1926).

34. Greene, *Pursuits of Happiness*, 186–90; Robert Gross, *The Minutemen and Their World* (New York: Hill and Wang, 1976), 10–15; David Hackett Fischer, *Albion's Seed: Four British Folkways in America* (New York: Oxford University Press, 1989), 571–73.

35. David Cannadine, *The Rise and Fall of Class in Britain* (New York: Columbia University Press, 1999), 28–38; Cadwallader Colden, "State of the Province of New York" (1765), in *Collections of the New-York Historical Society*, vol. 10 (New York: New-York Historical Society, 1877), 68–69.

36. Greene, *Pursuits of Happiness*; Margaret Newell, *From Dependency to Independence* (Ithaca, NY: Cornell University Press, 1998); McCusker and Menard, *Economy of British America*.

37. Bettye Hobbs Pruitt, "Self-Sufficiency and the Agricultural Economy of Eighteenth-Century Massachusetts," *William and Mary Quarterly*, 3rd ser., 41 (1984): 333–64; Carolyn Merchant, *Ecological Revolutions: Nature, Gender, and Science in New England* (Chapel Hill: University of North Carolina Press, 1989), 149–97; Benjamin Franklin, "Observations Concerning the Increase of Mankind" (1751), in *Writings* (New York: Library of America, 1987), 368–69.

38. "Comptroller Weare to the Earle of [Halifax]," *Collections of the Massachusetts Historical Society*, vol. 1 (1792), 71–72; John L. Bullion, "Escaping Boston: Nathaniel Ware and the Beginnings of Colonial Taxation, 1762–1763," *Huntington Library Quarterly* 45 (1982): 36–58; Bernard Bailyn, *The Peopling of British North America: An Introduction* (New York: Random House, 1986), 9–10.

39. Greene, *Pursuits of Happiness*, 198–200; Gross, *Minutemen and Their World*, 10–15; Dick Hoerder, *Society and Government, 1760–1780: The Power Structure in Massachusetts Government* (Berlin: John F. Kennedy Institute, 1972), 13–38; Benjamin Labaree, *Patriots and Partisans: The Merchants of Newburyport, 1764–1815* (Cambridge, MA: Harvard University Press, 1962), 13–15; Nash, *Urban Crucible*, 28–37, 362–82.

40. Barry Levy, *Town Born: The Political Economy of New England from Its Founding to the Revolution* (Philadelphia: University of Pennsylvania Press, 2009); Michael Zuckerman, *Peaceable Kingdoms: New England Towns in the Eighteenth Century* (Boston: Knopf, 1970), 154–86; Gross, *Minutemen and Their World*, 11–15; Greene, *Pursuits of Happiness*, 138–39; Brendan McConville, *These Daring Disturbers of the Public Peace: The Struggle for Property and Power in Early New Jersey* (Philadelphia: University of Pennsylvania Press, 1999); Edmund Morgan, *American Slavery, American Freedom: The Ordeal of Colonial Virginia* (New York: Norton, 1975); Isaac, *Transformation of Virginia*.

41. Alexander B. Haskell, "Deference, Defiance, and the Language of Office in Seventeenth-Century Virginia," in *Early Modern Virginia: Reconsidering the Old Dominion*, ed. Douglas Bradburn and John C. Coombs (Charlottesville: University of Virginia Press, 2011), 158; Benjamin Colman, *Government the Pillar of the Earth* (1730); William Cooper, *The Honours of Christ demanded of the Magistrate* (Boston, 1740); Michael Zuckerman, "Endangered Deference, Imperiled Patriarchy: Tales From the Marshlands," *Early American Studies* (special issue on "Deference in Early America: The Life and/or Death of an Historiographical Concept") 3 (2005): 235–44; [George Keith], *Observator's Trip to America* (Philadelphia, 1726).

42. McConville, *These Daring Disturbers*.

43. Douglas Winiarski, *Darkness Falls on the Land of Light: Experiencing Religious Awakenings in Eighteenth-Century New England* (Chapel Hill: University of North Carolina Press, 2017), esp. 175–304; Linford Fisher, *The Indian Great Awakening: Religion and the Shaping of Native Cultures in Early America* (New York: Oxford University Press, 2012); *Boston Weekly Post-Boy*, Mar. 28, 1743; Catherine A. Brekus, *Sarah Osborn's World: The Rise of Evangelical Christianity in Early America* (New Haven, CT: Yale University Press, 2013); Richard L. Bushman, *From Puritan to Yankee: Character and the Social Order in Connecticut, 1690–1750* (Cambridge, MA: Harvard University Press, 1967), 192–96.

44. Rhys Isaac, "Evangelical Revolt: The Nature of the Baptists' Challenge to the Traditional Order in Virginia, 1765 to 1775," *William and Mary Quarterly*, 3rd ser., 31 (1974): 345–68; Marjoleine Kars, *Breaking Loose Together: The Regulator Rebellion in Pre-Revolutionary North Carolina* (Chapel Hill: University of North Carolina Press, 2002), 121–30, quotation p. 174.

45. Douglas Winiarski, "Souls Filled with Ravishing Transport: Heavenly Visions and the Radical Awakening in New England," *William and Mary Quarterly*, 3rd ser., 61 (2004): 3–46; Aaron Spencer Fogleman, *Two Troubled Souls: An Eighteenth-Century Couple's Spiritual Journey in the Atlantic World* (Chapel Hill: University of North Carolina Press, 2013), 44–50; Jane Merritt, *At the Crossroads: Indians and Empires on a Mid-Atlantic Frontier, 1700–1763* (Chapel Hill: University of North Carolina Press, 2003); Rachel Wheeler, *To Live beyond Hope: Mohicans and Missionaries in the Eighteenth-Century Northeast* (Ithaca, NY: Cornell University Press, 2008).

46. Alan Taylor, *American Colonies: The Settling of North America* (New York: Viking Penguin, 2001), 316–21; Merritt, *At the Crossroads*; Bailyn, *Peopling of British North America*, 17–33; Peter Silver, *Our Savage Neighbors: How Indian War Transformed Early America* (New York: Norton, 2008); Franklin, "Those Who Would Remove to America," in *Writings*, 978. When the British Army became involved in that warfare during the Seven Years' War, 1754–60, there was a marked upswing in British popular interest in the Indian, but as a nasty scalp-hunting savage instead of the subtly subversive Edenic man; Troy O. Bickham, *Savages within the Empire: Representations of American Indians in Eighteenth-Century Britain* (Oxford: Oxford University Press, 2005); Timothy Shannon, *Indian Captive, Indian King: Peter Williamson in America and Britain* (Cambridge, MA: Harvard University Press, 2018), 137–42.

47. Patrick Frazier, *The Mohicans of Stockbridge* (Lincoln: University of Nebraska Press, 1992), 146–71; Alan Taylor, *Liberty Men and Great Proprietors: The Revolutionary Settlement on the Maine Frontier, 1760–1820* (Chapel Hill: University of North Carolina Press, 1990), 181–220; Paul Moyer, "'Real' Indians, 'White' Indians, and the Contest for the Wyoming Valley," in *Friends and Enemies in Penn's Woods: Indians, Colonists, and the Racial Construction of Pennsylvania*, ed. William A Pencak and Daniel K. Richter (University Park: Pennsylvania State University Press, 2004), 221–37; Reeve Huston, "Popular Movements and Party Rule: The New York Anti-rent Wars and the Jacksonian Political Order," in *Beyond the Founders: New Approaches to the Political History of the Early American Republic*, ed. Jeffrey L. Pasley, Andrew W. Robertson, and David Waldstreicher (Chapel Hill: University of North Carolina Press, 2004), 355–86; John Brooke, *Columbia Rising: Civil Life on the Upper Hudson from the Revolution to the Age of Jackson* (Chapel Hill: University of North Carolina Press, 2010).

48. Daniel Williams, "Until They Are Contaminated by Their More Refined Neighbors: The Images of the Native American in Carver's *Travels Through the Interior* and Its Influence on the Euro-American Imagination," in *Indians and Europe: An Interdisciplinary Collection of Essays*, ed. Christian Feest (Lincoln: University of Nebraska Press, 1989), 199; Robert Coram, *Political Inquiries, to which is Added A Plan for the Establishment of Schools Throughout the United States* (Wilmington, DE, 1791); Thomas Paine, *Agrarian Justice* (1797), 6.

Chapter 3. · *Revolutionary Ideologies and Regulations*

1. Benjamin Trumbull, *A Discourse, Delivered at the Anniversary Meeting of the Freemen of the Town of New-Haven, April 12, 1773* (New-Haven: Thomas and Samuel Green, 1773), 30–31.

2. *Boston Gazette*, June 16, 1777, p. 3; A.B., "To Mr. Watson," *Connecticut Courant*, May 12, 1777, p. 1. The *Courant* was a particularly important, widely circulated newspaper during the war; Isaiah Thomas, *The History of Printing in America*, 2nd ed. (1874; repr., New York: Weathervane Books, n.d.), 308. I use the political and economic definitions for "liberal" provided by the *Oxford English Dictionary*. "*Pol.* supporting or advocating individual rights, civil liberties, and political and social reform tending towards individual freedom or democracy with little state intervention"; and "*Econ.* favouring or characterized by unrestricted trade." Adam Smith in *Wealth of Nations* used liberal in the latter sense, and it certainly fits the economic ideas presented by A.B. and similar writers.

3. Jack Greene, *Pursuits of Happiness: The Social Development of Early Modern British Colonies and the Formation of American Culture* (Chapel Hill: University of North Carolina Press, 1988); John J. McCusker and Russell R. Menard, *The Economy of British America, 1607–1789* (Chapel Hill: University of North Carolina Press, 1985); Bettye Hobbs Pruitt, "Self-Sufficiency and the Agricultural Economy of Eighteenth-Century Massachusetts," *William and Mary Quarterly*, 3rd ser., 41 (1984): 333–64.

4. Bernard Bailyn, *The Ideological Origins of the American Revolution* (Cambridge, MA: Harvard University Press, 1967), 28–47. Hulme's *Essay* was frequently discussed in Philadelphia newspapers in the mid-1770s to critique the persistence of property requirements for voting in the province; see *Pennsylvania Gazette*, May 15, 1776, and *Pennsylvania Packet*, Sept. 17, 1776.

5. Michael Winship, *Godly Republicanism: Puritans, Pilgrims, and a City upon a Hill* (Cambridge, MA: Harvard University Press, 2012); Marjoleine Kars, *Breaking Loose Together: The Regulator Rebellion in Pre-Revolutionary North Carolina* (Chapel Hill: University of North Carolina Press, 2002).

6. *Boston Independent Advertiser*, Jan. 25, 1748. This was originally in Thomas Gordon, "Of Public Spirit," *Cato's Letters*, 7th ed., 4 vols. (1755; Indianapolis: Liberty Fund, 1995), 2:12, no. 35, July 1, 1721.

7. Joseph Tinker Buckingham, *Specimens of Newspaper Literature: with Personal Memoirs, Anecdotes, and Reminiscences*, 2 vols. (Boston: Charles C. Little and James Brown, 1850): 1:156–62; Denver A. Brunsman, "The Knowles Atlantic Impressment Riots of the 1740s," *Early American Studies* 5 (2007): 324–66; Greene, *Pursuits of Happiness*, 170–200.

8. Cf. "commonwealth," definitions predating 1600, *Oxford English Dictionary*; James Otis, *The Rights of British Colonies Asserted and Proved* (Boston: Edes and Gill, 1764), 31; Joseph Warren, Boston, to Edmund Dana, Mar. 19, 1766, reprinted in Richard Frothingham, *Life and Times of Joseph Warren* (Boston: Little, Brown, 1865), 20–21.

9. Joyce Appleby, *Economic Thought and Ideology in Seventeenth-Century England* (Princeton, NJ: Princeton University Press, 1978), 243–57; Samuel Fleischacker, "Adam Smith's Reception among the American Founders, 1776–1790," *William and Mary Quarterly*, 3rd ser., 59 (2002): 897–924; Ned Landsman, *From Colonials to Provincials:*

American Thought and Culture, 1680–1760 (Ithaca, NY: Cornell University Press, 1997); Daniel Walker Howe, "Why the Scottish Enlightenment Was Useful to the Framers of the American Constitution," *Comparative Studies in Society and History* 31 (1989): 576–83. For David Hume's critique of Harrington, see his *Essays Moral, Political, and Literary*, 2 vols. (1742, 1752; New York: Longmans, Green, 1899), 1:481.

10. Barbara Clark Smith, *The Freedoms We Lost: Consent and Resistance in Revolutionary America* (New York: New Press, 2010), 95–117; Nathaniel Ames, *An Astronomical Diary; or, Almanack for the Year of our Lord Christ 1768* (Boston, 1767); Timothy Barnes, "The Loyalist Press in the American Revolution, 1765–1781" (PhD diss., University of New Mexico, 1970), 106–19. On September 1, 1769, Jonathan Hunt, a student at Harvard College, proudly assured his father in Concord that he and his colleagues had attended ceremonies "in Homespun" during the past two years and that the seniors "have unanimously agree'd to take their Degrees in their own Manufactury"; Jonathan Hunt, Cambridge, to Deacon Hunt, Concord, Sept. 1, 1769, box 1, folder 3, United States Revolution Collection, American Antiquarian Society, Worcester, MA.

11. *The Commercial Conduct of the Province of New York Considered* (New York, 1767), 11–12; Trumbull, *A Discourse, Delivered*; Worthington C. Ford et al., *Journals of the Continental Congress, 1774–1789*, 36 vols. (Washington, DC, 1904–37), 1:75–79; Richard D. Brown, *Revolutionary Politics in Massachusetts: The Boston Committee of Correspondence and the Towns, 1772–1774* (Cambridge, MA: Harvard University Press, 1972), 234–35; Benjamin Labaree, *Patriots and Partisans: The Merchants of Newburyport, 1764–1815* (Cambridge, MA: Harvard University Press, 1962; New York: Norton, 1975), 36–38; Edward Countryman, *A People in Revolution: The American Revolution and Political Society in New York, 1760–1690* (Baltimore: Johns Hopkins University Press, 1981), 138; Cathy Matson, *Merchants and Empire: Trading in Colonial New York* (Baltimore: Johns Hopkins University Press, 1997), 308 (number of ships seized); "To the Inhabitants of Berks County," *Pennsylvania Gazette*, Jan. 11, 1775; Steven Rosswurm, *Arms, Country, and Class: The Philadelphia Militia and the "Lower Sort" during the American Revolution* (New Brunswick, NJ: Rutgers University Press, 1987).

12. Thomas Nevil et al., Committee of Privates, *To the Several Battalions of Military Associators*, June 26, 1776 (Philadelphia, 1776).

13. Andrew Marvell [pseud.?], *Pennsylvania Packet*, Nov. 26, 1776, p. 2; Terry Bouton, *Taming Democracy: "The People," the Founders, and the Troubled Ending of the American Revolution* (New York: Oxford University Press, 2007), 31–41.

14. Allan Kulikoff, *From British Peasants to Colonial American Farmers* (Chapel Hill: University of North Carolina Press, 2000), 256–68; *Newport Mercury*, Mar. 27, 1775; May 13, June 20, 1776; *New York Gazette*, Apr. 22, 1776; Eric Foner, *Tom Paine and Revolutionary America* (New York: Oxford University Press, 1976), 151–52; Smith, *Freedoms We Lost*, 138–42.

15. Smith, *Freedoms We Lost*, 48–54; E. P. Thompson, "The Moral Economy of the English Crowd in the Eighteenth Century," *Past and Present* 50 (1971): 76–136.

16. William E. Nelson, *The Common Law in Colonial America*, vol. 1, *The Chesapeake and New England, 1607–1660* (New York: Oxford University Press, 2008), 57–58; Bruce Mann, "The Transformation of Law and Economy in Early America," in *Cambridge History of American Law*, vol. 1, *Early America (1580–1815)*, ed. Michael Grossberg and Christopher

Tomlins (New York: Cambridge University Press, 2008), 370–71; Jon Teaford, *The Municipal Revolution in America: Origins of Modern Urban Government, 1650–1825* (Chicago: University of Chicago Press, 1975), 2–30; Matson, *Merchants and Empire*, 31–33, 93, 114–16, 214, 230–38; N. Phelps Stokes, *The Iconography of Manhattan Island, 1498–1909*, 6 vols. (New York: Robert H. Dodd, 1915–28), 4:571, 737 (quoting 1763 petition); Edward Country-man, "Moral Economy, Political Economy, and the American Bourgeois Revolution," in *Moral Economy and Popular Protest: Crowds, Conflict and Authority*, ed. Adrian Randall and Andrew Charlesworth (New York: St. Martin's Press, 2000), 148–49.

    17. Barry Levy, *Town Born: The Political Economy of New England from Its Founding to the Revolution* (Philadelphia: University of Pennsylvania Press, 2009), 26–50; Teaford, *Municipal Revolution in America*, 22–23, 36, 50–52; Richard B. Morris, *Government and Labor in Early America* (1946; New York: Octagon Books, 1965), 21; Kars, *Breaking Loose Together*; Brendan McConville, *These Daring Disturbers of the Public Peace: The Struggle for Property and Power in Early New Jersey* (Philadelphia: University of Pennsylvania Press, 1999); Allan Kulikoff, *Tobacco and Slaves: The Development of Southern Cultures in the Chesapeake, 1680–1800* (Chapel Hill: University of North Carolina Press, 1986); Rhys Isaac, *The Transformation of Virginia, 1740–1790* (Chapel Hill: University of North Carolina Press, 1982).

    18. *Acts and Resolves, Public and Private, of the Province of the Massachusetts Bay* (Boston: Wright and Potter, 1886), 5:669; *New London (CT) Gazette*, Mar. 22, 1776; "Journal of Proceedings of the Convention at Dracut, in November 1776," *Collections of the New Hampshire Historical Society*, vol. 2 (Concord, NH: Jacob Moore, 1827), 58–66; *Mass. Acts and Resolves*, 5:669; Charles Hoadly, *The Public Records of the State of Connecticut* (hereafter *Conn. State Rec.*), vol. 1, *From October, 1776, to February 1778* (Hartford: Case, Lockwood & Brainerd, 1894), 62, 63.

    19. Rhode Island, *An ACT to prevent Monopolies and Oppression, by excessive and unreasonable Prices for many of the Necessaries and Conveniences of Life, and for preventing Engrossers, and for the better Supply of our Troops in the Army with such Necessaries as may be wanted* (Providence: J. Carter, 1777), 1–5; Mass., *An act to prevent monopoly and oppression* (Boston, 1777); Boston, *Boston, Feb. 19th, 1777. In pursuance of an act of the General Assembly of this state, entitled "An act to prevent monopoly and oppression"* (Boston, 1777); Conn., "Act to Prevent Monopolies and Oppressions," *Connecticut Courant*, Feb. 17, 1777, pp. 2–3; New Hampshire, *Laws, etc. An act for regulating the prices of sundry articles, therein enumerated* (Exeter, NH, 1777); Morris, *Government and Labor*, 95–96; Hugh Rockoff, *Drastic Measures: A History of Wage and Price Controls in the United States* (New York: Cambridge University Press, 1984), 28–29.

    20. Benjamin Rush's notes of debates, *Letters of Delegates to Congress, 1774–1789*, ed. Paul Smith et al., 25 vols. (Washington, DC: Library of Congress, 1976–2000), 6:275–77; Morris, *Government and Labor*, 100. Rush was badly distorting Hume, who actually used that phrase to describe the Crusades; David Hume, *History of England*, 6 vols. (1754–61; Boston: Little, Brown, 1854): 1:243. Smith, *Freedoms We Lost*, is literally correct when she writes that none of the congressmen opposed to regulation argued "that price controls infringed on individual rights, or that the purpose of the Revolution was individual economic freedom." However, subsequent liberal appeals against price controls, beginning in May 1777, *did* make both of those arguments, and those concepts were known and embraced by these men at the time.

21. Newburyport, *In pursuance of an act from the great and General Court* (Newbury-Port: John Mycall, 1777). For additional examples, see *Connecticut Courant*, Jan. 27, 1777, pp. 1–2; *Norwich Packet*, Feb. 17, 1777, p. 4; Salem, *The Price Act; or, the bill now in force in the town of Salem . . . February 1, 1777* (Salem: E. Russell, 1777); Ipswich (MA), *The Price Act; or, the list of prices now in force in the town of Ipswich, for the prevention of monopoly and oppression . . .* Feb. 10, 1777 (Salem: E. Russell, 1777); Ipswich, *Whereas by an act of the great and General Court . . . the following articles shall not be sold for a higher price in the town of Ipswich* (Salem: E. Russell, [1777]); New Haven town meeting, Jan. 30, 1777, in Jolene Roberts Mullen, *Connecticut Town Meetings during the American Revolution*, 2 vols (Berwyn Heights, MD: Heritage Books, 2011), 2:20; New London, *At a Meeting . . . in New-London, 21st January, 1777* (New London, CT: Timothy Green, 1777); Barbara Clark Smith, *After the Revolution: The Smithsonian History of Everyday Life in the Eighteenth Century* (New York: Pantheon Books, 1985), 36.

22. Boston Committee of Correspondence, *Boston, February 27. 1777* (Boston, 1777); *Boston Continental Journal*, Apr. 17, 1777; Proclamation, Lebanon, Connecticut, Feb. 26, 1777, Trumbull papers, doc. 51a, vol. 6, Connecticut Colonial Official Papers, Connecticut Public Library, Hartford, CT.

23. Springfield town meeting, Jan. 16, 1777, Hampden County, Town Records, 1736–99, vol. 5, Mormon microfilm no. 480836, p. 443, Massachusetts State Archives, Boston; Robert Treat Paine, Taunton, to William Baylies, Dighton, Mar. 3, 1777, and Baylies to Paine, Mar. 6, 1777, both in *The Papers of Robert Treat Paine*, ed. Edward W. Hanson, 3 vols., *Collections of Massachusetts Historical Society* 89 (Boston: Massachusetts Historical Society, 2005), 3:355–58; *Selections from the Correspondence of the Executive of New Jersey, From 1776 to 1786* (Newark, NJ: Daily Advertiser, 1848), 34–48. Initially the final version did include at the end a few price control measures, but even those were rejected by delegates from Pennsylvania, Delaware, and Maryland; see *Selections*. For examples of newspaper articles highlighting the connections between prices and currency, see the *Connecticut Courant*, Dec. 23, 1776; Jan. 13, Oct. 21, and Dec. 2, 1777.

24. Boston, Committee of Correspondence, Feb. 27, 1777, *Gentlemen, At a Time When Degenerate Britons . . .* (Boston, 1777); William Pynchon, *The Diary of William Pynchon of Salem [1776–1786]: A Picture of Salem Life, Social and Political, a Century Ago*, ed. Fitch Edward Oliver (Boston: Houghton, Mifflin, 1890), 24; *New England Chronicle*, Apr. 24, 1777 (on problems reported at a Worcester meeting of that county's committees of safety); Abigail Adams to John Adams, Apr. 21, 1777, *Adams Family Papers: An Electronic Archive*, Massachusetts Historical Society, http://www.masshist.org/digitaladams/. On March 26, 1777, Boston's committee on the act had reported to a general meeting that some in the town were willing to "sacrifice the public Interest to satisfy their Lust & Appetites" by violating the act and depreciating the Continental and state currencies; Boston, Town Meeting minutes, mss., p. 113, Boston Public Library, Rare Books.

25. Chap. 46, passed May 10, 1777, in *Mass. Acts and Resolves*, 5:642–47, and in *Boston Gazette*, June 23, 1777; *Boston Gazette*, June 16, 1777, p. 3, on report from Plympton convention; Abigail Adams to John Adams, July 31, 1777, *Adams Family Papers*; Pynchon, *Diary*, 34–35; Morris, *Government and Labor*, 101, 125. For examples of Massachusetts towns enacting tougher enforcement measures, see Concord Town Meeting, June 2, notebook 12, vol. 5, pt. 1, 1746–80, 71a, Special Collections, Concord Free Library; Newburyport,

June 30, Town Records, 1764–89, p. 282, Mormon microfilm no. 890253; Rowley, July 9, Town Meetings, vol. 3, 1771–1807, p. 43, Mormon microfilm no. 887752; Shelburne, June 30, Town Records, 1768–95, p. 75, Mormon microfilm no. 886748; Springfield, Town Records 1736–99, vol. 5, p. 447, Mormon microfilm no. 480836; Westborough, June 30, Town Records, Proceedings, Miscellaneous, 1717–1810, p. 350, Mormon microfilm no. 867881; Watertown Records, vol. 4, pt. 6, 161.

26. A.B., "To Mr. Watson," *Connecticut Courant*, May 12, 1777, p. 1; T.M. "To Mr. Watson," *Connecticut Courant*, May 26, 1777, p. 2, cols. 2–3; Boston meeting minutes, May 26, 1777, pp. 126–27, Boston Public Library. Smith, *Freedoms We Lost*, 166, believes that this measure was pushed through the town meeting by commercial interests, although no direct evidence supports that hypothesis. One month later, a Providence town meeting similarly asked its representatives to repeal Rhode Island's acts; Morris, *Government and Labor*, 103.

27. Daniel R. Mandell, "A Natural & Unalienable Right": New England Revolutionary Petitions and African American Identity," in *Remembering the Revolution: Memory, History, and Nation-Making from Independence to the Civil War*, ed. Robert Aldrich et al. (Amherst: University of Massachusetts Press, 2013), 46–47.

28. Mass., Chap. 6, 1777–78, *Mass. Acts and Resolves* 5:738; *Journals of the House of Representatives of Massachusetts*, vol. 54, pt. 1, 15–40; Mass. Archives, 144:34–47 (handwritten report of the conference to the Massachusetts General Court; "inconveniences" is on p. 43); *Conn. State Rec.*, vol. 1, 366, 413–15, 599–606; Mass., Chaps. 5 and 6, both passed Oct. 13, 1777, *Mass. Acts and Resolves*, 5:733–38, 1012; Boston town meeting records, p. 145, Boston Public Library; Smith, *Freedoms We Lost*, 167; "Town Meeting of the Town of Providence on the 13th Day of September AD 1777," doc. 1297, Providence Town Papers, 1639–1832, Rhode Island Historical Society, Providence; Connecticut Act "To Encourage Fair Dealing and to Restrain and Punish Sharpers and Oppressors," passed Oct. 11, 1777, reprinted in *Connecticut Courant*, Nov. 15, 1777, p. 2.

29. "Boston, September 8," *Boston Gazette*, Sept. 8, 1777, p. 4 ("avaricious designs"); "A Countryman," *Boston Independent Chronicle*, Aug. 29, 1777, p. 3; "Tertius Cato," *Boston Independent Chronicle*, Sept. 11, 1777, p. 1 ("natural right"); Cato, "To the Courant," *Connecticut Courant*, Dec. 2, 1777, pp. 1–2 ("punish an extortioner"); Westminster to Massachusetts General Court, Nov. 1777, box 3, folder 3, United States Revolution Collection, 1754–1928, American Antiquarian Society, Worcester, MA; Cato, "To the Courant," *Connecticut Courant*, Dec. 2, 1777, pp. 1–2 ("fat and nasty"); Dec. 16, 1777, pp. 1–2 ("monopolists and engrossers"). "Cato" was also the pen name chosen by the writer of the *Connecticut Courant* series on currency, Oct. 21, 1777, p. 1, col. 3, to p. 2, cols. 1–3; and Nov. 15, 1777, p. 1, col. 1. That name was one of the most popular pseudonyms in the eighteenth century.

30. *Journals of the Continental Congress*, 9:956–57; Mass. Archives, 144:65–67 (transcribed convention report); *Conn. State Rec.*, 1:607–20, and *Mass. Acts and Resolves*, 5:1013–15 (published convention reports); *Connecticut Journal*, Mar. 18, 1778, p. 2 (passage of regulatory act); Richard C. Bull, "Constitutional Significance of Early Pennsylvania Price-Fixing Legislation," *Temple Law Quarterly* 11 (1936–37): 322–23; *Mass. Acts and Resolves* 5:1016–17 (Apr. 27 joint committee report); Oliver Wolcott to Laura Wolcott, Apr. 7 and 14, 1778, *Letters of Delegates to Congress*, 9:387, 415 (on call by Congress and expected repeal by

Connecticut); Wolcott and Samuel Huntington to Governor Jonathan Trumbull, Apr. 29, 1778, *Letters of Delegates to Congress,* 9:542; Kenneth Scott, "Price Control in New England during the Revolution," *New England Quarterly* 19 (1946): 453–73; "An Act for Suspending," *Pennsylvania Packet,* June 3, 1778, p.1; *Journal of the Continental Congress,* 7:569–70 (price limits as "ineffectual"). Congress asked all the states from Delaware north to meet in New Haven on January 15; Virginia, Maryland, and North Carolina to meet at Fredericksburg on the same day; and South Carolina and Georgia to meet in Charlestown a month later. But only the New Haven convention occurred.

31. Committee of Congress to the Several States, Nov. 11, 1778, *Letters of Delegates to Congress,* 11:201–5. This is contrary to the generally accepted idea that the significance of committees declined after 1776 as Revolutionary leaders reestablished more familiar governmental structures at the state level; Willi Paul Adams, *The First American Constitutions: Republican Ideology and the Making of the State Constitutions in the Revolutionary Era* (Chapel Hill: University of North Carolina Press, 1980), 27–48.

32. Foner, *Tom Paine,* 152–56, 165–66; Drinker diary quoted by Steven Rosswurm in *Life in Early Philadelphia: Documents from the Revolutionary and Early National Periods,* ed. Billy Smith (University Park: Pennsylvania State Press, 1995), 258–62.

33. *Pennsylvania Packet,* May 27, 1779, p. 2; Philadelphia Committee for Enquiring into the State of Trade, *Whereas the Rapid and Alarming Depreciation of the Currency . . .* (Philadelphia: F. Bailey, 1779); Rosswurm, *Arms, Country, and Class,* 181–83; John Watson, *Annals of Philadelphia and Pennsylvania,* 2 vols. (Philadelphia: Carey and Hart, 1845), 2:303–5; *Committee-room, May 28, 1779* (Philadelphia: Francis Bailey, 1779); transcript, *Pennsylvania Packet,* May 29, 1779, p. 1; *Committee-room, June 26, 1779* (Philadelphia: Francis Bailey, 1779). A "Pennsylvanian" in the *Pennsylvania Packet* justified the committee's powers as politically "consistent with the welfare of the people"; *Pennsylvania Packet,* June 6, 1779, pp. 1, 4.

34. Countryman, *A People in Revolution,* 180–81. Countryman cites the minutes of this convention in manuscript, Matthew Visscher folder, Albany Institute, Albany, New York. The institute has since misplaced or lost this material; John Brooke to Mandell, email correspondence in author's possession, Mar. 9, 2010.

35. *Pennsylvania Packet,* June 29, 1779, p. 2; *Mass. Acts and Resolves,* 5:1253–55; Boston merchant committee, chairman John Rowe, resolves, June 16, 1779, Boston town records, loose documents, Boston Town Library, Boston. In early 1779, merchant John Rowe had remarked on the "Great distress" in the city, and hearings held by a town committee investigating "Forestallers, Engrossers, and Monopolizers" resulted in a state law that tried to bar those evils but had little effect; John Rowe diaries, Massachusetts Historical Society, vol. 15, Aug. 13, 1778–July 18, 1779, pp. 2444–59; Boston town records, loose documents, commission and report by committee, Jan. 16–Feb. 1, 1779, Boston Public Library; John Tudor, *Deacon Tudor's Diary,* ed. William Tudor (Boston: Wallace Spooner, 1896), 77–78; Mass., Act Against Monopoly and Forestalling, reprinted in *Boston Gazette,* Feb. 15, 1779, p. 1.

36. Boston town resolve, June 17, 1779, Boston town records, loose documents, commission and report by committee, Jan. 16–Feb. 1, 1779; *Pennsylvania Packet,* June 29, 1779, p. 2; *Mass. Acts and Resolves,* 5:1253–55; Morris, *Government and Labor,* 108, 122–23; *Proceedings of the convention begun and held at Concord . . . on the 14th day of July, 1779* (Boston: Edes and Sons, 1779); convention of eighteen towns in Worcester County, *Proceedings of the Convention*

(Worcester, 1779); *Proceedings of a Convention of Delegates from Eighteen Towns in the County of Essex* (Danvers: E. Russell, 1779); convention of delegates from towns in Middlesex and Suffolk counties, *Thomas's Massachusetts spy*, Aug. 16 and 26, 1779; *Boston Independent Chronicle*, Sept. 6, 9, 23, Oct. 14, 1779; *Boston Gazette*, Sept. 6, 1779; Providence (RI), Committee of Correspondence, *Providence, July 26, 1779. Sir; By the annexed vote of the town of Providence...* (Providence: John Carter, 1779); (Providence, R.I.) *American Journal and General Advertiser*, Sept. 2, 1779; New Hampshire, Portsmouth Town Meeting, Oct. 1, 1779 (Portsmouth, 1779); *Connecticut Courant*, Sept. 14, 1779, p. 3, col. 1, and Oct. 12, 1779, p. 3.

37. *Virginia Gazette*, July 24, 1779, pp. 1–2; Williamsburg, *To Wit: ever attentive to the interests of their country ... some publick spirited inhabitants of this city* (Williamsburg: Dixon & Nicolson, 1779).

38. Kulikoff, *From British Peasants*, 260; Foner, *Tom Paine*, 171–73; Pelatiah Webster, "An Essay on Free Trade and Finance," in *Political Essays on the Nature and Operation of Money, Public Finances and Other Subjects* (Philadelphia: Joseph Crukshank, 1791), 9, 24 (Webster through this volume identified himself as the author of the *Essay*).

39. *Pennsylvania Packet*, Sept. 10, 1779, pp. 1, 4; John Alexander, "The Fort Wilson Incident of 1779: A Case Study of the Revolutionary Crowd," *William and Mary Quarterly*, 3rd ser., 31 (1974): 600.

40. *Pennsylvania Packet*, Sept. 10, 1779, pp. 2–3. On the labor theory of value, see James L. Hutson, "The American Revolutionaries, the Political Economy of Aristocracy, and the American Concept of the Distribution of Wealth, 1765–1900," *American Historical Review* 98 (1993): 1180–81, 1090–91.

41. *Pennsylvania Packet*, Sept. 25, 1779, p. 3; Rosswurm, *Arms, Country, Class*, 91–193; Penn., *Journal of the Council of Censors* (Philadelphia: Hall and Sellers, 1784), 135; Alexander, "The Fort Wilson Incident," 600–605.

42. Boston, *To the Gentlemen who represented the Country Towns* (Boston, 1779); *Mass. Acts and Resolves*, 5:1255–57, 1114.

43. *Conn. State Rec.*, 2:567–68; Rockoff, *Drastic Measures*, 34; Henry Marchant to Rhode Island Governor William Greene, Oct. 12, 1779, *Letters of Delegates to Congress*, 14:64; Samuel Holten to the Massachusetts Council, Nov. 11, 1779, *Letters of Delegates to Congress*, 14:175; *Journal of Continental Congress*, 15:1289–92; *Conn. State Rec.*, 2:562. Connecticut's recommended ceiling was 20 times higher than prices and wages had generally been in 1774.

44. *Mass. Acts and Resolves*, 5:1264; Morris, *Government and Labor*, 115; Foner, *Tom Paine*, 179–80.

45. Penn., *Journal of the Council of Censors*, 135; Mathew Carey, ed., *Debates and Proceedings in the General Assembly of Pennsylvania on the Memorials Praying a Repeal or Suspension of the Law Annulling the Charter of the Bank [of North America]* (Philadelphia: Seldon & Pritchard, 1786), 87; Penn., *Journal of the Council of Censors*, 134 (the *Journal* spells his name "Finley"); Andrew Shankman, *Crucible of American Democracy: The Struggle to Fuse Egalitarianism and Capitalism in Jeffersonian Pennsylvania* (Lawrence: University Press of Kansas, 2004), 6, 8. The title page of the *Journal of the Council of Censors* lists 1783 as its publication date, but that must be inaccurate because most of the volume contains proceedings after December 31, 1783, and WorldCat lists the same edition (judging by publisher and page numbers) published in both 1783 and 1784.

46. Robert Coram, *Political Inquiries, to which is Added A Plan for the Establishment of Schools Throughout the United States* (Wilmington, DE, 1791), 22.

47. Woody Holton, *Unruly Americans and the Origins of the Constitution* (New York: Hill and Wang, 2007); Bouton, *Taming Democracy*.

48. Seth Cotler, *Tom Paine's America: The Rise and Fall of Transatlantic Radicalism in the Early Republic* (Charlottesville: University of Virginia Press, 2011), esp. 123–60; Bouton, *Taming Democracy*; Mark S. Schantz, *Piety in Providence: Class Dimensions of Religious Experience in Antebellum Rhode Island* (Ithaca, NY: Cornell University Press, 2000); Karen V. Hansen, *A Very Social Time: Crafting Community in Antebellum New England* (Berkeley: University of California Press, 1994); William Manning, *"The Key of Liberty": The Life and Democratic Writings of William Manning, "A Laborer," 1747–1814*, ed. Michael Merrill and Sean Wilentz (Cambridge, MA: Harvard University Press, 1993). In 2016, I searched for "assize" in the full text of newspapers published throughout the United States, 1780–1850, on the database *America's Historical Newspapers*, and came up with 11,397 "hits." Narrowing the search to "assize of bread" reduced the "hits" to 7,310. Among other things, the search showed assizes of breads regularly enacted during the late 1840s in, among other places, the cities of Washington, DC, and Charleston, South Carolina.

Chapter 4. · *Wealth and Power in the Early Republic*

1. Johann David Schoepf, *Travels in the Confederation* [1783–84], trans. Alfred J. Morrison, 2 vols. (1788; Philadelphia: William J. Campbell, 1911), 1:99, 2:205.

2. Eumenes, "Letter II, on Liberty," *New Jersey Journal*, May 10, 1780, reprinted in *Documents Relating to the Revolutionary History of the State of New Jersey*, ed. William Nelson, 5 vols. (Trenton, NJ: State Gazette Printing, 1914–17), 4:365–66; Kentucky inhabitants to Congress (as submitted by Virginia delegates), Jan. 2, 1784, in *Papers of Thomas Jefferson*, ed. Julian Boyd (Princeton, NJ: Princeton University Press, 1952), 6:553; "In the House of Representatives," *Connecticut Courant*, June 11, 1787, p. 1. The *Courant* does not give Welton's first name, but a list of Connecticut assembly men from October 1787 shows a "John Welton" as one of two delegates from Waterbury, and several Waterbury histories describe him as an important man in the community elected to the Assembly beginning in 1782.

3. A True Patriot, *New Jersey Gazette*, Apr. 25, 1781, in *Documents Relating to the Revolutionary History*, 5:238; Observator, no. II, *New Haven Gazette*, Sept. 1, 1785, p. 1; Lucius, *Independent Chronicle*, Dec. 1, 1785, p. 2; Thomas Dawes Jr., Esq., "Part of an Oration, Delivered at Boston, on the 4th of July, 1787," *American Magazine*, Aug. 1, 1788, p. 619; *Rudiments of Law and Government, Deduced from the Law of Nature* (Charlestown, SC: John McIver, Jr., 1783), 19; Peter H. Lindert and Jeffrey G. Williamson, "American Incomes before and after the Revolution," National Bureau of Economic Research, July 2011, rev. Feb. 2013, http://www.nber.org/papers/w17211.pdf.

4. John Adams, *A Defence of the Constitutions of Government of the United States of America* (Philadelphia, 1787), 359; "A Farmer of New Jersey," *Observations on Government, Including Some Animadversions on Mr. Adams' Defense* (New York: Ross, 1787), 46; Noah Webster Jr., *An Examination in the Leading Principles of the Federal Constitution* (Philadelphia: Prichard & Hall, 1787), 47; Harrison Gray Otis, *An Oration Delivered July 4, 1788* (Boston: Russell, 1788), 22.

5. Drew McCoy, *The Elusive Republic: Political Economy in Jeffersonian America* (Chapel Hill: University of North Carolina Press, 1980).

6. *Principles and Articles Agreed on by the Members of the Constitutional Society, in Philadelphia; and Proposed for the consideration of the Lovers and Supporters of Civil Government in other Parts of the State* (Philadelphia: Bailey, 1780); Woody Holton, *Unruly Americans and the Origins of the Constitution* (New York: Hill and Wang, 2007), 46–54; Lycurgus, "Observations on the Present Situation," no. II, *New-Haven Gazette and Connecticut Magazine*, no. 2 (Feb. 23, 1786): 9.

7. A True Patriot, *New Jersey Gazette*, Apr. 25, 1781, in *Documents Relating to the Revolutionary History*, 5:235–38; *Rudiments of Law and Government, Deduced from the Law of Nature* (Charlestown, SC: John McIver, Jr., 1783), 19, 20; David Daggett, *An Oration, Pronounced in the Brick Meeting-House, in the City of New-Haven, on the Fourth of July, AD 1787* (New Haven: Greens, 1787), 4, 23; Robert Coram, *Political Inquiries, to which is Added A Plan for the Establishment of Schools Throughout the United States* (Wilmington, DE: Andrews and Brynberg, 1791), 24, 97, 89; David Ramsay, *The History of the American Revolution* (1789), ed. Lester Cohen, 2 vols. (Indianapolis: Liberty Fund, 1990), 1:30; Mercy Otis Warren, *History of the Rise, Progress and Termination of the American Revolution* (1805), ed. Lester H. Cohen, 2 vols. (Indianapolis: Liberty Fund, 1994), 1:14.

8. Samuel Stillman, *An Election Sermon, Preached before the Honorable Council and the Honorable House of Representatives of the State of Massachusetts Bay . . . at Boston, May 26, 1779, Being the Anniversary for the Election of the Honorable Council* (Boston: T. and J. Fleet, 1779), 8, 18; *Independent Gazetteer* (Philadelphia), Aug. 24, 1787, reprinted in the *Massachusetts Gazette* (Boston), Oct. 2, 1787; *Thoughts Upon the Political Situation of the United States of America: in Which that of Massachusetts is more Particularly Considered, With some Observations on the Constitution for a Federal Government, Addressed to the People of the Union. By a Native of Boston* (Worcester: Isaiah Thomas, 1788), 55, 57. On the concept of a natural aristocracy, see J. R. Pole, *The Pursuit of Equality in American History*, 2nd ed. (Berkeley: University of California Press, 1993), 43; on John Adams's ideas and writings, see Gordon Wood, *The Creation of the American Republic, 1776–1787* (Chapel Hill: University of North Carolina Press, 1969), 569–92.

9. A Foreign Spectator [Nicholas Collin], "An Essay on the Means of Promoting Federal Sentiments in the United States," no. 10, *Independent Gazetteer*, Aug. 24, 1787.

10. Herman Husband, *Proposals to amend and Perfect the Policy of the Government of the United States of America* (Baltimore, 1782), 3–4, 20–21; *Rudiments of Law and Government*, 24; Cassius [Aedanus Burke], *Considerations on the Society or Order of Cincinnati* (Charlestown, SC: A. Timothy, 1783), 18.

11. *Boston American Herald*, Feb. 4, 1788; Walter Brewster, *Norwich Packet*, Sept. 8, 1791.

12. Daniel R. Mandell, "'A Natural & Unalienable Right': New England Revolutionary Petitions and African American Identity," in *Remembering the Revolution: Memory, History, and Nation-Making from Independence to the Civil War*, ed. Robert Aldrich et al. (Amherst: University of Massachusetts Press, 2013), 38–53; James Oliver Horton and Lois E. Horton, *In Hope of Liberty: Culture, Community, and Protest among Northern Free Blacks, 1700–1860* (New York: Oxford University Press, 1997).

13. Agrippa [James Winthrop], Letter XII, *Massachusetts Gazette*, Jan. 11, 1788; Robin L. Einhorn, *American Taxation, American Slavery* (Chicago: University of Chicago Press,

2006), 81–83; Ramsay, *History of the American Revolution*, 1:35; Annette Gordon-Reed and Peter S. Onuf, *"Most Blessed of the Patriarchs": Thomas Jefferson and the Empire of the Imagination* (New York: Liveright, 2016), 58–61.

14. Burke, *Considerations on the Society or Order of Cincinnati*, 21–22; "Free Republican, No. III," *Boston Magazine*, May 1784, 271, 272; "Free Republican, No. V," *Boston Magazine*, Aug. 1784, 420–22; Martin J. Burke, *The Conundrum of Class: Public Discourse on the Social Order in America* (Chicago: University of Chicago Press, 1995), 22–50.

15. Adams, *Defence of the Constitutions*; Burke, *Conundrum of Class*, 25–27.

16. Oscar Handlin and Mary Handlin, eds., *The Popular Sources of Political Authority: Documents on the Massachusetts Constitution of 1780* (Cambridge, MA: Harvard University Press, 1966), esp. 487, 520; Alexander Keyssar, *The Right to Vote: The Contested History of Democracy in the United States*, rev. ed. (New York: Basic Books, 2009), 15–16.

17. James K. Martin and Mark E. Lender, *A Respectable Army: The Military Origins of the Republic, 1763–1789*, 2nd ed. (Somerset, NJ: Wiley and Sons, 2005), 196–97; "A Querist," *New-Jersey Journal* (Chatham, NJ), Sept. 10, 1783, no. 239.

18. Burke, *Considerations on the Society or Order of Cincinnati*, 6. Burke's influence was extensive: his pamphlet was reprinted in Hartford, Connecticut; Newport, Rhode Island; New York; and Philadelphia; and in Massachusetts and Connecticut newspapers. A decade later, one of the first New England historians, Hannah Adams, noted that "the public odium against the officers" caused by the pension issue "was augmented by" these concerns about the society and that Burke's pamphlet "greatly contributed to spread the flame of opposition"; Adams, *A Summary History of New-England: from the first settlement at Plymouth, to the acceptance of the federal Constitution: Comprehending a general sketch of the American war* (Dedham: H. Mann and J. H. Adams, 1799), 485; John C. Meleney, *The Public Life of Aedanus Burke: Revolutionary Republican in post-Revolutionary South Carolina* (Columbia: University of South Carolina Press, 1989), 88. See generally William Doyle, *Aristocracy and Its Enemies in the Age of Revolution* (New York: Oxford University Press, 2009), 95–136.

19. Holton, *Unruly Americans*, 56–65; Terry Bouton, *Taming Democracy: "The People," the Founders, and the Troubled Ending of the American Revolution* (New York: Oxford University Press, 2007), 116–20; "A Friend to the Rights of Mankind," *New Hampshire Gazette*, June 3 and July 1, 1785 (quotation); Ruth Bogin, "Petitioning and the New Moral Economy of Post-Revolutionary America," *William and Mary Quarterly*, 3rd. ser., 45 (1988): 420–24.

20. Robert Gross, ed., *In Debt to Shays: The Bicentennial of an Agrarian Rebellion* (Charlottesville: University Press of Virginia, 1993); David Szatmary, *Shays' Rebellion: The Making of an Agrarian Insurrection* (Amherst: University of Massachusetts Press, 1980).

21. John Larson, *Internal Improvement: National Public Works and the Promise of Popular Government in the Early United States* (Chapel Hill: University of North Carolina Press, 2001), esp. 10; Andrew Schocket, *Founding Corporate Power in Early National Philadelphia* (DeKalb: Northern Illinois University Press, 2007), 3–6.

22. Bouton, *Taming Democracy*, 78–80, 84–100, 131–37; Mathew Carey, ed., *Debates and Proceedings in the General Assembly of Pennsylvania on the Memorials Praying a Repeal or Suspension of the Law Annulling the Charter of the Bank* (Philadelphia: Seldon & Pritchard, 1786), 17.

23. Carey, *Debates and Proceedings*, 38, 65, 88, 96; Schocket, *Founding Corporate Power*, 54, 76–80; Atticus, "Letter the Fourth," *Freeman's Journal*, June 14, 1786, reprinted in

Pennsylvania Packet, June 28, 1786; Jerry Markham, *A Financial History of the United States*, 2 vols. (New York: M. E. Sharpe, 2002), 1:87–88.

24. "The Politician, no. VII," *Massachusetts Magazine*, Jan. 1, 1790, p. 12; printed petition, broadside format, with signatures, undated but circa 1793, to the Pennsylvania legislature, House file, Canal and Navigation Companies, Roads, Turnpikes, 18th session-1, 1793–94, box 1, ser. 7.11, Record Group 7, Records of the General Assembly, House of Representatives, Pennsylvania Archives, Harrisburg; Bouton, *Taming Democracy*, 111–13; Tim Wu, "The Right to Avoid Regulation," *New Republic*, June 3, 2013.

25. Printed petition circa 1793 to the Pennsylvania legislature; handwritten petition with signatures opposed to rechartering the Bank of North America, undated but circa 1799, to the Pennsylvania legislature, House file, 24th session-1, 1799–1800, folder 1, box 1, ser. 7.11, Record Group 7, Records of the General Assembly, House of Representatives, Pennsylvania Archives, Harrisburg; Schocket, *Founding Corporate Power*, 55.

26. [William Ogilvie], *An Essay on the Right of Property in Land: With Respect to its Foundation in the Law of nature, its present establishment by the municipal laws of Europe, and the regulations by which it might be rendered more beneficial to the lower ranks of mankind* (London: J. Walter, 1781), 169; Richard Price, *Observations on the Importance of the American Revolution* (London, 1784; Hartford, CT: Barlow and Babcock, 1785), 48–49. Adams's copy of Ogilvie is in the collection of the Boston Public Library and has been digitized for public use: http://archive.org/details/essayonrightofprooogil. New England newspapers reprinting Price's "The Unequal Distribution of Property" included the *Boston Independent Ledger,* Feb. 14, 1785; *Salem Gazette,* Feb. 1, 1785; *Boston Independent Chronicle,* Mar. 10, 1785; *Norwich (CT) Packet,* Mar. 17, 1785; *Vermont Gazette,* Mar. 28, 1785; *Fowle's New-Hampshire Gazette,* Apr. 1, 1785; and *Falmouth (ME) Gazette and Weekly Advertiser,* Apr. 2, 1785.

27. Anon., *Thoughts on the Five Per Cent* (Providence, RI: Carter, 1782), 4; *Rudiments of Law and Government*, v, 15, 20, 26.

28. Benjamin Trumbull, *A Discourse, Delivered at the Anniversary Meeting of the Freemen of the Town of New-Haven, April 12, 1773* (New-Haven: Thomas and Samuel Green, 1773), 30; John Murray, *Jerubbaal, or Tyranny's Grove Destroyed, and the Altar of Liberty Finished: A Discourse on America's Duty and Danger* (Newbury-Port: John Mycall, 1784), 56.

29. *Boston Gazette*, July 19, 1779, p. 1, and June 17, 1780, p. 1; Paskalos to Isaiah Thomas, *Massachusetts Spy*, June 28, 1781, p. 4, and Aug. 2, 1781, p. 2; *Connecticut Courant*, June 11, 1787, p. 1, col. 1. One reader in Worcester County wrote Thomas to applaud the idea and called on others in the county to push for similar town resolves; An Honest Man, *Massachusetts Spy*, Aug. 2, 1781.

30. William Plumer to John Hale, Sept. 20, 1786, in Colonial Society of Massachusetts, *Transactions*, 12 (Boston, 1910), 390–92, quotation 392; *New Haven Chronicle*, Feb. 1787; Henry Knox to George Washington, Oct. 23, 1787, in *Documentary History of the Ratification of the Constitution*, ed. John P. Kaminski and Gaspare J. Saladino, 21 vols. (Madison: State Historical Society of Wisconsin, 1976–), 13:93; Camillus, "Observations on the late insurrection in Massachusetts," *American Museum* (Philadelphia), Oct. 1787, 320.

31. Alexander Hamilton, "Conjectures about the New Constitution," in *The Debate on the Constitution*, ed. Bernard Bailyn, 2 vols. (New York: Library of America, 1993), 1:284; Foreign Spectator [Nicholas Collin], "Essay on the Means of Promoting Federal Sentiments," *Independent Gazetteer*, Aug. 24, 1787; Publius, Federalist X, *New York Daily*

Advertiser, Nov. 22, 1787, in Bailyn, *Debate on the Constitution*, 1:408; John Adams, New York, to Richard Price, Apr. 19, 1790, in *The Works of John Adams, Second President of the United States*, ed. Charles Francis Adams, 10 vols. (Boston: Little, Brown, 1856), 9:564; Adams in the *Raleigh (NC) Star*, May 18, 1809, quoted in Robert A. Gross, "A Yankee Rebellion? The Regulators, New England, and the New Nation," *New England Quarterly* 82 (2009): 117.

32. Carey, *Debates and Proceedings*, 87, 122; printed broadside circa 1793, to Pennsylvania legislature, House file, 18th session-1, 1793–94, box 1, ser. 7.11, Record Group 7, Pennsylvania Archives, Harrisburg. Seth Cotler argues that these "vague conventional assertions of the sanctity of property rights" served as "preemptive strikes against the charge of levellerism"; Cotler, *Tom Paine's America: The Rise and Fall of Transatlantic Radicalism in the Early Republic* (Charlottesville: University of Virginia Press, 2011), 135.

33. Carol Shammas, Marylynn Salmon, and Michel Dahlin, *Inheritance in America: From Colonial Times to the Present* (New Brunswick: Rutgers University Press, 1987); Stanley Katz, "Republicanism and the Law of Inheritance in the American Revolutionary Era," *Michigan Law Review* 76, no. 1 (Nov. 1977): 1–29; Eric Nelson, *The Greek Tradition in Republican Thought* (New York: Cambridge University Press, 2004), 213, and generally chap. 6; Webster, *An Examination*, 46, 48; Thomas Jefferson, "Autobiography" (1821), in *Writings*, ed. Merrill Peterson (New York: Library of America, 1984), 32, 44; Holly Brewer, "Entailing Aristocracy in Colonial Virginia: 'Ancient Feudal Restraints' and Revolutionary Reform," *William and Mary Quarterly*, 3rd ser., 54 (1997): esp. 318–20, 345.

34. "Speech of the hon. Charles Pinckney, Esq., delivered at the opening of the [constitutional] convention of South Carolina, May 14, 1788," *American Museum*, Sept. 1788, 157–58; *Laws of the State of Delaware*, 2 vols. (Newcastle: Samuel and John Adams, 1797), 2:582; Stanley Katz, "Republicanism and the Law of Inheritance in the American Revolutionary Era," *Michigan Law Review* 76, no. 1 (Nov. 1977): 13–15 (p. 14 quoting North Carolina law); Nelson, *Greek Tradition in Republican Thought*, 220–24 (on language in debates over the constitution), 230–32 (on the situation in state laws at the end of the century); "For the General Advertiser," *General Advertiser* (cont. as *Aurora General Advertiser* in November 1794), Mar. 13, 1793; *American Daily Advertiser*, Apr. 30, 1790. In 1789 Massachusetts abolished the right of primogeniture but may have been the only state to do so; "American Intelligence," *American Magazine*, June 1, 1789, p. 607; "Hartford, Jan. 21," *American Daily Advertiser*, Feb. 16, 1791.

35. *Rudiments of Law and Government*, 22; "From the Rough Hewer," *New York Independent Gazette, or the New-York Journal*, Jan. 24, 1784, p. 1.

36. Gilbert Chinard, *The Commonplace Book of Thomas Jefferson* (Baltimore: Johns Hopkins University Press, 1926), 259; Jefferson to James Madison, Oct. 28, 1785, in *Writings*, 841; "Rough Hewer," *Independent Gazette*; Bouton, *Taming Democracy*, 120; "Queries and Remarks on a Paper, entitled 'Hints for the Members of the Convention, No. 2,' in the *Federal Gazette* of Tuesday, November 3, 1789," *Independent Gazetteer*, Dec. 4, 1789, p. 2; Einhorn, *American Taxation*, 103.

37. See especially Jürgen Heideking, *The Constitution before the Judgment Seat: The Prehistory and Ratification of the American Constitution, 1787–1791* (Charlottesville: University of Virginia Press, 2012), 8, 34, 85, 93, 120–133.

38. Noah Webster Jr., *A Collection of Essays and Fugitive Writings on Moral, Historical, Political and Literary Subjects* (Boston: I. Thomas and E. T. Andrews, 1790), 326.

39. Heideking, *Constitution before the Judgment Seat*, 340–57, 362; David Waldstreicher, *In the Midst of Perpetual Fetes: The Making of American Nationalism, 1776–1820* (Chapel Hill: University of North Carolina Press, 1997), 55, 72–92; Alfred Young, *The Shoemaker and the Tea Party: Memory and the American Revolution* (Boston: Beacon Press, 1999), 128.

40. Andrew Shankman, *Original Intents: Hamilton, Jefferson, Madison, and the American Founding* (New York: Oxford University Press, 2018), 67–91.

41. A Farmer [George Logan], *Letters, addressed to the yeomanry of the United States* (Philadelphia: Eleazer Oswald, 1791), 25; Archimedes, "Plan for a Nobility in the United States," *American Museum*, May 1792, 240–42; Shankman, *Original Intents*, 93–102.

42. Madison, "Parties," *National Gazette*, Jan. 23, 1792, p. 98; A Farmer [George Logan], *Five Letters, Addressed to the Yeoman of the United States* (Philadelphia: Eleazer Oswald, 1792), 10, 11, 21 (originally published in the *National Gazette*, Mar.–Apr. 1792).

43. Walter Brewster, "The Mechanick on Taxation no. 3," *Norwich Packet*, Apr. 19, 1792; Brewster, "Copy of a letter sent to his Excellency Samuel Huntington," Mar. 26, 1792, in *American Mercury* (Hartford, CT), May 21, 1792, p. 2; *New-York Journal*, Feb. 25, 1792 (Tammany toasts); Bouton, *Taming Democracy*, 101.

44. Cotler, *Tom Paine's America*, 70–72; A Farmer [George Logan], *Five Letters*, 4, 6; John Adams to Thomas Brand Hollis, June 11, 1790, in Adams, *Works of John Adams*, 9:570.

45. Waldstreicher, *In the Midst of Perpetual Fetes*, 72–92; Gary Nash, "The American Clergy and the French Revolution," *William and Mary Quarterly*, 3rd ser., 22 (1965): 392–412; Boston festival, *General Advertiser*, Feb. 5, 1793, pp. 2–3; Abigail Adams to John Adams, Feb. 1 and Jan. 22, 1793, in *Adams Family Papers: An Electronic Archive*, Massachusetts Historical Society, http://www.masshist.org/digitaladams/aea/browse/letters_1789_1796.html.

46. Bouton, *Taming Democracy*, 91–101, 199–241; Thomas Slaughter, *The Whiskey Rebellion: Frontier Epilogue to the American Revolution* (New York: Oxford University Press, 1986).

47. Jeffrey Pasley, *The First Presidential Contest: 1796 and the Founding of American Democracy* (Lawrence: University Press of Kansas, 2013).

48. Ruth Bogin, *Abraham Clark and the Quest for Equality in the Revolutionary Era, 1774–1794* (Rutherford, NJ: Fairleigh Dickinson University Press, 1982), 155, quoting *Wood's Newark Gazette*, Mar. 12, 19, 26, 1794; A Back-Woods Man, "For the Aurora," *Aurora General Advertiser*, Feb. 8, 1796, p. 2, cols. 2–3; George Warner, *Means for the Preservation of Public Liberty* (New York: Greenleaf and Judah, 1797), 12; Richard Beresford, *Aristocracy the Bane of Liberty* (Charleston: W. P. Young, 1797), 29; William Manning, *"The Key of Liberty": The Life and Democratic Writings of William Manning, "A Laborer," 1747–1814*, ed. Michael Merrill and Sean Wilentz (Cambridge, MA: Harvard University Press, 1993), esp. 137; Charles Warren, *Jacobin and Junto; or, Early American Politics as Viewed in the Diary of Dr. Nathaniel Ames, 1788–1822* (Cambridge, MA, 1931), 106–10; *Independent Chronicle*, June 17 and 20, 1799.

49. Cotler, *Tom Paine's America*, 145–56.

50. Perez Fobes, *A Sermon, Preached before His Excellency* (Boston: Young & Minns, 1795), 7, 9, 22.

51. Philip Freneau, "On Some of the Principles of American Republicanism," *New York Time Piece*, May 5, 1797, pp. 1–2.

52. Holton, *Unruly Americans*; *New York Journal*, July 22, 1795.

53. *National Gazette*, Mar. 30, 1789, Sept. 18, 1793; [Vicesimus Knox], *The Spirit of Despotism* (Philadelphia: Lang and Ustick, for Carey, 1795), 84; *Pennsylvania Gazette*, Dec. 5, 1795; *Aurora General Advertiser*, May 27, 1796; William Godwin, *An Enquiry Concerning Political Justice* (Philadelphia: Bioren and Madan, 1796). Cotler notes that "the demo conversation about economic inequality reached a high point in 1796–97 with the American publication of Volney's *Ruins*, William Godwin's *Political Justice*, and Paine's *Agrarian Justice*," which were frequently excerpted in newspapers; *Tom Paine's America*, 150.

54. Thomas Paine, *Agrarian Justice* (Baltimore: Keatinge, 1797), 8–12; "In Press," *Aurora General Advertiser*, May 20, 1797, p. 2.

55. Coram, *Political Inquiries*, 17, 18, 33, 53, 22; Seth Cotlar, "Property for All: Robert Coram and the American Revolution's Legacy of Economic Populism," in *Revolutionary Founders: Rebels, Radicals, and Reformers in the Making of the Nation*, ed. Alfred Young, Gary Nash, and Ray Raphael (New York: Alfred A. Knopf, 2011), 339–55.

56. Coram, *Political Inquiries*, 93; Webster, *A Collection of Essays*, 24, 26; *Rudiments of Law and Government*, 26; "The Free Republican, No. II," *Boston Magazine*, Mar. 1784, p. 193; Benjamin Rush, *A Plan for the Establishment of Public Schools and the Diffusion of Knowledge in Pennsylvania* (Philadelphia: Thomas Dobson, 1786).

57. "On New England Republicanism," *American Museum*, Dec. 1792, 303; Beresford, *Aristocracy the Bane of Liberty*, 14, 19–20; Coram, *Political Inquiries*, 93; Manning, *"The Key of Liberty."*

58. "For the *City Gazette*," *Charleston City Gazette*, Feb. 22, 1793, p. 2, col. 1; Charles William Janson, *The Stranger in America* (London: Albion Press, 1807), ix, 87; see also "Equality," *General Advertiser*, Feb. 5, 1793, p. 2, col. 2. On the decline of honorifics, see Gordon Wood, *The Radicalism of the American Revolution* (New York: Knopf, 1992), 23, 232–34. On the racialization of social hierarchy, see Lois Horton, "From Class to Race in Early America: Northern Post-Emancipation Racial Reconstruction," *Journal of the Early Republic* 19 (1999): 629–49; James B. Stewart, "Modernizing 'Difference': The Political Meanings of Color in the Free States, 1776–1840," *Journal of the Early Republic* 19 (1999): 691–712.

59. John Van Atta, *Securing the West: Politics, Public Lands, and the Fate of the Old Republic, 1785–1850* (Baltimore: Johns Hopkins University Press, 2014), 1–84; Jamie Bernstein, *Two Nations, Indivisible: A History of Inequality in America* (Santa Barbara: Praeger, 2016), 14.

60. [Herman Husband], *A Dialogue Between an Assembly Man and a Convention Man on the Subject of the State Constitution of Pennsylvania* (Philadelphia: Spotswood, 1790), 8, 11; M.S., "For the *Carlisle Gazette*," *Gazette*, July 9, 1794; Slaughter, *Whiskey Rebellion*, 207, citing Carlisle petition, Aug. 14 (dated Aug. 29), 1794, in Rawle Family Papers, I, 31, 132, Historical Society of Pennsylvania, Philadelphia.

61. Columbus [Tucker], *Cautionary Hints to Congress, Respecting the Sale of Western Lands* (Philadelphia: M. Carey, 1796), 6–7, 14; Elhanan Winchester, *A Plain Political Catechism, Intended for the Use of Schools, In the United States of America* (Greenfield, MA: T. Dickman, 1796), 56; McCoy, *Elusive Republic*, 48–75; Jefferson, *Writings*, 818, 836–37, 918.

62. John Mellen, *The great and happy doctrine of liberty. A discourse, delivered at Hanover, Commonwealth of Massachusetts, February 19, 1795* (Boston: Samuel Hall, 1795), 15; William Brown, *An Essay on the Natural Equality of Man, The Rights That Result From It, and On the Duties Which it Imposes* (Philadelphia: William W. Woodward, 1793), 20, 23.

63. "Public Notice Extraordinary," *Martinsburg Potomak Guardian*, May 5, 1796, quoted in Pasley, *First Presidential Contest*, 233.

64. Pasley, *First Presidential Contest*, 218–407; Cotler, *Tom Paine's America*, 55, 83, 98; Henry Cumings, *A Sermon Preached at Billerica, December 15, 1796* (Boston, 1797), 24–25.

65. Nathaniel Emmons, *A Discourse, Delivered May 9, 1798. Being the Day of Fasting and Prayer Throughout the United States* (Newburyport: Angier, 1798), 42; Stanley Elkins and Eric McKitrick, *Age of Federalism: The Early American Republic, 1788–1800* (New York: Oxford University Press, 1995), 549–90.

66. Thomas Day, *An Oration, On Party Spirit* (Litchfield, CT: T. Collier, 1798), 14; Jonathan Maxcy, *An Oration Delivered in the First Congregational Meeting-House in Providence* (Providence: John Carter, 1799); Elkins and McKitrick, *Age of Federalism*, 694–726.

67. John Ferling, *Adams vs. Jefferson: The Tumultuous Election of 1800* (New York: Oxford University Press, 2004), 128–30; Sean Wilentz, *Chants Democratic: New York City and the Rise of the American Working Class, 1788–1850* (New York: Oxford University Press, 1984), 39–103; Ron Chernow, *Alexander Hamilton* (New York: Penguin, 2004), 606–10.

Chapter 5. · Raising Republican Children

1. James O. Horton and Lois E. Horton, *In Hope of Liberty: Culture, Community and Protest among Northern Free Blacks, 1700–1860* (New York: Oxford University Press, 1977), 150–54.

2. Gretchen Adams, "'Pictures of the Vicious ultimately overcome by misery and shame': The Cultural Work of Early National Schoolbooks," in *Children and Youth in the New Nation*, ed. James Marten (New York: New York University Press, 2009), 149–69; Ruth Miller Elson, *Guardians of Tradition: American Schoolbooks of the Nineteenth Century* (Lincoln: University of Nebraska Press, 1964); John A. Nietz, *Old Textbooks* (Pittsburgh: University of Pittsburgh Press, 1961); David Jaffee, "The Village Enlightenment in New England, 1760–1820," *William and Mary Quarterly*, 3rd ser., 47 (1990): 345.

3. Jacqueline Reinier, *From Virtue to Character: American Childhood, 1775–1850* (New York: Twayne, 1996), 21–29.

4. E. Anthony Rotundo, *American Manhood: Transformations in Masculinity from the Revolution to the Modern Era* (New York: Basic Books, 1993), 11–18 (quotation p. 18); Sarah Knott, *Sensibility and the American Revolution* (Chapel Hill: University of North Carolina Press, 2009), 189–201; Jan Lewis, "The Republican Wife: Virtue and Seduction in the Early Republic," *William and Mary Quarterly*, 3rd ser., 44 (1987): 689–721.

5. Reinier, *From Virtue to Character*, 31; Jeffrey L. Pasley, *The First Presidential Contest: 1796 and the Founding of American Democracy* (Lawrence: University Press of Kansas, 2013), 69; *General Advertiser* (Philadelphia), Feb. 5, 1793, pp. 2–3.

6. John Locke, *Some Thoughts Concerning Education and of the Conduct of the Understanding* (London: A. and J. Churchill, 1693), 33; Reinier, *From Virtue to Character*, 32–43.

7. John Adams, "Dissertation on Canon and Feudal Law," *Boston Gazette*, 1765; Thomas Dawes Jr., Esq., "Part of an Oration, Delivered at Boston, on the 4th of July, 1787," *American Magazine*, Aug. 1, 1788, pp. 619–20; "On New England Republicanism," *American Museum, or, Universal Magazine* 12 (Dec. 1792): 303.

8. Thomas Jefferson, "A Bill for the More General Diffusion of Knowledge" (1778), *Writings*, ed. Merrill Peterson (New York: Library of America, 1984), 365–73; Jefferson to Peter Carr, Sept. 7, 1814, *Writings*, 1346–52; *Rudiments of Law and Government, Deduced from the Law of Nature* (Charlestown, SC: John McIver, Jr., 1783), 26.

9. Governor George Clinton, speech to the New York legislature, July 11, 1782, in *State of New York, Messages from the Governors*, ed. Charles Z. Lincoln (Albany: J. B. Lyon, state printers, 1909), 2:183; "The Free Republican, No. II," *Boston Magazine* (Mar. 1784), 193; Benjamin Rush, *A Plan for the Establishment of Public Schools and the Diffusion of Knowledge in Pennsylvania* (Philadelphia: Thomas Dobson, 1786), 10, 17, 3–4; Rush, *Thoughts upon Female Education, Accommodated to the Present State of Society, Manners and Government in the United States of America* (Boston: Samuel Hall, 1787), 6; Noah Webster, *On the Education of Youth in America* (Boston, 1790), reprinted in *Essays on Education in the Early Republic*, ed. Frederick Rudolph (Cambridge, MA: Harvard University Press, 1965), 41–77, quotation p. 70.

10. Clinton, speech, July 11, 1782, in *Messages from the Governors*, 2:183; Rush, *Plan for the Establishment of Public Schools*, 14, 20; Noah Webster, *A Collection of Essays and Fugitiv [sic] Writings* (Boston: Thomas and Andrews, 1790), 24, 26; Carl Kaestle, *Pillars of the Republic: Common Schools and American Society, 1789–1860* (New York: Hill and Wang, 1983), 8.

11. Rudolph, *Essays on Education in the Early Republic*, xv; Samuel Harrison Smith, *Remarks on Education* (1798), in Rudolph, *Essays on Education in the Early Republic*, 188, 187, 210–1; Samuel Knox, *An Essay on the Best System of Liberal Education* (1799), in Rudolph, *Essays on Education in the Early Republic*, 368; Aaron Bancroft, *A Sermon . . . May 27, 1801, the Day of General Election* (Boston: Young and Minns, 1801), 23.

12. Robert Coram, *Political Inquiries* (Wilmington, DE: Andrews & Brynberg, 1791), 92–93; Michael Merrill and Sean Wilentz, eds., *The Key of Liberty: The Life and Democratic Writings of William Manning, "A Laborer," 1747–1814* (Cambridge, MA: Harvard University Press, 1993), 127–64; Eve Cornfield, *Creating an American Culture, 1775–1800* (Boston: Bedford-St. Martin's Press, 2001), 34–36.

13. Kaestle, *Pillars of the Republic*, 1–61; Adams, "Pictures of the Vicious," 150–53; Jason M. Opal, *Beyond the Farm: National Ambitions in Rural New England* (Philadelphia: University of Pennsylvania Press, 2008), 98–122.

14. [Eleazar Moody], *The School of Good Manners* (Boston: Hall, 1790), 7, 25; *The School of Good Manners* (Windsor, VT: Jesse Cochran, 1815), 7; d'Alte Aldridge Welch, "A Bibliography of American Children's Books Printed Prior to 1821," *Proceedings of the American Antiquarian Society* 77 (Apr. 1963): 137; C. Dallett Hemphill, *Bowing to Necessities: A History of Manners in America, 1620–1860* (New York: Oxford University Press, 2002), 233n24. Welch found that much of the work was taken from J. Garretson's *The School of Manners*, printed in England beginning in 1685; Hemphill's more recent work notes that Garretson had translated an even earlier French work on behavior.

15. Reinier, *From Virtue to Character*, 34–35; Elizabeth Harrison, *The Friendly Instructor; or, A companion for young ladies and young gentlemen* (Philadelphia: Joseph Crukshank, 1782), 26–28. "Carriage to Superiors and Inferiors," like many other English children's stories, was reproduced by American publishers in their own collections without attribution; see, for example, *A Collection of Easy and Familiar Dialogues for Children*, 5th ed. (Windsor, VT: Alden Spooner, 179-), 20. Spooner is well-known for publishing children's works first published in England, including Hannah More's writings; conversation with

Laura E. Wasowicz, Curator of Children's Literature, American Antiquarian Society, Worcester, May 22, 2015.

16. *The Sister's Gift; or, the Naughty Boy Reformed. Published for the advantage of the rising generation* (Worcester: Thomas, 1786). The initial publication year of 1769 is given by George Watson, ed., *The New Cambridge Bibliography of English Literature*, 5 vols. (Cambridge: Cambridge University Press, 1969–1977), 2:1021. Alice Morse Earle printed the 1772 list, from an advertisement in the *Boston Gazette and Country Journal*, January 20, 1772, to show what children in New England were reading at the time; Earle, ed., *Diary of Anna Green Winslow: A Boston School Girl of 1771* (Boston: Houghton, Mifflin, 1894), 115–16.

17. M. (Arnaud) Berquin, *The Children's Friend*, 4 vols. (Newburyport, [Mass.]: John Mycall, [1789–90?], 2:36, 47. The work was first published in France, 1782–83, translated and published in London in 1786, and quickly reproduced widely in the United States. William Bentley in his diary entry for Sept. 24, 1790, noted the use of the book in Salem's schools; Bentley, diary.

18. Berquin, *The Children's Friend*, 2:255–56.

19. Harry B. Weiss, *Hannah More's Cheap Repository Tracts in America* (New York: New York Public Library, 1946), 3–9; Hannah More, *Village Politics: Addressed All the Mechanics, Journeymen, and Day Labourers, in Great Britain. By Will Chip, a Country Carpenter*, 5th ed. (York: G. Walker, 1793), quotation p. 4.

20. Hannah More, "The Shepherd of Salisbury-Plain," in *Cheap Repository Tracts*, 2 vols. (Boston: E. Lincoln, 1802), 1:4–5, 10; More, "The History of Diligent Dick," in *Cheap Repository Tracts*, 1:206; Welch, "Bibliography of American Children's Books," 151.

21. Gary J. Kornblith and John M. Murrin, "The Making and Unmaking of an American Ruling Class," in *Beyond the American Revolution: Explorations in the History of American Radicalism*, ed. Alfred Young (DeKalb: Northern Illinois University Press, 1993), 29, 44, 60–63; Gordon Wood, *The Radicalism of the American Revolution* (New York: Knopf, 1991), 194–210 (John Adams quoted on p. 195).

22. More, "The History of Mr. Fantom, the New Fashioned Philosopher, and His Man William," in *Cheap Repository Tracts*, 1:234; Gideon Hawley, Mashpee, to Jeremy Belknap, Aug. 25, 1796, Belknap Papers, P-380, reel 6 of 11, no. 161. B. 159, Massachusetts Historical Society, Boston; Elhanan Winchester, *A Plain Political Catechism. Intended for the Use of Schools, In the United States of America* (Greenfield, MA: T. Dickman, 1796), 69. *Catechism* was published the same year in Philadelphia and in 1806 in Norfolk, Virginia. See generally Christopher Grasso, "Skepticism and Faith," *Common-Place* 9 no. 2 (Jan. 2009), http://www.common-place.org/vol-09/no-02/grasso/; and on Paine and the *Age of Reason*, see Jill Lepore, "A World of Paine," in *Revolutionary Founders: Rebels, Radicals and Reformers in the Making of a Nation*, ed. Alfred Young et al. (New York: Knopf, 2011), 93–96.

23. Winchester, *Plain Political Catechism*, 95; Noah Webster Jr., *A Grammatical Institute of the English Language* (Hartford: Hutson and Goodwin, 1783), 11; Webster Jr., *An American Selection of Lessons in Reading and Speaking, Calculated to Improve the Minds and Refine the Taste of Youth* (1785; New York: Evert Duyckinck, 1804).

24. Jedidiah Morse, *Geography Made Easy . . . Calculated particularly for the Use and Improvement of Schools in the United States* (New Haven, CT: Meigs, Bowen and Dana, 1784), 68, 69; Elijah Parish, *A Compendious System of Universal Geography* (Newburyport, MA: Thomas and Whipple, 1807), 32.

25. Adams, "Pictures of the Vicious," 155–56; Jedidiah Morse, *A Sermon Exhibiting the Present Dangers, and Consequent Duties of the Citizens of the United States of America* (Charlestown: Samuel Etheridge, 1799), 11. A few wrote specifically New England histories, including Hannah Adams with *A Summary History of New-England* (Dedham, MA: H. Mann and J. H. Adams, 1799) and *An Abridgement of the History of New England, For the Use of Young Persons, Now Introduced into the Principal Schools in this Town* ([Boston], 1805); and Jedidiah Morse and Elijah Parish, *A Compendious History of New England, Designed for schools and private families* (1804). There is no record of histories of Pennsylvania, New York, Virginia, or states or regions having been published at the turn of the century. Parish was born in Lebanon, Connecticut, in 1762, graduated from Dartmouth College in 1785, and from 1787 until his death in 1825 served as minister of Byfield (Newbury), Massachusetts; [Moses Parish?], *Sermons, Practical and Doctrinal, by the Late Elijah Parish, D.D., with a Biographical Sketch of the Author* (Boston: Crocker and Brewster, 1826), iv–vi. Winchester was born in Brookline, Massachusetts, began preaching at age nineteen after experiencing a "New Light" conversion, and for the rest of his life moved between Calvinist Baptist and Universalist churches; he is considered one of the founders of Universalism. See Robin Parry, "The Baptist Universalist: Elhanan Winchester (1751–97)," Center for Baptist History and Heritage (Oct. 29, 2011), https://www.academia.edu/8643336/_The_Baptist _Universalist_Elhanan_Winchester_1751_97. On Morse, see Joseph Phillips, *Jedidiah Morse and New England Congregationalism* (New Brunswick, NJ: Rutgers University Press, 1983). On the political and moral beliefs held by the ministers who formed the core of this informal alliance, see Jonathan D. Sassi, *A Republic of Righteousness: The Public Christianity of the Post-Revolutionary New England Clergy* (New York: Oxford University Press, 2001), 11–18, 75–82.

26. Johann David Schoepf, *Travels in the Confederation* [1783–84], trans. Alfred J. Morrison, 2 vols. (1788; Philadelphia: William J. Campbell, 1911), 2:205; Webster, *American Selection of Lessons*, 97. On the extent and nature of deference in early America, see the debate in a special issue of *Early American Studies* 3, no. 2 (Fall 2005).

27. [Moody], *School of Good Manners*, 7, 25; Robert Dodsley, *The Economy of Human Life* (Albany, NY: C. R. and G. Webster, 1801), n.p.; Lindley Murray, *The English Reader* (1799; Hallowell, ME: Calvin Spaulding, 1821), 62; Parish, *Compendious System of Universal Geography*, 32, 28.

28. Christopher L. Tomlins, *Law, Labor, and Ideology in the Early American Republic* (New York: Cambridge University Press, 1993); Charles Sellers, *The Market Revolution: Jacksonian America, 1815–1846* (New York: Oxford University Press, 1991); Gary Kulik, "Dams, Fish and Farmers: Defense of Public Rights in Eighteenth-Century Rhode Island," in *The Countryside in the Age of Capitalist Transformation*, ed. Steven Hahn and Jonathan Prude (Chapel Hill: University of North Carolina Press, 1985), 25–50; Sean Wilentz, *Chants Democratic: New York City and the Rise of the American Working Class, 1788–1850* (New York: Oxford University Press, 1983).

29. Johann Neem, *Democracy's Schools: The Rise of Public Education in America* (Baltimore: Johns Hopkins University Press, 2017), 1–57; Daniel Howe, *What Hath God Wrought: The Transformation of American, 1815–1848* (New York: Oxford University Press, 2007), 453–54; Lawrence Cremin, *American Education: The National Experience, 1783–1876* (New York: Harper and Row, 1980), 132–42, 154–57.

30. Neem, *Democracy's Schools*; Coventry, Rhode Island, "Report of the School Committee for 1847," in *Reports and Documents Relating to the Public Schools in Rhode Island for 1848* (Providence: State Printers, 1849), 137.

31. Howe, *What Hath God Wrought*, 449–53; Cremin, *American Education*, 301 (figures on schoolbook production 1820–50), 391–95 (on the readers and history textbooks published circa 1790–1850).

32. Abner Alden, *The Reader . . . Being the Third Part of a Columbian Exercise* (Boston: Thomas and Andrews, 1802); Daniel Adams, *The Understanding Reader; or, Knowledge Before Oratory, Being a New Selection of Lessons, Suited to the Understanding and the Capacities of Youth, and Designed for their Improvement*, 2nd ed. (Leominster, MA, 1804); Titus Strong, *The Common Reader*, 2nd ed. (Greenfield, MA: Denio and Phelps, 1819). Alden's 1802 edition was also published in Worcester, Albany, and Baltimore; a fifth edition was published in Boston in 1822. See Henry Stevens, *Catalogue of the American Books in the Library of the British Museum* (London, 1867), 14.

33. Charles Shaw, *A Topographical and Historical Description of Boston* (Boston: Oliver Spear, 1817), 170–72; William A. Mowry, *Recollections of a New England Educator, 1838–1908* (New York: Silver, Burdett, 1908), 27; Murray, *English Reader*, 19; William Herndon, *Life of Lincoln* (Cleveland: World Publishing, 1949), 34.

34. John Pierpont, *The American First Class Book; or, Exercises in Reading and Recitation: Selected Principally From Modern Authors of Great Britain and America; and Designed for the Use of the Highest Class in Publick and Private Schools* (Boston: William B. Fowle, 1823), 22, 2 (adoption by Boston school committee); Pierpont, *The National Reader: A Selection of Exercises in Reading and Speaking, Designed to Fill the Same Place in the Schools of the United States that is held in those of Great Britain by the Compilations of Murray, Scott, Enfield, Mylius, Thompson, Ewing, and Others* (1827; Norfolk, England, 1829), 153; "Pierpont's National Reader," City of Boston Archives, https://cityofbostonarchives.omeka .net/items/show/2; Henry Barnard, Commissioner of Public Schools, *Reports and Documents Relating to the Public Schools in Rhode Island for 1848* (Providence: State Printers, 1849), 95. Pierpont's works were among the most popular American textbooks before the Civil War; Nietz, *Old Textbooks*, 68.

35. Howe, *What Hath God Wrought*, 430–39; Paul Gilje, *The Road to Mobocracy: Popular Disorder in New York City, 1763–1834* (Chapel Hill: University of North Carolina Press, 1987), 235–88; Noah Webster, *Instructive and Entertaining Lessons for Youth: With Rules for Reading with Propriety, Illustrated by Examples: Designed for use in Schools and Families* (New Haven: CT: S. Babcock and Durrie and Peck, 1835), 170.

36. Webster, *Instructive and Entertaining Lessons*, 229; Elson, *Guardians of Tradition*, 270–80.

37. Rufus Claggett, *The American Expositor; or, Intellectual Definer. Designed for the Use of Schools*, 2nd ed. (Boston: Gould, Kendall and Lincoln, 1836), v, 62, 94, 102, 106, 166. For a biography of Claggett, see Elisha Dyer, "The Old Schools of Providence," *Narragansett Historical Register* 5 (1886): 231–32.

38. Lydia H Sigourney, *The Boy's Reading Book* (New York: J. Orville Taylor, 1839), 153–54, 122–24; Daniel Adams, *The Monitorial Reader, Designed for the use of Academies and Schools; and as a Monitor to Youth, Holding up their view Models Whereby to form their own Character* (Concord, NH: Boyd and White, 1839), 212–19.

39. Samuel Goodrich, *The Tales of Peter Parley* (Boston: Goodrich, 1827); Goodrich, *Peter Parley's Common School History* (1837), rev. ed. (Philadelphia: E. H. Butler, 1859). WorldCat lists existing editions published every year between 1837 and 1859 except 1847. It was listed among the books used by Providence grammar schools in 1847; Barnard, *Reports and Documents*, 95.

40. Samuel G. Goodrich, *Recollections of a Lifetime; or, Men and Things I have Seen; in a Series of Familiar Letters to a Friend*, 2 vols. (New York: Miller, Orton and Mulligan, 1857), 1:64, 119n; Goodrich, *Fireside education*, 2nd ed. (New York: F. J. Huntington, 1838), 391.

41. Samuel G. Goodrich., *The Fourth Reader, For the Use of Schools* (Boston: Otis, Broaders, 1839), 71,123–25, 253. The *Reader* was also published in Louisville, Kentucky.

42. William H. McGuffey, *The Eclectic Second Reader* (Cincinnati: Truman and Smith, 1836), quotation p. 46, https://archive.org/details/McGuffeys_Readers_The_Eclectic _Second_Reader_1836/page/n7; United States, National Park Service, "William Holmes McGuffey and His Readers," *Museum Gazette*, Jefferson National Expansion Memorial, Experience Your America (Jan. 1993), http://www.nps.gov/jeff/learn/historyculture/upload /mcguffey.pdf; Nietz, *Old Text Books*, 70–80.

43. William H. McGuffey, *The Eclectic Second Reader, Consisting of Progressive Lessons in Reading and Spelling, for the Younger Classes in Schools*, 41st ed. (Cincinnati: Winthrop B. Smith, 1843), 45–47.

Chapter 6. · Clashes over America's Political Economy

1. Seth Luther, *An Address to the Working Men of New England on the State of Education and On the Condition of the Producing Classes in Europe and America*, 2nd ed. (New York: George H. Evans, 1833), 7, 2, 6–7, 16, 26; Luther, *An Address on the Origin and Progress of Avarice, and its Deleterious Effects on Human Happiness, with a Proposed Remedy for the Countless Evils Resulting from an Inordinate Desire for Wealth. Delivered before the Union Association of Working Men in the Town Hall, Charlestown, Mass., Jan 30, 1834* (Boston, 1834), 5, 12, 10, 15, 20–21.

2. For one account of the rural origins and focus of those who embraced ambition and disruptive change during this period, see Jason M. Opal, *Beyond the Farm: National Ambitions in Rural New England* (Philadelphia: University of Pennsylvania Press, 2008).

3. Paul K. Conkin, *Prophets of Prosperity: America's First Political Economists* (Bloomington: Indiana University Press, 1980), 17–26.

4. "Circuit Court Proceedings," *Independent Chronicle* (Boston), June 17, 1799, p. 3, and June 20, 1799, p. 2; Michael Merrill and Sean Wilentz, introduction to *"The Key of Liberty": The Life and Democratic Writings of William Manning, "A Laborer," 1747–1814* (Cambridge, MA: Harvard University Press, 1993), 72–73.

5. Michael J. Thompson, *The Politics of Inequality: A Political History of the Idea of Economic Inequality in America* (New York: Columbia University, 2012), 60–80; Joyce Appleby, *Capitalism and a New Social Order: The Republican Vision of the 1790s* (New York: New York University Press, 1984).

6. Conkin, *Prophets of Prosperity*, 30–40; D. P. O'Brien, *The Classical Economists Revisited* (Princeton, NJ: Princeton University Press, 2014), 1–3, 13–15.

7. Jane Marcet, *Conversations on Political Economy: In Which the Elements of that Science Are Familiarly Explained* (1816; Philadelphia: Moses Thomas, 1817); John Larson, "An Inquiry into the Nature and Causes of the Wealth of Nations," *Journal of the Early Republic* 35 (2015): 15–17. Translations of *Conversations* were published in Paris, Geneva, Germany, and the Netherlands. It was frequently reprinted in London until 1839, and there was one additional edition in 1861.

8. Scott Nelson, *A Nation of Deadbeats: An Uncommon History of America's Financial Disasters* (New York: Knopf, 2012), 48–65; Loammi Baldwin, *Thoughts on the Study of Political Economy* (Cambridge, MA: Hilliard and Metcalf, 1809); Thompson, *Politics of Inequality.*

9. Association of the Mechanics of Boston, *Constitution of the Associated Mechanics of the Town of Boston* (Boston: Folsom, 1795); Sean Wilentz, *Chants Democratic: New York City & the Rise of the American Working Class, 1788–1850* (New York: Oxford University Press, 1984), 68–71; George Burrill, *An Oration, Delivered before the Providence Association of Mechanics and Manufacturers, at their annual election, April 11, 1796* (Providence: B. Wheeler, 1796), 16–18; William Duane, *Politics for American* (Washington City [DC]: R. C. Weightman, 1807), 82.

10. Wilentz, *Chants Democratic*, 70–76, toast quoted p. 71; William Thornton, *Political Economy Founded in Justice and Humanity in a Letter to a Friend by W.T.* (City of Washington: Samuel Harrison Smith, 1804); Seth Cotler, *Tom Paine's America: The Rise and Fall of Transatlantic Radicalism in the Early Republic* (Charlottesville: University of Virginia Press, 2011); Drew McCoy, *The Elusive Republic: Political Economy in Jeffersonian America* (Chapel Hill: University of North Carolina Press, 1980); Appleby, *Capitalism and the New Social Order*; Tristam Burges, *The Spirit of Independence* (Providence: B. Wheeler, 1800).

11. Alan Taylor, "Expand or Die: The Revolution's New Frontier," *Journal of the Early Republic* 37 (2017): 604–10; Jessica Choppin Roney, "1776, Viewed from the West," *Journal of the Early Republic* 37 (2017): 658–62; Colin Calloway, *The Scratch of a Pen: 1763 and the Transformation of North America* (New York: Oxford University Press, 2006), 61–65; Peter Silver, *Our Savage Neighbors: How Indian War Transformed Early America* (New York: Norton, 2008), 282–97; Lindsay G. Robertson, *Conquest by Law: How the Discovery of America Dispossessed Indigenous People of Their Lands* (New York: Oxford University Press, 2005); Edward Baptist, *The Half Has Never Been Told: Slavery and the Making of American Capitalism* (New York: Basic Books, 2014), 18–21.

12. Conkin, *Prophets of Prosperity*, 53–74.

13. Samuel Blodget, *Thoughts on the Increasing Wealth and National Economy of the United States of America* (Washington, DC: Way and Groff, 1801); Blodget, *Economica: A Statistical Manual for the United States of America* (Washington City, 1806).

14. John Larson, *Internal Improvement: National Public Works and the Promise of Popular Government in the Early United States* (Chapel Hills: University of North Carolina Press, 2001), 52–58; Nelson, *Nation of Deadbeats*, 48–59.

15. Andrew Shankman, *Crucible of American Democracy: The Struggle to Fuse Egalitarianism and Capitalism in Jeffersonian Pennsylvania* (Lawrence: University Press of Kansas, 2004); Andrew Schocket, *Founding Corporate Power in Early National Philadelphia* (DeKalb: Northern Illinois University Press, 2007), 51; *Aurora*, May 27, 1805; Thompson,

Politics of Inequality; James Cheetham, *A Dissertation Concerning Political Equality, and the Corporation of New York* (New York: D. Denniston, 1800), 89.

16. Bruce Laurie, *Artisans into Workers: Labor in Nineteenth-Century America* (New York: Hill and Wang, 1989), 50–51; Eric Foner, "Free Labor and Political Ideology," in *The Market Revolution in America: Social, Political, and Religious Expressions, 1800–1880,* ed. Melvyn Stokes and Stephen Conway (Charlottesville: University Press of Virginia, 1996), 99–127; Ronald Schultz, *The Republic of Labor: Philadelphia Artisans and the Politics of Class, 1720–1830* (New York: Oxford University Press, 1993), 160; Wilentz, *Chants Democratic,* 56–59, 96–100; Thompson, *Politics of Inequality,* 81–85.

17. Laurie, *Artisans into Workers,* 47–52; Shankman, *Crucible of American Democracy;* "Ambition," *City Gazette and Daily Advertiser* (Charleston, SC), June 6, 1789, reprinted in *American Political Writing during the Founding Era, 1760–1815,* ed. Charles Hyneman and Donald Lutz, 2 vols. (Indianapolis: Liberty Fund, 1983), 2:712; Baldwin, *Thoughts on the Study of Political Economy,* 64.

18. Jason Opal, "Enterprise and Emulation: The Moral Economy of Turnpikes in Early National New England," *Early American Studies* 8 (2010): 642; Schocket, *Founding Corporate Power,* 69–76; Nelson, *Nation of Deadbeats,* 53–69.

19. Baptist, *The Half Has Never Been Told,* 90–93; Jessica M. Lepler, *The Many Panics of 1837: People, Politics, and the Creation of a Transatlantic Financial Crisis* (New York: Cambridge University Press, 2013), 27; David Jaffee, *A Nation of Goods: The Material Culture of Early America* (Philadelphia: University of Pennsylvania Press, 2010), 17–45; Robert Walsh to Robert Wickliffe, Lexington, KY, Nov. 29, 1815, in Wickliffe-Preston Papers, University of Kentucky, Lexington, quoted in Sarah Kidd, "'To be harassed by my Creditors is worse than Death': Cultural Implications of the Panic of 1819," *Maryland Historical Magazine* 95 (2000): 169.

20. Gary Nash, *The Urban Crucible: Social Change, Political Consciousness, and the Origins of the American Revolution* (Cambridge, MA: Harvard University Press, 1979), 125–27, 184–97, 253–56, 325–38; Paul E. Johnson and Sean Wilentz, *The Kingdom of Matthias: A Story of Sex and Salvation in Nineteenth Century America* (New York: Oxford University Press,1994); Conrad Wright, *The Transformation of Charity in Post-Revolutionary New England* (Boston: Northeastern University Press, 1992); Seth Rockman, ed., *Welfare Reform in the Early Republic: A Brief History with Documents* (Boston: Bedford-St. Martins, 2003), 9–14.

21. Pennsylvania Society for the Promotion of Public Economy, *Report of the Library Committee* (Philadelphia: Merritt, 1817), in Rockman, *Welfare Reform in the Early Republic,* 46 ("Habitual drunkards") and generally 43–48; M. M. (Mordecai Manuel) Noah, *Essays of Howard on Domestic Economy* (New-York: G. L. Birch, 1820), 6; Charles Sellers, *The Market Revolution: Jacksonian America, 1815–1846* (New York: Oxford University Press, 1991), 200–30.

22. SPPE, *Report of the Library Committee,* in Rockman, *Welfare Reform in the Early Republic,* 47; New York Society for the Prevention of Pauperism, *Report of a Committee on the Subject of Pauperism* (New York: Samuel Wood and Sons, 1818), in Rockman, *Welfare Reform in the Early Republic,* 49–56; Herman Humphrey, *On Doing Good to the Poor* (Pittsfield, MA: Phinehas Allen, 1818), in Rockman, *Welfare Reform in the Early Republic,* 58; Stephen Nissenbaum, *The Battle for Christmas* (New York: Random House, 1996), 219–50.

23. Samuel W. Dana, *Observations on Public Principles and Character* (Washington, DC: Gales & Seaton, 1820), 29–32; John Watson, *Annals of Philadelphia and Pennsylvania,*

2 vols. (Philadelphia: Carey and Hart, 1845), 2:303–5; Le Chevalier Felix de Beaujour, *Sketch of the United States of North America . . . From 1800 to 1810, . . . Translated from the French by William Walton* (London, 1814), 145, 155.

24. Nelson, *Nation of Deadbeats*, 62–73.

25. Baptist, *The Half Has Never Been Told*; James L. Hutson, *Securing the Fruits of Labor: The American Concept of the Distribution of Wealth, 1765–1900* (Baton Rouge: Louisiana State University Press, 1998), 63–65.

26. Murray N. Rothbard, *The Panic of 1819: Reactions and Policies* (1962; Auburn, AL: Ludwig von Mises Institute, 2007), 39–231.

27. Mordecai M. Noah, *An address delivered before the General Society of* Mechanics *and Tradesmen of the City of New-York, on the opening of the Mechanic Institution* (New York; William A. Mercein, 1822), 18; Mathew Carey, *Address to the Wealthy of the Land* (Philadelphia: Wm. F. Geddes, 1831), in Rockman, *Welfare Reform in the Early Republic*, 146; Kidd, "To be harassed by my Creditors is worse than Death," 160–78; Edward Pessen, *Riches, Class, and Power before the Civil War* (Lexington, MA: D. C. Heath, 1973).

28. Daniel Raymond, *Thoughts on Political Economy, in 2 parts* (Baltimore: Fielding Lucas, Jr., 1820), esp. 215, 230; Conkin, *Prophets of Prosperity*, 83–104.

29. George Goodfellow, *The Lounger* 1, no. 26 (June 15, 1816); John Brooke, *Columbia Rising: Civil Life on the Upper Hudson from the Revolution to the Age of Jackson* (Chapel Hill: University of North Carolina Press, 2010), 395–97; Conrad Weiser [pseud.?], *To the Free and Independent German Electors of the Commonwealth of Pennsylvania* (1817); Cornelius Blatchly, *Some Causes of Popular Poverty*, in Thomas Branagan, *The Pleasures of Contemplation* (Philadelphia: Eastwick and Stacy, 1817), 194–220, 206 quotation; Schultz, *Republic of Labor*, 206–8.

30. Philip Foner, *William Heighton: Pioneer Labor Leader of Jacksonian Philadelphia* (New York: International Publishers, 1991), 10; Schocket, *Founding Corporate Power*, 162–63; Cornelius Blatchly, *An Essay on Common Wealths* (New York: New York Society for Promoting Communities, 1822); Wilentz, *Chants Democrat*, 159–61.

31. Arthur Bestor, *Backwoods Utopias: The Sectarian Origins and the Owenite phase of Communitarian Socialism in America, 1663–1829*, 2nd ed. (Philadelphia: University of Pennsylvania Press, 1970), 60–83; Wilentz, *Chants Democrat*, 162–63.

32. John Gray (1799–1883), *A Lecture on Human Happiness . . . [and] Articles of Agreement Drawn up and Recommended by the London Co-operative Society* (Philadelphia: D. & S. Neall, 1825), 27–29, 43; Schultz, *Republic of Labor*, 214–16; Foner, *William Heighton*, 13–15.

33. Wilentz, *Chants Democratic*, 87–95, 169–70; Schultz, *Republic of Labor*, 207–8; Paul Johnson, *Sam Patch, the Famous Jumper* (New York: Hill and Wang, 2004), 68–71; Baptist, *Half Has Never Been Told*; Bertram Wyatt-Brown, *Honor and Violence in the Old South* (New York: Oxford University Press, 1986).

34. Langdon Byllesby, *Observations on the sources and effects of unequal wealth* (New York: Lewis J. Nichols, 1826), 36, 53, Wilentz, *Chants Democratic*, 164–65; Conkin, *Prophets of Prosperity*, 234–36.

35. Byllesby, *Observations*, 55, 75, 101; Wilentz, *Chants Democratic*, 164–65; Conkin, *Prophets of Prosperity*, 234–36.

36. William Heighton, *An Address, Delivered Before the Mechanics, and Working Classes Generally, of the City and County of Philadelphia, at the Universalist church in*

Callowhill street, on Wednesday evening, November 21, 1827, by the "Unlettered Mechanic" (Philadelphia, 1827), in Foner, *William Heighton,* 70, 75, 78, 84.

37. Foner, *William Heighton,* 21–33, 42, 45–46, 51–52; John R. Commons et al., eds., *A Documentary History of American Industrial Society,* 10 vols. (Cleveland: Arthur H. Clark, 1910–11), 5:84 (quotations), 84–90 generally. Shortly after the 1830 election, Heighton disappeared from all records.

38. Thomas Skidmore, *The Rights of Man to Property! Being a Proposition to Make it Equal among the Adults of the Present Generation* (New York: Alexander Ming, Jr., 1829); Wilentz, *Chants Democratic,* 184–88; Conkin, *Prophets of Prosperity,* 237–39.

39. Commons et al., *Documentary History,* esp. 5:146, 147, 150; Wilentz, *Chants Democratic,* 190–214. In August 1832, Skidmore died in a cholera epidemic that swept the city.

40. Foner, *William Heighton,* 117n104, 33–35; Commons et al., *Documentary History,* 5:93, 94–107, 110, 108; "Workingmen," *Baltimore Mechanics' Banner and Workingman's Shield,* Mar. 29, 1834; "Remedies for Existing Ills, #3, Inequality of Taxation," *Mechanic's Free Press,* Jan. 30, 1830, p. 2; Luther, *Origin and Progress of Avarice,* 36.

41. Mark Schantz, *Piety in Providence: Class Dimensions of Religious Experience in Antebellum Rhode Island* (Ithaca, NY: Cornell University Press, 2000); William Sutton, *Journeymen for Jesus: Evangelical Artisans Confront Capitalism in Jacksonian Baltimore* (University Park: Pennsylvania State University Press, 1998).

42. Sutton, *Journeymen for Jesus,* 131–34; Lawrence A. Peskin, "Class, Discourse, and Industrialization in the New American Republic," in *Class Matters: Early North America and the Atlantic World,* ed. Simon Middleton and Billy G. Smith (Philadelphia: University of Pennsylvania Press, 2008), 138–55.

43. Joseph Buckingham, *An Address delivered before the Massachusetts Charitable Mechanic Association, Oct. 7, 1830* (Boston: John Cotton, 1830), in *Christian Examiner & General Review* (Nov. 1, 1830): 250–68.

44. Henry Charles Carey, *Principles of Political Economy* (Philadelphia: Carey, Lea & Blanchard, 1837), 339; Laurie, *Artisans into Workers,* 50–52; Schantz, *Piety and Providence,* 46, 158–59, 165.

45. Jonathan Mayhew Wainwright, *Inequality of Individual Wealth the Ordinance of Providence, and Essential to Civilization. [Election sermon], January 7, 1835* (Boston: Dutton and Wentworth, 1835).

46. Francis Wayland, *Elements of Political Economy* (New York: Leavitt, Lord & Company, 1837), 109, 112, 126.

47. Samuel Tibbett DeFord (1787–1870), *An Address Delivered Before the Brutus Fire Society, in Newburyport, at their annual meeting, Jan. 6, 1831* (Newburyport, MA: E. W. Allen, 1831), 4; "The Propriety of Distinctions," *Horae Collegianae* (Oct. 1, 1837): 11–12; "Essay on the Phrenological Causes of the different Degrees of Liberty enjoyed by different Nations," *Annals of Phrenology,* Sept. 1, 1834.

48. Wainwright, *Inequality of Individual Wealth,* 41–42, 45; Willard Phillips, *A Manual of Political Economy* (Boston: Hillard, Gray, Little, and Watkins, 1828), 150–52; Wayland, *Elements of Political Economy,* 454; Censor, *An Appeal to the State* (Columbia, SC, 1831), 5; *Philadelphia National Gazette,* July 10, 1830, p. 2, reprinted in Commons et al., *Documentary History of American Industrial Society,* 5:107–8.

Chapter 7. · Separating Property and Polity

1. Massachusetts, *Journal of Debates and Proceedings in the Convention of Delegates, Chosen to Revise the Constitution of Massachusetts: Begun and Holden at Boston, November 15, 1820, and Continued by Adjournment to January 9* (Boston: Daily Advertiser, 1821), 254–55, 279–80.

2. Mass., *Journal of Debates*, 247–48; William Story, *Life and Letters of Joseph Story* (Boston: Little Brown, 1851), 1:392–94.

3. Mass., *Journal of Debates*, 250–58, quotation p. 253.

4. Alexander Keyssar, *The Right to Vote: The Contested History of Democracy in the United States*, rev. ed. (New York: Basic Books, 2009), 4–5; Willi Paul Adams, *The First American Constitutions: Republican Ideology and the Making of the State Constitutions in the Revolutionary Era* (Chapel Hill: University of North Carolina Press, 1980), 208–9.

5. Keyssar, *Right to Vote*, 9; Holly Brewer, *By Birth or Consent: Children, Law, and the Anglo-American Revolution in Authority* (Chapel Hill: University of North Carolina Press, 2005), 96–126.

6. Keyssar, *Right to Vote*, 5–7; Adams, *First American Constitutions*, 199–207; Gary Nash, *The Urban Crucible: Social Change, Political Consciousness, and the Origins of the American Revolution* (Cambridge, MA: Harvard University Press, 1979), 63, 266, 351.

7. Adams, *First American Constitutions*, 16, 203, 205, 206; Keyssar, *Right to Vote*, 16–17; Oscar Handlin and Mary Handlin, eds., *The Popular Sources of Political Authority: Documents on the Massachusetts Constitution of 1780* (Cambridge, MA: Harvard University Press, 1966).

8. Adams to James Sullivan, May 26, 1776, in *The Works of John Adams, Second President of the United States,* ed. Charles Francis Adams, 10 vols. (Boston: Little, Brown, 1856), 9:378; Keyssar, *Right to Vote*, 340–41; Adams, *First American Constitutions*, 206–8, 293–307; Handlin and Handlin, *Popular Sources of Political Authority*, 437.

9. Adams, *First American Constitutions;* Jackson Turner Main, "Government by the People: The American Revolution and the Democratization of the Legislatures," *William and Mary Quarterly*, 3rd ser., 23 (1966): 391–407. The states that did not specify wealth standards for elected office were Connecticut, Rhode Island, New York, Pennsylvania, and Virginia. Information on income and wealth ca. 1774 is from Jackson Turner Main, *The Social Structure of Revolutionary America* (Princeton, NJ: Princeton University Press, 1965), 78–79.

10. Keyssar, *Right to Vote*, 20 (quotation). In two Connecticut rural towns, the percentage excluded went from 21 percent in 1740 to about 35 percent in 1800; Chilton Williamson, *American Suffrage: From Property to Democracy, 1760–1860* (Princeton, NJ: Princeton University Press, 1960), 27, 123, 166.

11. Keyssar, *Right to Vote*, 17–18; Fletcher Green, *Constitutional Development in the South Atlantic States, 1776–1860* (Chapel Hill: University of North Carolina Press, 1930), 143.

12. Woody Holton, *Unruly Americans and the Origins of the Constitution* (New York: Hill and Wang, 2007); Gordon Wood, *The Radicalism of the American Revolution* (New York: Knopf, 1992), 229–50.

13. Holton, *Unruly Americans*, 182–196.

14. Keyssar, *Right to Vote*, 21–24.

15. Reginald Horsman, *The Frontier in the Formative Years, 1783–1815* (New York: Holt, Rinehart and Winston, 1970), 88–89; John Van Atta, *Securing the West: Politics,*

Public Lands, and the Fate of the Old Republic, 1785–1850 (Baltimore: Johns Hopkins University Press, 2014), 62–66.

16. "On New England Republicanism," *American Museum*, Dec. 1792, 303. This was one of the last issues of the periodical.

17. Keyssar, *Right to Vote*, 23–24; Williamson, *American Suffrage*, 120–23; *The Federalist: The New Jersey Gazette* (Trenton), Dec. 24, 1798, quoted in Williamson, *American Suffrage*, 121.

18. Keyssar, *Right to Vote*, xxiv, 28–29; Green, *Constitutional Development in the South Atlantic States*, 161.

19. Charles G. Steffen, *The Mechanics of Baltimore: Workers and Politics in the Age of Revolution, 1763–1812* (Urbana: University of Illinois Press, 1974), 121–35, quotation p. 131; *Address to the People of Connecticut* (New Haven, 1804); Burgess quoted in Green, *Constitutional Development in the South Atlantic States*, 193; Philo Thropo, "For the Alexandria Herald," *Alexandria (VA) Herald*, Dec. 4, 1811, pp. 2–3.

20. Kyle F. Zelner, *A Rabble in Arms: Massachusetts Towns and Militiamen during King Philip's War* (New York: New York University Press, 2009); 33; Thomas Jefferson, "Virginia Convention," *Niles Weekly Register* 26 (May 15, 1824): 179; *Niles Weekly Register* 20 (April 21, 1821): 113.

21. Williamson, *American Suffrage*, 106–7; Timothy Ford [Americanus], *The Constitutionalist* (Charleston, 1794); Rachel Klein, *Unification of a Slave State: The Rise of the Planter Class in the South Carolina Backcountry, 1760–1808* (Chapel Hill: University of North Carolina Press, 1990), 224–28.

22. "A Quid for Citizen Livingston," *New York Gazette*, July 18, 1798, p. 2; Donald H. Stewart, *The Opposition Press of the Federalist Period* (Albany: State University of New York Press, 1969), 879, 881; Noah Webster, *An Oration, Pronounced before the Citizens of New Haven, On the Anniversary of the Declaration of Independence* (New Haven, CT: Morse, 1802), n18; "From the *Connecticut Courant;* 'Features of the Free Republican Government of Connecticut,'" *Independent Republican, & Miscellaneous Magazine*, Aug. 1, 1805, 12–14.

23. Van Atta, *Securing the West*, 18, 31, 37–44, 50–82; Horsman, *The Frontier in the Formative Years, 1783–1815* (New York: Holt, Rinehart and Winston, 1970), 85–87; Kentucky Constitution of 1792, at http://felonvoting.procon.org/sourcefiles/1792_KY_Constitution.pdf.

24. Horsman, *Frontier in the Formative Years*, 88–91; Van Atta, *Securing the West*, 62–66; William Henry Smith, "A Familiar Talk about Monarchists and Jacobins," *Ohio Archaeological and Historical Publications* 2 (1900): 187–97, St. Clair quotation p. 193; Williamson, *American Suffrage*, 212. In 1808, Congress similarly gave the right to vote for members of Indiana's territorial legislature to men who owned town lots worth at least $100; Horsman, *Frontier in the Formative Years*, 91.

25. Horsman, *Frontier in the Formative Years*, 89–90; Charles Kettleborough, ed., *Constitution Making in Indiana*, 2 vols. (Indianapolis: Indiana Historical Commission, 1916), 1:74; Williamson, *American Suffrage*, 212; 8th Cong., 2nd sess., Doc. 192, *American State Papers*, Miscellaneous, 1:422–23; chapter LXVII, approved Mar. 2, 1819, in *U.S. Statutes at Large iii*, 490 (Alabama authorization); Malcolm Cook McMillan, *Constitutional Development in Alabama, 1798–1901: A Study in Politics, the Negro, and Sectionalism* (Chapel Hill: University of North Carolina Press, 1955), 32.

26. Keyssar, *Right to Vote*; Horsman, *Frontier in the Formative Years*, 89–90; Kettleborough, ed., *Constitution Making in Indiana*, 1:90, 92, 107; McMillan, *Constitutional*

Development in Alabama, 35–36; "The Mississippi Constitution of 1817," *Mississippi History Now,* http://mshistory.k12.ms.us/index.php?s=extra&id=267.

27. "The Right and Power of Suffrage," *Niles Weekly Register* 19 (Oct. 21, 1820): 115–16. The writer also compared voting requirements in Virginia (where only freeholders could vote), New York (only freeholders voted for the senate and governor), Pennsylvania (all taxpayers vote), and Maryland (where all white men could vote)—and the arguments against each standard.

28. Keyssar, *Right to Vote.*

29. *Address to the People of Connecticut, at a Meeting of Delegates from 97 towns in August 1804* (New Haven, 1804); Michael Servetus [pseud.], "The Age of Improvements," *Hartford Times,* Mar. 25, 1817, in *Original Discontents: Commentaries on the Creation of Connecticut's Constitution of 1818,* ed. Richard Buel Jr. and George J. Willauer (Hamden, CT.: Acorn Club, 2007), 33–34.

30. Douglas Arnold, ed., *The Public Records of the State of Connecticut, from May through October 1818,* vol. 19 (Hartford: Connecticut State Library, 2007), 36, 112, 114, 115, 119.

31. *Connecticut Courant,* June 30, 1818, in Arnold, *Public Records,* 111–12; Judd, "The Constitution," No. V, *Hartford Times,* Aug. 18, 1818, in Arnold, *Public Records,* 123–25.

32. "Constitution of Connecticut, 1818," in *New York Convention Manual,* pt. 1, *Constitutions,* 1867, pp. 111–12, https://www.cga.ct.gov/asp/Content/constitutions/1818 _Constitution.pdf; A Freeman, *Connecticut Courant,* Sept. 22, 1818, p. 155, and Sept. 29, 1818, p. 163, in Buel and Willauer, *Original Discontents.*

33. Mass., *Journal of Debates,* 246–54, 279–80; Story, *Life and Letters,* 392–93; Keyssar, *Right to Vote,* 40–41.

34. Merrill Peterson, ed., *Democracy, Liberty, and Property: The State Constitutional Conventions of the 1820s* (1966; Indianapolis: Liberty Fund, 2010), 115–27; John Brooke, *Columbia Rising: Civil Life on the Upper Hudson from the Revolution to the Age of Jackson* (Chapel Hill: University of North Carolina Press, 2010), 172–227, 382–97.

35. New York, *Reports of the Proceedings and Debates of the Convention of 1821* (Albany: E. and E. Gosford, 1821), 215–22, 230–31, 253–54; Peterson, *Democracy,* 172, 174–75. Kent compared this call for universal suffrage in the state to the desire of "the radicals of England" to "sweep away the property, the laws, and the liberties of that island," probably referring to the Hamden Clubs and other unionization efforts; Peterson, *Democracy,* 175.

36. New York, *Reports of the Proceedings and Debates of the Convention of 1821,* 226, 238, 239, 257, 258; Peterson, *Democracy,* 120–25.

37. Philo Thropo, "For the Alexandria Herald," *Alexandria (VA) Herald,* Dec. 4, 1811, pp. 2–3; *Niles Weekly Register* 20 (Apr. 14, 1821); Thomas Jefferson, Monticello, to Samuel Kercheval, July 12, 1816, *Writings* (New York: Library of America, 1984), 1395–1403 (quotation p. 1396); "Chronicle," *Niles Weekly Register* 10 (Aug. 3, 1816): 383; "Staunton Convention," *Niles Weekly Register* 11 (Sept. 7, 1816): 17–21.

38. "Virginia Legislature, House of Delegates, Saturday, January 11," *Richmond Inquirer,* Jan. 14, 1817, p. 3.

39. *Niles Weekly Register* 20 (Apr. 14, 1821): 101; "Virginia," *Niles Weekly Register* 28 (June 4, 1825): 210; Philo, "On the Convention. To the Freeholders in Virginia," *Richmond Inquirer,* Sept. 3, 1824, p. 1; *Richmond Whig,* May 4, 1824; "Virginia," *Niles Weekly Register* 28 (June 4, 1825): 210; *Richmond Impartial Observer,* in Green, *Constitutional Development in*

the South Atlantic States, 193; Peterson, *Democracy, Liberty, and Property*, 245;"Virginia Convention," *Niles Weekly Register* 36 (Aug. 22, 1829): 410.

40. *Proceedings and Debates of the Virginia State Convention of 1829–30* (Richmond: Richie and Cook, 1830), 43–44.

41. *Proceedings and Debates of the Virginia State Convention*, quotations pp. 57, 58, 85.

42. *Proceedings and Debates of the Virginia State Convention*, 66–71, 74–79, 156–62, 164, 292, quotations pp. 156, 157.

43. Harold J. Counihan, "The North Carolina Convention of 1835: A Study in Jacksonian Democracy," *North Carolina Historical Review* 46 (1969): 335–64; Keyssar, *Right to Vote*, 41; David Reid, "To the People of North Carolina," June 28, 1850, *North-Carolina Standard*, July 3, 1850; Lindley S. Butler, ed., *The Papers of David Settle Reid*, vol. 1, *1829–1853* (Chapel Hill: University of North Carolina Press, 1993), xxxix, 55, 250, 252–53.

44. Daniel Howe, *What Hath God Wrought: The Transformation of America, 1815–1848* (New York: Oxford University Press, 2007), 599; Freeman, *Hints to the Farmers of Rhode Island* (Providence: John S. Greene, 1829), 14; Seth Luther, *An Address on the Right of Free Suffrage . . . April 19, and Repeated April 26* (Providence: S. R. Weeden, 1833), 4; Francis Wayland, *Elements of Political Economy* (New York: Leavitt, Lord, 1837), 137.

45. Howe, *What Hath God Wrought*, 600–2; Kirk H. Porter, *A History of Suffrage in the United States* (Chicago: University of Chicago Press, 1918), 93–102.

46. E. Anthony Rotundo, *American Manhood: Transformations in Masculinity from the Revolution to the Modern Era* (New York: Basic Books, 1993), 10–12.

47. Rotundo, *American Manhood*, 18–21.

48. Amy Greenberg, *Cause for Alarm: The Volunteer Fire Department in the Nineteenth-Century City* (Princeton, NJ: Princeton University Press, 1998), 59–70, 113–15.

49. James Oliver Horton and Lois E. Horton, *In Hope of Liberty: Culture, Community, and Protest among Northern Free Blacks, 1700–1860* (New York: Oxford University Press, 1997), 162–73; Nicholas Guyatt, *Bind Us Apart: How Enlightened Americans Invented Racial Segregation* (New York: Basic Books, 2016).

50. Williamson, *American Suffrage*, 104–5; Keyssar, *Right to Vote*, 340–41, 350–51; Green, *Constitutional Development in the South Atlantic States*, 201, 161; Malcolm Cook McMillan, *Constitutional Development in Alabama, 1798–1901: A Study in Politics, the Negro, and Sectionalism* (Chapel Hill: University of North Carolina Press, 1955), 30–36. It is telling that the Cherokee Nation, whose leaders in the 1810s embraced many aspects of American culture, including race-based plantation slavery, wrote a constitution in 1827 (in part to demonstrate its civility to US policymakers) that barred blacks and their children from voting or holding office; "Cherokee Constitution of 1827," in *Cherokee Removal: A Brief History with Documents*, ed. Theda Perdue and Michael Green, 2nd ed. (Boston: Bedford St. Martin's, 2005), 60–69.

51. Keyssar, *Right to Vote*, 349–52; Arnold, *Public Records of the State of Connecticut*, 112, 274.

52. *National Register*, Jan. 31, 1818; New York, *Reports of the Proceedings and Debates of the Convention of 1821*, 180, 190–93; Sean Wilentz, *The Rise of American Democracy: Jefferson to Lincoln* (New York: Norton, 2006), 192–94; Peter J. Galie, *Ordered Liberty: A Constitutional History of New York* (New York: Fordham University Press, 1996), 76–77.

53. Nicholas Wood, "'A Sacrifice on the Altar of Slavery': Doughface Politics and Black Disenfranchisement in Pennsylvania, 1837–1838," *Journal of the Early Republic* 31 (2011): 75–106; Christopher Malone, *Between Freedom and Bondage*, 91–98; Keyssar, *Right to Vote*, 55.

54. Elisha Williams, quoted in Booke, *Columbia Rising*, 382.

55. *Speech of the Honorable Ely Moore . . . In House of Representatives, May 5, 1836* (Washington, DC: Blair and Rives, 1836), 4–5; James R. Leib, *Thoughts on the Elective Franchise* (Philadelphia: John C. Clark, 1839), 14–15.

Chapter 8. · Reviving the Tradition

1. *The Radical, In Continuation of the Workingman's Advocate,* February 1842, 17–19, rear leaf; Helene Sara Zahler, *Eastern Workingmen and National Land Policy, 1829–1862* (New York: Columbia University Press, 1941; New York: Greenwood Press, 1969), 21–36. *The Radical* lasted from June 1841 to April 1843.

2. Jamie Bronstein, *Land Reform and Working-Class Experience in Britain and the United States, 1800–1862* (Palo Alto: Stanford University Press, 1999), 16–17.

3. Donald F. Durnbaugh, "Communitarian Societies in Colonial America," in *America's Communal Utopias,* ed. Donald E. Pitzer (Chapel Hill: University of North Carolina Press, 1997), 14–36.

4. Arthur Bestor, *Backwoods Utopias: The Sectarian Origins and Owenite Phase of Communitarian Socialism in America: 1663–1829,* 2nd ed. (Philadelphia: University of Pennsylvania Press, 1970), 20–35; Yaakov Oved, *Two Hundred Years of American Communes* (New Brunswick, NJ: Transaction Publishers, 1988), 19–33; Karl J .R. Arndt, "George Rapp's Harmony Society," in Pitzer, *America's Communal Utopias,* 60–82.

5. Priscilla J. Brewer, "The Shakers of Mother Ann Lee," in Pitzer, *America's Communal Utopias,* 37–49; Calvin Green and Seth Wells, *A Summary View of the Millennial Church; or, United Society of Believers, (Commonly Called Shakers) . . . Published by Order of the Ministry* (Albany, 1823), 23–24; Bestor, *Backwoods Utopias,* 24–26, 31–32.

6. Brewer, "Shakers of Mother Ann Lee," 44–47, quotation p. 46.

7. Donald E. Pitzer, "Robert Owen and New Harmony," in Pitzer, *America's Communal Utopia,* 111–12; Carl J. Guarneri, *The Utopian Alternative: Fourierism in Nineteenth-Century America* (Ithaca, NY: Cornell University Press, 1991), 80–81, 438n62; Horace Greeley, "A Sabbath with the Shakers," *Pennsylvania Inquirer and Daily Courier,* July 23, 1838.

8. Daniel Walker Howe, *What Hath God Wrought: The Transformation of America, 1815–1848* (New York: Oxford University Press, 2007), 313–19, 723–31; J. Spencer Fluhman, "Communitarianism and Consecration in Mormonism," in *The Oxford Handbook of Mormonism,* ed. Terry L. Givens and Philip L. Barlow (New York: Oxford University Press, 2015), 577–82; Leonard J. Arrington, Feramorz Y. Fox, and Dean L. May, *Building the City of God: Community and Cooperation among the Mormons,* 2nd ed. (Urbana: University of Illinois Press, 1992), 43–60, 63–78.

9. Howe, *What Hath God Wrought,* 285–89, 302–3; Gerrard Winstanley, "England's Spirit Unfoulded; Or, an Incouragement to The *Engagement*" (1650), ed. G. E. Aylmer, *Past and Present* 40 (1968): 10; Gerrard Winstanley et al, *The True Levellers Standard Advanced; Or, The State of Community Opened, and Presented to the Sons of Men* (London, 1649).

10. Cornelius Blatchly, *Some Causes of Popular Poverty*, in Thomas Branagan, *The Pleasures of Contemplation* (Philadelphia: Eastwick and Stacy, 1817), 194–220, 206 quotation; Ronald Schultz, *The Republic of Labor: Philadelphia Artisans and the Politics of Class, 1720–1830* (New York: Oxford University Press, 1993), 206–8; Dan McKanan, "The Dialogue of Socialism," *Harvard Divinity Bulletin* 38 (2010), http://www.hds.harvard.edu /news-events/harvard-divinity-bulletin/articles/the-dialogue-of-socialism.

11. Robert P. Sutton, *Communal Utopias and the American Experience: Secular Communities, 1824–2000* (Westport, CT: Praeger, 2004); Pitzer, "Robert Owen and New Harmony," 107; McKanan, "The Dialogue of Socialism"; Langdon Byllesby, *Observations on the Sources and Effects of Unequal Wealth* (New York: Lewis J. Nichols., 1826), 88–136.

12. Sutton, *Communal Utopias*, 1–18; Pitzer, "Robert Owen and New Harmony."

13. Isidore Lowenstern, *Les Etats-Unis et la Havane souvenirs d'un Voyage* (1842), 181.

14. Orestes Brownson, *The Laboring Classes, An Article from the Boston Quarterly Review*, 3rd ed. (Boston: Benjamin Greene, 1840), 11; Guarneri, *The Utopian Alternative*, 37–38; 63–68; Stephen Nissenbaum, *The Battle for Christmas* (New York: Knopf, 1996), 90–257; Alfred F. Young, *The Shoemaker and the Tea Party: Memory and the American Revolution* (Boston: Beacon Press, 2000), 132–80.

15. Sutton, *Communal Utopias*, 23–25; Guarneri, *The Utopian Alternative*, 1–32.

16. Oved, *Two Hundred Years*, 130–32; Sutton, *Communal Utopias*, 25–27; Guarneri, *The Utopian Alternative*, 36–44; Bronstein, *Land Reform and Working-Class Experience*, 103.

17. H[enry] H. Van Amringe, *Association and Christianity, Exhibiting the Anti-Moral and Anti-Christian Character of the Churches and the Social Relations in Present Christendom: and Urging the Necessity of Industrial Association, Founded on Christian Brotherhood and Unity* (Pittsburgh: J. W. Cook, 1845), 9, 25, 38.

18. Sutton, *Communal Utopias*, 26; Guarneri, *The Utopian Alternative*, 64–69; Oved, *Two Hundred Years*, 131.

19. Christopher Clark, *The Communitarian Moment: The Radical Challenge of the Northampton Association* (Ithaca, NY: Cornell University Press, 1995), 2; Chris Jennings, *Paradise Now: The Story of American Utopianism* (New York: Random House, 2016), 188–202; Anne C. Rose, *Transcendentalism as a Social Movement, 1830–1850* (New Haven, CT: Yale University Press, 1981), 132–35.

20. Rose, *Transcendentalism as a Social Movement*, 140–59.

21. Rose, *Transcendentalism as a Social Movement*, 118–130; "root is selfishness" in Alcott to SJM, Aug. 10, 1840, p. 118; "man has no moral claim," in Alcott, "Diary," entry for Aug. 12, 1841, quoted p. 119; and "we do not recognize purchase of land," quoted p. 122, all in Rose, *Transcendentalism as a Social Movement*.

22. Clark, *Communitarian Moment*.

23. Robin Einhorn, *American Taxation, American Slavery* (Chicago: University of Chicago Press, 2006).

24. Edward Countryman, *A People in Revolution: The American Revolution and Political Society in New York, 1760–1790* (Baltimore: Johns Hopkins University Press, 1981), 15–25; Reeve Huston, *Land and Freedom: Rural Society, Popular Protest, and Party Politics in Antebellum New York* (New York: Oxford, 2000); Oscar Handlin and Irving Mark, "Chief Daniel Nimham v. Roger Morris, Beverly Robinson, and Philip Philipse—An Indian Land Case in Colonial New York, 1765–1767," *Ethnohistory* 11 (1964): 193–246.

25. Huston, *Land and Freedom*, 39, 46, 59, 63–86.

26. Huston, *Land and Freedom*, 90–124; Handlin and Mark, "Chief Daniel Nimham v. Roger Morris."

27. Huston, *Land and Freedom*, 98–134.

28. Lewis Masquerer, *Sociology* (New York, 1877), 95, 132–34; Thomas Devyr, *Odd Book of the 19th Century* (Greenpoint, NY, 1882), 40–43; Gregory Claeys, "Lewis Masquerader and the Later Development of American Owenism, 1835–1845," *Labor History* 42 (2001): 230–37; Edward Pessen, *Most Uncommon Jacksonians: The Radical Leaders of the Early Labor Movement* (Albany: State University of New York Press, 1967), 71–75; Huston, *Land and Freedom*, 137; *Working Man's Advocate*, Mar. 16, 1844, p. 1.

29. "Equal Rights to Land," *Working Man's Advocate*, Mar. 16, 1844, p. 2.

30. John R. Van Atta, *Securing the West: Politics, Public Lands, and the Fate of the Old Republic, 1785–1850* (Baltimore: Johns Hopkins University Press, 2014), 35–40; Roy M. Robbins, *Our Landed Heritage: The Public Domain, 1776–1970*, 2nd ed. rev. (Lincoln: University of Nebraska Press, 1976), 6–14.

31. Van Atta, *Securing the West*, 35–40, 50.

32. Van Atta, *Securing the West*, 53, 56, 62–66; Daniel Feller, *The Public Lands in Jacksonian Politics* (Madison: University of Wisconsin Press, 1984), 26–32.

33. Van Atta, *Securing the West*, 108–10, 124, 186–91, 207–10.

34. Evans, "To the Public," *Working Man's Advocate*, Mar. 16, 1844, p. 1.

35. "Our Principles," *Working Men's Advocate*, Apr. 6, 1844, p. 2.

36. "To the People of the United States," *Working Man's Advocate*, July 6, 1844, p. 1; "Which is Best, The Life of the Indian Savage or the White Operative?," *Working Man's Advocate*, Aug. 10, 1844, p. 4.

37. "Constitution of the NRA," *Working Man's Advocate*, Mar. 30, 1844, p. 4. The Committee was made up of a delegate elected from each ward in New York City and Brooklyn plus one delegate from Williamsburg village and one from Jersey City.

38. "Remarks of Mr. Commerford at Meeting March 20," *Working Men's Advocate*, Mar. 30, 1844, p. 4. On Commerford, see Sean Wilentz, *Chants Democrats: New York City and the Rise of the American Working Class, 1788–1850* (New York: Oxford University Press, 1984), 225, 233–35.

39. Zahler, *Eastern Workingmen*, 42–54; Mark Lause, *Young America: Land, Labor, and the Republican Community* (Urbana: University of Illinois Press, 2005), 16–31. For example, the "Working Men's Meeting" in Columbiana County, Ohio, had eight demands including six unrelated to NRA goals; *Working Men's Advocate*, Jan. 4, 1845, p. 1.

40. Thomas Devyr, *Our Natural Rights: A Pamphlet for the People*. Originally Published in Belfast, Ireland, 1835. (Williamsburg, NY, 1842), 25, 38, 60, 55, 57; Devyr to the *Helderberg Advocate*, Feb. 22, 1842, reprinted in Devyr, *The Odd Book of the Nineteenth Century* (Greenpoint, NY, 1882), pt. 2, 42–43.

41. *Working Men's Advocate*, Jan. 4, 1845, p. 3; Hutson, *Land and Freedom*, 145, 139.

42. *Young America*, June 28, 1845, p. 2; *The Jubilee: A Plan for Restoring the Land of New-York or (Incidentally) of any Other State to THE PEOPLE* (New York, 1845), 3, 5, 8–9. Although the columns reprinted in *Jubilee* were authored anonymously, Devyr seems the most likely author because the writer notes at one point that he had been a member of a

committee "of the first National Convention of Reformers," which seems to have been the Anti-Rent Convention called by Devyr in early 1845.

43. Hutson, *Land and Freedom*, 138–49.

44. Hutson, *Land and Freedom*, 150–74; Devyr, *Odd Book*, 2: 42–51; Lause, *Young America*, 40.

45. "Industrial Convention," *Young America*, Oct. 18, 1845, p. 2, col. 2 (resolutions passed by the Convention), col. 3 ("Anti-Slavery men," etc.); "Constitution of the Industrial Congress," *Young America*, Oct. 25, 1845, p. 3, col. 1 ("Rights" and "Redeem"); Lause, *Young America*; 30–46.

46. Guarneri, *Utopian Alternative*, 71 (on Van Amringe); *Niles National Register*, Mar. 14, 1846, p. 24; Zahler, *Eastern Workingmen and National Land Policy*, 73, 133–34.

47. *Journal of the House of Representatives of the United States, being the first session of the thirtieth Congress, begun and held at the city of Washington, December 6, 1847* (Washington: Wendell and Van Benthuysen, 1848–49), 540; Zahler, *Eastern Workingmen and National Land Policy*, 134–35; George W. Julian, "The Spoliation of the Public Lands," *North American Review* 141 (Aug. 1, 1885): 179.

48. Lause, *Young America*, 68–71; *The Harbinger* 3 (June 30, 1846) (on the NEWA meeting).

49. Lause, *Young America*, 93–97, 107–8; David M. Potter, *The Impending Crisis, 1848–1861* (New York: Harper, 1976), 75, 80–82, 142–43. The November 2, 1850, issue is the last one in the collection of the American Antiquarian Society.

50. Zahler, *Eastern Workingmen and National Land Policy*, 98n44; "Land Office," *Portland (ME) Pleasure Boat*, Apr. 12, 1849, p. 1; "Land Limitation and Homestead Exemption," and "Freedom of the Public Lands," both in *Young America*, Oct. 12, 1850, p. 4; Lause, *Young America*, 106. Nearly half of the petitions came from New England and the Mid-Atlantic states, a third from the Midwest, and the remainder from the South (Lause, 106).

51. Julian, "The Spoliation of the Public Lands," 175–85; Johnson, "The Homestead," *Congressional Globe*, 31st Cong., 1st sess. Dec. 3, 1849–Sept. 30, 1850, 951.

52. Zahler, *Eastern Workingmen and National Land Policy*, 99–106, 147–75; Julian, "The Spoliation of the Public Lands," 175–85.

53. Zahler, *Eastern Workingmen and National Land Policy*, 174–90.

Chapter 9. · Reconstruction and the Rejection of Economic Equality

1. Laura M. Towne, *Letters and Diary . . . Written from the Sea Islands of South Carolina, 1862–1884*, ed. Rupert S. Holland (Cambridge, MA: Riverside Press, 1912), 103; Steven Hahn, *Nation under Our Feet: Black Political Struggles in the Rural South from Slavery to the Great Migration* (Cambridge, MA: Harvard University Press, 2003), 127–38.

2. *United States Chronicle* (Providence, RI), June 21, 1787; "Debate on the Missouri Bill," *Daily National Intelligencer*, Aug. 10, 1820; "Discourse Delivered at Walden, July 4, 1825," *Evangelical Witness*, Sept. 1, 1825; "The Jubilee," *Saratoga Sentinel*, July 4, 1826; "The Sorrows of Anglo," *Freedom's Journal*, June 8, 1827; "On the Anniversary of our Independence," *Beran*, Aug. 22, 1826, reprinted from the *Norfolk Herald*; "National Jubilee," *Boston Recorder and Telegraph*, June 2, 1826.

3. Gary B. Nash, *The Liberty Bell* (New Haven: Yale University Press, 2010), 37–40. By July 4, 1839, a long article ("The Traveller: Liberty Bell") in *Youth's Cabinet*, a children's magazine, seemed to assume that was the official name of the Bell. I searched the American Antiquarian Society's periodical database for "liberty bell" and "slavery" in the "full text" field, and the first relevant article, "The Liberty Bell," appeared in the *Anti-Slavery Record* in February 1835. "Liberty Bell," *USHistory.org*, http://www.ushistory.org/libertybell/, reports that the first association of the bell as a symbol of abolitionism was in the frontispiece of the 1837 edition of *Liberty*, published by the New York Anti-Slavery Society.

4. "The Year of Jubilee," *Puritan Recorder*, Jan. 10, 1850.

5. "Jubilee Catechism," *Monthly Jubilee*, Sept. 1, 1855, 63, 62; "Land-Monopoly and Chattel Slavery," *Vanguard*, June 13, 1857, p. 116; "Causes and Cure of Poverty," no. 9, "Mania of Speculation in America," *Principia*, Nov. 17, 1860, p. 424. For more on the Associated Working Men and Women and its Jubilee, see Anthony F. C. Wallace, *Rockdale: The Growth of an American Village in the Early Industrial Revolution* (New York: Knopf, 1978), 454.

6. James Horton and Lois Horton, *In Hope of Liberty: Culture, Community and Protest among Northern Free Blacks, 1700–1860* (New York: Oxford University Press, 1997), 91, 170–72; Richard Archer, *Jim Crow North: The Struggle for Equal Rights in Antebellum New England* (New York: Oxford University Press, 2017), 31–39; Maurice Jackson, *Let This Voice Be Heard: Anthony Benezet, Father of Atlantic Abolitionism* (Philadelphia: University of Pennsylvania Press, 2009), 276–78.

7. Robert L. Tsai, "John Brown's Constitution," *Boston College Law Review* 51 (2010): 151–206; "What Is To Be Done With the Slaves?," *Weekly Anglo-African* (New York), Nov. 21, 1861, University of Detroit Mercy, Special Collections, Black Abolitionist Archive, http://research.udmercy.edu/find/special_collections/digital/baa/item.php?record_id =1383&collectionCode=baa.

8. "Notes From the Capital," *The Independent* (New York), Aug. 8, 1861, p. 8; "Facts and Phases of the War," *Circular*, Dec. 19, 1861, p. 179; Edward McPherson, *The Political History of the United States, During the Great Rebellion* (Washington, DC: Philp & Solomons, 1865), 195; "Confiscation Bill," *Advent Herald,* Dec. 21, 1861, p. 397.

9. Adam Gurowski, *Diary, from March 4, 1861, to November 12, 1862* (Boston: Lee and Shepard, 1862), entry for Dec. 1861, 129–30.

10. *Congressional Globe*, 37th Cong., 2nd sess., 1861–62, 60–67 (McDougall), 185–86 (Harding), 137–38 (Dolittle), 1074–76 (Morrill), 174 (Spaulding); "Congress," *Independent*, May 8, 1862, p. 8; "The Confiscation and Emancipation Bill," *Morning Star* (Dover, NH), July 23, 1862, p. 67.

11. Charles Sumner, *His Complete Works*, 20 vols. (Boston: Lee and Shepard, 1900), 9:74–75; George W. Julian, *Political Recollections, 1840–1872* (Chicago: Jansen, McClurg, 1884), 215; *Congressional Globe*, 37th Cong., 2nd sess., 1861–62, 184–85, 171–74.

12. McPherson, *Political History of the United States,* 196–98; Julian, *Political Recollections,* 219.

13. Steven Hahn et al., eds., *Freedom: A Documentary History of Emancipation, 1861–1867*, ser. 3, vol. 1, *Land and Labor, 1865* (Chapel Hill: University of North Carolina Press, 2008), 685, 713–14; Rene Hayden et al., eds., *Freedom: A Documentary History of Emancipation, 1861–1867*, ser. 3, vol. 2, *Land and Labor, 1866–1867* (Chapel Hill: University of

North Carolina Press, 2013), 757–58; Towne, *Letters and Diary*, 103; "Freedmen to Become Landholders," *Principia*, reprinted in *American Missionary* (Nov. 1, 1863): 250.

14. Douglas R. Egerton, The *Wars of Reconstruction: The Brief, Violent History of America's Most Progressive Era* (New York: Bloomsbury Press, 2014), 99; "Wendell Phillips at Cooper Institute," *New York Times*, Dec. 23, 1863; "The Abolition Programme," *The World*, from the *National Anti-Slavery Standard* (New York), Jan. 2, 1864, p. 1; "A Good Word for the Freedman," *National Anti-Slavery Standard*, Feb. 13, 1864, p. 2.

15. *Congressional Globe*, 38th Cong., 1st sess., 1863–64, 1185–89, 2249–53 (quotations, 2251); LaWanda Cox, "A Promise of Land for the Freedmen," *Journal of American History* 45 (1958): 414; Julian, *Political Recollections*, 238, 242, 246. On widespread Republican support for breaking up southern plantations and providing farms for freedmen, see generally Cox, "Promise of Land."

16. Various *New Orleans Tribune* articles, 1864–65, quoted in Hahn, *Nation under Our Feet*, 142–43; "Our Freedmen," *Zion's Herald and Wesleyen [sic] Journal*, June 15, 1864, p. 93; Eric Foner, *Politics and Ideology in the Age of the Civil War* (New York: Oxford University Press, 1980), 131–32; Cox, "Promise of Land."

17. Hahn, *Freedom*, 1:396–97; "Gen. Sherman Taking Advice of the Negroes," *Anti-Slavery Standard*, Feb. 18, 1865, p. 3.

18. Cox, "Promise of Land"; "An Act to Establish a Bureau for the Relief of Freedmen and Refugees," *Freedmen's Record*, May 1, 1865, p. 82.

19. Annette Gordon-Reed, *Andrew Johnson* (New York: Henry Holt, 2011), 17–34, 98–111; "A Straw," *Independent* (New York), April 27, 1865, p. 4.

20. Hahn, *Freedom*, 1:8–10; Gordon-Reed, *Andrew Johnson*; M. C. Miegs, Quartermaster General, to General O. Howard, Aug. 22, 1865, in Hahn, *Freedom*, 1:427–28; Richard White, *The Republic for Which It Stands: The United States during Reconstruction and the Gilded Age, 1865–1896* (New York: Oxford University Press, 2017), 35–39.

21. Hahn et al., *Freedom*, 1:174–78, 398–401, 618; White, *Republic for Which It Stands*, 41–43, 56–57, 59; Circular No. 13, July 28, 1865, in Hahn et al., *Freedom*, 1:423–24; Egerton, *Wars of Reconstruction*, 106.

22. Thaddeus Stevens, "Reconstruction" speech, Sept. 6, 1865, in *The Selected Papers of Thaddeus Stevens*, ed. Beverly Wilson Palmer and Holly Byers Ochoa, 2 vols. (Pittsburgh: University of Pittsburgh, 1998), 2:14–26. The speech was printed in the *Lancaster Daily Evening Express* and in many newspapers throughout the nation, including the *New York Times*, September 10, 1865, p. 2.

23. James McPherson, *The Negro's Civil War: How American Negroes Felt and Acted during the War for the Union* (New York: Pantheon Books, 1965), 29 ("Tell Lincoln"); Hahn et al., *Freedom*, 2:215–16, 715–16, 757–58; Egerton, *Wars of Reconstruction*, 98, 108–11, 208 ("All de land").

24. Hahn et al., *Freedom*, 1:713–14; 2:215–16, 357–58, 715–716, 757–58 (quotation 357); Joe A. Mobley, *James City: A Black Community in North Carolina, 1863–1900* (Raleigh: Division of Archives and History, North Carolina Department of Cultural Resources, 1981), 43–68.

25. Jonathan E. Smith to Howard, Freedmen's Bureau Commissioner, June 22, 1865, in Hahn et al., *Freedom*, 1: 100; bureau assistant commissioner's testimony quoted in Hahn et al., *Freedom*, 1:798; Hahn, *Nation under Our Feet*, 130.

26. Egerton, *Wars of Reconstruction,* 112; letters regarding Rexford, in Hahn et al., *Freedom,* 1:29–31, quotation p. 131; commander of detachment of Mississippi black soldiers to Howard, Bureau Commissioner, July 8, 1865, in Hahn et al., *Freedom,* 1:618; Capt. O. Brown, Assistant Bureau Commissioner, for Virginia, to General Howard, Bureau Commissioner, June 6, 1865, in Hahn et al., *Freedom,* 1:337; Grant to President Johnson, December 18, 1865, *Congressional Globe,* 39th Cong., 1st sess., 1864–65, 78.

27. Col. J. P. Shined Gobin, Commander of the fourth subdistrict of the eastern district of South Carolina, to Maj. Gen Gillmore, Commander of the Department of South Carolina, Aug. 17, 1865, on role of black soldiers, in Hahn et al., *Freedom,* 1:381–83; for reports of the beliefs in this "gift," see Hahn et al., *Freedom,* 1:290, 293, 381, 477, 480, 736n, 809, 814, 820–21, 835–37, 841, 854, 862, 866, 869, 878, 892, 897, 946, 995; Freedmen's Bureau acting sub-assistant, Georgia District, to Commissioner Howard, Nov. 28, 1865, in Hahn et al., *Freedom,* 1:855–56; on the four seals, see Edwin Magdol, *A Right to the Land: Essays on the Freedmen's Community* (Westport, CT: Greenwood Press, 1977), 141.

28. Magdol, *Right to the Land,* 140; Egerton, *Wars of Reconstruction,* 112–14; Hahn, *Nation under Our Feet,* 153.

29. Hahn et al., *Freedom,* 1:401–5; "The Freedman's Bureau Again," *Independent,* Oct. 12, 1865, p. 4.

30. Mary Ames, *From a New England Woman's Diary in Dixie in 1865* (Springfield, MA, 1906), 95–97; Henry Bram, Ishmael Moultrie, and Yates Sampson to General Howard, Oct. 19, 1865, in Hahn et al., *Freedom,* 1:440–41; Bram et al. to President Johnson, Oct. 28, 1865, in Hahn et al., *Freedom,* 1:443; Hahn, *Nation under Our Feet,* 144.

31. J. S. Fullerton, Adjutant of the Freedmen's Bureau Commission, South Carolina, to the Commissioner, July 28, 1865, in Hahn et al., *Freedom,* 1:148; Peter Johnson, North Carolina freedman, to the President, Nov. 23, 1865, in Hahn et al., *Freedom,* 1:723–24, quotation p. 724; "Report of a Speech by a Virginia Freedman" (Wyatt), in Hayden et al., *Freedom,* 2:338. See generally Magdol, *Right to the Land,* 170–72.

32. Magdol, *Right to the Land,* 165–70; Hayden et al., *Freedom,* 2:49–52, 55–56, 213–25; "The Freedman's Bureau Again," *Independent,* Oct. 12, 1865, p. 4; "Distress Among the Freedmen." *Liberator,* Dec. 1, 1865.

33. Egerton, *Wars of Reconstruction,* 124–27; Magdol, *Right to the Land,* 159; Stevens, *Selected Papers,* 2: 81.

34. *Congressional Globe,* 39th Cong., 1st sess., 1865–66, 716; Hayden et al., *Freedom,* 2:886–92; Magdol, *Right to the Land,* 160; Michael Lanza, *Agrarianism and Reconstruction Politics: The Southern Homestead Act* (Baton Rouge: Louisiana State University Press, 1990).

35. Eric Foner, *Reconstruction: The Unfinished Revolution* (New York: Harper Collins, 1988; History Book Club edition, 2005), 264–77; Egerton, *Wars of Reconstruction,* 217–21.

36. *Congressional Globe,* 40th Cong., 1st sess., 1867, 15, 49–51.

37. *Congressional Globe,* 40th Cong., 1st sess., 1867, 205; Foner, *Politics and Ideology,* 135.

38. *Congressional Globe,* 40th Cong., 1st sess., 1867, 208, 51; Foner, *Reconstruction,* 309; *Philadelphia Inquirer,* Apr. 19, 1867, p. 4; Foner, *Reconstruction,* 305, 309, generally 304–6; Heather Cox Richardson, The *Death of Reconstruction: Race, Labor, and Politics in the Post-Civil War North, 1865–1901* (Cambridge, MA: Harvard University Press, 2001), 54–55; Egerton, *Wars of Reconstruction,* 252, 225; *Boston Daily Advertiser,* June 13, 1867, p. 2;

"Gerrit Smith's Speech at Richmond," *New York Herald*, May 16, 1867, p. 6; Louisiana Republican newspaper quoted in Foner, *Reconstruction*, 306.

39. *Congressional Globe*, 40th Cong., 1st sess., 1867, 51–52, 467; Charles Sumner, *The Works of Charles Sumner* (Boston: Lee and Shepard, 1870–83), vol. 15 (1877): 124–35.

40. *Congressional Globe*, 40th Cong., 2nd sess., 1867–68, 108, 110, 112, and generally 108–17; Hans L. Trefousse, *The Radical Republicans: Lincoln's Vanguard for Racial Justice* (New York: Knopf, 1969), 371–74, 436–39.

41. *Congressional Globe*, 40th Cong., 2nd sess., 1867–68, 112.

42. General Davis Tillson, speech to Georgia convention (printed), Oct. 31, 1865, in Hahn et al., *Freedom*, 1:295; White, *Republic for Which It Stands*, 61; General Order 13, Mississippi Freedmen's Bureau Assistant Commissioner, Oct 31, 1865, in Hahn et al., *Freedom*, 1:290; generally White, *Republic for Which It Stands*, 65–66.

43. Foner, *Politics and Ideology*, 100–2, 104; White, *Republic for Which It Stands*, 57–61, 76–77; Hayden et al., *Freedom*, 1:72–74; General O. O. Howard, Aug. 28, 1865, address to midwestern freedmen's aid reps, reprinted in *The Radical Republicans and Reconstruction, 1861–1870*, ed. Harold M. Hyman (New York: Bobbs-Merrill, 1967), 214.

44. Foner, *Politics and Ideology*, 103–25; Egerton, *Wars of Reconstruction*, esp. 118, 113–32; Hayden et al., *Freedom*, 68–69, 74; White, *Republic for Which It Stands*, 46–48, 31–33.

45. *Liberty, and Equality Before the Law. Proceedings of the Convention of Colored People of Virginia, held in the City of Alexandria, Aug. 2, 3, 4, 5, 1865* (Alexandria: Cowing and Gillis, 1865), 9, 22; Richardson, *Death of Reconstruction*, 54–55; Foner, *Reconstruction*, 304–306.

46. *Congressional Globe*, 39th Cong., 1st sess., 1865–66, 536; Foner, *Reconstruction*, 133; *Boston Daily Advertiser*, June 13, 1867; "Land for the Landless," *The Nation*, May 16, 1867, p. 395.

47. *Boston Daily Advertiser*, June 13, 1867; *Congressional Globe*, 40th Cong., 1st sess., 50–51; "How Pardons Might be Purchased; Agrarianism in a New Dress," *New York Times*, July 9, 1867; James Huston, *Securing the Fruits of Labor: The American Concept of Wealth Distribution, 1765–1900* (Baton Rouge: Louisiana State University Press, 1998), 328–36.

48. *Boston Daily Advertiser*, June 13, 1867; Foner, *Politics and Ideology*, 147–48; "The Agrarians—Division of Property," *DeBow's Review* 6 (Dec. 1867): 586–87.

Epilogue

1. Staughton Lynd, *Intellectual Origins of American Radicalism* (New York: Pantheon Books, 1968), 86–88; Ronald Schultz, *The Republic of Labor: Philadelphia Artisans and the Politics of Class, 1720–1830* (New York: Oxford University Press, 1993), 212–22.

2. Michael J. Thompson, *The Politics of Inequality: A Political History of the Idea of Economic Inequality in America* (New York: Columbia University, 2012), 63.

3. Richard Hofstadter, *The American Political Tradition and the Men Who Made It* (1948; New York: Knopf, 1973), 217.

4. Thompson, *Politics of Inequality*, 118–25; Jamie Bronstein, *Two Nations, Indivisible: A History of Inequality in America* (Santa Barbara, CA: Praeger, 2016), 37, 45–55.

5. John L. Thomas, *Alternative America: Henry George, Edward Bellamy, Henry Demarest Lloyd, and the Adversary Tradition* (Cambridge, MA: Harvard University Press,

1983); Thompson, *Politics of Inequality*, 109–17; Bronstein, *Two Nations, Indivisible*, 40–44, 49–52; Richard White, *The Republic for Which It Stands: The United States during Reconstruction and the Gilded Age, 1865–1896* (New York: Oxford University Press, 2017), 345–54, 649–53. The Knights welcomed all workers including women and blacks but regarded Chinese as subservient slaves, and the Great Upheaval of 1885—the first nationally organized strike that grew to be larger than the 1877 Uprising—began as an effort to drive Chinese workers from western mines; White, *The Republic for Which It Stands*, 518–51.

6. Thomas, *Alternative America*; White, *Republic for Which It Stands*, 747–51; Ganesh Sitaraman, *The Crisis of the Middle-Class Constitution: Why Economic Inequality Threatens Our Republic* (New York: Knopf, 2017), 143–50; Milford Howard, *The American Plutocracy* (New York: Holland Publishing, 1895), 121.

7. Bronstein, *Two Nations, Indivisible*, 60–75; Thompson, *Politics of Inequality*, 127–34.

8. Thompson, *Politics of Inequality*, 127–34 Sitaraman, *Crisis of the Middle-Class Constitution*, 165–84.

9. Bronstein, *Two Nations, Indivisible*, 77–95; Thompson, *Politics of Inequality*, 134–40; Sitaraman, *Crisis of the Middle-Class Constitution*, 186–202.

10. Richard F. Berkhofer Jr., *The White Man's Indian: Images of the American Indian from Columbus to the Present* (New York: Knopf, 1978), 178–79; Thompson, *Politics of Inequality*, 139.

11. Bronstein, *Two Nations, Indivisible*, 97–130; Sitaraman, *Crisis of the Middle-Class Constitution*, 202–220.

12. *Class Matters* (New York: Times Books / Henry Holt, 2005); Chris Hayes, *Twilight of the Elites: America after Meritocracy* (New York: Crown Books, 2012); William R. Black, "Let's Bring Back the Sabbath as a Radical Act against 'Total Work,'" *Aeon*, Sept. 14, 2018, https://aeon.co/ideas/lets-bring-back-the-sabbath-as-a-radical-act-against-total-work.

13. Bronstein, *Two Nations, Indivisible*, Thompson's *Politics of Inequality*, and Sitaraman's *Crisis of the Middle-Class Constitution* are the only three in this tide of analyses on recent economic inequality that included considerations of how Americans regarded and managed wealth and power before the 1880s. Bronstein is a historian whose short work (215 pages) focuses on the roots and persistence of economic inequality. Thompson is a political scientist, and Sitaraman is a professor of law and policy; both of their works are intended as analyses of and solutions for current problems rather than studies of the evolution of the idea of economic equality.